FIRE CANNOT KILL A DRAGON

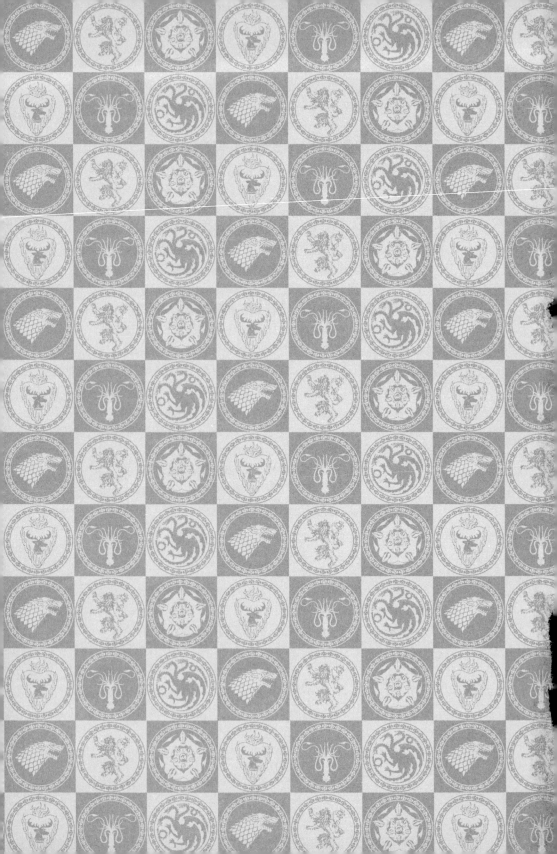

FIRE CANNOT KILL A DRAGON

GAME ᴏꜰ THRONES
AND THE OFFICIAL UNTOLD STORY
OF THE EPIC SERIES

JAMES HIBBERD

DUTTON

DUTTON

An imprint of Penguin Random House LLC

penguinrandomhouse.com

LIBRARY OF CONGRESS CATALOGING-IN-PUBLICATION DATA
has been applied for.

ISBN 9781524746759 (hardcover)
ISBN 9781524746766 (ebook)

Printed in the United States of America
1 3 5 7 9 10 8 6 4 2

BOOK DESIGN BY KRISTIN DEL ROSARIO

For my mom,
who read the stories

CONTENTS

CONTENTS

CONTENTS

FIRE CANNOT KILL A DRAGON

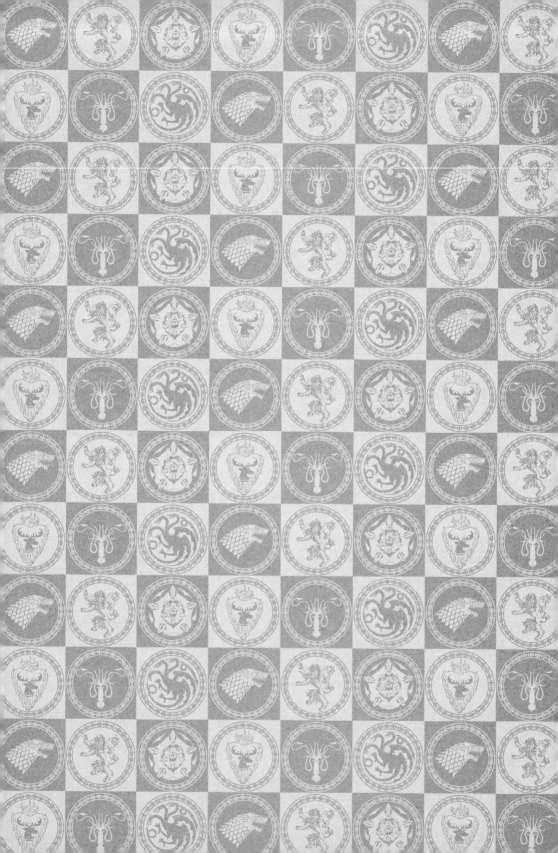

FINDING WESTEROS

Hundreds of men are screaming.

The armored soldiers charge forward, howling with rage, their swords and shields clashing, their boots struggling for purchase in the thick mud. Slowly, agonizingly, some of the fighters are pushed back against a looming tower of corpses. The body pile is a mixture of slain men and horses, gorily intertwined like some gothic rendition of hell. In the distance, flayed men burn on crucifixes.

"You are dying!" yells an assistant director. "That's the main thing to remember, you are dying!"

It's October 2014. There are six hundred crew members, five hundred actors, and seventy horses in a Northern Ireland field to film the Battle of the Bastards.

At the center of the mayhem is Kit Harington, who plays the reluctant hero Jon Snow. He's been fighting Bolton soldiers for days, furiously swinging a hefty broadsword at one attacker after another. During one take, he performs a dozen intricately choreographed strikes that he has drilled perfectly into his muscle memory.

Well, *almost* perfectly. Harington suddenly gets knocked down into the field's boggy, mudlike soup. Weeks of battle filming have transformed the soil into a foul mix of dirt, horse manure, urine, fake snow, sweat, saliva, and bugs.

The star gets wearily back onto his feet.

"'Become an actor,' they said," Harington groans. "'Think of all the fame and glory,' they said . . .'"

W atching this battlefield spectacle from the sidelines, I marveled at the audacity of making *Game of Thrones*.

My journey with the HBO drama series had begun years earlier when I accepted a routine assignment. In George R. R. Martin's novels, the smallest decision in a character's life can have the greatest of consequences. But back on November 11, 2008, I had never heard of him.

I was a senior writer working for *The Hollywood Reporter* when I interviewed a pair of first-time showrunners, David Benioff and Dan Weiss. HBO had just green-lit the duo's pilot based on Martin's books, and the show was an . . . adult fantasy drama? What, you mean like *The Lord of the Rings*?

Not like *The Lord of the Rings*, Benioff and Weiss explained. No wizards, no elves, no dwarfs—well, maybe one dwarf.

"It's not a story with a million orcs charging across the plains," Weiss said, while Benioff added: "High fantasy has never been done on TV before, and if anybody can do it, it's HBO. They've taken tired genres and reinvented them—mobsters in *The Sopranos* and Westerns with *Deadwood*. . . ."

My resulting story was utterly routine. The headline—"HBO Conjuring Fantasy Series"—didn't even include the title *Game of Thrones*. The idea that TV's most prestigious Emmy-winning network would take a crazy gamble on an expensive fantasy show for grown-ups was considered the most newsworthy hook.

And that should have been the end of my *Thrones* journey. But Benioff and Weiss's intriguing description of Martin's story stuck in my head. I bought a copy of the first *A Song of Ice and Fire* novel, *A Game of Thrones*. Like countless others, I fell headlong into Martin's daringly original world. Within a few weeks, I finished the third book in his saga,

A Storm of Swords, which was the most exciting and horrifying stretch of page-turning twists and turns I had ever read.

I began obsessively covering the progress of HBO's pilot. Colleagues would ask: *Why do you write so much about that one show?* I would reply: *Because if they can pull off adapting the books—and I don't think anybody can—it will change television.*

By the time the first season of *Game of Thrones* premiered in 2011, I had moved to *Entertainment Weekly,* where I embarked on a series of annual visits to the *Thrones* set. I was in the desert when Daenerys stood outside the gates of Qarth; bared witness to Sansa and Tyrion's awkward wedding; watched Joffrey suffer his well-deserved demise; was among the crowd for Cersei's Walk of Shame; trekked on a frozen lake during Jon Snow's quest beyond the Wall; and paced Winterfell's ramparts during the climactic Long Night.

Over the years, I grew to admire the cast and crew's dedication to making the best possible show, a commitment that often resulted in outright suffering. We're so accustomed to seeing life on movie and TV sets depicted as soft and easy: stars lounging between takes in posh RVs, directors riding around in golf carts on sunny studio back lots, a cast of heroes filming against a green-screen backdrop for computer animators to later insert them into fabrications of harsh environments and deadly peril.

The glamorous and comfortable vision of the entertainment world does exist if you're on a big-budget production in Hollywood filming on a major studio lot. That was never *Thrones.* The show was unlike any production, film or television, I have ever seen before or since. Working on *Thrones* was being wet and freezing for eleven hours, night after night, week after week, and learning to accept that sometimes you were going to be utterly miserable in order to get a shot just right. *Thrones* was being six-foot-six-inch Rory McCann, an actor made even bigger by his character's heavy costume and boots, whose only way to rest after shooting an exhausting action sequence was to curl up on the hard floor of a tiny utilitarian trailer, his face half-covered in suffocating latex, a space heater making the drafty caravan either too hot or too cold. And while the production sometimes relied on green screen, more often *Thrones* actors worked on wholly immersive sets that made you feel like you had literally been transported into another world.

By the time the show concluded in 2019, I had written hundreds of stories covering the series. Yet there was much to the making of *Game of Thrones* that was left untold. *What was Benioff and Weiss's first fateful meeting with Martin really like? What went down during the filming of the show's unaired original pilot? How did* Thrones *pull off its first major battle in season two? What happened with the Dorne storyline? Why did the showrunners decide to end the series after eight seasons? What were those grueling fifty-five consecutive nights filming "The Long Night" really like? And hey, why didn't Lady Stoneheart ever show up?*

My list of lingering questions, along with a desire to create a unified story from my decade of experience covering the show, is the reason for this book. *Fire Cannot Kill a Dragon* includes more than fifty exclusive new interviews with *Game of Thrones* producers, executives, cast, and crew that were conducted after the series finale. There are also many quotes that were previously published by *EW,* as well as occasional quotes that were reported in other outlets (which are attributed in the text along the way).

Of course, no single book can capture the entirety of making a production as long-running and complex as *Thrones.* But it's my hope that readers will find some fascinating behind-the-scenes stories here about the characters and moments they love the most. *Thrones* was also, it should be said, controversial—from literally its first episode to its last—and many of those topics are likewise addressed by the show's producers, directors, and cast (surely not to the satisfaction of all, but you'll now learn *why* certain choices were made).

Mainly this book seeks to chronicle the colossal effort that went into making an extraordinary show. There is nothing more rare in pop culture than to build an alternate world so popular, sophisticated, and engrossing that it's globally embraced as a place almost as real as our own. J. R. R. Tolkien did it with *The Lord of the Rings*. So did George Lucas with *Star Wars*, J. K. Rowling with the Harry Potter series, and Marvel with its cinematic universe. *Game of Thrones* gave rise to a living, breathing world due to the passionate and tireless efforts of thousands of people.

But it's worth remembering that it all started with one man. . . .

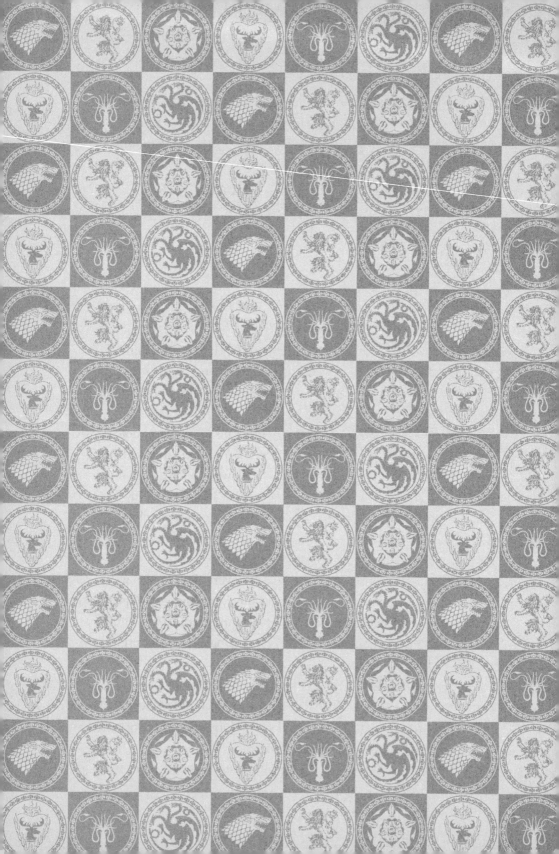

CHAPTER ONE

A DREAM OF DRAGONS

Before the Starks and the Lannisters, the Dothraki and the direwolves, before the continent of Westeros had formed and the first dragon had been born, there was a boy whose imagination could not easily be contained.

George Raymond Richard Martin grew up in a federal housing project in 1950s New Jersey. His father was a longshoreman, and his mother worked as a factory manager. He wasn't allowed to have dogs or cats but was permitted to own tiny dime-store turtles, along with a toy fortress to put them in. His first fantasy story—the first he can remember, at least—was titled "Turtle Castle." He imagined his tiny reptiles were competing for power and vying for a little plastic throne.

One day, Martin made a shocking discovery: His turtles were dying. Despite his best efforts to keep his pets alive, his heroes still perished. It was a twist he hadn't seen coming. So Martin began to weave their fates into his fantasy. Perhaps his turtles were killing each other off in sinister plots?

As the years passed, Martin put his fantasies to paper. He wrote monster stories and sold them to other kids for a dime apiece. He fell in love with comic books. He later sold short stories to pulp magazines, and then penned sci-fi and horror novels.

In 1984, Martin moved to Hollywood and landed a job writing on

CBS's reboot of *The Twilight Zone.* Martin's first aired episode was, as fate would have it, a fantasy tale about medieval knights and magic. "The Last Defender of Camelot" was an adaptation of Roger Zelazny's short story about Sir Lancelot living in modern times. The climax is set in an otherworldly version of Stonehenge, where Lancelot fights an enchanted suit of armor—a silent mountain of a warrior called the Hollow Knight.

In Martin's original script, Lancelot and the knight fought on armored horses, but that idea was deemed unworkable by the show's line producers. "They told me, 'You can have Stonehenge or you can have horses,'" recalled Martin. "'But you cannot have Stonehenge *and* horses.' I called my friend Roger Zelazny to pose the question to him. He sucked on his pipe a minute and said, 'Stonehenge,' and so it was. They fought on foot."

Undeterred, Martin moved on to another CBS fantasy show, 1987's *Beauty and the Beast,* where his scripts continued to bump up against the network's creative limitations. "Counting how many times we could say 'damn' or 'hell,' telling us a corpse's makeup couldn't be 'too horrific,' eliminating a news report on a TV in the background because it might be 'too controversial,'" Martin said. "Bullshit changes, sheer cowardice, afraid of anything that was too strong, anything that anyone might be 'offended' by—those [restrictions] I hated and railed against."

Martin grew frustrated, disillusioned. He returned to writing novels full-time in 1991 and a couple of years later he had an idea for a fantasy story—a "reaction," he once dubbed it, to his years spent writing for television. It was a sprawling epic like J. R. R. Tolkien's *The Lord of the Rings,* a saga that Martin adored, except Martin's tale was inspired by actual European historical events such as the Wars of the Roses and reflected the true brutality of the Dark Ages. The first book, *A Game of Thrones,* was published in 1996. Sales were, as Martin later wrote on his blog, "nothing spectacular."

In rapid succession, Martin followed up with two more books in the saga. Their popularity spread by word of mouth, enthralling an ever-growing fandom with a complex story that shattered the fantasy genre's long-held rules. Beloved heroes died horribly, loathsome villains became strangely sympathetic, the wise and cunning were toppled by the slightest procedural error, and the power of magic was considered unreliable at best.

Along the way, Martin threw in all the horses and castles and sex and violence he wanted. This wasn't the story of one fantasy kingdom but seven! Each realm had its own distinct history, leadership, and culture (plus there was a whole *other* continent of diverse cities across the Narrow Sea). There were more than two thousand named characters, a figure that doubled the count from Tolkien's saga. Plus there were massive battles—one involved four armies, tens of thousands of soldiers, and hundreds of ships. Even meals in Westeros could be extravagant, such as a banquet that included seventy-seven distinct courses. Often such feasts were lavishly described ("elk roundels with blue cheese, grilled snake with fiery mustard sauce, river pike poached in almond milk . . ."). The books' adult content was equally voluminous, with shocking acts of torture, rape, and incest. Martin penned paragraphs that single-handedly would have consumed an entire season of a network TV show's budget, gotten a show kicked off the air, or both.

He called this epic *A Song of Ice and Fire*.

Hollywood took notice. By the early 2000s, Peter Jackson's *The Lord of the Rings* trilogy was blowing up the box office. Then, in 2005, Martin's fourth installment in his saga, *A Feast for Crows*, debuted at number one on the *New York Times* bestseller list ("A fantasy realm too vile for hobbits," declared the *Times*). Martin's novels made the rounds among agents and producers. His phone rang with offers of easy money and silver-screen glory.

Martin, then fifty-seven and enjoying a quiet life in Santa Fe, was wary. . . .

GEORGE R. R. MARTIN (*author, co–executive producer*): The Peter Jackson movies were big. Everybody was looking for a feature fantasy series for films. Everything was being optioned. I started [A *Song of Ice and Fire*] thinking it couldn't be filmed. I was like: "How are you going to make a feature out of this that's two and a half hours? You can't get it all in." Jackson took three movies to do Tolkien's books, but all three of Tolkien's books were as long as just one of mine. How are you going to do this?

The answers I got back were not ones I wanted to hear, like: "[Fan-favorite Stark bastard] Jon Snow is the central character, we'll focus on him and cut the rest away." Or they pitched, "We're not going to cut anything, we'll keep it all, but we'll just make the first film and then make more if it's a big hit." Well, what if it's *not* a big hit? You're saying it's going to be *The Lord of the Rings*, but what if it's more like Philip Pullman's [failed 2007 *His Dark Materials* adaptation *The Golden Compass*]? You make one movie, it bombs, and then you have a broken thing. No. I wasn't interested in anything like that.

Martin's literary agent sent copies of the *Song of Ice and Fire* novels to David Benioff, a thirty-five-year-old novelist and screenwriter, and suggested he might consider trying to adapt them for a feature film. Benioff was an up-and-comer in the industry, having penned the acclaimed 2002 crime thriller *25th Hour,* along with the screenplays for the films *Troy* and *The Kite Runner.*

Eight chapters into reading *A Game of Thrones,* Benioff was stunned when seven-year-old Bran Stark—who had just witnessed an act of incest between the queen of Westeros and her brother—was mercilessly shoved out a tower window. A few hundred pages later, when Martin killed off the book's main character, the honorable and heroic Ned Stark, Benioff phoned his friend and writing partner, Dan Weiss.

Weiss, thirty-four, had met Benioff a decade earlier while the two were studying literature at Trinity College Dublin. They'd bonded over things like Irish literature and "trying to find a functional gym in Dublin in 1995," as Weiss told *Vanity Fair.* Weiss was an author as well, having published his debut novel, *Lucky Wander Boy,* in 2003. Benioff asked Weiss to read Martin's books "to make sure I wasn't crazy."

"We'd been reading fantasy books since childhood and never encountered anything as good as what George had written," Benioff said.

Benioff and Weiss, like others before them, wanted to adapt *A Song of Ice and Fire.* But they quickly ruled out making the books into a movie, deciding instead that only a TV series could capture the scope of Martin's narrative. At least, the duo hoped it could—neither had ever worked on a TV show before.

Martin agreed to meet Benioff and Weiss for lunch at the Palm Restaurant in Los Angeles to hear their pitch. The meeting lasted four hours and would ultimately produce a pop-culture dragon: the biggest global television phenomenon of the twenty-first century. Yet it all might have been derailed by Martin asking a single unexpected question.

DAN WEISS (*showrunner*): We were nervous. When you start working in Hollywood, every meeting is nerve-wracking because you feel if you don't do it right it's the last meeting you're ever going to have. I had gotten long past that. You get used to meetings, and most never amount to anything. But this felt like the first meeting I'd ever taken all over again because we knew this was a one-of-a-kind opportunity and if we didn't get this job we'd never have a chance to work on something like this again, because nobody had ever seen anything like this before. There was one keeper of the keys, and that was George. If George didn't say yes, all of our dreams were dead in the crib. So we were under pressure to get it right.

DAVID BENIOFF (*showrunner*): Part of the meeting was talking about where George came from and the science fiction writers he knew. Part of it was talking about his books and our passion for them, for him to see that we had really read them. Having worked in Hollywood before, George knew about people who read [a synopsis of a book] and then say,

"Oh, this could work as a *Lord of the Rings* knock-off." The fact we read the books and could speak to them with some degree of knowledge I think meant something to him.

DAN WEISS: When converting to Judaism, the rabbi's job is not to convince you to convert but to talk you out of it. There was an element of that with George explaining to us that the reason he left television to do full-time writing was to write things you *couldn't* produce. George told us about the horses and Stonehenge. He said: "My imagination is bigger than 'the horses and Stonehenge'; I want Stonehenge and the horses *and* another twenty Stonehenges *and* another million horses." He wrote the books to use the entirety of his imaginative capacity and wrote it almost intentionally to be unfilmable.

DAVID BENIOFF: George created a world so rich that you're coming into the story 95 percent of the way into it. So much happened in the past— like the Targaryen invasion of Westeros—and you need to understand that stuff in order for the current story to make sense. Books have a more elegant way of putting backstory in. On television, you either do a flashback or boring exposition. So one of George's questions was: "How are you going to let the audience know all this stuff that's so crucial?" I don't remember what our answer was. We probably came up with some bullshit.

DAN WEISS: In the course of making the show, you develop your approach to those things. But looking back on it, the history he built, even if you take out 90 percent, it's like the scaffolding on a building. You don't see the scaffolding after you take it away, but the fact it was there is what makes the building look right. You feel that 90 percent of history through the 10 percent that's on-screen. There's this overarching sense of backstory and connection and logic to why characters feel the way they feel about each other. It's never just people fighting because it's dramatic.

GEORGE R. R. MARTIN: They were very persuasive. They loved the books and wanted to adapt the books to a different medium, not change them or "make it their own." I hate that in Hollywood, when I go in pitching a book and meet with writers and they're like, "Here's my take on it." I don't want your take on it! Don't reimagine it, don't make it your own, just adapt it.

I told them, "I want a faithful adaptation. I don't want it to be one of those things where you take a title and write a whole new story." And I wanted to be part of it. I wanted to be a producer on it and write some scripts. "And it can't be for a [traditional broadcast network]. I don't want the sex and violence cut out. A season for each book." So we were on the same accord.

The meeting was going well. The lunch crowd had long since departed, and the restaurant staff was preparing for dinner. Then Martin asked Benioff and Weiss a question that might have ended their tentative partnership right there. One of the biggest mysteries in Martin's novels is the secret of Jon Snow's parentage. The Stark bastard is described as the son of Ned Stark and an unnamed mistress he met during Robert Baratheon's rebellion against Aerys II Targaryen, "the Mad King." Martin had scattered clues along the way hinting at Jon Snow's true identity, and fans had several theories.

GEORGE R. R. MARTIN: I did famously ask them the question: "Who is Jon Snow's mother?" They said they read the books. I wanted to see if they had *really* read the books and how much they had paid attention.

DAVID BENIOFF: We were weirdly prepared for that question. We had discussed that the day before. We had just started to talk about it and came up with our theory, which just happened to be right.

GEORGE R. R. MARTIN: They knew the answer, which was good.

DAVID BENIOFF: After we got the Jon Snow–mother question right, he gave us the backing to try and go out there and sell it.

GEORGE R. R. MARTIN: It was a strange situation. It's hard to remember now, but when we sat down, I had way more television experience than David and Dan. I spent ten years in television. I had gone through the ranks from staff writer to a supervising producer. If fate had been a little different I might have ended up a showrunner myself. And here were these two guys who were very talented writers but had never done anything in TV before. So a part of me wanted to do it myself, but I hadn't finished writing the books. I still haven't finished the books. I didn't see *that* happening.

Pitching *Game of Thrones* as a television series was the first of many uphill battles the producers would fight to get the show on the air. While the *Lord of the Rings* films were hits and other parties had approached Martin about making a possible movie, fantasy on television was associated with low-budget, all-ages syndicated fare like *Xena: Warrior Princess* and *Hercules: The Legendary Journeys*. Martin's books were very R-rated, and fantasy for grown-ups was a largely untested market. "You talked dragons, you got smirks," as Harry Lloyd, who played Viserys Targaryen, put it. And even a scaled-down version of *A Song of Ice and Fire* would be prohibitively expensive. There were only a few networks at the time that allowed adult content and might be able to afford the show.

Benioff and Weiss drafted a confident-sounding (and, it turned out, prophetic) proposal that included lines such as, "People are hungry for *Game of Thrones*. . . . They will watch it, and keep watching it, and tell everyone they know to watch it, and never stop talking about it at dinner, at work, at home. When we give them this show, they will lose their fucking minds." In their pitch, the duo promised the show would have "none of the things that can make fantasy feel creaky, corny, or kiddie."

They tried to sell their adaptation to three outlets. One potential buyer was DirecTV, which was looking to fund original content but was also considered a rather unexciting option with a limited platform. Benioff and Weiss also pitched Showtime, which was interested, but the CBS-owned cable network was known for modest spending. Said Benioff, "We intuitively knew that even the most expensive Showtime show ever made couldn't come close to getting this where it needed to be."

That left HBO, which Martin, Benioff, and Weiss had agreed over lunch would be the ideal home. And if you wanted HBO to buy your pitch, there was one person in particular you had to impress: then–programming president and nineteen-year HBO veteran Carolyn Strauss. The executive's power at the network, combined with her inscrutable demeanor and penchant for wearing all black, gave Strauss a reputation for being, as Benioff put it, "the scariest person in Hollywood."

DAVID BENIOFF: We were told, "She's not going to smile at anything you say, she's not going to laugh, just be prepared for that."

CAROLYN STRAUSS (*former programming president at HBO; executive producer*): The idea [for *Thrones*] wasn't something I necessarily gravitate toward. But being an executive is not necessarily about doing everything you like to do.

Benioff and Weiss booked a pitch meeting with Strauss and other executives.

GINA BALIAN (*former vice president of drama at HBO*): The vibe in the room was very quiet. We were listening intently. The pitch was very similar to the story of the pilot. They walked us through that first hour and ended with the cliffhanger. My mouth was gaping open. *The kid was pushed out a window?*

DAVID BENIOFF: We talked about how fantasy was the most popular genre there is. Loosely defined, *Star Wars* is fantasy, Harry Potter is fantasy, and even [superhero movies] are their own kind of fantasy.

CAROLYN STRAUSS: There were a fair number of reasons not to do it. There are many ways a fantasy series can go south. Any show that relies on a mythology that isn't thought out in enormous detail can go off the rails. You're maybe good for a season or two and then after that you start running into brick walls. Plus, this was clearly going to be expensive.

DAVID BENIOFF: We said most shows begin only knowing their first season. Because of the work George had done, we had a sense of where this was going for many seasons. Even then we knew—though George's books hadn't gotten there—that [exiled heroine Daenerys Targaryen] would come back to Westeros and fight for the throne. We had a good sense of the show five years down the road, and that's a rare privilege for television.

CAROLYN STRAUSS: The way they told the story in that meeting made it sound much more involved and complex and character-driven than I usually feel from fantasy stories. It was not a story of good vs. evil but characters who had elements of both those things.

DAVID BENIOFF: At one point, Carolyn laughed and we were like, "Oh my God, we're in! We made Carolyn Strauss laugh." We felt good by the end of the meeting that they were interested.

GINA BALIAN: This wasn't your usual HBO show. So after the pitch I ran down to Carolyn's office: "We're going to buy this, right?"

HBO agreed to take *Game of Thrones* to the next step: negotiating with Martin for the rights to *A Song of Ice and Fire*. This alone ended up taking nearly a year due to legal hang-ups.

GEORGE R. R. MARTIN: The big sticking point was the merchandising. We didn't know that would be big going in, but HBO's lawyers didn't want to set the precedent of giving away something they hadn't given away before. I was saying, "I can't give you everything you want. I already have a video game in the works, a role-playing game in the works. I've already given the rights to a guy to make replica coins." Who knew *Game of Thrones* replica coins would be a thing? So we were in this endless negotiation of parsing individual items, like, "You can have bobblehead dolls, I get key rings. . . ."

Then came another stumbling block. Strauss, who had become a strong advocate for the show behind the scenes, stepped down from HBO in 2008. Strauss shifted to join *Thrones* as an executive producer, but regime change at a network often spells doom for titles developed under the previous boss. Somehow, Benioff and Weiss had to convince a new leadership structure led by HBO co-president Richard Plepler and programming president Michael Lombardo to spend at least $10 million on a pilot that was wildly unlike anything else HBO—or any network—had ever made.

MICHAEL LOMBARDO (*former HBO programming president*): HBO was still coming out of *The Sopranos, The Wire,* and *Deadwood.* We were getting questions like, "Why did you not get *Mad Men?* How come you didn't pick up *Breaking Bad?*" We had been the place for all things quality drama and were looking to regain our footing. But *Game of Thrones* didn't seem to fall into our category. This didn't scream "Emmy voters." This was not a genre embraced by the voices HBO traditionally listened to for drama series. It had a lot going against it.

But Carolyn said, "This is a really good script, you should read this," and it read like a page-turner. The writing was sharp and clear. You get to Jaime pushing Bran out the window and I was like, "Holy shit, this isn't like anything I've read." Still, *The Lord of the Rings* had been out and was done pretty damn well. How do we compete with that? How can this feel, from a production standpoint, as textured and credible? We knew it had to be able to stand next to projects in this genre being done on the big screen, yet with a more limited budget.

Hanging over *Thrones* was the fallout of another HBO title, 2005's *Rome,* an ambitious and compelling period drama co-produced with the BBC that cost a staggering $100 million for its first season. HBO had axed *Rome* due to low ratings before its second season aired. The network was understandably reluctant to sink tens of millions into another swords-and-shields costume drama when they just had one that didn't work.

Benioff and Weiss tried to assure HBO executives that *Thrones* would remain far less expensive than *Rome,* which, of course, wasn't remotely true.

DAN WEISS: A story of this scale had never been told within filmed entertainment, to my knowledge. Nowadays it's economically viable to make a television show at this scale. Back then, it just wasn't done. HBO had tried with *Rome,* which was a step in that direction. One thing we felt like we had going for us is we said, "It's not a symphony, it's a chamber piece."

DAVID BENIOFF: The lie we told was that the show was "contained" and it was about the characters.

DAN WEISS: We knew most of the people making the decisions were not going to read four thousand pages [of Martin's books] and get to the dragons getting bigger and the [major battles]. The show was exactly what we told them it wasn't. We were banking on them not finding out until it was too late.

MICHAEL LOMBARDO: I'm not sure I ever really believed that. We knew it was a gamble. We were budgeting it and scratching our head whether we should go ahead and green-light this. We were trying to figure out the production challenges.

There was something else going against *Thrones* as well. Benioff and Weiss had never worked on a television show before (at least, not one that made it past the pilot stage). Typically in such situations a network would bring in a veteran writer-producer to take the lead on the project. But HBO insiders said Benioff and Weiss continually impressed them with their insights during the show's development process.

CAROLYN STRAUSS: I'd worked with series producers where we forced them to hire other writers. But Dan and David were always confident they could do it, and they were very open to learning what they didn't know. They're incredibly fast learners. We would bring in producers or department heads who were more experienced and had a certain conventional wisdom, and time and time again Dan and David would prove their instinct was the right one. Bit by bit, they earned our trust.

In the fall of 2008, the decision of whether to order the *Game of Thrones* pilot was hanging over the network. Lombardo went to his gym, the Equinox in West Hollywood. As it so happened, Weiss went to the same gym.

MICHAEL LOMBARDO: And I see Dan on one of the bicycles. He was reading this dog-eared copy of the first book, and it had underscores and yellow highlights [on the pages]. He didn't know I saw him. And I thought, "We're going to figure this out. These guys breathe this show in a way that doesn't happen all the time." I found that little window into Dan in that quiet moment, that this is what he was doing in his free time. It was such an acknowledgment of everything I suspected about those guys, and it made me determined to figure this thing out.

RICHARD PLEPLER (*former co-president and CEO of HBO*): You could see they were breathing this. There's a feeling when great artists are talking about their passion and are immersed in a subject. It's the same feeling you get when [*The Wire* creator] David Simon pitches something or when Armando Iannucci pitched *Veep* or Mike Judge pitched *Silicon Valley*. I just had that feeling about them.

In November, Benioff and Weiss got the news they had waited three years to hear. HBO had agreed to green-light a pilot for *Game of Thrones*. The duo was relieved and elated. But before they could celebrate, they wanted to make sure of one last thing.

GINA BALIAN: David and Dan told me, "We can't have you guys come back to us later and say we can't kill the lead character because suddenly you really like him." So when we got the okay to make the pilot I remember running to Mike and barging in and going: "Just double-, double-, *double*-checking: We're killing the lead and there's dragons."

CHAPTER TWO

CASTING TALES

Nothing about making *Game of Thrones* was easy. When building a new fantasy world on a relatively limited budget, nearly every aspect of production comes with an unprecedented degree of difficulty—starting with the casting.

First there was the sheer number of roles. *Thrones'* debut season had dozens of speaking parts and twenty core cast members, or "series regulars." Tougher still, many of these roles were for children. Finding one excellent child actor can be hard enough. *Thrones* needed six Stark kids who could look and act like a cohesive family while also handling adult content and making a years-long commitment to the show.

Though HBO gave *Thrones* a generous budget (roughly $20 million was eventually spent on the pilot and then another $54 million on the rest of the season), the money was needed to build out Martin's new fantasy universe. When you create sets for a period drama set in medieval times, or in ancient Egypt or Rome, you can replicate designs from a historical record. Every set, costume, and prop in Martin's books needed to be unique. For instance, Martin describes the seat of power in Westeros, the Iron Throne, as a towering monstrosity of spikes and jagged edges; twisted metal forged from a thousand swords into a piece of furniture so jagged and uncomfortable that it can literally kill a person (and has). How do you adapt that description into a realistic-looking chair that blends with its environment and that actors can sit in for hours during filming?

Then there were all the computer-generated (CG) special effects—far fewer than in the show's latter seasons, but almost certainly more effects than any other TV show at the time.

So there wasn't much left in the budget for hiring a lot of well-known stars. The producers would instead have to largely cast *Thrones* the hard way—by hunting through thousands of audition tapes.

"On paper, *Game of Thrones* is the stupidest idea on the planet to invest in," noted actor Liam Cunningham, who came on board in season two to play Davos Seaworth. "To have a production hanging on nine-year-old children in the pilot to get you through the rest of the show eleven years later."

Filling at least one major role seemed like it would be rather easy (because the perfect actor was obvious), but it was also nerve-wracking (because he wasn't initially interested). Tyrion Lannister, the cunning and sarcastic black sheep of the powerful Lannister family, is a fan favorite from Martin's books. Peter Dinklage was considered the ideal choice, as evidenced by his work in *The Station Agent* and his scene-stealing roles in *Elf* and *Living in Oblivion*.

Yet Dinklage was coming off another fantasy role in 2008's *Prince Caspian,* Disney's modestly performing sequel to *The Lion, the Witch and the Wardrobe,* and was looking for something different. Dinklage was also wary of the genre's stereotypical use of little people. He once cited *The Lord of the Rings'* infamous dwarf-tossing joke as particularly galling and would later use his first Golden Globes acceptance speech in 2012 to draw attention to a real-life dwarf-tossing victim.

GEORGE R. R. MARTIN (*author, co–executive producer*): We thought right away that role would be the trickiest. We all agreed we wanted an actual dwarf to play Tyrion; we didn't want to do what *Lord of the Rings* did where they take John Rhys-Davies and shrink him down to play Gimli. If Peter had turned us down we would have been screwed.

PETER DINKLAGE (*Tyrion Lannister*): I wouldn't go anywhere near that stuff—fantasy. As soon as I heard about [*Thrones*] I was like, *"No."* In fantasy, everybody speaks in broad strokes. There's no intimacy. There's dragons and big speeches, and there's nothing to hold on to. And for somebody my size, it's fucking death, the opposite of [the activism] I was involved with.

But Dinklage knew and respected showrunner David Benioff's writing, and it didn't hurt that the actor was friends with Benioff's wife, actress Amanda Peet. So when Dinklage read the *Thrones* pilot script, he had a change of heart.

PETER DINKLAGE: David and Dan are incapable of doing [fantasy tropes]; they're too good. I told them that I love turning people's expectations on their heads. You overcome stereotypes when people least expect it. You do it quietly. You don't do it through a bullhorn. And I felt like that's what they were doing with Tyrion. In another show it would be focused on the people on the throne looking down on me.

Dinklage had at least one rule: no beard, which is why Tyrion is clean-shaven during the show's first few years despite the character having a beard in the books. The actor later eased off that requirement and grew a modest beard after his character was firmly established. "I just didn't want a long beard in a dwarf–in–*The Lord of the Rings* way," he explained.

The actor also urged his longtime friend Lena Headey (*Terminator: The Sarah Connor Chronicles*) to try out for the role of Tyrion's ambitious and cunning sister, Cersei. "We met lots of others too, but it was clear she was the most interesting and best choice," said Nina Gold, who served as *Thrones'* casting director along with her partner Robert Sterne.

While the producers were looking to stand apart from *The Lord of the Rings*, they nonetheless cast Sean Bean in the role of the honorable Stark patriarch Eddard (a.k.a. Ned). Bean had played another ill-fated fantasy warrior from a noble family, Boromir in *The Fellowship of the Ring*. "Sean was somebody we talked about from the very beginning; he seemed like the prototype of the Guy," said Gold.

Dinklage would be the show's only American actor for most of the series. Gold and Sterne searched for the rest of the roles out of London. Westeros was based on what's now known as the UK, and there was a long tradition of historical-style dramas using actors with British accents. Benioff, Weiss, and Martin were heavily involved in the selection process, as was the director of the series' original pilot, Tom McCarthy, who was brought on board having previously directed Dinklage in *The Station Agent* as well as acted with Peet in the film *2012*.

GEORGE R. R. MARTIN: I was a big part of casting in the early seasons. They would send me a link every day with like twenty-three different people who read for various roles. I would watch every one of them. I would write David and Dan these really detailed six-page evaluations.

Also weighing in on casting—unofficially—were Martin's readers. *A Song of Ice and Fire* fans lobbied online for certain actors to be considered for key roles, sometimes quite successfully. The fans were also quick to make their disapproval known when a casting choice fell short of their expectations for a character—such as when Danish film star Nikolaj Coster-Waldau landed the role of Cersei's legendarily handsome and arrogant knight brother, Jaime Lannister.

NIKOLAJ COSTER-WALDAU (*Jaime Lannister*): I had a meeting with Dan and David and Carolyn Strauss, and they told me the whole story and it sounded amazing. Then about a half hour into the conversation they said, "Oh, yeah, he has a special relationship with his sister—they're lovers." I thought that was interesting. Then there was some discussion [among fans] about my nose—that I had the wrong nose.

DAVID BENIOFF (*showrunner*): We learned to cast the actor who was best for the role, not whose face matches whose in the books. That means

we got certain complaints in the fan community. People complained Peter was too tall and that Nikolaj's nose was too big. [Theon Greyjoy actor Alfie Allen] doesn't look anything like the character in the book, but his audition blew everybody else out of the water.

Allen didn't originally think he would make a great Theon either. The English actor first tried out to play Jon Snow, and producers were inspired to ask him to come back and read for the role of the traitorous Stark ward (this wasn't unusual, as many *Thrones* actors tried out for multiple parts on the show).

Yet Martin's fans scored a bull's-eye by suggesting Jason Momoa, an American actor best known for *Stargate: Atlantis,* for the role of the fearsome Dothraki warrior Khal Drogo.

Momoa arrived at his audition wearing an open black chest-baring shirt and a tribal-looking necklace. Given Drogo's lack of dialogue, Momoa asked producers if he could perform a Maori-warrior haka dance to visually demonstrate some of his physical menace before reading his lines. The actor furiously stomped, chanted, and pounded his chest while giving a threatening Drogo-like glare.

JASON MOMOA (*Khal Drogo*): I was born to play this role. When I read they were casting Khal Drogo, I couldn't believe it was happening. I had to have that role. I've never gone out for something before where I was like, "No one is going to take this from me." I was pretty adamant about it. I just remember giving it my all and leaving it going, "Good luck finding someone who's going to play Drogo."

Northern Ireland television and theater veteran Conleth Hill tried out to play the bald eunuch royal advisor Varys, despite some initial reluctance.

CONLETH HILL (*Varys*): I resisted for so long. I remember telling my agent I wasn't interested. I thought it would be like Dungeons & Dragons.

But Belfast was only an hour away and I loved Tom McCarthy's movies, so I figured I would go meet them. I taped for King Robert, but when I came out, I saw Mark Addy was up for that part as well. I knew he was perfect, so I thought that was a no-go.

The producers said, "We'll come back to you." I thought that was bullshit—nice bullshit, but bullshit. Then they had me back in again doing Varys's big speech where he talks about his past. I was thinking, "What a journey for this character." They asked, "Do you mind getting your head shaved?" I had never shaved my head before, and [at first] I was very depressed.

For Scottish actor Rory McCann, landing the role of Prince Joffrey Baratheon's fearsome bodyguard Sandor "the Hound" Clegane wasn't just another acting gig but a matter of actual survival. The actor told *The Independent* in 2019 that before being cast on *Thrones,* he was homeless, sleeping in a tent, and stealing food.

DAVID BENIOFF: We had trouble finding someone for the Hound. That's a tricky role. It's gotta be someone who's genuinely intimidating but who you also believe has a soul. Nina and her team would put all these videos online and there were hundreds of Hound interviews. Then we got an email from George saying, "Have you looked at Rory McCann?" We clicked on that one. It's when he's yelling at Sansa and goes: *"Look at me!"*—the way he snarled at camera made us both [lean back]. Rory is a very sweet, gentle person, but he definitely has that anger within him.

Northern Ireland actor Kristian Nairn was tapped for the role of hulking yet sweet, mono-word-uttering House Stark servant Hodor.

KRISTIAN NAIRN (*Hodor*): I was in the middle of my day and got a phone call from a guy who had acted as my agent saying, "We have an audition for you. You need to find a child." I obviously didn't have one with me. But he told me about a birthday party where one would be.

GEORGE R. R. MARTIN: Then we got this tape of Kristian Nairn and he's in a backyard staggering around with a kid on his back, shouting, "Hodor!"

German actress Sibel Kekilli paid out of pocket to fly to London for the opportunity to audition for Tyrion's wily prostitute lover Shae in person. After the meeting, however, Kekilli changed her mind about the role. The script pages she'd read during the scene were originally closer to the book's portrayal of Shae as a heartless opportunist, and she felt uncomfortable playing such a character opposite Dinklage.

SIBEL KEKILLI (*Shae*): When I got the part, my first reaction was I didn't want do it. I said, "No, thank you!" I knew Peter Dinklage was a great actor, but I was thinking [based on the audition lines] that they wanted to make fun of little people—make fun of the situation. David and Dan sent me a beautiful letter saying, "Please-please-please, you are our Shae. You did a great audition and we're going to change Shae a bit. We'll do it different than the books," and they convinced me.

Scottish actor Iain Glen already had some Hollywood genre-movie experience thanks to major roles in films such as *Resident Evil: Apocalypse* and *Lara Croft: Tomb Raider* when he tried out for banished Westerosi knight Ser Jorah Mormont.

IAIN GLEN (*Jorah Mormont*): No one knew anything really about it except that it was HBO and so many [British actors] were going out for it. I met with them, felt pretty good about it, then it all went silent. I said to my wife—and I never usually say this—"I really, *really* want that job." She asked why. "Honestly, I don't know," I said. "Because I know nothing about it. I just got a funny feeling. . . ."

For the pivotal role of exiled princess Daenerys Targaryen, the producers originally cast English actress Tamzin Merchant, who was coming off

Showtime's period drama *The Tudors*. Daenerys was one of several younger characters that had been slightly reconceived to fit the chosen actor.

GEORGE R. R. MARTIN: I based the books on the Middle Ages, when girls were getting married at thirteen. The entire concept of adolescence didn't exist; you were either a child or an adult. So Dany is thirteen years old in the books. But it was against British law to cast anyone in a sexual situation who is under seventeen. You can't even cast a seventeen-year-old to play a thirteen-year-old if it's a sexual situation. So we wound up with a twenty-three-year-old playing a seventeen-year-old and had to adjust the timeline.

For bullying teenage prince Joffrey, producers auditioned many young actors who read their lines as an obvious "demon seed," an *Omen*-like child villain.

DAVID BENIOFF: We were auditioning for Joffrey, and we found a kid we thought was perfect, so we thought we were done with that role. Then we went to Dublin to cast for other characters and there was one kid who had been scheduled to read for Joffrey and we didn't want to cancel on him. So basically, just as a courtesy, we agreed to see Jack Gleeson. He started speaking and changed our concept of the character. We didn't expect to spend as much time with Joffrey until we cast Jack. There's something so loathsome yet so believable about [the performance]. He's not supernatural, he's not the servant of darkness, he's just a believably awful human being.

Seventeen-year-old Gleeson's most notable prior credit was a small part in *Batman Begins*. The young Irish actor said he had looked to other big-screen villains for inspiration.

JACK GLEESON (*Joffrey Baratheon*): My characterization came from those first sides that I got and a collection of evil characters I've seen over the years. Joaquin Phoenix's Commodus in *Gladiator* had a big impact—the smirk. Also the monster Hexxus from *FernGully*. Those would be the two biggest. He's a product of his setting and context. Everyone has met Joffrey in some shape or form.

The toughest role to fill on *Thrones* was Arya Stark—the crafty, strong-willed young heroine who defies gender stereotypes and endures monumental hardships throughout the series.

GEORGE R. R. MARTIN: I despaired for a while that we couldn't find an Arya. We read more girls for Arya than anyone else. Most child actors in sitcoms, they just have to be cute and snap off one-liners. This part deals with real violence and grief and fear. Three-quarters of the girls we saw were just reciting lines; there was nothing else going on there. It's a big thing for a ten-year-old to recite those lines, but there was no acting. The rest were kids who obviously had gone to acting classes and some coach had told them they had to emote and they were emoting all over the place. They were all grimacing and rolling their eyes. I'm looking at this saying, "We're doomed."

Then twelve-year-old English actress Maisie Williams, in her second audition for a role ever, recorded a tape playing Arya during her lunch break at school.

GEORGE R. R. MARTIN: Holy hell. Her facial features weren't at all what I had described in the books, but she was perfect. She was Arya! She was alive!

For Arya's prim, idealistic sister, Sansa Stark, thirteen-year-old Sophie Turner was urged by her drama teacher to try out for the role. She later said the taping just seemed like "a fun, jokey thing to do." She didn't even tell her parents about the role until she made it to the final seven.

NINA GOLD (*casting director*): Sophie likes to say we found her in a field somewhere in Warwickshire, which isn't quite true, but it's almost true.

ROBERT STERNE (*casting director*): We went to her school, and she just clearly from the start had some connection with the material.

Williams and Turner met for the first time at one of their auditions and were partnered together for a chemistry read.

MAISIE WILLIAMS (*Arya Stark*): I came out of it thinking: "Even if I don't get the part of Arya, I want Sophie to get the part of Sansa."

DAVID BENIOFF: Maisie and Sophie liked each other right away. There was real chemistry even though the characters are not supposed to like each other at that point. From then on, they would be, like, giggling and laughing together, then the second you say, "Action," they were at each other's throats in a completely believable way. Being friends makes it easier for actors to play hostility between them. It was the same with Peter and Lena.

NINA GOLD: From the first read-through, they just became inseparable.

Williams and Turner would later get matching tattoos of the date "07.08.09," commemorating their casting.

SOPHIE TURNER (*Sansa Stark*): That date always meant a lot to us, and we always said we were gonna get it done. We'd been filming [season seven] for a week and were having the best time ever, and so we were like, "Fuck it, let's just do it!"

English actor Isaac Hempstead Wright had no interest in performing until he joined a drama club at school. He was just ten when he was cast as Bran Stark, the boy who winds up disabled, yet with a mystical destiny.

ISAAC HEMPSTEAD WRIGHT (*Bran Stark*): I had three auditions and then just forgot about it over the summer. I was running around playing football or whatever. Then one day I came out from school and got in my mum's car and she said, "Congratulations, Bran Stark." Oh. Cool!

Scottish actor Richard Madden was twenty-two when he was chosen for the eldest Stark son, Robb. (He shifted his accent to closer match Bean's Yorkshire dialect.) Like Joffrey, Robb is a character that the showrunners expanded from the books due to the strength of their actor's performance. "At first we just liked Richard because he was the odds-on favorite for 2009's Best-Dressed Man in Scotland Award," Weiss said in the book *Inside HBO's Game of Thrones: Seasons 1 & 2*. "He did indeed win, and in addition to his clothes, we got an amazing talent." Madden would later tell *Jimmy Kimmel Live!* that he was so destitute at the time he was cast, the role saved him from having to move back in with his parents. (Perhaps he spent too much on clothes?)

English actor Kit Harington was also only twenty-two and without any screen credits when he auditioned for the role of Stark bastard Jon Snow. But he was already acclaimed in the London acting community for his starring role in a West End production of *War Horse*.

KIT HARINGTON (*Jon Snow*): Every young male actor in the UK went in for the role. I psyched myself up massively. I remember thinking, "This is one I might be right for." Actors generally are perceptive to the energy in a room. David and Dan had been sitting in the room all day looking for a person they liked, and you could feel them . . . [*leans forward*]. After the second audition I thought I was on to something and if I lost it I would be upset.

To help sort through the audition tapes, the producers enlisted the help of Bryan Cogman, a screenwriter and a Julliard-trained actor whose wife worked as a nanny for Benioff and Peet. Cogman devoured Martin's novels and became an expert on *A Song of Ice and Fire*'s mythology.

Initially hired as Benioff's assistant, Cogman would rise through different roles throughout the series as he wrote episodes, supervised on set, and became a co-executive producer. "They gave me way too much responsibility early on, considering I had no experience," Cogman said. "But you know what? They didn't either! I think they valued the fact that I was an actor and had some training."

BRYAN COGMAN (*co-executive producer*): This is embarrassing. We were casting ladies for the character that became Ros. At that point the character was just "redheaded and a whore." One day, David, Dan, and Tom McCarthy weren't available and I was tasked with auditioning actors for this role. This Northern Irish actress comes in. I was terrified because it was this randy scene and what the fuck did I know? The sides were all these double entendres and the young lady did a nice job but she kept looking at me funny and I didn't know why.

I said, "Okay, let's try one more." Because I guess we should do more than one? She read it again, and I said, "Okay, that's great!" And she stood there for a minute and said, "Well, I guess I'll go now. . . ." The next day Nina Gold calls me and goes, "You didn't have her strip to her underwear!" She had been waiting to be told to take off her clothes. I guess that's normal when casting those roles. I felt immense guilt. Later, Esmé Bianco came in and won the role.

NINA GOLD: We don't *have* actors take their clothes off in the audition, I have to say. Though some take them off on their own accord.

ESMÉ BIANCO (*Ros*): "The Redheaded Whore" was the character name then, and she was originally just going to be in the pilot. I auditioned in my underwear. They do that because some actresses will say they are okay with doing nudity at an audition but then on the day of shooting will not be okay with it. At the time I was doing burlesque shows and lingerie modeling, so this was like just another day in the office. When the show got green-lit, the producers reached out: "Would you be interested in doing more scenes?" It was George R. R. Martin who said, "Maybe you should give her a name instead of referring to her as 'the Redheaded Whore' for the entire season."

English actor Joe Dempsie was coming off the provocative UK hit show *Skins* when he was cast as Robert Baratheon's abandoned bastard son Gendry.

JOE DEMPSIE (*Gendry*): I auditioned for two or three parts before getting Gendry. I initially thought when I wasn't getting those parts that they thought I was terrible. In hindsight, they identified people they wanted to work with and after that they were figuring out what piece in the jigsaw you are. That we have a bunch of actors that get on so well and have such good work ethics and professionalism is not by chance. David and Dan created that atmosphere. Nobody is bigger than the show. So there was very little ego.

DAVID BENIOFF: We have a lot of friends who [write on TV shows] and the problems we had to deal with over the years in terms of cast misbehavior was so minuscule compared to what most people deal with. I don't know if it's a UK thing or what, but we got so lucky given the size of the cast it's incredible. We only had like one or two dicks in minor roles.

NINA GOLD: One actress—who got the part but shall remain nameless—was reading for Robert [Sterne], and to everybody's great surprise suddenly she straddled him and started trying to take his shirt off. Robert, being a complete trouper, didn't say, "Stop, cut, how dare you," and just went with it. I could see Robert's hair slightly standing on end as he was thinking, "How do I get out of this one?" And didn't she try to kiss you?

ROBERT STERNE: Yeah, it's all about being committed to it, and sometimes they want somebody to hang on to when doing these kinds of scenes.

But the pilot's best audition story belongs to British actor John Bradley, who had just graduated from drama school when he got an opportunity to read for lovable yet blundering Night's Watch conscript Samwell Tarly.

JOHN BRADLEY (*Samwell Tarly*): I wasn't thinking it was one of the most important days in my life. It's only since then that I see it that way. I had to go to London from Manchester, where I live. So I gave myself four hours to make the two-hour journey, only to find the direct train to London had been canceled. So I had to take this huge detour.

DAN WEISS: We'd probably seen seven or eight Samwells in person that weekend during a four-day stretch. We had found a guy who was great—and it was not John Bradley. Nina said, "There's a fellow who's coming in and his train is late, would you mind waiting?" We're thinking, "It's hot up here and we're kind of hungry. But he took the train from Manchester; we can't just not see him."

JOHN BRADLEY: I've always been an overplanner and overthinker. I probably would have overthought myself into distraction and tied myself into knots about the audition if I had time on the train. But I was going at such a breakneck pace I didn't have time to think.

DAN WEISS: He ran from the station. Then he found out the elevator was out.

JOHN BRADLEY: So I ran up three flights of stairs and burst into their office. I was so grateful they didn't decide to just call it a day. I had to go in completely breathless and with all this nervous energy, which fed into my interpretation of Sam.

DAN WEISS: He looked like he was ready to pass out. He was drenched in sweat. And within thirty seconds we realized he had just cost this other guy his job, because he was completely perfect.

CHAPTER THREE

"YOU GUYS HAVE A
MASSIVE PROBLEM"

T he original *Game of Thrones* pilot began shooting on October 24, 2009. Filming lasted twenty-six days. But first, the producers had to make a decision: Where, exactly, was Westeros?

While the series would ultimately film in many countries and locations, the team needed a primary production hub as their base of operations. Picking somewhere in the British Isles made the most sense as the show was inspired by historical wars in what's now the United Kingdom. Shooting in England and Wales was quite expensive, which left Ireland, Scotland, and Northern Ireland. David Benioff and Dan Weiss were familiar with Ireland, having attended college in Dublin. But its neighbor to the north offered lucrative tax breaks that would offset the show's production cost. Northern Ireland's capital city of Belfast also had some existing studio infrastructure and crew, and its surrounding countryside had plenty of rustic filming locations and medieval ruins.

"Northern Ireland offers a broad array of diverse locations within a short drive," Benioff wrote in *Inside HBO's Game of Thrones: Seasons 1 & 2*. "Windswept hilltops, stony beaches, lush meadows, high cliffs, bucolic streams—we can shoot a day at any of these places and still sleep that night in Belfast." At the time, Northern Ireland was considered a bold choice, as the country had only recently emerged from a period of urban violence known as the Troubles. Yet picking Belfast was a decision that would define the look of the show, help transform the country's economy, and provide *Thrones* with a crew of local workers long known for their rugged fortitude.

The production set up camp around Belfast's cavernous Paint Hall studio hangar. The site is on the grounds of the abandoned shipyard that once built the RMS *Titanic,* and the hall is where White Star Line ships were once painted. The hangar sits on a windy gray corner of the world, with cold, dark water lapping against a rocky shore. A series of tall poles on an adjacent concrete slab mark the outline of the RMS *Titanic* as an eerie memorial.

The site was tough to beat, not only as a practical choice but also as an unintended metaphor. The birthplace of what was once the world's biggest and most lavish ship was about to create the world's biggest and most lavish TV drama. Yet the show's first pilot—the production's maiden voyage, if you will—almost sank the series.

DAN WEISS (*showrunner*): It was a frightening time because it was our first time running a production of any scale. And there are many, many moving parts, human and otherwise, that go into any production, especially one of this size.

Like Martin's saga, the pilot opened with a trio of Night's Watch rangers venturing beyond the Wall—a seven-hundred-foot-high border wall made of ice inspired by Hadrian's Wall (a fortification in England that once marked the border of a Roman Empire province). The Rangers have a fateful encounter with the supernatural White Walkers, an ancient race of winter demons. Only as initially conceived, the White Walkers spoke in their own fictional language, called Skroth, and their costume design wasn't ready by the time shooting began.

DAVID BENIOFF (*showrunner*): The original White Walkers looked so terrible. We just punted it.

DAN WEISS: For the first White Walker, we stuck a guy in a green suit and thought we'd figure out what he looked like later with CGI. Nobody said, "That's an enormously expensive approach to the problem you have." The thing to do was come up with [a costume], even if it's not 100 percent of the way there, and then fix it later with CGI as opposed to coming up with nothing and designing it entirely in CGI. That would have taken half the budget of the pilot just to do that.

But the pilot's finished costumes for other roles had problems too. "All the costumes looked brand-new," Benioff told *Vanity Fair*. "They all looked like they'd just been made the day before. . . . The costumes needed to look lived-in. This is a period where people weren't taking their things to the dry cleaner's. Aside from maybe the queen, everyone's clothes [should] look dirty and sweat stained."

Scotland tourist attraction Doune Castle was used for Winterfell, the seat of House Stark. It didn't make financial sense to build a Winterfell set from scratch, as the project had not been picked up to series. But Doune had an overly familiar look and was leaned on heavily for the pilot.

GEORGE R. R. MARTIN (*author, co–executive producer*): Doune Castle was where they filmed *Monty Python and the Holy Grail*. The gift shop was selling plastic coconuts.

BRYAN COGMAN (*co–executive producer*): Everything was at Winterfell in the first pilot. All the King's Landing scenes were cut from the script to save money—like Jaime and Cersei and Jon Arryn's dead body. So we met the Lannisters when they arrived at Winterfell.

And one of the Starks almost didn't survive the cutbacks.

GEORGE R. R. MARTIN: They were doing a faithful adaptation, but I knew they'd have to cut some things. The biggest thing was Dan and

David called me up and had the idea of eliminating Rickon, the youngest of the Stark children, because he didn't do much in the first book. I said I had important plans for him, so they kept him.

For the youngest actors, being in the pilot simply felt like a thrilling adventure.

ISAAC HEMPSTEAD WRIGHT (*Bran Stark*): It was like summer camp. I was ten years old, I was getting to go leave school, go to a place I've never been, get put up in a hotel, and play around with swords. The only thing was our hotel stank of sewage—people like Sean and Nikolaj were in this posh hotel and us kids were in this other one.

For the veteran actors, however, there were worrisome signs that this *Game of Thrones* thing might not be on solid footing.

NIKOLAJ COSTER-WALDAU (*Jaime Lannister*): Nobody knew what they were doing or what the hell this was. During King Robert's arrival I remember finding the whole thing ridiculous. The absurdity of doing this parallel universe with these very noble men. It's a very fine balance between being serious and believing it and just being cosplayers. There was certainly not a sense that this was going to be some game-changer for anyone. But we had a lot of fun.

MARK ADDY (*Robert Baratheon*): We were trying to establish the rules and order of this new world. In the Winterfell courtyard scene, nobody kneeled when the king arrived in the first pilot. You can't play being the king. You can't display "look at how powerful I am." People have to give you that by showing subservience. It has to be afforded to you by others. In the reshoot, everybody kneeled. It makes a huge difference in terms of establishing who's in charge.

LENA HEADEY (*Cersei Lannister*): I looked like a Vegas showgirl in the pilot—furs and massive hair, like a medieval Dolly Parton. Not that I'm complaining, I loved it.

BRYAN COGMAN: When we first shot the scene where the Starks find the direwolves—this was the version you never saw—the wonder of what a direwolf was wasn't coming across. It didn't seem important enough to the characters. And I'm little assistant Bryan running around the set yelling to anyone who would listen: "These are *direwolves*! No one has seen these in a million years! This is like seeing dinosaurs! It's not like finding puppies!" And everyone's sort of chuckling.

ESMÉ BIANCO (*Ros*): I thought it was going to be for a niche audience because it was described to me as a fantasy. So I just had a really fun day on set with Peter Dinklage, who's a generous actor and charming and sweet. I think our scene was the only scene from the pilot that wasn't reshot. Nobody had any sense of the magnitude of what was coming.

CHRISTOPHER NEWMAN (*producer*): Joffrey had a different haircut. In the original pilot, it was more pageboy cut, slightly pudding bowl–ish, like Henry the Fifth. It wasn't that it didn't suit him being a little shit, but it softened the edge. The modern cut in the version that aired gave him more spitefulness.

DAVID BENIOFF: At first it seemed to us like it was going well, but that was because we didn't know any better.

DAN WEISS: As we went on, the cracks turned into bigger cracks, which turned into fissures. You started to feel the wheels coming off by the time we got to Morocco.

In Morocco, the production staged the sequence where the smug sociopath Viserys Targaryen sells his sister, Daenerys (then played by Tamzin Merchant), into an arranged marriage to the menacing Dothraki warrior Khal Drogo. Except this version shot Daenerys's wedding at night, among several other differences.

GEORGE R. R. MARTIN: I went to Morocco for Dany's wedding in the first pilot. I played a Pentoshi nobleman with beard extensions and an enormous hat. I looked like an idiot, but it was fun.

HARRY LLOYD (*Viserys Targaryen*): I had a different wig. It was titanium and silver, and it was shorter and a bob. Looking back, it was a mistake. There were consultations: "I'm not like Draco Malfoy, I'm not like Legolas . . . how do we do this?"

IAIN GLEN (*Jorah Mormont*): It was a bit ragged and, in some ways, ill conceived, and no one had great conviction. Since the wedding was shot at night, quite a lot of money had been spent on seeing absolutely fuck-all.

GEORGE R. R. MARTIN: There are a couple of stories. As a wedding gift, Khal Drogo gives Daenerys a silver horse and she rides away. For a moment you think she's fleeing. Then she turns the horse around and leaps the horse over a big campfire. Drogo is very impressed, and it starts the relationship on a good note. We tried to film this scene. We got a top stunt rider and a top horse, a silver filly, but the filly would not jump that campfire. She got close and then was like, "There's fire there!" and would turn the other way. We tried to film it a half dozen ways. So the director goes, "Put out the fire and we'll do the fire with CGI." They put out the fire and the horse would still not jump the dead fire. It's a smart horse. It knows it's not burning now, but it was burning a little while ago! So they had to scrap that sequence, which was unfortunate, as it was a bonding moment between Dany and Khal Drogo.

Then came the filming of the wedding night. In the Emilia Clarke version, it's rape. It's not rape in my book, and it's not rape in the scene as we filmed it with Tamzin Merchant. It's a seduction. Dany and Drogo don't have the same language. Dany is a little scared but also a little excited, and Drogo is being more considerate. The only words he knows are "yes" or "no." Originally it was a fairly faithful version.

So we're by this little brook. They tied the horses to the trees and there's a seduction scene by the stream. Jason Momoa and Tamzin are naked and "having sex." And suddenly the video guy starts to laugh. The silver filly was not a filly at all. It was a colt. And it was getting visibly excited by watching these two humans. There's this horse in the background with this enormous horse schlong. So that didn't go well either.

The pilot filming wrapped. Benioff and Weiss then presented a rough cut of their pilot to family and friends to get a sense of how the episode was playing. The experience was, to put it mildly, unpleasant.

DAVID BENIOFF: I showed it to my brother-in-law and sister-in-law and just watched their reactions. You could tell watching their faces that they were bored. It wasn't anything they said. They were trying to be nice.

DAN WEISS: You listen to how sharply the pitch of somebody's voice turns up when they tell you it's good—"It's *good!*" How much higher than their average register is the word *good*? That's a gauge of how fucked you are. Our *good* was in dog-whistle territory. There were others who weren't trying to be nice but were actually trying to be helpful. [Veteran television producer] Craig Mazin told us: "You guys have a massive problem."

GINA BALIAN (*former vice president of drama at HBO*): Their screening was the final confirmation for them that we had problems.

One frequently cited issue at HBO was that the pilot lacked "scope."

Thrones was supposed to be an epic fantasy, but the production felt "small," particularly for its steep budget and exotic locations.

MICHAEL LOMBARDO (*former HBO programming president*): There were some concerns about whether we were getting enough wide shots. Are we getting the coverage we need? We hired the best costume designer and the best art director and shot this in Northern Ireland and Morocco, yet there was very little scope. I remember the quote was, "We could have shot this in Burbank."

IAIN GLEN: Some bigwig at HBO said, "Why the fuck did we go to Morocco? You can't see fucking diddly squat, we could have shot it in a car park!"

GINA BALIAN: Somebody said, "It looked like it was shot in my backyard."

The tone also felt off, like a series set in the world of *Downton Abbey* or a Merchant Ivory film, instead of Westeros and Essos.

MICHAEL LOMBARDO: Some scenes were fantastic, like at Winterfell with the family. Arya, Sansa, Tyrion. But there was something about it that felt vaguely similar to British period dramas.

Another concern was caused by hand-wringing over the project's fantasy elements. *A Song of Ice and Fire* is an intensely realistic drama with moments of supernatural magic. But nobody was exactly sure how much *Thrones* should have of each genre, and it showed.

BRYAN COGMAN: Is it fantasy with dramatic trappings? Is it a drama with fantasy trappings? There was a nervousness about the pilot leaning into the fantasy too much—ultimately to a fault. Key exposition was cut to make the dialogue sound more "real," and as a result, the pilot didn't make much sense. The impulse to not be over-the-top Shakespearian and Tolkien-esque was right—you're trying to make it as grounded as possible—but this is still an epic fantasy, and if you ignore that, it's to the detriment of your story.

One confusing aspect wasn't entirely the filmmakers' fault—they couldn't afford to stage any King's Landing scenes, which more firmly established the Lannister family in the reshoot. But the dialogue didn't help either. The shocking punch of Jaime pushing Bran out the window seemed nonsensical, as viewers didn't realize that Jaime and Cersei were sibling lovers trying to protect their treasonous secret. The producers also tried to help explain the show's backstory by adding at least one flashback (of Ned Stark's father and brother being killed by the Mad King), but that idea was later scrapped as it just seemed to add to the narrative muddiness.

GEORGE R. R. MARTIN: I liked the pilot. I realized later that I was a poor person to judge because I was too close to it. Some didn't know Jaime and Cersei were brother and sister. Well that wasn't a problem for me! My great familiarity with the material made it hard for me to objectively judge. I liked that they kept a considerable level of complexity. I'm told I'm under penalty of death if I ever show it to anyone.

DAVID BENIOFF: HBO was very much on the fence. It's a traditional thing at any studio that the last regime's projects are going to be less appealing to the new regime. And this was a very expensive project.

DAN WEISS: It seemed like Mike was leaning toward no. He was not at all pleased, and for good reason. He decided maybe it would be better to just take the loss on this one.

MICHAEL LOMBARDO: We were in the conference room and had the producers in for a "come to Jesus" meeting. The question was whether the showrunners thought they nailed it. Because if you're on a different page, that's really a concern. How do we show this pilot to our CEO and convince him to pick this up to series? How do we convince him this is a gamble worth taking? We go into a mode of "how do we fix this."

The producers knew they were in deep trouble. "I was just staring at Mike's face—it was like a horror movie," Weiss recalled to *Vanity Fair.* "To his credit, he didn't want me to feel terrible. He was trying to keep his face impassive."

Benioff and Weiss drew up a list of what they knew wasn't working and how to fix each issue.

DAN WEISS: We'd done a lot of soul searching. The one thing I think we did right is we owned all the mistakes. We didn't point fingers. We said: "We know this isn't good, and here is what went wrong and how we would do it differently the next time." We just went down the line. I think they got the sense, which was honest, that we weren't coming in trying to explain why the bugs were features. We were all on the same page that where we want to be is many levels up from this.

CAROLYN STRAUSS (*former programming president at HBO; executive producer*): There was a lot of begging and pleading. I think what was clearly evident was that there was a show here. This is why you do a pilot, because you're looking at what works and what doesn't and whether this thing has legs. Once certain things were fixed, this would be a story you can tell over many episodes that keeps moving, with characters that keep evolving, but not so fast that you run out of story.

The rough pilot and the revision plan were handed to HBO's co-president Richard Plepler, who was the ultimate decision-maker. The company had already sunk $10 million into this dragon drama. Would they double down?

DAVID BENIOFF: We knew going into that screening that his decision was going to make or break us. It was a very tense hour while waiting for a phone call from Gina.

DAN WEISS: The line about pain being a great teacher is true. It was so deeply unpleasant to have been given the opportunity to make something like this, an opportunity we knew would most likely never come along again, and then to have the sense there was a 52/48 chance you fucked it up. It was one of the most horrible feelings I can remember.

DAVID BENIOFF: Then Richard came out and said, "You know, let's make this."

RICHARD PLEPLER (*former co-president and CEO of HBO*): You could see that some of the casting and the narrative was off. It needed to be fixed; it needed to be reshot. But the overall emotional response was that you could feel how engaging it could be. So just as you could feel there were a range of problems that needed to be addressed, you could equally feel that there was magic in there.

DAN WEISS: To his credit, Richard saw through the mistakes to what this could be if the mistakes were fixed.

HBO ordered ten episodes of *Game of Thrones*, including a reshot pilot. Changes weren't only made to the script and the production plan but among the cast and crew as well. First-time TV director McCarthy was replaced on episode one by a top HBO veteran, Tim Van Patten, who had directed many acclaimed episodes of HBO dramas. Meanwhile, British-American actress Jennifer Ehle, who'd played Catelyn Stark in the original pilot, had changed her mind about the series, telling *The Daily Beast* she wanted to spend more time with her newborn daughter.

MICHAEL LOMBARDO: The actress who played Catelyn decided she didn't want to move to Northern Ireland. I'm like, "*What?*" Then you have a conversation with yourself about whether to force her to uphold her contract. In retrospect it was one of the best things that could have happened. Michelle Fairley took over the role and was fantastic.

Benioff had spotted Fairley in a London production of *Othello,* where she played Emilia, whose tragic final scenes of breakdown and murder are not unlike the eventual fate of Catelyn Stark. "Emilia's not a character I generally notice in *Othello,*" Benioff recounted in the book *Inside HBO's Game of Thrones: Seasons 1 & 2.* "Iago's wife? Who cares? But Michelle was so absurdly good that I left the theater thinking, 'Who the hell was that? And is she available?'"

But the team's most difficult decision was to recast Daenerys Targaryen. One source said that breaking the news to Merchant was "the hardest phone call [the producers] ever had to make."

MICHAEL LOMBARDO: There was a piece of casting we had to rethink, [a role] that was compromised. We all knew Daenerys's journey was critical. Her scenes with Jason just didn't work.

JASON MOMOA (*Khal Drogo*): [Merchant] was great. I'm not sure why everything was done. But when Emilia got there that's when everything clicked for me. I wasn't really "there" until she arrived.

BRYAN COGMAN: Everybody involved in making the original pilot scored such a bull's-eye with so many of our actors. I thought Tamzin did a really good job. It's hard to say why things didn't work out. Ultimately, it's obvious Emilia Clarke was born to play that part.

CHAPTER FOUR

"My Book Come to Life"

Second chances in Hollywood are rare. You take a big swing, you miss, and you're done—definitely with that project, and sometimes with your entire career. *Game of Thrones* was granted a very rare second chance. The producers, cast, and crew were determined not to blow it. Filming resumed in July 2010 with a newfound sense of meticulousness and urgency. "We were very lucky to be given a ten-million-dollar rehearsal," said Harry Lloyd (Viserys Targaryen). "Then the reshoot was bigger. There was an investment on a grander scale."

Massive new sets were created by British production designer Gemma Jackson at the Paint Hall (including the Red Keep in King's Landing, with its iconic Iron Throne, and the Eyrie in the Vale of Arryn, with its perilous Moon Door). Jackson also constructed a new Winterfell at the historic Castle Ward, a step up from the ruins of Doune Castle, and an expansive courtyard for Castle Black at Magheramorne quarry, a set that included a fully operating winch elevator. And costume designer Michele Clapton took the cast's already impressive outfits to another level with a feeling of lived-in authenticity. The crew's preparations stunned the actors when they arrived on set as they bonded and settled into their roles.

KRISTIAN NAIRN (*Hodor*): I remember the first day walking into the Paint Hall and seeing they had built a castle inside of this big shed. I'm a complete fantasy nerd, and I was blown away. Nothing looked fake; it all looked correct and real.

KIT HARINGTON (*Jon Snow*): I was dazzled by all of it. I've since worked out that most film sets are not as magnificent as *Thrones*. So I just assumed this is what every film set was like. Looking back, I realize how special it was.

MARK ADDY (*Robert Baratheon*): The sets were huge and surprised me. You feel like you're in the world. There was so much with the costumes and the sets that made your job easier. Very little green screen.

PETER DINKLAGE (*Tyrion Lannister*): It was so great not to be wearing a costume with Velcro on it.

As Richard Madden once described his hefty, layered costume to Westeros.org: "It took some forty minutes to put it on. I needed help because there were all these straps and buckles. I loved it, because it really affected my performance and helped me as an actor. It changed the way I walk, the way I breathe, the way I stood and hold my posture. At 4 A.M., putting on the costume could be a killer, but it was really useful for me in helping to build the character of Robb."

JOHN BRADLEY (*Samwell Tarly*): Walking onto the Castle Black set the first time, it hit home that this is a real thing. That brought a considerable amount of pressure to it. Until then, I had the satisfaction of getting the job and my friends and family back in Manchester back-slapping. Then you get on that set and see how many people it took to make this thing, and you're around actors at a level I've never been at before. Kit already had a great reputation in theater; he was revered by a lot of people I went to acting college with. And people like Owen Teale [Ser Alliser Thorne] and James Cosmo [Commander Jeor Mormont] and other actors had achieved so much.

There was also a 360-degree element to the set. There was nothing to distract you. The smoke, the smell of burning flambeaux—it may not be pleasant, but it really did immerse you. You're feeling like your character would feel and smelling what your character would smell. If you can sacrifice some comfort, it helps the process.

So on my first day, I was just given my sword and told, "Be useless with that." I'm useless with that in real life. So the fact I could barely pick it up and didn't really know what I was doing was perfect.

KIT HARINGTON: Alfie, Richard, and I clicked instantly as the young lads. We were guys straight out of drama school, so we might as well become best mates, and we became best mates. Then obviously Maisie and Sophie and Isaac fell into being little siblings. We felt protective over them. And they, I think, looked up to us as the older kids. We felt like a family quite quickly.

Harington filmed one of his most important scenes in the series very early on, though the actor didn't know how meaningful it was at the time—Jon Snow's farewell to his father, who cryptically assured him, "You may not have my name, but you have my blood."

KIT HARINGTON: I remember that scene better than most. I remember it being my big scene, and my only scene with just Sean. I thought, "This does mark Jon out as having a secret." I would have put a lot of work into that scene had I known what it meant.

TIM VAN PATTEN (director): I didn't want that scene to be overly sentimental. And we decided to do it at these crossroads in order to play the fact that they never see each other again.

ISAAC HEMPSTEAD WRIGHT (*Bran Stark*): Kit, Richard, and Alfie became like big brothers to me. I was thinking, "They're so cool!" I went out and bought a jacket that looked like Kit Harington's. We would all hang out in the greenroom teaching each other card games.

MARK ADDY: The boys, Kit, Richard, and Alfie, were just young lads who were very excited about getting to carry a sword and wear armor.

Williams decided during the first season to learn to how use a sword with her left hand, just like Arya in the books, despite being right-handed herself. Keeping up the continuity of Arya's being left-handed would end up being a bit of a nightmare. "Eight years later, and I'm still paying for that mistake," she told *Vogue* UK in 2019. "In the beginning, I just had to do a little sparring. Now, I'm doing entire fight sequences with the wrong hand, and I'm like, 'Why did I ever think this was a good idea?'"

MAISIE WILLIAMS (*Arya Stark*): I look back at when I was twelve and I can tell [watching scenes] when I was really tired that day on the set. I was thinking, "I'm hungry, I'm tired," all those silly twelve-year-old things.

DAVID BENIOFF (*showrunner*): I remember we had dinner with Sophie and her mom and it was the first time she had ever eaten shrimp.

SOPHIE TURNER (*Sansa Stark*): My mom read the books. I wasn't allowed to read much of it because of the explicit stuff. But I read [the Sansa-point-of-view] chapters to know what was going through my character's mind.

Wright had to learn about "the explicit stuff" in order to understand his scene in the pilot when Bran discovers Jaime and Cersei. "I was told what was going on, but it meant that my mum had to give me the sex talk a little earlier—with some topics that probably aren't covered by general sex talks," Wright told *Jimmy Kimmel Live!*

But Bran was mostly paired for scenes with Kristian Nairn's Hodor.

ISAAC HEMPSTEAD WRIGHT: As an icebreaker when we first met, Kristian handed me his iPhone. I was playing the Harry Potter Spells app. He said, "Whatever you do, don't drop my phone." Then I threw it and smashed his phone into a thousand pieces. From then on we had a very fun relationship.

KRISTIAN NAIRN: When Joffrey and the Lannisters arrive in Winterfell, that's one of my best memories. It was probably one of the biggest gatherings of the cast. Everyone was still alive among the Starks, Robert Baratheon, the Lannisters. Apart from Daenerys, the whole cast was there. That was the day I realized what a big production it was going to be and what I was a part of. That was a fantastic day—everyone together for one of the first and last times.

MARK ADDY: One day, Lena Headey was in hysterics due to the discovery that Sean Bean had a nail brush in his bathroom. It was such a serious scene and between takes we were enjoying the fact that Sean might have a soap on a rope at home.

GETHIN ANTHONY (*Renly Baratheon*): My first day was a small council scene and it was terrifying. I was fairly green, and these were guys I'd looked up to when growing up. You're worried somebody is going to fire you at any moment. I only had one line—"If you can't keep the king's peace, perhaps the City Watch should be commanded by somebody who can"—and I still managed to mess it up. Director Brian Kirk came over to me: "Hey, how you doing, buddy?" I was like, "I'm good! I'm good. . . ." He was like, "Don't worry. I'm pretty nervous too." That settled me down. He could read the room.

Later, I had my first time filming one-on-one with Sean. In my mind, this is the point where you prove you know your lines. The rehearsal of the scene started, and there was this big hanging pause. I looked at Sean. Sean looked at me. And nothing happened. I'm thinking, *Is he going to talk or what?* It's a bit awkward. Then the first AD goes—looking at me—"Not to worry, chaps, let's go again!" Then again, we just stood there staring at each other for what seemed like an unendurable age. Then they stop again, going, "Okay, guys, this doesn't seem to be, um . . ." And Sean's looking at me. He asks: "You all right?" And I'm going, "Yeah! I'm fine." And I'm thinking, "*Oh God, oh God, what am I doing wrong? Am I supposed to signal him or something? What's happening?!*" I felt pure terror. Eventually, one of the writing assistants comes over to Sean and says, "Is everything okay? This is your first line." Sean goes, "Oh, we're doing *that* scene!" He thought it was our next scene where it did start with me. He had been working so incredibly hard and had like fifty scenes in his head.

AIDAN GILLEN (*Littlefinger*): One of my first scenes was an obvious Littlefinger character establisher—"distrusting me was the wisest thing you've done since you climbed off your horse"—and I was very happy that it dropped into place so easily, that we could inhabit this fantastical world but for it all to seem rooted in truth. I'd admired Sean as an actor from way back—the 1988 film *Stormy Monday*, to be precise—and he was as I'd expected him to be: magnetic and solid, but still vulnerable and fairly quiet. Sean's not the kind of guy who feels he has to talk all the time between takes, and neither am I. I wouldn't say I got to know him terribly well, but I got to know Ned Stark terribly well.

GETHIN ANTHONY: I was once walking along the parking lot in the rain and wearing this amazing leather outfit that I was trying not to get wet while carrying an umbrella. Sean had his driver swerve to go through a puddle to spray me. I look up, and Sean got out of the car giggling, "Yeah, yeah, I told him to do that!"

ESMÉ BIANCO (*Ros*): It was fun at that stage because nobody knew what was going to happen and how big the show was going to be. No one was carrying on their backs this burden of the fandom and everybody's expectations. It was a time of great freedom. Everybody was having so much fun and, you know, drinking a lot. It was quite the party that season.

The first season wasn't quite as enjoyable for the producers and directors. The team was scrambling to pull off ten hugely ambitious episodes on a relatively limited budget despite having a lack of collective experience, particularly with creating epic fantasy. *Thrones* was also filming its episodes out of order, which was highly unusual for a television drama and more like the production of a feature film.

It was decided that Irish director Brian Kirk would tackle episodes three, four, and five—which would be the first ones shot—and then a trio of top HBO veterans would film the rest of the season: Tim Van Patten helmed episode two and the reshot episode one; Daniel Minahan was assigned six, seven, and eight; and Alan Taylor took on nine and ten. The production was divided into two filming units that would often shoot scenes at the same time in different locations. One was called Dragon, and the other was Wolf.

Hanging over everything was the painful knowledge that the production had already failed once and was being trusted not to screw up again. The creatives were determined to avoid their past mistakes, yet there was only so much they could plan in advance when each day presented unexpected problems—everything from torrential storms to discovering, for instance, that you cannot have ravens and food on set at the same time or else the birds will dart off camera and eat it.

BRYAN COGMAN (*co–executive producer*): It was the Wild West. We didn't know what we were doing, and because it was being all shot out of order, it was hard to tell while shooting it if it was working. It was new territory for HBO, given the genre. It was new territory for David and

Dan, as they'd never done a TV show. I'd only done five months in a writers' room on a failed NBC series. Even the directors and the designers and everybody who had amazing credits behind them had never done a show like this. Northern Ireland had some previous film production, but this was far and away the biggest operation they ever had. We were all learning how to make a TV show. HBO gave us the freedom to fall flat on our face and try things. I also think they were also concentrating, candidly, on making *Boardwalk Empire* and *Luck* while we were far away in Belfast, so there was some degree of being left alone.

TIM VAN PATTEN: I was, foolishly, very initially reluctant to do this. I was coming off *Sopranos* and *Boardwalk Empire*. I don't much get into fantasy, and I was so exhausted from [*Boardwalk*] and on my hiatus. HBO sent me the book, and it was so dense, I couldn't digest it. They were saying, "What do we do with this thing?" I was like, "I don't get it, I don't know why you're doing this." I kept saying no. It took them a month to wear me down. I [joined the production] out of complete loyalty to the company because they had been so great to me. The one thing going for it was that the script was so tight that I "saw" it, you know? But I went into it having no idea what the result would be. And it was grueling because they'd already done a pilot and they needed this to work, so the pressure was on.

DANIEL MINAHAN (*director*): I got to Belfast, and I was cross-boarding three episodes at once. I went into the throne room, and I was like, "Holy shit." The throne room was just this huge empty room! How do you block something in here? I'm thinking, "These people are trying to kill me. If we leave for the airport now, by the time they discover we are gone it will be too late." So we just used people as foreground and background. They became like a wall. We used every character as set dressing.

BRYAN COGMAN: We were even figuring out what the look of the show was. Like: How is the show lit? There was a lot of emphasis in those days on making all environments lit very specifically to make each distinct, so the viewer would know when they were in King's Landing as opposed to Winterfell. We were really trying to orient the viewer and learn from all the mistakes of the pilot.

One inspiration was the films of legendary Japanese director Akira Kurosawa, whose titles, including *Seven Samurai, Yojimbo,* and the aptly titled *Throne of Blood,* defined epic cinema and inspired a generation of modern filmmakers. Benioff and Weiss devoured Kurosawa's movies before starting production and encouraged their directors and director of photography, Alik Sakharov, to attempt to capture Kurosawa's classical style. It's an influence that's particularly noticeable when the three Night's Watch rangers ride out beyond the Wall in the first episode. Even during the reshoot, however, there wasn't any sense that the show's opening scene would look particularly impressive once it was finished.

TIM VAN PATTEN: There was a studio executive visiting when we were shooting the first scene out in a quarry outside Belfast. You could see a preexisting quarry wall, and nothing you were looking at told you there was going to be [a seven-hundred-foot ice wall in the shot]. All day long, it was just three guys on horses. I remember feeling these seeds of doubt around the monitors. Like, "What are we doing here? What is this, exactly?" I could understand their nervousness because even I was thinking, "Oh God, I hope this works." But you got to have confidence. Even if you're not confident, act like it, because people feed off your confidence.

Naturally, the fledgling production had some growing pains.

DANIEL MINAHAN: It was so cold in Paint Hall, but it's supposed to be like [King's Landing's Mediterranean climate]. We were shooting this sequence with Cersei. The handmaidens behind her were only wearing these gauzy togas. And one of them just fell flat, fainted, because she was so overcome with cold. At first I thought it was a joke, then we ran up there.

KRISTIAN NAIRN: I got a back injury that season I'm probably going to have for the rest of my life. My first day was the scene where Tyrion gives Bran the plans for the saddle. They had me carry Isaac up and down that hall seventy-four times. Probably halfway through that my back had given up. I was afraid to say no. It was my first day on set, so I couldn't not do this. It's my own fault for not being honest. You wanted to appear bulletproof.

ISAAC HEMPSTEAD WRIGHT: Kristian Nairn still sends me bills from his chiropractor.

PETER DINKLAGE: We shot one scene on horseback on the side of a cliff during a serious windstorm. The horses were very nervous. One guy was thrown from the horse just literally a couple feet away from the edge of a cliff.

Michelle Fairley recalled that incident as well. "Peter, whose legs just reach the height of the saddle . . . hadn't a lot of horse-riding experience," the Catelyn Stark actress told the Popcorn Taxi film festival in Australia. "The horse goes ballistic. This [other] actor in a complete suit of armor was being thrown all over the place; everybody is jaw on the ground. The horse does one final buck and this actor goes flying through the air. Literally, he's in slow motion and you just see this suit of armor go flat on his back. We're like, 'Oh my God, he's dead! He's dead!' And he doesn't move. The horses are in shock as well. You could hear a pin drop. Even the wind stopped. And the next thing was he moved two fingers and everybody went over. And Peter's like, 'Are these horses trained? Are these horses trained?'"

PETER DINKLAGE: So that was a bit difficult in terms of, like, life and death.

DANIEL MINAHAN: There was a scene where they opened up the stomach of a stag [when the Starks find the direwolves in the reshot version of the first episode]. They did it for real, and it releases this horrible smell. All the actors—the boys—threw up.

TIM VAN PATTEN: That is a fact. Instead of using a taxidermy stag and then cutting to show some organ meats, we had an actual dead stag. It was bloated and filled with gas. We did everything in the scene up to opening up the stag's belly. Then we got to that moment when we drive the knife into it. Nobody was expecting this: The entrails fell out, and the odor sent the crew scrambling and vomiting.

BRYAN COGMAN: I've still never smelled anything so terrible, and I wasn't even anywhere near it. I was across the meadow in a producer's tent. Just thinking about it, I can smell it right now.

TIM VAN PATTEN: I was sick and gagging and crying laughing.

DAVID BENIOFF: We didn't even have security in season one. We did a scene where Ned is looking for the armory where he's going to find Gendry. He's walking by racks of swords and daggers. These German tourists were coming by and just picking stuff up. I ran over, "No, no, put that down!" They were just kind of staring at me like, "Who is this dumb American yelling and telling me I can't pick up this sword?"

Reshooting the pilot also meant actors had to redo scenes they thought were finished, which in some cases was awkward. The scene of Jaime having sex with Cersei had to be, well, repositioned.

TIM VAN PATTEN: It was a lot to ask of the actors, to come back and redo something. For Lena, having to go back to that scene had to be incredibly difficult. In fact, I know it was, because we had conversations about it. And I totally get it. The scene wasn't working in the [original] pilot. I can't be specific about it. It was a matter of taste. The scripted stuff was the same, but it needed to be shot from another perspective, and she needed to be protected in that scene.

Then there was the matter of pulling off the season on the show's budget. HBO was generous, but the production couldn't come close to covering the scale of Martin's novel.

GEORGE R. R. MARTIN (*author, co–executive producer*): We were told we would have a good budget but not as high as *Rome*. "We don't want you to cost as much as *Rome*." So there were a number of points we had to cut back. The jousting tournament was one of them. A tournament in the Middle Ages sponsored by the king in the capital [was] a huge thing. And Bryan wrote a faithful version. There were dozens of knights, you saw eight different jousts, you got this sense of pageantry and competitors rising and falling and the commoners betting. We should have at least been as big as *A Knight's Tale,* but we couldn't even achieve that. The only jousts we saw were essential to the plot. Still, I thought it worked pretty well.

DAN WEISS (*showrunner*): The bulk of the joust sequence worked very, very well. We maybe could have put some more people in there. You're making thousands and thousands of decisions over the course of a show, and some of them are not going to be the best. It's really more about batting average.

GEORGE R. R. MARTIN: Where we really fell down in terms of budget was my least favorite scene in the entire show, in all eight seasons: King Robert goes hunting. Four guys walking on foot through the woods carrying spears and Robert is giving Renly shit. In the books, Robert goes off hunting, we get word he was gored by a boar, and they bring him back and he dies. So I never did [a hunting scene]. But I knew what a royal hunting party was like. There would have been a hundred guys. There would have been pavilions. There would have been huntsmen. There would have been dogs. There would have been horns blowing—*that's* how a king goes hunting! He wouldn't have just been walking through the woods with three of his friends holding spears hoping to meet a boar. But at that point, we couldn't afford horses or dogs or pavilions.

Or battles. In Martin's first *A Song of Ice and Fire* book, there were two clashes between the Stark and Lannister armies. The first, the Battle on the Green Fork, described Tyrion and his Lannister army riding out to fight a host that they had been tricked into believing was Robb Stark's entire army, when it was actually a relatively small force of just two thousand men that Robb sent as a diversion.

DAVID BENIOFF: We did have plans to show Tyrion marching into battle behind the Mountain. We had a whole way we wanted to shoot it following Tyrion's eye level as the Mountain is just [cutting soldiers down]. Ultimately we had to make some really tough decisions. We ran out of time to shoot it properly, and we'd much rather have a great scene with our characters than a crappy version of a battle.

DAN WEISS: We didn't want battles to look like a PlayStation 2 game. We wanted it to look at the same level [of quality] as the rest of the show.

ALAN TAYLOR (*director*): We settled on the idea of knocking Tyrion out. I loved what that offered. My favorite dramatic structures are when you build up something and then pull the carpet out from underneath it. So the fact that Tyrion has this rousing speech and we're building to what we think will be a huge battle and then we missed it was fun. I also really loved the imagery I got to play with to bring him back to consciousness. He's floating over the terrain of the battlefield, a shot I unapologetically stole from *Gladiator*.

The book's other major clash was the Battle of the Whispering Wood, where the majority of Robb's forces take Jaime Lannister's army by surprise, thanks to the distraction provided by the Battle on the Green Fork and the Starks' forging an alliance with House Frey. The producers always knew there wouldn't be enough resources to stage the Whispering Wood clash (which isn't shown in the books anyway) and instead had a tense scene where Catelyn anxiously waited to see which army would emerge victorious from the forest. Then Robb triumphantly rode out with Jaime as his hostage.

ALAN TAYLOR: I remember reading: "40,000 horsemen ride out of the woods." We ran forty horses out of the woods. But it worked fine. As long as you think there's a lot more horses in those woods, you buy it. It's all puny and adorable from the standpoint of what the show became later, but at the time you had to be inventive and let the audience fill in the gaps.

The *Thrones* team was also introduced to what would become their greatest nemesis throughout the series: Northern Ireland's temperamental weather systems. The production would eventually develop coping strategies to stay on schedule during even severe downpours, but in the first season their plans were knocked off course by freezing rain and wind.

BRYAN COGMAN: Weather killed us those first few months. We were slashing script pages left and right to make the day. We had this five-page scene we had to cut to one because we didn't have time and the rain was not letting up. It was this big sequence at a feast in the pavilion tournament where Robert gets drunk and hits Cersei by accident and there's all this business. Then the Hound offers to escort Sansa back to the Red Keep. But because we had to cut the entire sequence that established the Hound escorting Sansa, we ended up not being able to use a scene we shot earlier from the book where the Hound gives Sansa his origin story.

So at the last second we gave the Hound's origin story to Littlefinger to tell it to Sansa. We gave the pages to [Littlefinger actor] Aidan Gillen that same day. That's how it was in season one, and we never really did pages-on-the-day after that.

For Gillen, the switch meant he suddenly had to introduce Littlefinger's relationship with Sansa—a complex allegiance that extends through most of the series—on very short notice. While the monologue was entirely about the Hound, Gillen's performance makes the viewer think about Petyr Baelish, whose conspiratorial demeanor hinted that his interest in the young Stark daughter was less than innocent.

AIDAN GILLEN (*Petyr "Littlefinger" Baelish*): I've always liked getting handed things last minute. It smashes any other anxieties around other scenes that day into relief as you've now got to learn and perfect this new thing as best you can in twenty minutes or whatever. It's also what excited me about screen acting from before I even did it. I knew François Truffaut and Woody Allen and Federico Fellini had a normal practice of handing dialogue out to actors on the day. It keeps you on your toes.

That scene worked very well for Baelish in that oblique way, talking about one thing while thinking something else; charming and disarming and looking for clues. [His monologue] was really for the benefit of both Stark sisters, not just Sansa. A good time later, I was talking to [the Hound actor Rory McCann], who told me he'd been down to deliver those lines, but they went my way instead. I was mortified because if I'd known I'd have said something about it to him beforehand. As it worked out, it seemed right. It established an aspect of my character quite strongly and kindled that tricky Sansa-Baelish dynamic.

While filming Daenerys's wedding in Malta—which replaced Morocco as the season's desert location—the production also ran into some bad luck with the weather.

CHRISTOPHER NEWMAN (*producer*): The first day of shooting, a huge storm came in and took out our set. Within a three-hour period, the whole set was submerged and blown away. So we lost days of shooting, and you just try to recover the best that you can.

Cutting pages from the scripts, due to either budget, weather, or a lack of time, had an unintended consequence: HBO's supposedly epic hour-long drama series was making sitcom-length episodes.

BRYAN COGMAN: We discovered that when you cut a page from a script, you're cutting a minute of screen time. So if you cut enough pages, your episodes will come in at thirty minutes. Episodes three, four, and five were coming in at only half an hour.

GINA BALIAN (*former vice president of drama at HBO*): It was late in the process, you're thinking you're almost done, and then you realize your episodes are short. And the way the cast was scheduled meant they weren't all still there. We also didn't have every set at our disposal. So the producing team said: "You've got these actors, these sets . . . what can you do?"

BRYAN COGMAN: As a result, we wrote all of these new scenes that ended up defining the style of the show. They were these wonderful, lengthy [conversations between two characters, or "two-handers"], because we needed scenes that would fill the time, use our series regulars, and use our existing sets, but not cost money or take too long to shoot. As a result you get scenes like the one with Robert and Cersei. If that problem hadn't happened, I don't think we would have had as rich and successful of a show.

The quiet episode five scene between Robert and Cersei was a six-minute showstopper depicting a royal marriage in ruins. The scene was not in Martin's novel, as his books employ a structure where each chapter is told from the viewpoint of a specific character and neither Cersei nor Robert was a "viewpoint character" (though Cersei becomes a viewpoint character in the later books).

"I felt something for you once, you know," Cersei told Robert. "Was it ever possible for us? Was there ever a time, ever a moment?"

"No," Robert replied. "Does that make you feel better or worse?"

"It doesn't make me feel anything."

The scene was also one of the first to prove that *Thrones* could deliver intimate, character-driven moments on par with any "serious" drama.

DAVID BENIOFF: There are lots of scenes over the season that came from that "what if" process. George created this world that's so fully fleshed out and dimensional that you think about what the people in this story are doing when they're not in the main line of the plot. Robert and Cersei may hate each other, but they can't avoid each other 100 percent of the time. Every once in a while they will find themselves alone together, and what will they say?

MARK ADDY (*Robert Baratheon*): It was a fantastic scene largely because of Lena. My memory of shooting it was terror. I was handed that scene the morning we were shooting the boar hunt. So I'm out there doing the boar hunt while trying desperately to memorize this seven-page scene. They promised they'd break it down into little chunks, but that never happened. We needed to do the whole thing, and again and again. Lena was brilliant and I was just remembering words. It's a lovely scene. I just wish I had longer to learn it.

LENA HEADEY (*Cersei Lannister*): The scene had a melancholy low energy, which had to do with these two people being tired of it all—of their marriage. We also shot it at the end of a very long day and were just knackered.

BRYAN COGMAN: And that's when Cersei really came to life. Up until that point, she's Ice Queen Cersei as seen through the eyes of our heroes. It really freed us to leave the strict character POV structure of the books and explore these characters and have fun with pairing them up. In some ways, such scenes break all the rules of screenwriting—the rule is that every scene must propel the narrative forward, and most of these did not. But fuck it, that rule's wrong.

ALAN TAYLOR: What surprised me was how long some of the scenes were. I remember getting cranky with Dave and Dan about scenes that were eight pages of dialogue or thirteen pages walking and talking. I'd beg them to reduce them, and they would always refuse, and then we would shoot and it would be fine. But they're daunting when you first read them.

Another scene spawned from that last-minute scramble was a three-and-a-half-minute chat between the devious master of coin, Petyr Baelish, and the enigmatic master of whisperers, Varys, in the throne room.

DAN WEISS: You have these two master connivers and, perhaps with the exception of Tyrion, the two smartest guys in the story. It's like the head of the KGB and the head of the CIA getting together for a coffee break.

CONLETH HILL (*Varys*): Varys was very enigmatic, always. That's easy to do. You just play the moment and let people wonder. It's a very cerebral part. I never fight anyone. I never have sex with anyone. He had a way of speaking in court and council meetings that had a marked difference from when he talked with someone he trusted. Initially, there was talk of Varys being a master of disguise, which we never did. I thought it was going to be an Alec Guinness or Peter Sellers role or something.

GEORGE R. R. MARTIN: Conleth Hill is such a marvelous Varys. You meet Conleth, he's nothing like Varys. You can't even recognize him. He just vanishes into Varys.

DAN WEISS: Aidan almost turned Littlefinger into a mystical embodiment of will to power and thriving on chaos. There's something so impenetrable about everything that he does that he's like an onion that you keep peeling away the skins of and there's never an end to the skin.

Along the way, there were constant discussions over staging even the smallest elements of this new world. One example was a debate between Benioff and Weiss about a scene where blind Maester Aemon was doing a bit of busywork during his chat with Jon Snow at Castle Black.

DAVID BENIOFF: You see [Maester] Aemon chopping meat. . . .

DAN WEISS: He's chopping meat. Why can't a blind guy chop meat?

DAVID BENIOFF: He can definitely. I just think you would probably have your steward do it. I looked at the dailies, and I called Dan: "Why is this blind hundred-year-old man chopping meat?"

DAN WEISS: The actor doing the chopping, Peter Vaughan, is legally blind. So whatever he was doing, he's a blind person doing it. I stand behind that.

The first five episodes of the first season solidly established the show's world and characters. The sixth hour, "A Golden Crown," written by Jane Espenson, was when *Thrones* began to take off. Suddenly the show's individual components were working together as a whole, the narrative pace picked up, and some dark humor seeped in.

One standout sequence was in the mountain castle of the Eyrie, where Tyrion first emerged from the show's packed ensemble as a particularly likable and sympathetic character. Held captive by Lysa Arryn (Kate Dickie), Tyrion launches into a profane and defiant speech and hires rogue sellsword Bronn (Jerome Flynn) to represent him during trial by combat. The contrast between the practical and unscrupulous Bronn and his opponent—an "honorable" knight weighted down by clunky armor—was a splendid example of *Thrones'* brutal pragmatism overturning traditional Arthurian hero storytelling.

DANIEL MINAHAN: Jerome did most of his own work because he wasn't wearing a helmet. He made the choice not to do that and just hang back like a boxer during the fight.

DAVID BENIOFF: Gemma Jackson, our production designer, did a fantastic job [on the Eyrie set] with very little time and budget. That Moon Door, the level of detail. You see a shot of these two guys turning a wheel, you see the door open, you assume it's the magic of photography making that happen. But she designed it so the wheel really does open the door.

DAN WEISS: The Moon Door was real enough for Jerome Flynn to have fallen through it and nearly killed himself.

At the conclusion of the sequence, Tyrion happily gives his thuggish jailer Mord a sack of coin. The moment is the first time the audience is shown, not merely told, "a Lannister always pays his debts."

PETER DINKLAGE: God, that's a lifetime ago. I loved Bronn the mercenary fighting the Tin Man. You know, when I threw the coin to the jailer, paying his debt? That's when I really keyed in [to the character]. At first I was like: "Who is this guy? He's got whores around and has a lot of money. . . ." But when he gives Mord the jailer that tip and the actor made this face . . . that's who Tyrion is. He's like a great director, thinking of everything, and will follow through on everything.

The hour also contained one of the show's best lines, a two-word summation of the tale's focus on survival and an affirmation of life. Arya's

Braavosi instructor, Syrio Forel, played by British actor Miltos Yerolemou, asked if she prayed to the gods. Arya said she indeed prays to the Old Gods and the new. Forel replied: "There is only one god and his name is Death, and there is only one thing we say to death: *'Not today.'*"

DANIEL MINAHAN: I was concerned when I saw Miltos's audition as Syrio Forel because he was going too "big" in his performance. Then I realized he was a self-dramatizing character. He's theatrical, like a showman. I thought they had a great chemistry together.

DAVID BENIOFF: I was recently at dinner with my wife and my parents. My mom, who's eighty-two, asked: "Who wrote ['Not today']?" For a minute I couldn't remember. I was like, "Oh, I think that was in the books." As I said that, I'm like, "Wait a second. . . ."

DAN WEISS: Take credit, especially for your mom. There was a version of that scene in the first draft written by Jane Espenson, which didn't have that line.

DAVID BENIOFF: Then Dan did a really good rewrite. It just had a different ending. Then I said, "Oh, I have one idea for something." I remember thinking, "Dan better not critique this or I'm going to be mad." And you said, "Dude, I think that's pretty good."

DAN WEISS: That's better than pretty good.

DAVID BENIOFF: I don't remember what religious or quasi-religious impulse led to that line. I guess it's sad that the line I'm most proud of writing was from the first season.

The following episode also had standout scene, which introduced the imperious Tywin Lannister. Actor Charles Dance skinned a stag (which happens to be the sigil of House Baratheon) while simultaneously dressing down his son Jaime.

DANIEL MINAHAN: We weren't going to make the mistake they made with cutting open the deer's belly in the first episode. The producers got us two stags that were already dressed from a butcher and put rubber entrails inside of them. So what Charles had to do was go through the motions. I asked Charles if he'd like to meet with the butcher, and he said, "No, I've done this before." Okay, wow. They showed him once, and he was impeccable.

LIAM CUNNINGHAM (*Davos Seaworth*): From an acting point of view, you're doing a two-to-three-page speech that gives your entire reason for being in the show, while also informing your incredibly arrogant son that he's not doing his job properly. To explain everything about your character while you're skinning a deer, most actors would not pull that off. He did it with a style and elegance that makes you completely understand the motivations of everything he did.

DANIEL MINAHAN: It was written beautifully so that you understood Tywin right off the bat, but not in a declarative way. It also completely humanized Jaime. We saw him as this little boy who was damaged by this guy. It was one of those scenes where you think, "Okay, we're firing on all pistons here."

The production assembled rough cuts of the early episodes, which began to circulate among the writers and HBO executives.

DAVID BENIOFF: You're doing all this work and have no idea if it's just gonna sink into the ocean without a trace.

MICHAEL LOMBARDO (*former HBO programming president*): We started seeing dailies. The journey to King's Landing, the scenes with Sansa and

Joffrey, were so moving. It felt like something I hadn't seen before. The production value was coming through. It didn't look like something that was less than $100 million films. You started to feel like there was a confidence building. It started to feel like this was going to work.

TIM VAN PATTEN: For me, the scene that defined the show, the one that was the most informative for me, was when Ned executes the deserter—it gave you a lot of valuable information about who you were dealing with in the Starks. That code of honor and making Bran watch it. And we caught a beautiful day on the hillside.

BRYAN COGMAN: I knew it was working when we got back a rough cut of episode two. Jon says goodbye to Arya and gives her Needle. Jon says goodbye to Robb. Catelyn gives Jon that look of loathing. And it culminates with a scene of Ned telling Jon, "The next time we meet, we'll talk about your mother." At the end of that I was crying and realized, "Okay, we've got a show." Because I knew even then that ultimately the show is about this family, a family that has been split apart, and finding a way to bring all that together again. For me, that was always the core. And you feel that they were a family with a history even though you only see them together for an episode and a half. That's enough to sustain you so that when you fast-forward to season six and Sansa and Jon run to each other and embrace, you're weeping—even though Sansa and Jon never had a previous scene together! It's because the Starks at Winterfell were so well established in those opening episodes.

Even the show's toughest critic was impressed. Craig Mazin, the producer who famously told the showrunners they had a "massive problem" after seeing the original pilot, later recalled on the *Scriptnotes* podcast: "I said to [Benioff], 'That is the biggest rescue in Hollywood history.' Because it wasn't just that you had saved something bad and turned it really good. You had saved a complete piece of shit and turned it into something brilliant. That never happens."

GEORGE R. R. MARTIN: The first finished thing I saw was the scene between Arya and Ned. He's saying, "You'll grow up and you'll marry a lord and bear sons and live in a castle." And she says, "No, that's not me." It was straight out of my imagination, and it was perfect. The dialogue was wonderful. It's not a hugely important scene, but it was important to me emotionally. I thought that I could relax, they were going to do a great job on this. It was my book come to life.

CHAPTER FIVE

ENTER THE DRAGON

G *ame of Thrones* needed a new Daenerys Targaryen. HBO initially thought to replace Tamzin Merchant with another known star and quietly approached some familiar names (such as *28 Weeks Later* actress Imogen Poots) before having a casting call open to relative newcomers.

Emilia Clarke, then twenty-two, had recently graduated from drama school and only performed in a few small roles when she got the call from her agent about the opportunity. "The part called for an otherworldly, bleached-blond woman of mystery," the English actress wrote in *The New Yorker*. "I'm a short, dark-haired, curvy Brit. Whatever."

During her final audition, Clarke asked the producers if she could do anything else. Benioff replied that she could do a dance. After all, Momoa had done the haka when trying out for Drogo, and it had worked out pretty well for him. Clarke burst into renditions of the Funky Chicken and the Robot. "I could have ruined it all," Clarke wrote. "I'm not the best dancer." As she was walking out, the producers went after her and said: "Congratulations, Princess!"

EMILIA CLARKE (*Daenerys Targaryen*): I was unemployed when I was cast, but I was coming from three years of really intense training in drama school. We trained twelve hours a day, and I would rate myself—I was the cruelest person I could be to myself. We were trained to do horseback riding and fighting and, well, maybe not the nudity, but we did all of these intense things.

When I started on *Thrones* the first thing I vividly remember was the [assistant directors] always wanted to know where you were—obviously, you are the product. If you don't turn up, they can't do a filming day and you've ruined millions of dollars and everyone's time. They're like, "Emilia is going to the loo," and "Emilia is eating a cherry," and you're like, *"What the . . ."*

The other thing was that in drama school you take time to prepare before every scene. I was used to writing all my notes in my book and thinking through my process. I didn't know how to prepare for a scene while having a conversation with a director—I do now, just not then. So I would go off and hide to prepare. I would crouch between cars, and I'd hear the ADs being like, "We don't know where Emilia is! Eyes on Emilia?" I didn't want anyone to know where I was because no one's going to let me do my weird preparations that I felt like I needed. I was like: "Don't fuck it up, don't fuck it up, don't fuck it up."

If the pressure of suddenly being given the lead role in a massive production right out of drama school weren't enough, Clarke had the added burden of knowing that the first actress cast in her role hadn't met expectations, and she feared she would get replaced too.

EMILIA CLARKE: From day one, I was like, "Looking silly is not an option." And the only way to not look silly is to just be completely balls-in the whole way. Because I thought if anything's going to end up looking stupid, it's going to be because of me, not in spite of me. I was too naive to know [others' messing up] was even a possibility.

Clarke received reassurance and support from her more experienced scene partners Iain Glen and Jason Momoa.

IAIN GLEN (*Jorah Mormont*): One of Emilia's great qualities is she has no idea how good she is, but that also causes her to doubt her ability and causes neurosis. She worries. So I always wanted to be reassuring. She would always want to talk through the possibilities in a scene.

JASON MOMOA (*Khal Drogo*): Emilia and I got along instantly, like a house on fire. I ran up and gave her a big hug and lifted her up.

EMILIA CLARKE: Jason tackled me to the ground and said, "Wifey!"

The group's exterior scenes during the first season were largely shot in Malta, which served as Essos (Martin's Mediterranean-and-Asian-like continent located across the Narrow Sea from the Europe-inspired Westeros). There Momoa had a challenging time on the set as well, since his role required giving a subtle and largely nonverbal performance as the imposing embodiment of primitive masculinity.

JASON MOMOA: It was all very extreme. You were either freezing or sweating. I was basically in leather pants. Sweating in leather pants is no fun. Freezing in leather pants is no fun. People would say [my role was] easy—"You're just sitting there!" But it's extremely hard to be intimidating and say everything but not say anything.

One of my first scenes was when I rode up and I look down at Daenerys. I see her there, and I ride up and kind of make a grunt and take off. I remember a feeling washing over me like I have never had until that point in my acting career. I remember feeling very, very powerful. It was a cool moment to disappear into something with that big of a stature.

Daenerys's forced marriage to Drogo eventually blossomed into a more equitable romance, with Daenerys dubbing Drogo her "sun and stars."

Yet their first night together was one of the show's most notorious scenes. In Martin's book *A Game of Thrones,* and in the original pilot, Daenerys has consensual sex with Drogo on their wedding night. In the reshot version, Daenerys is the victim of marital rape.

GEORGE R. R. MARTIN: Why did the wedding scene change from the consensual seduction scene that excited even a horse to the brutal rape of Emilia Clarke? We never discussed it. It made it worse, not better.

Benioff and Weiss point out they filmed the version in the book, but they say the result didn't translate well to the screen. One oft-overlooked plot point from the novel is that after their wedding night, Drogo harshly abuses Daenerys until she takes charge of their sex life. So in the first season's original scripts, Daenerys was forced into a relationship with a stranger that rapidly progressed from an initial meeting, to consensual sex, to abusive sex, and then back to consensual again.

DAVID BENIOFF (*showrunner*): Originally we scripted it pretty much exactly as the book, and we shot it that way for the pilot. While it worked in the book, seeing it on-screen, here's a girl who is absolutely terrified of this barbarian warlord she's being married off to, it's the last thing in the world she wants, yet somehow by the end of this wedding night she seems to be in a complete joyful sexual relationship with him. It didn't entirely work for us.

DAN WEISS (*showrunner*): Also, in the second episode she has to go back to the less consensual, rougher relationship. In the book that works, but we just didn't have that amount of time and access to the character's mind. It turns too quickly. It was something the actors themselves felt wasn't gelling. They weren't able to find an emotional handhold.

DAVID BENIOFF: When Emilia Clarke or Jason Momoa comes to us with something like this, we give it a lot of thought. It doesn't always

mean we change it, but Emilia mentioned the wedding night and the issues she was having with it, and that meshed with issues we were having
ourselves.

The scenes also required nudity, something Clarke has expressed
mixed feelings about over the years. During our later on-set interviews,
the actress staunchly defended nude scenes. ("This is all me, all proud,
all strong," she said after filming a season six scene where a bare Daenerys triumphantly emerges from the fiery destruction of Vaes Dothrak.
"I'm just feeling genuinely happy I said yes [to the scene]. That ain't no
body double.") But she's also talked about feeling uncomfortable on
the set—particularly during the show's first season, when the production
was still figuring out how to shoot scenes effectively, let alone sensitively. "Those were tough days," she said, and on the *Armchair Expert*
podcast added, "I've had fights on set before where I'm like, 'No, the
sheet stays up,'" while praising Momoa and Glen for being helpful and
protective.

IAIN GLEN: In moments when she felt exposed because of what she was
required to do, I was always very protective of her on set, making sure
that the protocol was followed and everyone knew to treat her with respect.

EMILIA CLARKE: I was so desperate to be the most professional actor I
could be that I'd be like, "Yeah, sure," for anything they threw at me. "I'll
just cry about it in the bathroom later, whatever, you won't know."

Clarke also pointed out that the show's male actors weren't publicly
scrutinized for their nude scenes nearly as much as she was.

EMILIA CLARKE: How many times has Michiel Huisman [who played
Daario Naharis] been asked about the fact he's taken his clothes off a
bunch? Is that even a discussion?

It's true male actors were also encouraged to strip, as Jason Momoa, Eugene Michael Simon, and Kristian Nairn can attest.

DAVID BENIOFF: The first sex scene we ever shot [was a reshoot pickup] between Khal Drogo and Emilia where she gets on top of him and takes charge. It's the nice, romantic scene. We were nervous because we had never directed anything for real before. It seemed like it went fine, and then afterward Jason walks up to me and goes, "Hey, you did a great job." He shakes my hand, and I look down and he put the . . .

DAN WEISS: It's called a "cock sock."

DAVID BENIOFF: It's basically like a condom except a little bigger. He put it in my hand, and it had been on his cock the entire scene.

JASON MOMOA: That was because David had been like, "Momoa, just take it off!" You know, giving me shit. "Sacrifice! Do it for your art!" I'm just like, "Fuck you, bro. My wife would be pissed. That's for one lady only, man." David and I love giving each other shit.

So afterward I ripped the thing off and kept it in my hand and gave him a big hug and a handshake and was like, "Hey, now you have a little bit of me on you, buddy."

And then there was the time Hodor unexpectedly ran naked into a scene.

KRISTIAN NAIRN (*Hodor*): David and Dan asked if I would do a nude scene. First I asked if there's a child in the scene, which there was, so I asked if I could wear a prosthetic and they said yes. I was shit scared, but I did it because of the whole body-positive thing—*Game of Thrones* has a lot of people of different shapes and sizes, probably more than any other show ever. It was a very busy day on set, which was the opposite of what they told me. I've never seen a busier set! I had to get the prosthetic planted and weaved into my own body hair. It was liberating and mortifying. There was a lot of laughter on set that day.

DAVID BENIOFF: Equal-opportunity nudity. There's a line in the book about Hodor having the blood of giants, and you need to see him for that line to play. And we didn't want to do the coy *Austin Powers* joke where he's covered up by a French baguette or something.

The *Thrones* team will have more to say about the show's sexual content later in these pages. But for Daenerys, the Targaryen princess became pregnant with Drogo's child, while her loathsome brother Viserys felt increasingly frustrated and marginalized. One night Viserys became drunk and threatened Daenerys, so the khal poured a cauldron of boiling liquid gold over his head. It was a decisive moment for Daenerys as she finally stood up to her tyrannical older brother, but it was also the first glimpse of a dark and steely resolve within the character: "He was no dragon," Daenerys intoned as she stared impassively at her dying brother. "Fire cannot kill a dragon. . . ."

EMILIA CLARKE: You want me to *what?*! Okay, so this is the ultimate power play. Right. I need to hide between some cars and sit with this for a second and figure out what this is. So my loyalty is now to my husband. But Viserys is my brother. He's my blood, he's my family. Can I wrap my young brain around the dichotomy of a family member manipulating her? What's it like to be a kid that's been abused her whole life? How on earth can you have the wherewithal to rise above the only thing you've ever known? To take a breath of fresh air and go, "Whoa, my life is built on a lie." This was an education as to what Daenerys might end up feeling later on.

PETER DINKLAGE (*Tyrion Lannister*): What Emilia did there was so impressive because it *wasn't* mean. It was like, "You are so gone to me." If it was mean, it wouldn't have been as effective. He was gone to her, and she had this new person in her life that for some weird, crazy reason she was starting to fall in love with. That's what's so cool about this show. Relationships can start horribly and grow into love, or vice versa. Emilia's amazing because that's very tricky to do, because you could [act like], "Fuck you, brother, you deserve it," or go, "He doesn't deserve that," but it was neither. It was this in-between place that was so terrifying. Her transformation in season one was just incredible.

EMILIA CLARKE: It was a moment where shouting doesn't work. Anger doesn't work. Anger moves mountains, but in a woman it's perceived to be irrational and hysterical, over-the-top, and you white-noise it out. So the only thing to do is become the most powerful person in the room. And the most powerful person in the room is always the stillest. That was where Daenerys's steeliness came from. I remember being like, "This is harder, but this feels good." Because [Khal Drogo] can't not look at me. He can't tear his gaze away from the fact that I am fully able to watch a family member die in front of me and not even blink.

The scene proved a technical challenge as well, since Viserys's death was largely created using practical effects instead of CGI. Actor Harry Lloyd was outfitted with hidden pipes that pushed bubbling steam through tiny holes in his wig.

DANIEL MINAHAN (director): It wasn't easy to figure out how to pour molten gold over someone's head. And it was a very expensive wig. We were only going to be [able to] do one take of it.

HARRY LLOYD (Viserys Targaryen): I was really worried about the drunkenness looking ridiculous. The night before I was watching YouTube videos of drunks, and I wandered down the hotel corridor trying to stumble right. When it came time to shoot I was outside the tent in the freezing cold in Belfast with a hot toddy—tea and honey—and I had a little whiskey from the hotel and put some in there. The vulnerability in the scene came naturally, because it was fucking scary.

DANIEL MINAHAN: What surprised me was how nervous Jason Momoa was, because he was so unflappable and fearless. Before we shot, Jason caught my eye and held up his hand—it was trembling.

JASON MOMOA: I was really nervous. I didn't want to mess it up.

DANIEL MINAHAN: Drogo's gold jewelry was made of wax. We threw it in the cauldron, and it began to melt. Then we switched out the cauldron with this bubbling viscous fluid. Then Jason said to Harry, "Are you ready? I'm going to do it."

JASON MOMOA: There are moments in acting where you're really free and out of your head and you're really into a character. You don't have any anxiety about anything and you're listening and feeling and kind of in a zone. That moment was 100 percent that. I remember reaching out and holding Emilia's belly and having my back to Harry, then saying a word where [the Dothraki] grab him and I'm just trying to be cool and calm and collected. Drogo's no-nonsense. He's done this a thousand times.

HARRY LLOYD: I remember talking to a doctor about it beforehand. He said Viserys is dying from the gold piercing his brain and it would be like a single scream. Then on the day of shooting I was told to scream and make it a bit more demented. It felt like a fucking rush.

JASON MOMOA: As I'm pouring it over his head I got very excited. I just started watching him. I think Drogo would enjoy watching people's expressions—like watching him scream with the gold going over his mouth. Then I started to smell him because of the smoke coming up. It was so fucked up. I remember walking away from that going, "There's some ancestral shit going on in that one." Because I just really enjoyed myself.

DANIEL MINAHAN: And it all worked in one take.

One unusual moment when filming the Daenerys-Drogo storyline was the khal's gory fight with a Dothraki rider named Mago. Not only was the fight not in Martin's book, it wasn't even in the script.

JASON MOMOA: I told David and Dan one thing missing in the book for me was to see Drogo fight. The whole buildup and the myth of him is amazing, and George is phenomenal. But I want to see him fuck shit up. That's why I did the haka in the audition, so you could just see what it would be like if he went into battle. I said, "I can make this simple. I can just bob and weave and then we see his quickness."

DAVID BENIOFF: Jason had a high batting average of ideas he'd come to us [with] that we liked and ended up using. And one thing he said fairly early on was, "I'm supposed to be the baddest man on the planet, I got this long braid because I've never lost a fight, and everybody is afraid of me. But nobody sees me fight, and isn't that kind of lame?" We told him, "No, it's good, you're so badass you don't have to prove yourself. You're the victor of a thousand battles, Jason, go back to your trailer." But there was something kind of strange with not getting to see this guy do what he does best.

Despite the first season's limited budget and constant time pressure, a fight scene was conceived on the fly. The initial setup was that Mago would insult Daenerys, the two men would fight, and Drogo would chop off Mago's head.

JASON MOMOA: Then I had a dream where somebody dumped on my wife and I ripped his tongue out through his throat.

DANIEL MINAHAN: Jason said, "I don't think I should chop his head off; we've chopped off so many people's heads. I think I should cut his throat open and pull his tongue out through his throat." I'm like, "Okay, let me get a tongue made."

JASON MOMOA: The guy I'm fighting [Ivailo Dimitrov] was Bulgarian. He was my double for horse riding. We didn't have anyone else because it was so last-minute. But he didn't speak English and needs to give a speech in Dothraki. The producers were like, "You fucking hired him, you teach him!" So I had to teach a Bulgarian how to speak Dothraki when he doesn't speak English. And he did great. I still have that tongue on my desk.

A scratch from the fight would result in Drogo's demise (originally, Drogo was going to get the wound during an off-screen raid). Daenerys convinced her husband to let an enslaved sorceress treat him, which led to an infection and his death. It's a quintessential Martin twist—an undefeated warrior brought down by a slight miscalculation, his fate sealed by allowing his sentiment to override his caution.

JASON MOMOA: It's amazing what George sets up. Here are your lead characters, you're supposed to think about them one way, and you hate them, then you love them, and then they're killed, and it's a whirlwind of emotion. And all the little kids and even the smallest of characters just grow and grow and grow. He built a beautiful world. To play Khal Drogo was phenomenal, and I wished there was more stuff he could have done.

Khal Drogo was a career-making performance for Momoa, though for a while *Thrones* was a hindrance. The actor was so utterly convincing as a Dothraki warrior that he struggled for parts after the first season aired. Hollywood producers were convinced the Hawaiian-born actor either couldn't read dialogue or could only play strong, silent warrior types. As the years passed, Drogo became a fan favorite, and Momoa shot to stardom in films like *Aquaman*.

JASON MOMOA: For a while afterward, a lot of people bagged on me. It hurt me a lot. People thought I didn't speak English. They didn't know I was playing a role. I'm nothing like Drogo. I'm like Drogo when I'm being lovey and close to the woman I love and being nice, but his other half is not me. But then everyone fell in love with Drogo when they rewatched the show. It's been ten years since I was on, and it's still a frenzy. Now people come up all the time going crazy about Drogo.

CHAPTER SIX

LEARNING TO DIE

N ed Stark's execution was the traumatic loss of *Game of Thrones'* most traditional heroic protagonist. He was the steely and honorable patriarch chosen for a position of newfound power who uncovered a conspiracy against his longtime friend King Robert Baratheon. Up until that moment, every storytelling convention signaled to viewers that Ned would be the show's focus. *Thrones'* debut poster showed Ned on the Iron Throne, an assurance he was the lead character, one who was perhaps destined to rule Westeros. George R. R. Martin even told viewers in a pre-season publicity video that "Ned Stark is the center of the series."

Between HBO's crafty marketing and the ultra-cautious nature of most TV storytelling, Ned's death was arguably more shocking and groundbreaking in the series than it was in Martin's books. Thousands of TV shows had aired over the previous six decades, yet never before had a major series launched with an obvious lead character and then deliberately gotten rid of them in a debut season for strictly creative reasons.

Or, to use the Boromir meme, *"One does not simply . . ."* kill off your series lead in the ninth episode.

ALAN TAYLOR (*director*): ["Baelor"] was my first episode, and I knew it was a big deal we were doing this. Many people, especially those who did not know the books, would assume they'd be following Ned Stark's story for the next several seasons. We knew we were doing something radical in television terms.

GEORGE R. R. MARTIN (*author, co–executive producer*): The impact of Gandalf's death was enormous on me when I was a twelve-year-old kid reading *The Fellowship of the Ring*—"Fly, you fools!" and he goes into the chasm. "Holy shit, [J. R. R. Tolkien] killed the wizard! That's the guy who knew everything! How are they going to [destroy the ring of power] without him?" And now the "kids" have to grow up because "Daddy" is dead. If Gandalf could die, anybody could die. Then, just a few chapters later, Boromir goes down.

Those two deaths created in me the "anyone could die" thing. At that point I was expecting him to pick off the whole Fellowship one by one. But then, of course, he brings Gandalf back. He's a little strange at first, but then he's basically the same old Gandalf. I liked the impact we got from his being gone.

DAVID BENIOFF (*showrunner*): From your training in seeing so many movies and reading books, you know your hero is going to be saved. Is Arya going to pull this off? Does the queen have some trick up her sleeve? Someone has something planned, because they're not *really* going to chop off his head—right up until the moment when they chop off his head.

DAN WEISS (*showrunner*): The bluntness of George's prose made it even more brutal; there was nothing sentimental and saccharine about it. It was just: There he is up there, and [the sword] Ice is coming down on his neck, and that's it. It's faithful in the way it's translated to the screen, but it's still a very different thing because you have real live actors and little Maisie Williams watching and Ramin Djawadi's beautiful score. There were lots of things that made us nervous that season, but we knew with episodes nine and ten we were ending on a strong note.

SEAN BEAN (*Ned Stark*): I thought it was a very courageous move for a television company. I knew HBO had a track record of bold moves, but I thought, "This is pretty incredible if they can pull this off."

While fans of Martin's book knew Ned's death was coming, and the spoiler was readily available to anybody who looked at the book's Wikipedia page, the twist took the vast majority of the show's audience completely by surprise. The episode, "Baelor," managed to keep viewers guessing about Ned Stark's fate until the very last second.

In the episode's opening scene in the black cells, Varys assured Ned that if he falsely confessed to treason, his life and the lives of his family would be spared. Taylor uniquely lit the scene with a few flaming torches tied together to provide just enough illumination to shoot by.

"You think my life is some precious thing to me?" Ned asked Varys. "That I would trade my honor for a few more years of . . . *of what?* You grew up with actors. You learned their craft, and you learnt it well. But I grew up with soldiers. I learned how to die a long time ago." To which Varys replied: "Pity. Such a pity. What of your daughter's life, my lord? Is that a precious thing to you?"

Ned trusted the Lannisters would hold up their end of the bargain because his execution would likely lead to an uprising in the North—their deal would help both sides. Except nobody counted on Joffrey, crowned king in the wake of his father's death, flipping the script.

Ned was brought onto the platform at the Sept of Baelor for judgment and gave his halting confession, just as promised. A gleeful Joffrey then made a speech: "My mother wishes me to let Lord Eddard join the Night's Watch. Stripped of all titles and powers, he would serve the realm in permanent exile. And my lady Sansa has begged mercy for her father. But they have the soft hearts of women. So long as I am your king, treason shall never go unpunished. *Ser Ilyn, bring me his head!*"

Waves of shock and horror washed over Sansa, watching from the platform, and Arya, secretly watching from the crowd—and over the viewers as well.

ALAN TAYLOR: Our guiding principle was to tie ourselves very tightly to points of view and try and avoid generic coverage. In this case, to see the event through Arya's eyes, through Sansa's eyes, and through Ned Stark's eyes—the three characters who our hearts go out to the most. This is the scene about a father and two daughters.

In Martin's version, the Night's Watch brother Yoren coincidentally noticed Arya and took her away after the execution. The producers decided to have Ned spot Arya perched on the statue of Baelor and then tell Yoren her location as he passed him by. The importance of the moment is heightened by the rare use of a zoom shot as the camera dramatically pushed into a stunned Arya.

ALAN TAYLOR: It's unlike me to do something that zingy. But having decided it was about these two daughters, there's a matching shot like that off Sansa. It felt good to say, "This is about these two."

As pointed out in Kim Renfro's book *The Unofficial Guide to Game of Thrones,* throughout his life, Ned focused on protecting children—infant Jon Snow with his perilous birthright; young Daenerys, whom King Robert wanted to assassinate; even Cersei's children when he foolishly warned her to take them and leave the capital.

Ned managed to successfully protect one child, Arya, as his final act in the world.

DAVID BENIOFF: For us, it was more important that Ned be the one to see her and say that one word to him, "Baelor." We had the statue of Baelor [in the middle of the set] and had the name "Baelor" carved into it and thought we were being all smart. We failed to realize the crowd would be right in front of the word when we shot it. Luckily people seemed to figure it out anyway. It's the one last thing Ned can do to protect this girl he loves so much. He looks out there and sees she's gone, hopefully now she's safe. But it's also now just a sea of angry faces, and that's all he's left with. Sean Bean conveyed so much with no dialogue whatsoever.

ALAN TAYLOR: I was directing [Maisie and Sophie] as kids. It was pretty straightforward—"There's your dad, and this is bad." For Arya, the warrior in her comes out. For Sansa, she starts out all smiles, thinking this is all for the good and her dad is doing the right thing, then she absolutely crashes when the horror gets unleashed. They have very different hearts.

MAISIE WILLIAMS (*Arya Stark*): A lot of actors and actresses pull from past experiences. I'm really good at convincing myself somebody's killed my dad. That's the great fun about acting, is you can pretend to be somebody else all day.

JACK GLEESON (*Joffrey Baratheon*): I'm not gonna lie, it was a long shoot. That scene took three days. So it was hard sometimes to kind of feel the passion when there's two hundred actors in front of you, you're onstage, you have the lines, with these great actors behind you. But I was enjoying myself, and so I'm glad I looked like I was.

Executioner Ser Ilyn Payne beheaded Ned with the Stark patriarch's own broadsword, Ice. It's the same blade Ned used to execute the deserter in the first episode. (The executioner would later earn a spot on Arya's kill list, but Payne actor Wilko Johnson exited the series after season two due to receiving treatment for cancer.)

ALAN TAYLOR: Sean was whispering to himself [when the sword came down]. He asked somebody what an appropriate prayer would be for somebody of his belief. People have tried to guess what he said, but it's something private Sean created based on that.

SEAN BEAN: You just play what's on the page—he's a good man trying to do his best in the middle of this corruption. He's a fish out of water, he's used to being up north in Winterfell where people are pretty straight and pragmatic, and he comes down to a place where people are playing games and backstabbing. I love the character, that he's a principled man who tries to hold things together. This is a journey that he makes where ultimately his loyalty causes his downfall. But I just thought it was a wonderful piece of work.

DAVID BENIOFF: There's a parallel to the first episode, where Ned beheads a deserter and we're seeing it from Bran's perspective. Bran's told very specifically, "Don't look away," and we see the whole thing. In episode nine, we shift from Ned to Arya, and she's told, "Don't look, don't look," and Yoren restrains her from seeing. She'll be scarred anyway, but he doesn't want her to have this image in her mind. So we don't see what Arya doesn't see.

ALAN TAYLOR: I tried to heighten Ned's subjectivity. You hear his breathing; we dropped all the sound out and went to his point of view. Then I traded his view with Arya's, so you see her perspective as she watches the birds fly over and you hear *her* breathing—because she has inherited the Stark mantle.

DAN WEISS: We didn't want a gory Monty Python geyser, but we needed to see the blade enter his neck and cut on the frame where the blade was midneck. We needed it to be totally unambiguous. It was the longest discussion ever of where to cut a frame. We had very high-pitched arguments about whether to add another twelfth of a second. Two hours of discussion [about] whether [it should be] frame six or frame seven or frame eight.

ALAN TAYLOR: For the final shot, we designed this elaborate crane shot to reveal the architecture over the top of the Sept of Baelor. But there wasn't any architecture because we couldn't afford to put the VFX [visual effects] in later. The shot unfortunately is still in the show, where you do this grand crane up that for some reason tilts toward the sky and then back down again. It was meant to have like an arch going over it and instead it looks like the camera lost its mind for a second and had a stroke and then returned to business. I'm a little embarrassed by that.

Another minor oversight, likewise caused by the production running low on resources, ended up causing the team a much bigger headache. In the finale there's a shot of Ned Stark's severed head on a spike along with several others. In the first season's DVD commentary, Taylor noted one of the mock heads was of former president George W. Bush.

GEORGE R. R. MARTIN: I wanted to be a severed head on the wall where Joffrey makes Sansa look at Ned and the other severed heads. And I wanted to keep my severed head. David and Dan loved the idea, but they didn't have the budget. Do you know what a severed head costs?

BERNADETTE CAULFIELD (*executive producer*): It costs up to $5,000 for a good severed head, especially if you want eyes and human hair.

GEORGE R. R. MARTIN: It's very expensive. As it turned out, they would have been better off to pay the money. Because instead they bought a box of used severed heads somewhere. They're only seen for like three seconds. Nobody noticed anything until we did the Blu-ray and the director in his commentary said, "Notice two down from Ned, that's George W. Bush on a spike!" We had Rush Limbaugh going, "Cancel the show! They cut off the president's head! What disrespect!" It was like the whole world exploded.

GINA BALIAN (*former vice president of drama at HBO*): Yes, including us. We called David and Dan in the middle of the night saying, "We've got a problem here." They were really upset because it wasn't intentional. They weren't trying to make some statement.

HBO released a statement of their own, however, publicly slamming the move as "unacceptable, disrespectful and in very bad taste."

ALAN TAYLOR: I wasn't going to mention that because I got in trouble the last time I mentioned it. We didn't have enough heads. We had to use every head we had. [Bush's head] had been made for some comedy. So we had to use it. I remember making some not-very-brilliant joke at the time, like, "You go to production with the heads you have, not with the heads you want"—paraphrasing [Bush's secretary of defense] Donald Rumsfeld—because I was pretty angry at Bush and Rumsfeld at the time. I thought it was funny. Since then I've realized if someone made a joke like that about a president I believed in, I would have been offended too. I think I've probably mellowed a bit, though if you gave me the chance to use [Trump's] head I'd probably jump at it.

Otherwise, Ned Stark's demise had the impact that the *Game of Thrones* team had hoped. Every other drama on television suddenly looked like they were playing things safe, abiding by unwritten rules only *Thrones* dared to violate. Narratively, the execution raised the stakes by putting all the other heroes into greater peril—particularly the Stark children, who were thrown into a sea of predators, each now forced to make life-and-death decisions in order to survive. "The execution of the execution was so flawless that it ultimately didn't matter that I knew what was coming," wrote Uproxx's Alan Seppinwall. "That final scene was so gorgeously shot, and the weariness of Bean's performance and the horror of Maisie Williams's so perfectly conveyed the emotions of it, even as things seemed so chaotic."

AIDAN GILLEN (*Littlefinger*): What happened to Ned at the end of season one was what everything else that came after was built around, really, and the real hook that sold the show and novels on a human level. You really had to care, and with someone other than Sean playing that role, who knows how that would have worked out?

GINA BALIAN: I was watching [Ned's death] in editing and shedding a tear thinking, "We got here." *This* didn't feel like it was shot in Burbank. And I was so proud because there were so many points it could have gone awry.

GEORGE R. R. MARTIN: I have an ego. Normally I like things done the way I did it. But David and Dan improved that scene. In the books, Ned doesn't say anything or see Arya there and it's purely coincidence that Yoren finds her. It's a lovely moment, and I wish I had done it that way. The death of Ned Stark could not have been done any better.

DAN WEISS: Ned dying is telling a hard truth about the price of honor and the price of morality in a world where not everybody has the same values as you do. It's not a simplistic redemptive message, where you sacrifice yourself and it saves the day. A lot of times sacrifice ends up being futile.

DAVID BENIOFF: We wanted a strong reaction, and we got one. I think apathy is the worst thing when making a show like this. If people are infuriated, it's great that this fictional world has such an impact. It's a tough thing to build up a character and make somebody as memorable and impressive as Ned and then get rid of him. But at the same time it leads to a story that is so much more suspenseful because you truly have no idea what is going to happen and who is going to survive. You cling to the characters when you know you can lose them at any moment.

PETER DINKLAGE (*Tyrion Lannister*): It's a testament to George. He loves the outsiders. Ned Stark's great, he's a hero, but George is not as interested in the heroes so much as the people who stand behind the heroes. It still amazes me how shocking [killing Ned] was to people, and it's because it had never been done before. It still hasn't been done again.

Ned Stark's death was followed by the loss of another major character, Khal Drogo. Just as Ned's death propelled Arya and Sansa into greater jeopardy, Drogo's demise gave way to Daenerys seizing her destiny.

In the first-season finale, "Fire and Blood," Daenerys burned Drogo's body along with her three "petrified" dragon eggs and a sacrificial Mirri Maz Duur, the "witch" who betrayed Drogo after he led an attack on her people. Then Dany slowly entered the pyre's flames in a seemingly suicidal act. "Daenerys has an understanding that she has to give herself over to something larger than herself without knowing exactly what's going to happen," Weiss explained on *Making Game of Thrones*, HBO's behind-the-scenes production blog. "But she knows when she walks into that pyre that she's not going to burn up."

At dawn, Ser Jorah discovered his khaleesi unscathed—along with three live baby dragons. In the most stunning shot of *Thrones'* debut year, Daenerys rose from the ashes, Ser Jorah fell to his knees, and the Mother of Dragons was born.

ALAN TAYLOR: A stuntwoman walked into the flames for Emilia. I didn't think it was working because she was wearing a gossamer gown like Emilia was wearing and they had to put so much fire retardant on it that it looked like she just climbed out of a vat of Vaseline. I thought, "This is never going to work," but it seems to work fine.

Clarke's real-life emotions about performing Daenerys's rebirth nude were infused into her portrayal of the iconic moment, and she detailed her thoughts during each phase of the reveal.

EMILIA CLARKE (*Daenerys Targaryen*): On one side, that moment was incredibly powerful. And on the other side, I was butt naked in front of people I didn't know. Alan saw the fear on my face and said, "Let's lean into that then." So there's that close-up of me looking up at Ser Jorah, who's looking down. And that's exactly what I was going through: "I don't know what this is. I don't know what I'm expected to feel. I don't know what I'm expected to do. I'm fully aware that I couldn't be more . . . *open*."

So the shot went from sitting down where there was fear and then as I stood up I was like, "It's all out. So you just better own that shit." Then as you stand up, you think, "Okay, you've done the worst bit. You've stood up. No one is behind you. No one saw up your ass, so you can stand all the way up now." Suddenly that feels like a much more confident stance than just sitting cross-legged on the floor buck naked in front of people. Then I just naturally felt my shoulders go back.

ALAN TAYLOR: Emilia was rightfully worried about gratuitous nudity, but she understood that it was important for the character to be reborn in the flame. There's no way around it. [Not placing extras behind Clarke] was partly me being protective of her, and it was partly that we didn't have enough extras. All the extras were standing in front of her, where they could be on camera. And we were cheating by using the few extras we had over and over again from shot to shot.

EMILIA CLARKE: It was a glorious feeling of equal amounts adrenaline and equal amounts crippling fear. And those two things together described my whole journey on the show. There was one of those scenes every season where I'm like: "Beyoncé would be up here like, 'And what?!' and own this, but Emilia would not."

IAIN GLEN (Jorah Mormont): At the time, the dragons were just dots on Emilia's naked body. But the way she looked and the way the pyre went up, it all felt pretty amazing, and there was that buzz around the cameras that something magical was being created.

EMILIA CLARKE: They were like, "But what about the dragons?!" I decided I wasn't going to stand there and think I have dragons all over me. This is a stupid example, but if I had my dog, I wouldn't change my position because she was there. The dog would just exist, and just do whatever they're going to do.

ALAN TAYLOR: Her performance is so rich and layered in that scene. Also, Iain Glen's performance. It's one of those cinematic moments where you convey the wonder of what you're seeing partly by seeing it but mostly through the old Spielberg trick of watching somebody else react to it. Jorah's reaction when he sees Daenerys and the dragons and falls to his knee is so beautiful.

MICHAEL LOMBARDO (*former HBO programming president*): The biggest fear we had was whether the dragons would be credible. If they seemed cartoony or corny, we were fucked. But they worked, and people had an emotional response to them. So the good news was they worked. The bad news was we'd have to keep delivering at that level.

ALAN TAYLOR: Probably the thing I was most proud of was the aftermath. [The dragon reveal] in the novel takes place at night. I wanted to shoot it at dawn and got into a fight with David and Dan about it. I wanted to be able to pull back to see the landscape, and we couldn't afford to light that much landscape at night. They let me do it. I'm really happy with the shots that bring Jorah in and we do the slow reveal and the magic of the dragons, showing people awakening to this new world, then being able to drop back to a truly vast landscape. And what [composer] Ramin Djawadi does with the music there, so the last thing you hear is the dragons' cry.

The last line of the first book was "And for the first time in hundreds of years, the night came alive with the music of dragons." So that was a wonderful way to end. We know this world, and now it's been launched into whole new territory and you can't wait for next season.

CHAPTER SEVEN

FRESH BLOOD

G ame of Thrones premiered to 2.2 million viewers on April 17, 2011. The viewership was considered modest for such a costly show—HBO's short-lived *Rome* had opened to 3.8 million viewers.

Early reviews were somewhat mixed as well, with the nation's two most prestigious newspapers panning the drama after being sent advance copies of the first six episodes. *The New York Times* scathingly dismissed *Thrones* as "a lot of confusion in the name of no larger or really relevant idea beyond sketchily fleshed-out notions that war is ugly, families are insidious and power is hot," and expressed skepticism that female viewers would watch such "boy fiction," while *The Washington Post* dubbed *Thrones* a "groggy slog."

Others saw the show's promise straightaway, such as *Variety*'s Brian Lowry ("[*Thrones*] grabs the audience by the throat like an exceptionally loyal wolf"), Uproxx's Alan Sepinwall ("deposits me in a world I never expected to visit and doesn't leave me feeling stranded and adrift, but eager to immerse myself"), and *The Hollywood Reporter*'s Tim Goodman ("The ambition is immense, the fantasy world exceptionally well-conceived, the writing and acting elevating the entire series . . . the successful pairing of an acclaimed collection of fantasy books with a television series that illuminates and expands what's on the page").

And then, the show's second episode delivered another 2.2 million viewers.

GEORGE R. R. MARTIN (*author, co-executive producer*): We got okay ratings. But the second week, the ratings stayed level. I was in New York and had lunch with [HBO CEO] Richard Plepler at his club. He said, "The show is going to last ten years." I said, "There's only been two episodes, and the ratings are good, not great, so how do you know that?" He's all: "There's no drop-off. The second episode *always* goes down; the only question is by how much. This is level, and it's going to start going up." And that's exactly what happened.

HBO quickly green-lit another season of ten episodes based on Martin's second *A Song of Ice and Fire* novel, *A Clash of Kings*. The book chronicles Westeros in chaos as contenders for the Iron Throne vied for power, while across the Narrow Sea a nomadic Daenerys struggled to gain supporters. The new season required adding a rather enormous number of major roles to the show's already large cast, such as noble knight Brienne of Tarth, King Robert's uncompromising brother Stannis, principled smuggler Ser Davos, murderous sorceress Melisandre, Wildling warriors Ygritte and Tormund Giantsbane, Stark bannerman Roose Bolton, captive Wildling Gilly, treacherous lord Walder Frey, wily yet benevolent social climber Margaery Tyrell, and Margaery's sly grandmother Olenna Tyrell.

There was also new behind-the-scenes talent, most notably producer Bernadette "Bernie" Caulfield, who had previously worked on shows such as *The X-Files* and *Big Love*. Though Caulfield rarely received press attention (and certainly never courted it), Benioff and Weiss frequently credited her, along with fellow producer Christopher Newman, with keeping the show's railyards of trains running on time and for solving a seemingly never-ending stream of logistical problems.

The season also added a new filming location, Croatia, which would redefine the look of King's Landing and Essos. Croatia effectively replaced Morocco and Malta as the show's Mediterranean location of choice. As with selecting Northern Ireland, the producers picked a cost-efficient country with a relatively recent war-torn past that didn't feel like it was already overexposed by other Hollywood productions.

In particular, the Old Town area of Dubrovnik would be frequently used. Considered one of the world's most perfectly preserved medieval cities, the seaside tourist attraction served as an ideal Westeros doppelgänger. Its construction dates back to the seventh century, and its eighty-foot stone walls were built in the tenth century. From the air, Old Town's red-tiled roofs set against the Adriatic Sea very closely resemble King's Landing in the show (absent certain *Thrones* landmarks such as the imperial Red Keep and the grand Sept of Baelor).

As season-two pre-production and casting got under way, *Thrones'* ratings kept climbing and peaked with three million viewers watching the finale. Combined with repeat airings and DVR playback, the first season averaged around eight million viewers per episode. With the show edging into the territory of being a hit, the new cast members felt a type of pressure that the actors on the show's first season had managed to avoid.

LIAM CUNNINGHAM (*Davos Seaworth*): I first met Dan and David a year before [while auditioning] for a different character. I've never told anyone this, but it was for Ser Jorah. Within five pages you know if a script is going in the trash can or not, and these I couldn't put down. It's like for an actor you finally found what you're looking for. They told my agent they were "going a different direction," which is the nice way of saying you didn't get the job. They added, "We have some more characters coming in next season," and I'm thinking, "Yeah, sure, 'Don't call us, we'll call you.'" But they put me on the list to come in the following year. By then, everybody in the UK wanted *Game of Thrones* on their résumé. It was a badge of honor, a mission everybody wanted to be on.

CARICE VAN HOUTEN (*Melisandre*): I'd never played a character like this before. In [the Netherlands] I played light comedies and funny parts.

This was so serious. I completely fucked up my lines in the audition. I was over-conscious and intimidated by the whole thing. The show was already sort of a hit, and it was an uncreative room with five men in there. I had to audition with the "burning of the gods on the beach" speech, which is this big, epic scene. It's hard to portray that in a tiny Belfast office. But then they had me do another scene with Davos in a boat that was much more subtle. I think that saved me.

LIAM CUNNINGHAM: Carice and I did a movie together in South Africa, *Black Butterflies,* and then it wasn't long after we went up for our two roles. Both of us recommended the other one for the part, and both of us got them. The bizarre thing was we played lovers in the film and it was quite liberal. There was a lot of horizontal folk dancing in the movie, and I'll leave the rest to your imagination. She's wonderful to work with, and we looked after each other on that set.

NATALIE DORMER (*Margaery Tyrell*): I've never spoke about this previously: I didn't audition for Margaery Tyrell originally. I auditioned for Melisandre. Then I got a call from my agents saying, "They loved you but want you to audition for another role." And I'm like, "Damn, this Melisandre role looks fucking cool!" Dan and David said, "There's this character Margaery, and we're still exploring what we're going to do with her." You look back and realize Melisandre couldn't have been anyone else, Carice did an amazing job, but I always had a chuckle on the couch when a Melisandre scene came on.

Margaery brought a very sort of modern PR kind of angle [to the ensemble]. She was canvassing the common people's hearts and minds. I tried to think of her as like a hybrid of Michelle Obama and like a Kate Middleton or Princess Diana.

ROSE LESLIE (*Ygritte*): I was ecstatic. I was in the center of London and got a call from my agent and he told me the good news. I was jumping up and down like a maniac, and I didn't care that I was screaming in the middle of a crowded square.

GEMMA WHELAN (*Yara Greyjoy*): I was doing a lot of comedy, but I always wanted to do serious drama as well. It's quite hard when you're working in comedy to even be invited into the room for a drama casting. *Thrones* came about because I was at a comedy casting [which had the same] casting director. I was literally in the right place at the right time, even though I was at a comedy casting. I thought, "This is never going to be my first drama, I'll never get this." So I was quite relaxed in the audition because I thought I never had a chance.

KRISTOFER HIVJU (*Tormund Giantsbane*): I googled the character and read all the fan sites and blogs I could find about what fans had said about him. The fans gave me a very clear picture.

DAN WEISS (*showrunner*): Kristofer had the beard already, for some reason. And he had this giant unpeeled carrot in the audition, which makes no sense because Tormund lives in a frozen wasteland. But he's sitting there munching on this giant carrot, taking huge animal bites. There was something about it that was perfect even though nothing about it made any sense. I remember thinking, "I like what this guy is doing with the carrot. . . ."

DAVID BRADLEY (*Walder Frey*): I didn't have to audition, it was a direct offer, which is always nice. Some parts come through and I spend a lot of time struggling with how this person would be, how they would speak and move. With Walder, I knew how to play him as soon as I read it.

MICHAEL MCELHATTON (*Roose Bolton*): I went up for several [*Thrones*] roles and didn't get any of them. Then out of the blue I got an offer to play Roose Bolton. I didn't know anything about the character, and the very next day I was meeting the costume woman to fit me for boots.

MICHELLE MACLAREN (*director*): When I first got the job, I called up another director who worked on the show, David Nutter, and said, "I'm going to do *Thrones,* can I buy you lunch and get some advice?" And he goes, "Michelle, it's a Porsche. Get in and drive it." It was one of these things where the show was so massive and had such potential and such scope that you needed to go in and think of the impossible, to think of the biggest challenges you could. They wanted you to push the limits.

BRYAN COGMAN (*co—executive producer*): I remember thinking when we got to Brienne, "How are we going to find someone that can play this?" I was really worried the Hollywood thing would happen where they'd cast some willowy girl and just say, "Well, she's the best actress," and not cast what the role really needed. George watched Gwen's video first and said, "Oh my gosh, there she is." I wrote the script where Brienne was introduced, and I can't remember what it was like to write that character before it was Gwen. She was perfection in that role.

ROBERT STERNE (*casting director*): There were lots of things about Gwen that didn't look anything like Brienne of Tarth when she started out. The role's description talked about Brienne's muscularity and fitness and height—which was key. We'd seen Gwen in something completely different and got in touch with her, as it's unusual to have a part for Gwen's height. She read all the books and chopped her hair off, and by the time she came in she was flying with it.

GWENDOLINE CHRISTIE (*Brienne of Tarth*): The fans had seen pictures of me [after I was cast] on the Internet—some of which were frankly ghastly. I loved that fans said, "Who's this model?" I only ever wanted to be a model. All I've ever wanted is for people to say I'm pretty, but "*too* pretty"? Amazing. I've always been able to look very different very easily, so I worked with a trainer and went to a gym. But I was still incredibly nervous. I hadn't really done other filming, just bits and pieces. I trained for about four months to prepare for the role. Then I put the costume on, and that's when I started to experience the first sensation of transformation. The costume was incredibly painful, but that is how it would have felt for Brienne to wear it.

And then there was seventy-three-year-old screen legend Dame Diana Rigg, who was the ideal choice to play Tyrell matriarch Olenna, dubbed the "Queen of Thorns" for her piercing wit. Rigg was a Royal Shakespeare Company veteran whose credits included playing a Bond girl in *On Her Majesty's Secret Service* and sexpot Emma Peel in the 1960s *The Avengers* TV series. The *Thrones* team was delighted to cast actual British nobility to play Westeros royalty.

DAVID BENIOFF (*showrunner*): When we initially cast Diana Rigg, we had tea with her. Dames don't audition for you; you audition for them. We loved her. She was funny, she was bawdy, she was everything we wanted for that character.

DAN WEISS: She said with a big smile, "There's an awful lot of bonking, isn't there?" Then she came to the first table read having already memorized her entire role for the season.

DANIEL MINAHAN (*director*): Because I'm of an age where I, like, grew up watching reruns of *The Avengers*, I was like, "Oh my God, Emma Peel." A lot of the young people on set didn't understand who she was. They were like, "That old lady." I was like, "That 'old lady' was ten times wilder than you can ever imagine."

Then we went to the table read together, and Diana said, "I'm thinking I'm going to wear a wimple." Really quickly, I looked up "wimple." Okay, it's like something nuns wear? I was like, "So you don't want to wear a wig, right?" She didn't want to spend her days getting into a wig, and it takes about a quarter of the time to put on a wimple. Then we got to Dubrovnik in the summer and I think she really regretted wearing it, because it was eighty degrees and she's in this nun's habit.

As second-season filming got under way, new cast members strove to figure out their roles and the *Thrones* world, while returning actors sought to improve upon their first-season performances.

KRISTIAN NAIRN (*Hodor*): The atmosphere changed between seasons. The first season you had that sense of hope and expectation. The second season it was, "Oh, shit, that did really well. We have to do it again, but better."

JOHN BRADLEY (*Samwell Tarly*): In season one, we all got along so well, so you just hoped that atmosphere can carry on when you got separated from your core group.

HANNAH MURRAY (*Gilly*): I hadn't watched the show. I didn't even have a TV. I only watched it after I got cast. It was like I was auditioning John Bradley, because I knew we were going to be working so closely together. I really wanted him to be brilliant. Then he came on-screen and after about three seconds I was like, "Oh, this is going to be great." He brings so much warmth to that character; you care so much about him as soon as you see him.

JOHN BRADLEY: Hannah and I were aware this was going to be a relationship that was going to have a relatively long-term future. So there was a certain amount of trepidation. We want to have a good personal relationship as well as a good professional relationship. As soon as we met, a connection was definitely formed. We had similar attitudes about how to perform this relationship, and both had a distrust of anything that was too saccharine and manipulative.

GWENDOLINE CHRISTIE: My first filming day there was a hurricane. It was all extremely dramatic. We were all holed up in a little hotel with these open fires and a view of the coastline and the landscape. Everybody was just so open and warm, and we were all so excited to be on this show. We really bonded.

GETHIN ANTHONY (*Renly Baratheon*): Gwen's incredible. She insisted on organizing my real-life birthday party, on the basis that that was the kind of thing that Brienne would do for Renly, which was just amazing. I remember seeing her at the gym, and seeing physically how hard she prepared to play this role and it was really impressive.

PETER DINKLAGE (*Tyrion Lannister*): When we went out at night, we wouldn't talk about the weather. We talked about the show. We went out to dinner and were still talking about it, which is such a testament to the show.

GEMMA WHELAN: I was trying to get rid of my feeling of imposter syndrome. On sitcoms, humor and levity is the essence of what you're doing and you default to that. My introduction scene was with Alfie on a horse. We had quite a flatulent horse, and I found that extremely funny. And Alfie very gently said, "Listen, you have to not lose it to a giggle. You're on a big show now. Pull yourself together." He said it in the kindest possible way. You're on the Antrim Coast on a horse with limited time, so you don't fuck around. He made me think, "Okay, behave yourself." That was a kind piece of advice that was given early enough so I didn't make a fool of myself.

Later, there was a scene where Yara was meant to be chowing down on chicken in a scene. I don't eat meat and I was too shy and too nervous to tell them that. So I spent a day eating chicken and just tried to justify the fact that I was going Method for the day.

HANNAH MURRAY: One night it was three o'clock in the morning and we were all sitting around and Kit suddenly said, "This is such a ridiculous job that we do, isn't it? We're sitting in the woods in the middle of the night wearing cloaks." And [Night's Watch commander Jeor Mormont actor] James Cosmo goes: "Yeah, it *is* ridiculous, and the more seriously we take it, the more ridiculous it is."

That made such an impression on me. It was really wonderful advice for how to approach acting, because it really is silly and it's important to recognize that. I was twenty-two at the time and that made me not take myself or the work too seriously, and I had a lot more fun as a consequence.

The quartet of Liam Cunningham, Carice van Houten, Stephen Dillane (Stannis Baratheon), and Tara Fitzgerald (Selyse Baratheon) formed the core of a new storyline centered at Dragonstone castle, where King Robert's elder brother plotted to seize the Iron Throne from King Joffrey with the help of advisor Ser Davos and mysterious religious zealot Melisandre. Their first scene, where Melisandre burned statues of the Seven gods on the beach, served as the opening of season two.

DAN WEISS: Stannis wants the throne not just out of greed or power lust but because he's a man who's always done everything by the book and the book now says, "I should be king." He understands he's the rightful heir, and anyone who tries to prevent him from getting the throne is violating the law.

LIAM CUNNINGHAM: I loved the fact that Davos is from humble beginnings and is a small-time crook but had more humanity than any of the Lannisters and most of the Starks. He was never torn about his principles; they were just part of his DNA. Power had no interest for him. He's incredibly loyal and a decent man. I felt like occasionally he spoke for the audience. But we had to hit the ground running because these relationships were already formed [in the story].

CARICE VAN HOUTEN: It wasn't an easy part for me. My first shooting day I had to do the burning of the gods with so many great actors there.

It's not like me to be so sure of myself. I was so nervous and shy and insecure, but I couldn't use any of those feelings. I had to be all about the Lord of Light. Also, my dress was so fitted that I couldn't wear anything underneath. I had never been so cold in my life.

LIAM CUNNINGHAM: Carice would feel cold if she were dropped in a volcano. She constantly had a hot-water bottle pinned to her. She hates the cold.

CARICE VAN HOUTEN: It's true. I get cold in the summer. I'm the coldest person ever, which was not handy in this role. My character is never supposed to be cold. I got unlucky there.

Dillane earned a reputation as the show's most press-averse actor. He once explained to French outlet *Libération* that he had nothing to say about *Thrones* because he "understood neither the series nor its success" and candidly admitted to taking the role for, "among other things, the money."

CARICE VAN HOUTEN: Stannis is this not-pleasing character, and there's something very interesting about watching him. Maybe the actor trying to figure out what he was doing helped make him unpredictable. I never really got the relationship between all of them.

LIAM CUNNINGHAM: I have to defend Stephen. He's a fantastic actor, with quite a reputation, but Stephen is not good in interviews. Stephen wears his heart on his sleeve, and he will say things that are primed to be taken out of context. He's been much maligned for very much the wrong reasons. He's one of the most dedicated, fantastic people to work with; there's no ego that gets in the way of his work.

I'll give you an example: In the beginning of season three, I walk back into the room when it's been assumed Davos has died during the Battle of the Blackwater. Stannis is sitting on a chair looking out at Dragonstone.

When I walk in, a lesser actor would immediately stand up, take a moment, and say his line: "I thought you were dead." Whereas Stephen glances over his shoulder and says the line in an incredibly unemotional way. He doesn't do "trailer acting." He doesn't go with the easy choice.

Gethin Anthony had one scene with Dillane, a tense hilltop parlay on horseback between Renly and Stannis, with Catelyn Stark also in attendance. Both brothers refused to back down from their self-proclaimed claims to the Iron Throne. While Anthony didn't comment on Dillane, he rather cryptically described the filming of their scene as "educational."

GETHIN ANTHONY: I still feel almost confused by that scene. I learned a lot that day. I hope it came off well enough. I'm not sure it did. It was a strange experience. I think it was partly because I was so vested in it that it was hard to divorce myself from such a huge moment in this character's journey.

Then at the end of that scene, I said, "Can you believe I loved him once?"—a great one-liner—and then I'm supposed to gallop the horse up the cliff and away. Now, Michelle Fairley is a competition horse rider. She grew up in that area and used to ride without saddles. So she's brilliant. Yet she's supposed to follow me, which was embarrassing as a new horse rider. I managed it, but with much less confidence and slightly slow moving.

The Dragonstone group's gothic relationship had its oddest scene—the most bizarre in the whole series, really—when a naked and pregnant Melisandre gave birth to a shadow demon that went on to slay Renly.

GETHIN ANTHONY: People often criticize Renly for being militarily naive. I'm like, "No, he wasn't, he just didn't see magic coming." In a world where they don't believe in the magic, I think that's kind of fair enough, really.

The birthing scene was shot at Cushendun Caves on the Northern

Ireland coast in the early hours of the morning, with the "baby" created later using CGI.

LIAM CUNNINGHAM: It was insane. It looked like a cave, but it was more like a funnel, so there was a cold wind blowing through. Carice, that poor woman, was totally naked except for a pregnancy belly prosthetic. And there's three guys running pipework between her legs to make these air bubbles to make it move. The indignity of it. She's absolutely terrific in the scene under really difficult circumstances.

CARICE VAN HOUTEN: There I was with Liam next to me, pretending to give birth to this computer thing. Thank God for Liam, he really dragged me through it. It was so surreal. I was excited because this is something you don't normally get in a script, but it was also weird to give birth to something that was going to be CGI, so I had no idea what it was going to look like. It was also cold.

LIAM CUNNINGHAM: You have this gorgeous Dutch woman and you're supposed to stare straight between her legs and try to do that only between "action" and "cut." What am I supposed to be horrified by? Then "the baby" comes. They had this thing that looked like the Pillsbury Doughboy on a stick that was supposed to be the shadow baby that they used to help our eye line. But when I looked at the monitor I said to the director, "[The scene] looks like a Caravaggio painting," and the director said, "That's exactly what we're going for."

CARICE VAN HOUTEN: In retrospect, I think: "Did I really have to be naked for this? Was giving birth to the monster not enough? Was she described as naked in the books?"* I can live with it. I'm fine. I don't believe in regrets, but I do wonder in retrospect if that was really

---

* She was.

necessary. I've gotten more conscious in that regard. I've always defended Melisandre's nakedness because she uses it as a weapon, and that's true. But she used that weapon quite a lot.

Season two was frustrating for a few of the returning actors. Jaime Lannister actor Nikolaj Coster-Waldau, for example, spent the year chained outdoors in the mud for nearly all of his scenes.

NIKOLAJ COSTER-WALDAU (*Jaime Lannister*): As an actor, I hated it. "Hey, you can't just bench me, what the hell?" But it made sense for the journey he was on. He said it himself, that he is not quite well equipped for imprisonment. Sometimes you just have to be forced into not moving.

Robb and Catelyn Stark actors Richard Madden and Michelle Fairley spent much of the season in tents while the Young Wolf waged an off-screen war against the Lannisters. "I used to go, 'Not another bloody tent, Jesus,'" Michelle Fairley told the Popcorn Taxi film festival. "And that was simply because the budget didn't allow for the journeying. And every time they did a bit of the journey, they arrived and entered the tent. So that's why I spent so much of season two in a tent."

But Madden noted he relished such chances to flesh out Robb struggling to become a military leader despite his youthful inexperience. "He's got so little control over his own life for someone who became king," Madden told the Bahamas' *Tribune.* "He didn't want to be king, but he knew no one else was going to do this how it should be done, how his father would have done it, so he needed to try. Robb was putting up a mask all the time—and if I did doing the mask right you saw him as this quite intimidating foe to Jaime Lannister for example, or as this man who can lead an army, and then you get those scenes with his mother or with Theon where for a moment that mask slips and it's just a regular guy, he's just a boy."

Peter Dinklage, however, wasn't stuck in tents, chains, or caves. With Sean Bean gone, Dinklage was elevated to the show's top billing (a position he'd maintain for the rest of the series) and got to enjoy, along with his character, Tyrion's promotion to Hand of the King.

PETER DINKLAGE: Tyrion came from great wealth, but he was treated very poorly. Now there was a newfound respect. He was like, "Hmm, looks like I can get revenge on all those high school kids who made fun of me." Tyrion definitely enjoyed that part of himself and was trying desperately to hold on to it.

EUGENE MICHAEL SIMON (*Lancel Lannister*): There's the scene where Lancel is begging Tyrion to not reveal what he's been doing with Cersei. I remember trying to figure out how much Lancel should grovel—I mean, he's got a sword. We leaned into him properly begging [on his knees]. I knew it was working when Peter said, "I'm really liking this moment because Lancel is on the ground, literally beneath me." I don't know if there was any moment in *Thrones* when somebody was begging Tyrion that much. What struck me about it was Tyrion was probably capable of doing that to more than one person. He's got that power.

Palace intrigue at the Red Keep included Tyrion maneuvering against his conniving sister, Cersei.

LENA HEADEY (*Cersei Lannister*): The thing about Cersei is she's always covering her real feeling. There's a lot of reptilian in Cersei. I never truly believed her when I played her. There was one moment that season where she absolutely showed Tyrion her true self. He became like a confidant almost. I loved to be in those scenes with Pete. He's a great guy and we've known each other a long time, so there was an ease with it.

DAVID BENIOFF: Nobody understands Cersei as well as Tyrion—with the possible exception of Jaime. They share a certain worldview, but Cersei is more cynical. They were clearly raised by the same father, but her experience has left her a little more bitter than Tyrion, who still has a shred of optimism.

SIBEL KEKILLI (*Shae*): Even when the camera was on me, Peter would listen to me and act with me. Those kind of actors are really rare. Peter did make a lot of jokes about my English early on, and I didn't understand them. Then my English got better and Peter said, "I can't do jokes any-more because you're starting to understand them!"

SOPHIE TURNER (*Sansa Stark*): Peter was the most inspirational actor to watch. He'd say to the director: "This doesn't feel right, Tyrion needs to come over *here*." I wouldn't have had the courage to do that.

A grieving Sansa was cynically coming to believe that "the truth is always either terrible or boring," and began confiding in her handmaiden, Shae, who was secretly Tyrion's lover.

SOPHIE TURNER: The heads on spikes was a turning point for Sansa when she realized that she kind of has to be independent and strong and trust no one. So [in season two], all she was thinking about was surviving. She's suffering at the hands of Joffrey and literally has no one else. She went back to her roots of Winterfell with her clothing and her hair because she's missing home. I found it so hard to move around in the dresses, you're walking like a statue.

SIBEL KEKILLI: I remember one scene Sophie had to cry. She cried and cried, and then she couldn't stop! I felt like I should protect her, even though she's taller than me. And since I was single at the time, she would say, "Sibel, I have a single friend and maybe he'd be interested in you." I'm like, "Sophie, you're fifteen and I'm thirty! I cannot date your friends."

One recurring King's Landing location used for all manner of meeting scenes—the city's "tent," if you will—was Littlefinger's brothel. In Westeros, most nonfamily relationships are transactional and characters are considered foolish, sometimes fatally, if they make decisions for love.

Brothel scenes in Martin's novels and the series also demonstrated yet another way the powerful dominated the powerless.

Still, there was another, more pragmatic reason for the show's including brothel scenes: A pay-cable drama, especially at the time of *Thrones'* early seasons, was expected by subscribers to deliver sex, language, and violence at a level that ad-supported rivals could not. Early on, *Thrones* would occasionally package expository dialogue with nudity, a practice that blogger Myles McNutt famously dubbed "sexposition."

DAVE HILL (*co-producer*): People think brothel scenes must be fun to shoot as there's beautiful naked people running around simulating sex acts. They're actually stressful, because it's technical and detail oriented. Sex on a set is so incredibly awkward because it's obviously all fake and you're stopping and starting and getting the angles. It's not like being in a strip club. It's like being in the locker room of a strip club.

Also, a lot of those days are spent looking at extras. You're always making sure the extras all look right and are doing the right things. And sometimes the extras will go a little too far. You'd say, "No, you can't be distracting from the action."

INDIRA VARMA (*Ellaria Sand*): I loved doing my brothel scene. It's just so decadent. We worked with a great girl who was totally open about showing her body in a way that's so liberating and brilliant—not in a pornographic way, but just in an eloquent way, and I wish we could all be like that and feel that comfortable about ourselves. So we had to do a brothel scene where she was going down on me and snogging another girl and they were both naked and it was silly and fun.

GEMMA WHELAN: I was very nervous about my scene in a brothel. It's so strange to be thrown together with a stranger and then suddenly be so intimate. I was involved with a breast and a bottom, so that was quite overwhelming. She was such a nice girl, and we had a good giggle and then it became more relaxed. We made it work because she was so kind and made me comfortable and able to feel like I could help myself to someone's body in that way. You want to feel like you have permission but also look like you're not hesitating and being authentic, which is tricky to navigate.

ESMÉ BIANCO (*Ros*): Crash dieting and religious exercise—there was a lot of that going on for those scenes.

The show's most infamous brothel scene was during the first season, when Littlefinger delivered a menacing monologue while ordering Ros and another brothel worker named Armeca (Sahara Knite) to perform a rather vigorous sex act.

ESMÉ BIANCO: It was physically exhausting. It was boiling hot on the set, and I was pouring in sweat. The choreography of the scene was fairly basic, but there was quite a lot of, um, *movement* going on. I'm trying to remember things like, "Okay, at which point is Sahara's butt meant to be there and where's my leg supposed to be?"

DANIEL MINAHAN: We had a lot of Italian crew when shooting that in Malta. I remember having to chase away people who were hiding in the back watching Sahara and Esmé go at it.

ESMÉ BIANCO: It was supposed to be a closed set. I look behind me and there's three guys all holding one flag over a light. I'm buck naked. I'm like, "Hang on a second. Since when does it take three people to hold that? They need to leave!"

Littlefinger's speech revealed his history with Catelyn Stark, and it foreshadowed his eventual betrayal of Ned Stark: "Do you know what I learned losing that duel?" Littlefinger rhetorically asked. "I learned that I'll never win. Not that way. That's their game. Their rules. I'm not going to fight them. I'm going to fuck them. That's what I know. That's what I am. And only by admitting what we are can we get what we want."

DANIEL MINAHAN: I feel like Littlefinger's speech elevated it. We wanted it to be shocking, but also it was a big window into Littlefinger's character. It operates on all these different levels—it's pornographic, it's humorous, it's touching, it's menacing, and it just does these hairpin turns. It reminded me of that scene in *American Psycho* with Patrick Bateman and the two prostitutes; to me it was an homage to that. [Littlefinger actor Aidan Gillen] was unflappable. His head was in the game. And Esmé was a really good sport, but unfortunately when you look up "lesbian fisting," now her name pops up.

DAN WEISS: One of the benefits George had is that in books he could talk about what somebody was thinking. We needed to find other ways. [The brothel workers] were the only people Littlefinger could ever talk to about who he was and why he's doing what he was doing because they were so utterly powerless that he could afford to let down his guard long enough to say them.

AIDAN GILLEN (*Littlefinger*): The monologue and the [background] action were one and the same, really. It's one of those ones where I wished I'd pushed a little harder with an idea I had in terms of simple physical distance, but didn't. There wasn't too much time for messing around on that schedule, and one's ideas aren't always right anyways. I recall learning those lines walking along Eglantine Avenue in Belfast and the many ideas I was having and realizing for the first time that it was *all* about Catelyn. So whatever Esmé and Sahara were doing at my instruction, my mind was twenty years away in reverie, melancholic, turning bitter. Having played many scenes showing as much skin myself in the past, I see that all as a practicality and nothing that would faze me personally—and it definitely wouldn't faze Littlefinger.

ESMÉ BIANCO: It was my first time working with Aidan, and it was the only time I've ever been completely starstruck to the point where I couldn't form a coherent sentence. I don't know why it happened with

Aidan. He has this calm, mysterious, striking presence, and I had to do this full-on nude scene with him. Finally, my makeup artist was like, "Esmé, he's a really nice guy, stop being weird and say hello." I think Aidan realized something was going on, because he came up and was like, "Hello, Esmé. How are you?"—like very deliberate.

Gillen was later asked about Littlefinger's sex-symbol allure during an interview with Collider. "I'm not aware of being a sex symbol," he said. "I'm kind of surprised by that. . . . It's interesting given that some of the strands in the story are unsavory or could be seen that way and Littlefinger's relationship with Sansa Stark is quite unorthodox."

In 2018, HBO became the first network to require a new type of crew member for all scenes involving sex and/or nudity—the intimacy coordinator, a person tasked with ensuring the well-being of actors when filming sensitive scenes. But during *Thrones'* early years, actors in nude scenes on TV shows were largely left to advocate for themselves.

ESMÉ BIANCO: Back then, none of that usually entered the conversation. But Daniel Minahan had worked with us the day before shooting to create some choreography to figure out exactly how it would be shot so we'd be more comfortable—that's basically what an intimacy coordinator does now. And I think we need to be having those conversations prior to throwing actors into the deep end and letting themselves figure it out on set.

Shooting brothel scenes wasn't always awkward or strenuous, however. There were moments of levity as well—such as the time Diana Rigg stepped into Littlefinger's house of ill repute.

DAVE HILL: We were preparing for a scene where Olenna meets Littlefinger at the brothel. And Dame Diana Rigg looked around and went, "Shouldn't there be more sex toys? Shouldn't there be sheepskin condoms scattered about?" I'm all, "You're absolutely correct, Dame Diana!" We appreciated her knowledge of ancient sexual devices.

The Wall in the opening scene of the reshot pilot, "Winter Is Coming."

The Starks find direwolf pups.

The Stark family greets King Robert Baratheon (Mark Addy) at Winterfell.

On the Castle Black set.

Khal Drogo (Jason Momoa) and Daenerys Targaryen (Emilia Clarke)
receive a fateful wedding gift.

Syrio Forel (Miltos Yerolemou)
spars with Arya Stark
(Maisie Williams) as her father,
Ned Stark (Sean Bean), looks on.

Varys (Conleth Hill) and Littlefinger (Aidan Gillen) scheme at the Red Keep.

Petyr "Littlefinger" Baelish in his brothel.

King Robert Baratheon and Cersei Lannister (Lena Headey)
at the jousting tournament in "The Wolf and the Lion."

Tyrion Lannister (Peter Dinklage) demands trial by combat at the Eyrie.

Sellsword Bronn (Jerome Flynn) takes a stand.

A rare instance of Joffrey Baratheon (Jack Gleeson) showing sensitivity as his father, King Robert, lies mortally wounded in season one's "You Win or You Die."

The final moments of Ned Stark.

Arya looks on at her father's execution at the Sept of Baelor.

Arya is taken away by Night's Watch member Yoren (Francis Magee).

The Mother of Dragons is born.

A focused Emilia Clarke prepares to take the stage.

Melisandre (Carice van Houten) persuades Stannis Baratheon (Stephen Dillane).

A captive Jon Snow (Kit Harington) is led across a frozen lake
by Ygritte (Rose Leslie) and other Wildlings in Iceland.

The reduced crew on location at a frozen lake in Iceland.

Showrunners Dan Weiss and David Benioff on the set in Iceland.

Kit Harington fighting Simon Armstrong (playing Qhorin Halfhand) in Iceland.

The *Thrones* crew huddles around a monitor in Iceland.

The ship set, which was redressed and used for all ships throughout the series.

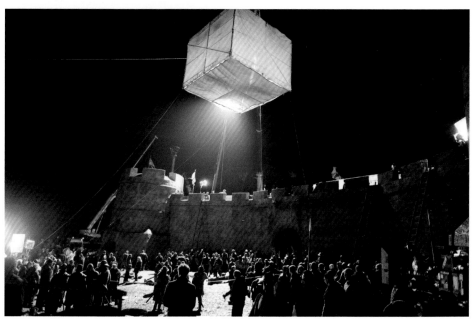

"Moonlight" over the Battle of the Blackwater.

King's Landing prepares for battle in "Blackwater."

Hollywood Reporter in 2008. "The most expensive effects are creature effects, and there's not much of that."

"Not much"—except depicting thousands of ships on fire and armies clashing on sea and land in a sequence that would blow out the budget of a feature film, let alone a TV show.

Game of Thrones had reached a pivotal moment, and it was before the production was truly ready. The outcome of this challenge would define the series. The showrunners knew Blackwater was only the first of several increasingly massive spectacles in Martin's books. *Thrones* was either going to continue as a character-driven drama with an occasional sword fight or direwolf, or it was going to evolve into a television-cinema hybrid unlike anything Hollywood had seen. At the time, an episode of *Thrones* was typically shot in about two weeks, but even a downsized version of Blackwater would need a minimum of three, plus additional funds for staging the on-the-ground action, extra cast, and special effects. The producers needed a multimillion-dollar stipend and, just as critical, to establish a clear precedent with the network and their fans that would make future battles not only possible but expected. The *Thrones* team didn't want Julius Caesar taking a nap.

DAN WEISS (*showrunner*): We were nervous, *really* nervous, going into the second season, about that episode. There was talk of turning Blackwater into a land battle, which would have been terrible.

DAVID BENIOFF (*showrunner*): Or doing it off-screen.

DAN WEISS: "M'lord, have you heard? They're at the bay!"

DAVID BENIOFF: We went down on bended knee: "Just this once. Please."

DAN WEISS: We begged and pleaded with Mike Lombardo. We were negotiating. We had a big conversation about how many boats could we do.

MICHAEL LOMBARDO (*former HBO programming president*): The question was, could you have a sophisticated, grounded drama, [with] fantasy tropes, and have epic battles? Could you do it all?

After considerable back-and-forth, Lombardo agreed to give *Thrones* an additional $2 million to stage a version of the battle, which included an extra week of filming. But the battle was still unworkable on paper. The episode's writer was Martin himself, so the author was tasked with the painful duty of downsizing his own vision while trying to maintain the fight's most crucial aspects—to keep the horses *and* Stonehenge, so to speak.

GEORGE R. R. MARTIN (*author, co–executive producer*): We had to scale down Blackwater considerably from the book. They told me right at the start that the bridge of boats would be impossible.

CHRISTOPHER NEWMAN (*producer*): What you see on the screen is ten times removed from not just the book but the first outline. Compromise was set in pretty early on.

One easy adjustment was setting the battle at night instead of day. Nighttime filming meant the production could save on having to pay for special effects to render detailed backgrounds and also helped the battle's visual storytelling (it made the flaming arrows and exploding boats look cool, in other words).

The producers also decided to make the battle as subjective as possible. Scripting scenes around the perspective of a single familiar character would help keep the audience engaged in the story while reducing the number of expensive wide shots of the battle that would require showing masses of ships and soldiers. Though this filming style was born from solving a budget problem, it would become a unifying element across all *Thrones* battles.

DAVID BENIOFF: There's the vast, epic way of shooting a battle, where you see an army of a hundred thousand and an attacking army of two hundred thousand. There's also the more ground's-eye view, where you're an infantryman and just seeing what's directly in front of you. And that can be a really visceral way of shooting a battle. We were trying to get it to feel real and gritty and dirty.

DAN WEISS: Any time you read any military account of an actual soldier's experience of battle, whether it was in ancient Rome or all the way up to Vietnam and beyond, it's never, "Then this flank moved over here and that flank." It's always, "This was a chaotic clusterfuck and I didn't know which way I was going and I was half the time not sure if I was shooting at my own guys."

And yet, even with the Blackwater battle cut down to its barest necessities, the plan still didn't fit their schedule.

GEORGE R. R. MARTIN: We had a director who kept saying, "Cut this! Cut that! I can't make the day." I kept removing elements, and it was getting to the point where it was getting as bad as the jousting tournament.

And then, just a few weeks before filming, the director had an unexpected family medical emergency and had to drop out. "I'd done quite a lot of work prepping that episode," the director said. "Very sadly, I had an illness in the family and I had to leave. I knew I was leaving them with a difficult time, but it was absolutely unavoidable."

Now the production had another problem. After all their pleading and negotiation with HBO for the money and latitude to stage a climactic battle, they were less than a month from shooting and didn't have a definitive plan or a director.

BERNADETTE CAULFIELD (executive producer): That was my first year on the show and probably my first fight with David and Dan. They were like, "Oh, let's get so-and-so." I said, "Ninety percent of this is action. We need somebody who really knows action. It's not easy. We should really look at Neil Marshall."

DAVID BENIOFF: Neil did *Centurion* and *Dog Soldiers,* movies where the guy is doing an incredible amount of really impressive action on a very thin budget.

BERNADETTE CAULFIELD: And other directors kept being mentioned, and I kept saying, "I'm telling you, we need an action director!" Then David calls me up. At the time we didn't know each other that well. And he goes: "Okay, Bernie, we're going with your idea to hire Neil."

I swear to God, my stomach dropped. I'm like, "Wait, *my* idea? This is a community decision!" I hung up the phone, and I thought, "Shit. Now it's *my* idea. I'm responsible for this guy doing our first battle."

NEIL MARSHALL (*director*): I was aware of *Game of Thrones* when season one was happening. I thought, "This is really my kind of thing," and had my agent contact HBO and say, "If there's any chance, I'd like to be able to direct an episode." Their response was like, "We have our directors, thank you very much."

Then a year or so later on a Saturday morning, I got an emergency call from Bernie to come and fix a situation that, from what I gathered, was a bit out of control. She asked if I would like to direct an episode. I was like, "Absolutely!" I'm thinking this will be in few months' time. Then she said, "It's on Monday morning, and you've got one week to plan."

DAVID BENIOFF: Neil had never seen the show before. We gave him a crash course on season one and talked to him about the story constantly. But he was such a fast learner and so enthusiastic and just fell in love with it. He ended up being a great choice.

NEIL MARSHALL: Dan and David weren't like, "This is it and you just gotta do it." They wanted ideas. Military history is a hobby of mine, so I brought a sense of strategy to the battle. Because in the script, forty thousand people arrive on a beach and they stand around a door. They had all this stuff at sea and the green fire, but once they got to the beach, it wasn't really clear who was trying to achieve what. Stannis basically marshaled the whole battle from the beach. I felt that that wasn't really in character and wasn't interesting. I was like, "They can't just stand around; they have to be doing other things, and we have to get Stannis in on the action."

GEORGE R. R. MARTIN: Neil Marshall reversed everything the previous director said. Marshall was like, "Put in more." He put so much back that I'd previously taken out and even added some stuff I hadn't thought of. He was the hero of that episode.

NEIL MARSHALL: I invented the boat that came in and was turned upside down with a battering ram suspended underneath to batter the gate. By bringing the ladders and the grappling hooks, it gave the scene more sense of purpose. And we had Stannis climb the wall and have a good fight up there and cut somebody's head off.

Once filming began, the challenges did not let up. The episode marked the first of several grueling nighttime battle shoots for the *Thrones* team. Such sequences would test the cast and crew's physical and mental stamina, and their ability to perform at their best in an environment that was universally described as torturous.

NEIL MARSHALL: With the exception of the action on the boat, it was all shot in Magheramorne quarry, where it was pouring with rain in October, freezing cold with mud up to our knees. There was an overall draining factor for everybody involved. Particularly for the extras, who just have to stand around in the rain. I was worried it would look like we were doing the cliché of a battle in pouring rain, but it's real rain, and we couldn't do anything about it.

CHRISTOPHER NEWMAN: It was moving like a locomotive. There was no way of stopping. Whatever we didn't finish on time wasn't going to be in the film. And the conditions were horrendous.

EUGENE MICHAEL SIMON (*Lancel Lannister*): We had three days of rain. On the fourth day it stopped. Suddenly everybody was like, "Oh shit, what are we going to do?" Because the continuity wouldn't match and we had tons of stuff to do. What happened was the most elaborate example of adapting I'd ever seen on a film set: There was a natural salt lake at the bottom of the quarry, but the water in it was below freezing—it didn't ice over because it was salt water. They ran a fire hose from the bottom of this freezing cold lake, and had a man hold a fire hydrant at the top of the wall for that scene where Tyrion is giving his speech—*"If I'm half a man, what does that make you!?"* The deadly cold water from the lake was fired up into the air so it would rain down on us while Peter had to expertly give this pro speech. You can see our breath evaporating since we're all freezing and it looks like we're in the North.

DAN WEISS: Peter Dinklage in those scenes didn't have to act tired because by four o'clock in the morning, he'd had rain pouring on him for eight hours straight. He was bleary, weary, and tired. It was miserable.

NEIL MARSHALL: But Peter was quite giddy that he was going to get out and start hitting people with an axe. He was really excited about leading this army and chopping a guy's legs off and stuff like that. It was a nice change for the character rather than, you know, drinking and whoring and whatever else.

PETER DINKLAGE (*Tyrion Lannister*): Some people rely on drunk, funny Tyrion. Funny and drunk lasts only so long.

GEORGE R. R. MARTIN: Tyrion's speech on the steps, pretty much verbatim from the books: "There are brave men out there, let's go kill them!" I love that scene.

PETER DINKLAGE: You gotta have a certain amount of confidence to pull that type of stuff off. I make it not my confidence, but the character's confidence. So maybe that might seem like I'm confident? It's really just the fact that this character, Tyrion, is sort of confident. I guess.

The battle scenes were intercut with Cersei awaiting her fate in Maegor's Holdfast, with the queen regent becoming intoxicated and mocking Sansa.

LENA HEADEY (*Cersei Lannister*): It was one of the first times we see Cersei so brazen. She's usually pretty snaky. Being drunk and thinking she may die, she's just letting Sansa have it direct. It's like this masochistic mentor relationship where she can't help but torture Sansa. And I think that's driven by envy and frustration that, as women, we're stuck. You know what I mean? She *thinks* she's helping her. But yeah, she's just horrid.

NEIL MARSHALL: I remember talking to Lena and saying, "Cersei is basically acting like the drunk aunt at a wedding. It's like she's had a few too many drinks and can't control her mouth." She was like, "I know exactly what you mean."

Headey could empathize with Cersei's envy. Her character told Sansa, "I'd rather face a thousand swords than be shut up inside with this flock of frightened hens." Headey likewise longed for bona fide action scenes.

LENA HEADEY: I kept begging them for a sword and a horse.

For the scenes in Blackwater Bay, the team constructed a boat in an entirely unremarkable "car park" (a.k.a. parking lot). The sea was added later with visual effects. The boat is probably the show's biggest and most repeatedly used visual effects cheat. Every sailing boat seen in the show—Baratheon, Targaryen, Lannister, or Greyjoy—is actually the same boat (except for the bow of Euron Greyjoy's *Silence*). So while most of the Blackwater cast was filming in a quarry, Cunningham was in a car park, eyeing an approaching "barge" filled with deadly wildfire.

LIAM CUNNINGHAM (*Davos Seaworth*): In reality that barge was just a little thing [about six feet long] with two pipes leaking green liquid out of it while two guys pushed it up the car park.

In the episode, Bronn fired a burning arrow to ignite Tyrion's wildfire trap. The resulting massive green explosion consumed the bulk of Stannis's fleet and blew away viewers. Finishing the effects by the episode's air date went down to the very last minute.

DAVID BENIOFF: We were turning in VFX shots on "Blackwater" a week before airing. HBO quality control got the tapes with twenty minutes to spare [before the deadline].

GEORGE R. R. MARTIN: When the wildfire explodes, it's glorious. It's one of my favorite episodes of the show. Certainly my favorite of the four I wrote [throughout the series].

CHRISTOPHER NEWMAN: "Blackwater" was a litmus test on whether we could pull things off. We had done something we didn't think was possible. The confidence that came out of doing it set the tone for the subsequent seasons.

LIAM CUNNINGHAM: Neil texted me a review from *Rolling Stone* that said, "This is possibly the best hour of television that's ever been made." And Neil, who had never done television before, wrote, "Not bad for a first-timer."

CHAPTER NINE

FIRE AND ICE

Daenerys, her clothes in tatters, stood at the towering gates of Qarth. The Mother of Dragons had survived a long trek through the expanse of the Red Waste, seeking shelter for the weary remnants of her khalasar. But the city's pampered leaders refused to let her inside. Emilia Clarke's stance was firm and defiant, her voice resounding across the desert: "When my dragons are grown, we will take back what was stolen from me and destroy those who wronged me. We will lay waste to armies and burn cities to the ground. Turn us away and we will burn you first!"

Showrunner Dan Weiss watched Clarke on a nearby monitor and marveled at the way she channeled the power of a fearsome Dothraki leader. "She looks really tough," Weiss said of the petite, five-foot-two actress. "I'm a six-foot-tall male, and if I try to stand tough I look like an asshole. We really need to sell that if she doesn't get into the city she's truly fucked."

It was September 2011 and Clarke's third day performing in a sun-drenched quarry in Croatia. The actress's long, dark hair was smushed into a bald cap glued onto her head, and then a tight blond wig was affixed on top of that. Standing in the heat, hour after hour, Clarke felt like her skull was baking. After filming the scene, the actress bowed out of a scheduled interview due to "heatstroke." As Clarke cheerfully explained later that week, "Oh, the other day? I just had a bit of a 'can't cope with the heat' moment. . . ."

Clarke wouldn't reveal the real reason behind her exhaustion for another eight years. After filming *Thrones* season one, she had suffered a brain hemorrhage at a gym in London. "I immediately felt as though an elastic band were squeezing my brain," Clarke wrote in *The New Yorker*. As she was rushed to the hospital, Clarke recalled lines of Daenerys Targaryen's dialogue to try to calm herself. The actress underwent emergency surgery and for several days couldn't even remember her own name, let alone speeches in Dothraki.

Somehow, just weeks later, Clarke returned to work on *Thrones* despite still having a second growth on her brain that a doctor said might—in theory, though it was unlikely—"pop at any time." Day after day on set, Clarke's performance gave no indication of her fatigue, fear, and pain.

EMILIA CLARKE (*Daenerys Targaryen*): It was crazy intense. We are in the desert in a quarry in like ninety-degree heat, and I had the consistent fear that I was going to have another brain hemorrhage. I spent a lot time just being like: "Am I gonna die? Is that gonna happen on set? Because that would be really inconvenient." And with any kind of brain injury it leaves you with a fatigue that's indescribable. I was trying so hard to keep it under wraps.

BRYAN COGMAN (*co–executive producer*): Only a very select few people knew about that. I was completely unaware. I heard a little bit that she had some problems between seasons, but nothing to that extent. And I had no clue while we were shooting.

ALAN TAYLOR (*director*): We were afraid for her. She's so brave, because it never affected her commitment to the work.

EMILIA CLARKE: If I had called my doctor, he would have been like, "Dude, you just need to chill out." But I still felt blind fear, and the fear was making me panic, and the panic was leading me to feel like I'm going to pass out in the desert. So they brought in an air-conditioned car for me—sorry, planet.

DAN WEISS (*showrunner*): It was terrifying because this amazing, sweet, wonderful human being came *this close* to not being around anymore—this person we loved so much after just one year. Obviously you need to make the show, but the important thing was making sure she was in a safe situation. You ask yourself: Is she as safe doing this show as if she was not doing it? If she was home, sitting on her couch? She was so gung-ho, the main thing for us was making sure she wouldn't put herself [in dangerous situations]. She would say: "Yeah, I just had brain surgery and if I need to gallop on a horse down a mountainside, I'll do it." You would have to tell her no because she would never say no.

EMILIA CLARKE: In all of my years on the show, I never put self-health first, which is probably why everyone else was worrying, as they could see that. They didn't want to work me too hard. I was like: "Don't think I'm a failure; don't think I can't do the job that I've been hired to do. Please don't think I'm going to fuck up at any moment." I had the Willy Wonka golden ticket. I wasn't about to hand that in.

By the time Clarke started filming season three, she felt considerably better—and was happier with her storyline, as well.

EMILIA CLARKE: Daenerys's storyline was a little funky in season two—"the tricky second album" is what I like to call it. Then in season three she was coming into her power and I felt like I was coming into my power. So season one, I was like, "I don't know what I'm doing"; by season three, I was like, "I know *exactly* what I'm doing."

The season contained one of the most critical moments for her character: Daenerys's gaining an Unsullied army. The sequence in Martin's

A Storm of Swords is an emotional high point and clever turn of events. Having sailed from Qarth to the Slaver's Bay city of Astapor in hopes of gaining an army, Daenerys patiently negotiated with the sadistic slave trader Kraznys (Dan Hildebrand), who assumed she didn't understand his insults spoken in Valyrian, while Kraznys's translator, Missandei (Nathalie Emmanuel), slyly hid his rudeness in an effort to keep the peace.

Daenerys agreed to give Kraznys a dragon, Drogon, in exchange for an army. But when the exchange was made, Daenerys revealed to the slave trader that she was, quite naturally, fluent in her ancestors' mother tongue. Daenerys ordered her soldiers, acquired just moments before, to slaughter the city's slave masters, and unleashed Drogon to torch Kraznys. "A dragon is not a slave," Daenerys declared. The moment was not merely about trickery, spectacle, or achievement but Daenerys's trusting her own instincts and playing the game of thrones for the first time.

EMILIA CLARKE: Up until that moment, Dany relies on everybody else's opinion to form her own because she didn't know any better. It's the biggest risk she's taken in her life and everyone around her is assuming she'll give Drogon up—which is ridiculous for the mother of a child. There's that moment of "Is this going to work or is it not going to work," whether the Unsullied are going to respect her, and everything hangs in the balance. It's the moment she becomes who she was always destined to be. There's a thin line between braveness and madness, and she dances on that line.

DAVID BENIOFF (*showrunner*): The best kind of surprises aren't the ones that come out of nowhere; they're the ones where after you see it you're asking yourself, "Why didn't I see that was coming?" I remember reading [that Daenerys was going to give up Drogon] going, "Oh, it's kind of disappointing that she's doing this." When her real plan is revealed I called Dan. It was one of those times when we were like, "We gotta make this fucking show." It's a hallmark of a number of scenes in this book, where in retrospect I should have seen it coming because George had laid out all the pieces; he had given you the clues.

The budget-straining sequence was shot in Morocco by director Alex Graves, who had to depict a slave uprising and the show's first major dragon attack using just a few concise shots.

ALEX GRAVES (*director*): It's one of those, "There's no money to this, but if you pull this off it's one of the greatest sequences of all time."

EMILIA CLARKE: I couldn't wait to stick it to the man. I had been practicing that speech for weeks in my room.

DAN WEISS: When we lit Kraznys on fire with the dragon, [special effects supervisor Stuart Brisdon] made a flamethrower on a pole up in the air. They shot this stuntman full in the face with a flamethrower. It was a shocking, powerful thing to watch, even as a stunt.

The scene concluded with Daenerys looking triumphant as a series of explosions ignited behind her from Drogon's attack.

ALEX GRAVES: I came up with what's been called "the *Apocalypse Now* shot." But we were filming in Morocco during the Arab Spring, when transporting high explosives into North Africa was not allowed. I didn't give up because that image of Emilia was so burned into my brain. So we smuggled the explosives into the country to do it. Emilia stood in front of these fireballs and you could feel the heat and the shock wave from the explosions, and she didn't flinch.

EMILIA CLARKE: Iain Glen, who was consistently my mentor, was like, "Darling, come here. Look at how well taken care of you are. All you have to do is stand in front of that and all this shit is happening." I realized that was all I needed to do. And it felt so good. It felt so electric. It was like everyone who had ever fucked me off in my life, they had them all lined up.

The sequence also gained Daenerys two allies who would accompany her through the final season and develop storylines of their own: savvy translator-turned-advisor Missandei and stoic Unsullied leader Grey Worm (Jacob Anderson).

NATHALIE EMMANUEL (*Missandei*): I was a really big fan of the show, and I had on a number of occasions phoned my London agent saying I really wanted to be on it. Then I saw a breakdown for a character where they specifically detailed Missandei should be of color between eighteen and twenty-three and I was like, "Wait, that's me!" I phoned my agent, and she was like, "I've already seen it, you've got an audition."

I did a bunch of research on the character and was reading the books as I wanted to be as prepared as possible. Because Missandei was from the Summer Isles, I thought maybe she might speak the Common Tongue with an accent. So I came up with an accent for her, like a [Received Pronunciation, or "posh," accent*]. My agent said, "No, no, you don't need to do an accent."

So I did the audition once, and casting director Robert Sterne said, "They haven't quite decided whether Missandei would have an accent or not." So I was so ready to go and did the accent. It's a testament to being prepared. I didn't hear anything for five weeks. When I got the call, I was on my way home from food shopping. I screamed and dropped my shopping and broke a jam jar and cried a lot.

---

* There are seven different accents floating around *Game of Thrones,* according to Chris Taylor, who broke them all down for a Mashable story in 2017. Sean Bean had a Yorkshire accent (which, fittingly, is from Northern England), and all the Stark boys and most of the Wildlings use it too. Sansa, Arya, Bran, and Rickon all took after their mother Catelyn's posh accent, which Daenerys has as well.

JACOB ANDERSON (*Grey Worm*): It was one of the worst auditions I have ever done. The only note I was given was to hold back any emotion. But it was the speech where Grey Worm talks about getting his name and I subconsciously cranked up my emotion because that was exactly what I've been told not to do. I couldn't help getting emotional about what I was saying. I was also self-conscious about my accent. They said, "Don't worry, you're not going to speak English." I'm like, "*What?*" I figured I'd definitely not gotten that part. To this day I have no idea how I got the job.

NATHALIE EMMANUEL: I went to a read-through [of the season-three scripts] in Belfast, and I was terrified. I stood in this room while all the cast of the show I'd been watching were coming in. Then [Loras Tyrell actor] Finn Jones—who I'd met before as he'd done a bit on *Hollyoaks,* a show I'd been on—saw me standing in a corner not moving and asked if I was all right. "I don't know, kind of overwhelmed." He was really sweet and helped me find my seat and introduced me to people.

JACOB ANDERSON: During my first week, I was like, "This could be quite boring playing this stoic character who doesn't have any thoughts or feelings." Then Dan said: "Grey Worm is walking trauma. If you imagine a robot built out of trauma, that's what he is." I found that a helpful guide to the rest of the show. If you're someone who has dealt with a lot of trauma, the last thing you want is to be present, because it can be re-traumatizing. Also, my costume was beautifully designed, but there was very little that was practical about it. I could barely walk, which is why I have a slightly funny walk in the show; it doesn't let up at all.

NATHALIE EMMANUEL: My first scene was when Missandei was showing her bravery when Daenerys said, "You may go hungry, you may fall sick, you may be killed." And it ends up with me saying, "All men must die," and Daenerys says, "Yes, but we are not men." It's such an iconic feminist moment in the script, with Missandei giving that small smile.

For the character, that's when she knew she was in safer hands and that this woman was a force to be reckoned with.

After that shot, David Benioff came up to me and he said, "You're officially on *Game of Thrones*," and it was the best thing anyone could have said to me. My little heart burst.

JACOB ANDERSON: Somebody later told me Benioff had said when I got cast that I was "good but way too skinny." But he never told me that! Had somebody told me that I would have worked out.

NATHALIE EMMANUEL: I was familiar with Jacob's work in *Adulthood* and was excited to work with him. We're the two characters of color in the show, and it's always great when you have someone around you've shared a certain experience with.

His first scene was when he gets chosen by the officers of the Unsullied army to be their leader and Daenerys says he gets to choose his freedom name. But it's all in Valyrian. I remember on his first take he delivered this incredible performance and Emilia and I looked at each other like, "Oh, damn, this is amazing." He delivered the speech with so much brilliance and conviction while saying essentially made-up words. "Whatever you just said, we believe you!"

JACOB ANDERSON: I remember being in awe of Emilia and Nathalie looking back at me in that scene. I didn't know anybody and they were really encouraging and friendly and I just needed that. I thought, "If this job is getting to work with these two, this is going to be a good job."

NATHALIE EMMANUEL: Jacob and Emilia and I just became this little gang and had so much fun together. Jacob was always aware and conscientious about us two being the only women around, and we loved him because of that.

The trio of actors became a tight-knit group for the rest of the series, with Clarke often arranging games to keep them entertained during downtime on the set (example: Everybody had to draw an animal in fifteen seconds and then they all compared the results; "We're like four-year-olds sometimes," she said).

One of Daenerys's season-three companions noticeably changed: The handsome Second Sons mercenary Daario Naharis was played by Ed Skrein in season three, then was switched to Michiel Huisman for seasons four through six. Skrein has previously told reporters the reason was "political." Insiders contend Skrein's voice wasn't quite right for the role and his lines were dubbed over.

MICHELLE MACLAREN (*director*): The guy was lovely and talented, it just wasn't the right combination, and those things do happen. I was impressed how [producers] dealt with it by not explaining anything. They were just like, "Okay, so there's a different actor but the same character, moving on. . . ."

While Daenerys gained allies in the desert, Jon Snow was getting captured by the Wildling army in the frozen wasteland beyond the Wall.

In a storyline that spanned the show's second and third seasons, Jon Snow infiltrated the Free Folk and posed as a Night's Watch deserter to learn their plans to invade the south. There he met the wildling Ygritte and, in defiance of his vows, fell in love.

Harington recalled the first moment he met Leslie, whom he would marry in real life seven years later.

KIT HARINGTON (*Jon Snow*): I googled Rose when I found out she was playing the part. Then I met her in a costume fitting—so the first time I ever saw Rose she was dressed as Ygritte. She offered me a ginger biscuit, which is very sweet. I was completely enamored. I was also bowled over by her portrayal of the character, which suggested brilliance to me.

DAVID NUTTER (*director*): I was the director the first day they met each other. The first scene we shot was when the Night's Watch take out the Wildlings and he puts the sword to her neck and he's about to kill her. Kit told me it was the happiest day of his life. You could tell there was a real spark.

ALEX GRAVES: They had charming, romantic scenes together where nobody got killed—and on *Game of Thrones,* that's weird. I don't think I realized that they were a couple until later. They were so damn happy together. We were like, "Are they dating? They ought to be if they're not."

KIT HARINGTON: I think I started to feel who Jon Snow was in season two. When Jon meets Ygritte, she tests him and puts him in a different ballpark. He's having to deal with some feisty different entity and she takes the piss out of him and through that you get to see who Jon really is. I don't think many people mark out season two as a particularly standout season, but for me it was the most special.

For the north-of-the-Wall sequences, producers wanted a landscape that was more desolate and convincingly wintery than what could be achieved by set-dressing a Northern Ireland location with fake snow and a dusting of CGI. The solution would be the show's first of several excursions to Iceland, a country that provided some of the show's most stunning visuals, as well as some of its toughest days.

BERNADETTE CAULFIELD (*executive producer*): [Producer] Chris Newman, whose wife is from Iceland, sent me a picture before season two: "I know we're going north of the Wall next year and I was thinking of Iceland, what do you think of this?" I'm like, "That's exactly what we need!" So I went to David and Dan, and they asked, "Do you think we can do that?" and that's always all I need to hear. "Of course we can do that!" Then I walked out of the office going, "How the fuck do we do that?"

So we came up with this whole plan to go to Iceland using a smaller crew for what little money we had at that point. And by the time shooting approached, wouldn't you know it, it's not snowing in Iceland. Every day I'd say to Chris: "Anything?" "Not yet." As producers, you feel responsible for things even that are not in your control.

CHRISTOPHER NEWMAN (*producer*): It was a little nerve-wracking for me, having persuaded everybody to go there.

BERNADETTE CAULFIELD: Eventually Chris says, "I'm going to have them pack a bag of [fake] snow in with our equipment." I'm all, "Chris, *one bag of snow* is not going to do it!" And he goes, "I know! But I have to do something!"

Just three days before we started shooting, it started snowing in Iceland.

But then it didn't stop.

DAVID BENIOFF: We got there, and it was a blizzard. I was driving to set in the morning up this tiny little road heading up the mountains. We had to pull over our Land Cruiser to let another car go by. We tried to get back on the road and our car got stuck in this massive snowdrift. We were completely stopped. We tried to shovel our way out and couldn't get out. So a production van came to give us a ride and we got about another half mile. Then the van got stuck in a gully. So a truck came and pulled the van out and the rope snapped. It was *that* hard to get to the set.

DAVID NUTTER: We were out scouting a location, and it was cliffside driving in a Jeep with four-feet-high snow. We went off the road. Fortunately, we went off on the hill side, not on the cliff side, but the car rolled over sideways, and I jumped out. I was like, "Okay, let's use that *other* location that's back down the hill."

CHRISTOPHER NEWMAN: At one point snow was coming in so heavy, we were stuck at the hotel and couldn't go anywhere except on foot. So we said to the director, Alan Taylor, "Just walk outside the hotel." We took the one camera we had, and he shot the scene where Samwell hears the three horns signaling the attack on the Fist of the First Men. They did that just outside, within sight of the hotel dining room. Yet it looks extraordinary as the hotel was right underneath a mountain. Sometimes you end up with a better scene when something doesn't work.

DAVID BENIOFF: The wind was blowing so hard. There was a shot where Samwell is talking to Jon. We're on Samwell and he's talking and he looks kind of normal, then you cut to Jon, and then you cut back to Samwell and he looks like Father Time—snow and ice frozen onto his face in just a matter of seconds.

BERNADETTE CAULFIELD: Then there were also all these rumors of Iceland's volcano blowing again, which would have been really bad. Chris and I were like, "Let's just not tell anybody that, let's keep that between us."

KIT HARINGTON: It was like guerrilla filmmaking. One day it was minus thirty-five, a frozen whiteout. There was a moment I had to yell, "Stop!" because Rose was walking backward around a five-hundred-foot drop. There was another when we were all on a frozen lake and you heard this huge *crack* underneath and we all had to run off.

ALAN TAYLOR: Every English person ran for the shore, but every Icelandic person just kept walking.

ROSE LESLIE (*Ygritte*): You're trudging through the snow and trying to make it look effortless on camera, because it's rather treacherous. This is Ygritte's home, she's incredibly comfortable in this particular surrounding, so you can't look like you're working so hard to trudge up a hill and I was, like, panting inside.

JOHN BRADLEY (*Samwell Tarly*): We said, "We're never going to complain about November in Belfast again," though of course we did. It also felt really special. It's an astonishingly beautiful place. You're standing on a glacier and you look a certain direction and there's not a trace of the modern world anywhere. It looks like it did a million years ago. I was looking at this view and I was with my friends and colleagues who I love and respect, and I realized how lucky I was.

DAN WEISS: I went up to Kit on his second day of shooting, and he looked like he was on ecstasy. He said, "I've never ever had a day of shooting that I loved as much as this day of shooting." He was just so in it and happy to be there that it became infectious.

When the *Thrones* team returned to Iceland for season three, filming was complicated by Harington's getting injured before filming began. "I left my keys in the house, so after a drunken night out I tried to climb up to the . . . window, but I fell backwards and broke my ankle in four places," Harington told the UK's *Daily Mail* at the time. "The doctors asked me if I'd been caught with another man's wife and had to jump out of the window. I had to say no, but that would have been far more exciting."

Harington sounded glib but privately felt terrible about the mishap and worried about how his injury would impact the show.

KIT HARINGTON: That's what happened. I didn't see the point in lying to anyone. I was an idiot. The invincibility of youth. The line producer had to rearrange everybody's schedules around me, and I bought him a nice bottle of whiskey because I felt so guilty. I'm sure they were cursing my name behind my back.

The schedule was shuffled to push all the Jon Snow scenes by two months. Publicly, the production downplayed Harington's injury and suggested the actor only had a bit of a limp. But a body double was used for some of Jon Snow's footage and Harington's action duties were scaled back.

ALEX GRAVES: He couldn't walk! At the time it was a big "let's keep this quiet" thing. We didn't want people watching the scenes wondering, "Is that him or not?" I designed a way to film and cut a scene where Kit would start walking, then I would cut to Ygritte, and then he would end up next to her. Then we did all the wide shots with a body double.

KIT HARINGTON: Even if it was just somebody walking, I had real problems with not going up to the guy doing the doubling and telling him how to do things differently. You don't think you create a walk for a character, but there were a couple shots where I checked his gait and I was like, "Nah, that's not right."

Between Clarke's brain surgery and Harington's ankle, the producers began to think about how easily the show could get permanently derailed due to a random and unforeseeable misfortune. *Thrones* had a large number of characters considered essential to its story. That some tragedy might befall a lead actor, or that a performer whose star was on the rise might quit the production to take a coveted movie role, was a background source of anxiety until the show's very last shot.

DAN WEISS: Accidents happen. But if Kit's fall had gone differently, then he's not in the show anymore. We had a lot of people, and the odds that something was going to happen that makes it impossible for them to continue started to feel pretty high.

During season three, Harington returned to Belfast for the rest of his storyline, which included Jon Snow and Ygritte's making love in a cave-sheltered hot spring. "[Harington] was, as ever, a gentleman," Leslie told reporters of the cave scene. "He made sure that I was comfortable with where he was going to be positioned, and he would always turn around when they called "cut" and the lovely wardrobe ladies would come in with a dressing gown, and then I would be covered. He made sure as much as possible that I didn't feel awkward standing in front of people with your tits out. So it's never going to be an enjoyable day, it's always going to be an awkward one, but he and the rest of the crew were incredibly considerate."

KIT HARINGTON: [The cave scene] was incredible. That scene in this really dire, dark world where nothing good happens and there's very little joy, that scene is one of the very few happy moments where you can escape from the grimness and horror of Westeros. There are promises made on film sets about water being warm. Bullshit, you know it's going to be cold. But they made a lovely warm bath for us.

ALEX GRAVES: Kit said he wanted to jump in the pool with Ygritte. I'm all, "Are you sure you want to do that with your ankle?" And he said he'd just use his other leg. So he got up naked and just jumped in.

Later, the duo scaled the Wall with their Wildling companions Tormund (Kristofer Hivju) and Orell (Mackenzie Crook). The Wall was actually a fifty-foot-high plaster-and-polystyrene "ice" surface constructed inside a studio. As with real ice, the actors could use axes to literally climb its surface.

KIT HARINGTON: Every time you walk onto a new set on *Thrones* you're like, "Fuck. They topped it again." I remember we tried to climb up the wall individually [before filming]. Mackenzie and I got a bit higher than Rose, but only by a little bit, by putting one ice pick in at a time until we couldn't pull ourselves up anymore with the costume and everything. Kristofer went up the whole wall in one try and nearly destroyed the thing. I have never met anyone who's more like their character.

The climb concluded with the most romantic shot in the series: doomed lovers Jon and Ygritte kissing on top of the world, a moment of bliss before the inevitable darkness to come.

KIT HARINGTON: The top-of-the-Wall shot is one of my favorite shots in all of *Thrones*. It's probably the best place Jon gets to in the show. Somewhere out there is a behind-the-scenes shot where you see there are also guys with fans turned on us and the AD and the art department and the director standing around. I think for me that sums up *Thrones*. Because you take all the green screen away and it's just this beautiful moment where I was kissing my future wife. I remember not wanting them to cut. I was like: "Please don't cut, this is perfect."

Shortly afterward, Ygritte figured out that Jon Snow was still loyal to the Night's Watch—and shot him with three arrows to express her annoyance. Their relationship came to its tragic end during the Wildling attack at Castle Black, which Neil Marshall returned to direct. It was another grueling, rain-soaked shoot. During one unexpected high point, the bullying Ser Alliser Thorne got to be the sword-swinging hero for a change, when he led a sortie against the Wildlings.

OWEN TEALE (*Alliser Thorne*): That was my Henry the Fifth moment. The rain was pouring so hard that night, it was like *Blade Runner*. They put some boards coming down like a boardwalk so you can walk into the courtyard because a huge amount of water was falling into a small area. But in the few minutes before we shot, so much water had come down, the boards had floated away. They said, "Just keep going!" There was something really exhilarating about it.

When Jon Snow found himself once again face-to-face with Ygritte, she had an arrow nocked and ready to fire into his heart. Jon couldn't help himself. He smiled, happy to see her.

NEIL MARSHALL (*director*): I suggested to Kit: "I don't care what's happened between you and her. You love her." And so there's that little moment of smile, and then it's crushed by the tragedy that follows, which just really helped that moment of payoff.

ROSE LESLIE: She wasn't shooting to kill him [earlier in the season]. She wasn't shooting to stop him. I think she was shooting to hurt him. That he couldn't just up and leave without any consequences. She wanted to make him pay. She's in love with him and couldn't bring herself to kill him. She could have killed him in one fell swoop with an arrow through the heart if she wanted to. She finally looks at him [at Castle Black] and can't bring herself to do it, hesitates. It's that hesitation that's the ruin of her. It's lovely she was in Jon Snow's arms.

In Martin's *A Storm of Swords*, Jon found Ygritte's dead body after the battle, the apparent victim of a random Night's Watchman's arrow. For *Thrones,* the writers initially scripted a scene where Jon walks toward Ygritte and she's shot in the back by an anonymous shooter. Then they realized that Ygritte's killer could be Olly (Brenock O'Connor), the bitter young orphan whose parents were killed by Wildlings.

NEIL MARSHALL: Olly was a character who was never supposed to be so involved in the show. He was supposed to have his parents killed and then run to the Wall and that was to be it. It's an example of the writers going, "Wait a minute, we got a bigger story here," and then he turns out to be the killer of Ygritte.

When Jon's cradling Ygritte in his arms, another thing I wanted to do was have the battle raging around them in slow motion. If we were still in the battle, it would have kind of killed that moment. I needed to separate them somehow in the viewer's mind. But slow motion wasn't a thing that was part of the visual language of *Game of Thrones* at that point, so there was a discussion with Dan and David. I'm really proud of that shot.

DAVID BENIOFF: From the moment he saw her to the moment she's dead, it's some of the most powerful seconds we'd put on-screen. People talk about chemistry. The chemistry between Kit and Rose was something that couldn't be faked no matter how good an actor or director might be.

ROSE LESLIE: They did a wonderful send-off. After my final take I was given my bow and arrow. Where I hold it with my left hand they replaced the grubby Wildling wrapping with white leather and put the emblem of a rose. It was absolutely beautiful. She's such a fiercely independent character, and I loved playing her.

————◇————

CHAPTER TEN

"This Is Going to Be Good"

Frigid rain pelted a lush green hilltop as a muddied Nikolaj Coster-Waldau took a break from filming. It was one of those miserable Northern Ireland nights where *Game of Thrones* crew members longed for the rare moment they could huddle next to a space heater or perhaps get a cup of hot tea. Yet there was Coster-Waldau, all smiles as the rain streamed down his grizzled face. "I actually really like it," the Jaime Lannister actor said, quite convincingly. "I don't mind having physical obstacles because it makes it easier to forget about the acting. You don't want to think about lines, you want to be in the moment. The hardest scenes are sitting around a table talking."

It was October 2012, and Coster-Waldau had found himself chained in the mud once again. At least this time, he had company since the actor was with Gwendoline Christie, playing Jaime's captor-turned-fellow-captive Brienne of Tarth. Christie displayed her bound wrists and happily beamed up at a visitor. "I can only shake hands with my eyes!" she said.

Though Jaime was first introduced in the series premiere and Brienne was added to *Thrones* early in season two, it wasn't until the third season that their characters came into focus. Just like how Ygritte helped reveal new sides to Jon Snow, Jaime and Brienne lured each other out of their respective emotional armor.

Behind the scenes, Coster-Waldau and Christie's relationship mirrored Jaime and Brienne's to a degree that was surreal and hilarious to witness. The duo would trade scathing insults mixed with occasional and seemingly reluctant admissions of profound respect. But they got off to a bumpy start on the day they first met.

GWENDOLINE CHRISTIE (*Brienne of Tarth*): I was hugely shy and had fallen in love with the character. I had also watched the show and never been involved with a show that I'd already watched. So this was a completely new experience to me. I saw Nikolaj and how imposing he was in the first season. I felt very intimidated.

On one of my first days of filming, I was told Nikolaj was in the makeup truck and that I should go and say hello. I didn't want to because I felt so shy. They said, "Don't worry, I'm sure he'll be nice." So I walked in and I said, "Hello, my name is Gwen . . . ," and then, "I'm playing Brienne."

He just looked me up and down like I was an alien from another planet, possibly a pile of manure, and then said: "Oh, so that's *you*, is it?"

I was really uncomfortable. I said, "Yeah." And he said, "Okay . . . ," and then he went back to looking at himself in the mirror. I felt awful.

NIKOLAJ COSTER-WALDAU (*Jaime Lannister*): She has this whole story about me being very rude to her when we first met. I don't remember that at all.

GWENDOLINE CHRISTIE: He has denied this! He has denied it publicly. He's denied it to my face in private. But when he denies it privately, he laughs. Nikolaj can have an incredibly selective memory.

NIKOLAJ COSTER-WALDAU: I do remember she was very upset about having to get her hair cut for the part. I'm such an insensitive guy. I probably didn't understand how upset she was about the loss of her hair and made some stupid joke and that clearly left an internal mark on her, so she keeps bringing it up over and over.

GWENDOLINE CHRISTIE: So then, the next day, we were shooting. The first thing he said to me was, "Do you know your lines?" And I said, "Good morning!" And he said, "Do you know your lines?" And I snapped back: "Yes, I know *my* lines. Do you know *your* lines?"

Then we got into the van to go down to the set and started bickering. We were annoying each other, but it was also making both of us laugh. It vacillated between being quite savage and very entertaining.

So I asked, "Are you Method?" And he said, "No, I am not Method. Are *you* Method? Because if you are, this is going to be exhausting." And I said: "I do what I like. . . ."

He was really winding me up. And then he said, "This is going to be good." There was something about him that made me know he wasn't being serious. And that set the tone.

NIKOLAJ COSTER-WALDAU: We both quickly agreed, to the annoyance of everybody around us, that we would just fall into those two characters. There was a constant carrying on of the banter between Jaime and Brienne on and off the set.

GWENDOLINE CHRISTIE: He tormented and tortured me. He did it in the evening. He did it at social events. He did it first thing in the morning. He did it when I was outside my trailer.

NIKOLAJ COSTER-WALDAU: Gwen is sharp as a razor and very funny. She'd cut me down, and I'd unsuccessfully try to get back at her.

GWENDOLINE CHRISTIE: He said to me while we were sitting in the truck having our hair done—it makes him seem very unintelligent, he lets himself down—he said, "You look like one of the dogs from *Beverly Hills Chihuahua* that I watched with my kids." And I'm all, "Every person involved with this production thinks you're an idiot."

Although when it came to their performances, the duo would get serious. One of their early standout scenes was on a bridge, when Jaime got his hands on a sword and tried to kill Brienne. Their fight was particularly meaningful to Christie, who trained for months to prepare for her first combat scene.

GWENDOLINE CHRISTIE: Nikolaj was already hugely adept at sword fighting. He learned the fight very quickly, maybe in an hour, and went off to Denmark. It took me much longer. Brienne obviously is supposed to have great skills and stamina and energy. So there was a lot of work I had to do. I trained for months; I mainlined protein.

DAN WEISS (*showrunner*): We talked for twenty-five minutes about creatine and whether or not you should use it.

Like many *Thrones* fights, the sequence wasn't only about winning or survival but also giving viewers new insight about the characters.

GWENDOLINE CHRISTIE: In the book, the sword fight was sensational because it told the story of the start of this relationship that is so many different things. For Brienne, she's fighting because she has to. She doesn't want to kill him. I thought that was very interesting because we're so used to seeing fights that are about the thrill or achieving power. With Brienne, fighting was always about enacting justice. For Jaime Lannister, it was about asserting status, and Brienne of Tarth was pulling him down from that stage. She was telling him who's boss.

The fight also showed their personalities. You saw Brienne was straightforward and steadier, but with great strength. His style was quick, mercurial, and devious. It was an illustration of their characters and their natures and their way of feeling each other out.

NIKOLAJ COSTER-WALDAU: To his surprise, Brienne is not fighting for her life. She's an honorable woman and made a promise to take him to

King's Landing. It was also a very different fight because I was still tied at my hands.

DANIEL MINAHAN (*director*): It had been raining for days, and this beautiful old bridge that we were shooting on—which the art department had covered with turf—became like walking on peanut butter. It was extremely viscous and slippery. So the actors had to navigate that, like fighting on a banana peel.

GWENDOLINE CHRISTIE: I loved every second of it. During that fight I found my inner butch, my strength as a woman—making myself larger and stronger. I felt a strength in my jaw and pushed my jaw forward, and I felt a power in that. I took great pleasure in being physical and not trying to appear dainty or sexual—just being overtly strong and pulling this difficult and irritating man back down to the level of prisoner. Nikolaj and I really got to know each other during that. He said, "God, you've worked really hard on this."

DAVID BENIOFF (*showrunner*): Gwen was really happy when Nikolaj said, "Can you hit me ten percent less hard?"

Further down the road, the duo were captured by Roose Bolton's sadistic hunter Locke. In one of the show's most jarring scenes, Locke chopped off Jaime's hand as punishment for trying to bribe him with the Lannister family's wealth and power. On the day of filming, Coster-Waldau was extremely sick with the flu, which added to his character's weariness.

NIKOLAJ COSTER-WALDAU: I was just lying down. Finally, I made it on set. I don't remember much from that scene other than screaming when it was cut off. I looked miserable, and I was. That was one of my few moments of Method acting.

DAVID NUTTER (*director*): Nikolaj impressed the hell out of me. He's into doing it rough and the way it should be, getting in the mud and going for it.

Perhaps too rough? When filming a scene where Locke kicks Jaime as he's writhing on the ground, one blow landed so hard that it broke one of Coster-Waldau's ribs. When asked about the incident, Coster-Waldau shrugged it off.

NIKOLAJ COSTER-WALDAU: He couldn't see where he was kicking and misjudged the kick.

Locke brought Jaime and Brienne to Harrenhal, where Roose Bolton (Michael McElhatton) granted the prisoners a respite from their ordeal. In the bathhouse, Jaime alarmed Brienne by joining her in a steaming tub, naked and uninvited. It was key scene from Martin's *A Storm of Swords* that Coster-Waldau had looked forward to shooting for years.

NIKOLAJ COSTER-WALDAU: For the first two seasons Jaime is building up to the bathtub scene. I knew that was going to be important for the character to become more than a moral-less, guarded, one-dimensional character—that's how he survives, using his arrogance and fighting skills and the fact he's a Lannister.

BRYAN COGMAN (*co–executive producer*): We went deep into the night shooting that. It turns out shooting in a bathtub is kind of hard. And the actors' being vulnerable like that—they both didn't have any clothes on, and they had to go to very emotional places during a long scene that took a lot of coverage.

NIKOLAJ COSTER-WALDAU: It was one of the best days on *Thrones*. Both for myself and for Gwen. It was a long day and you're in the water and there's a lot of obstacles.

ALEX GRAVES (*director*): I said to David and Dan at the time: "Jaime and Brienne are falling in love, right?" They always gave you as little information as possible. They said, "Yeah, but they don't know it."

At the start of the scene, Jaime was his usual rude self to Brienne. Then, after one insult too many, Brienne stood up in the tub to face him, exposing herself.

GWENDOLINE CHRISTIE: When Brienne stands up naked in front of him, it's an act of defiance. It isn't at all gratuitous. She's angry, she wants to get out of there, but he's in the way. In that moment she realizes the power of her womanhood without the armor, without the fighting, without killing anyone; that she's opposite this man that she has such a complex relationship with. He has saved her from being brutally raped, and she still cannot understand him. And he pushes her in that moment.

So many parts of my life that I've struggled with, that so many millions of others struggled with—about being an outsider, about feeling ugly, about having to overcome looking different to other people. She overcomes her own issues about her own femininity and vulnerability and gender and finds the power of not only what it means to be a woman but who she is as a woman. After that, nothing is the same again.

ALEX GRAVES: Jaime and Brienne have every reason to hate each other, but they can't get around the respect they have for one another. It's a great, sexless story about who people are. Jaime is affected by a woman who is like himself instead of being like Cersei, the only woman he's ever known. So the person who is overwhelmed in the scene isn't Brienne but Jaime.

NIKOLAJ COSTER-WALDAU: He'd never met anyone like her. He saw himself in her. His whole life was about secrets and not being able to trust anyone.

Brienne's reaction caused Jaime to do something we'd never seen him do before: apologize. Jaime then revealed to a stunned and speechless Brienne the true backstory of his most infamous act—killing the Mad King—and how he saved the populace of King's Landing by betraying his Kingsguard oath. Both characters were doing the one thing they found most difficult in the world: for Brienne, being physically vulnerable; and for Jaime, being emotionally vulnerable.

NIKOLAJ COSTER-WALDAU: He has this pride where he's refused to talk about what he feels is the immense injustice of what's happened to him with the Mad King. His pride has prevented him from saying, "By the way . . ." Finally, we see him open up.

ALEX GRAVES: We did a very long, slow push in on him during that speech, but the camera crane started making this horrible wheezing noise like every ten seconds as the camera moved in. It didn't do it in rehearsal; it was so evil. Nobody could figure out how to make it stop. Nikolaj said, "I don't want to loop this scene later, so let's go for it." Nikolaj learned the pattern of the sound and acted around it. This was really an actor going, "I'm going to do this, and nothing is going to stop me."

BRYAN COGMAN: I distinctly remember the take of him yelling, *"By what right does the wolf judge the lion?"* It was one of those transcendent moments where the actor just disappears.

GWENDOLINE CHRISTIE: When I think about it retrospectively, I was incredibly lucky to work with Nikolaj. He empowered me as an actor, and he never made me feel insecure or insignificant because of my lack of experience, and certainly never because of my gender. I was treated as an equal even though he was the actor with a bigger role and more experience. He recognized that I worked hard, and that made me unafraid to push him too. It was all incredibly enjoyable because—and I have to swallow here because a bad taste just came into my mouth—he's actually very talented.

CHAPTER ELEVEN

THE RED WEDDING

There were so many visceral and existential horrors compressed into the final moments of the season-three episode inconspicuously titled "The Rains of Castamere."

There was the death of Robb Stark, the likable hero and avenging son of Ned Stark. Robb was a handsome leader who won every battle yet lost his life for what seemed like a forgivable mistake (reneging on his pledge to marry Walder Frey's daughter). There was the death of Robb's mother, Catelyn, the Stark family's wary matriarch, who was still grieving the death of her husband (as well as, she mistakenly believed, the deaths of her sons Bran and Rickon). Catelyn was forced to witness Robb's murder and melted down in rage and anguish before being killed too. There was the death of Talisa Stark, Robb's healer wife, who was gruesomely stabbed in her pregnant belly. There was the fact the sequence took place during the traditionally safe harbor of a wedding, an occasion we associate with our own family, friends, and joyful memories. And it was a betrayal too. The Starks were killed not by their enemies but by people they thought were their allies. There was also Robb's direwolf, Grey Wind, stabbed whining and helpless in his crate. And there was the tragedy of Arya, who, having journeyed so far, discovered just outside the Frey castle that even more of her family were now dead.

The Red Wedding was horrifying for all those reasons, and then the writing, performances, and foreboding direction by David Nutter maximized its impact. From the moment Walder Frey's musicians began to play the ominous strings of the Lannister anthem "The Rains of Castamere" to the moment Catelyn's throat was cut was only about six minutes, yet it stays burned in your memory forever. "It's awful and horrible and everything the sequence needed to be," wrote *The A.V. Club*'s Emily Todd VanDerWerff after the episode aired, "and it marks a new high watermark for the series."

GEORGE R. R. MARTIN (*author, co–executive producer*): I knew [I'd kill off Robb Stark] almost from the beginning [of writing the first book]. Not the first day, but very soon. I like my fiction to be unpredictable. I like there to be considerable suspense. I killed Ned because everybody thought he's the hero and, sure, he's going to get into trouble, but then he'll somehow get out of it. The next predictable thing is that his eldest son will rise up and avenge his father. Everybody is going to expect that. So [killing Robb] became the next thing I had to do.

The Red Wedding was based on a couple real events from Scottish history. One was a case called the Black Dinner. The king of Scotland was fighting the Black Douglas clan. He reached out to make peace and offered the young Earl of Douglas safe passage. He came to Edinburgh Castle, and they had a great feast. Then at the end of the feast, [the king's men] started pounding a single drum. They brought out a covered plate and put it in front of the earl and revealed it was the head of a black boar—the symbol of death. As soon as he saw it, he knew what it meant. They put them to death in the courtyard.

The larger instance was the Glencoe Massacre. Clan MacDonald stayed with the Campbell clan overnight, and the laws of hospitality supposedly applied. But the Campbells arose and started butchering every MacDonald they could get their hands on.

No matter how much I make up, there's stuff in history that's just as bad, or worse.

DAVID BENIOFF (*showrunner*): In the book, when the band started playing "Rains of Castamere," you knew something bad is going to happen. It's the strongest physical reaction I've ever had to reading anything. I didn't want to turn the page.

DAN WEISS (*showrunner*): The Red Wedding was the thing we always told ourselves that if we got to that moment, and if we did it right, did it justice, then [the show would] be in a pretty good place. The energy that it injected into the story would be enough to get us through to the end of the show.

GEORGE R. R. MARTIN: Robb's wife in the show was maybe the first major departure from the books. David and Dan changed her backstory completely. In the show, Talisa is a healer from Volantis and very strong willed. In the books, Robb marries Jeyne Westerling, a daughter of a Lannister house he met while campaigning in the west. It's a Florence Nightingale thing where he was wounded and she nursed him back to health.

Also, Jeyne is still alive in the books. My version of Robb was: "Yeah, it's going to be dangerous going to the wedding, I don't think I'll take my wife with me, they're going to hate her, she's the one I married instead of one of their daughters. I'll keep her at Riverrun with my uncle guarding her."

RICHARD MADDEN (*Robb Stark*): I read [the books] season by season. I didn't want to preempt where Robb is going. But a thousand people spoiled it for me before I had a chance to pick up the third book. I also made the fatal flaw of googling. So that reinforced what people were hinting, saying something terrible was going to happen and giggling.

MICHELLE FAIRLEY (*Catelyn Stark*): I knew what was coming. It's something that anyone who's read the books will talk about, so people took great delight in knowing. There's something incredibly dramatic and brutal about the Red Wedding, the shock of it. I met somebody who read it on the plane and they were so heartbroken they left the book on the plane. For an actor to be given that part to play, you want to grab it and go straight into it.

OONA CHAPLIN (*Talisa Stark*): I knew it was going to deviate from the books. I also knew I was going to come to a demise at the end of season three. I was praying for a cool death, and when I read [the script], I was like, "Fuck, everyone dies!" But what it was on the page was nothing compared to what it was like on the day of shooting.

MICHAEL MCELHATTON (*Roose Bolton*): In the books, Roose is a much more obvious bad guy. In the show he played his cards close to his vest, so the audience wasn't sure. He was a sounding board for Robb for his battles. But Robb wasn't taking Roose's advice and things weren't going well for his family, or for the Lannisters, so he decided to get rid of him.

DAVID NUTTER (*director*): The most important part was the surprise element and making sure the audience was involved with the story. And the blocking was important. I spent several weeks sitting in preparations with a blank piece of paper doing schematics, figuring out the blocking. One Saturday morning, I felt like I cracked it and put it up on a white chalkboard, like how a football coach would explain stuff to his team. I said [to the producers], "This is how I think the tables should be, this is where we should put our heroes. . . ."

MICHAEL MCELHATTON: When I saw the room I was stunned by it. It looked like a Vermeer painting. It was smaller than you expected and the ceiling was lower, but the lighting was extraordinary. The Red Wedding had a very unique feel compared to any scene in the entire series.

The sequence at the Twins—the Starks meeting Walder Frey, Edmure Tully's wedding, and the fateful dinner—was filmed over the course of a week in Belfast.

MICHELLE FAIRLEY: We were very fortunate. We had a week to shoot the whole wedding sequence and did it chronologically as well. So every day we edged closer to the slaughter.

DAVID NUTTER: *Pretty* chronological; you can't do it too chronologically, but I made sure that the most powerful points were near the end of the shoot. These are beloved characters that everybody loved being around. You want to build up the emotional journey of the sequence.

OONA CHAPLIN: We had become such a family. I hadn't clocked that the end was nigh. I was in quite happy disbelief for all the scenes leading up to it.

RICHARD MADDEN: We had put it out of our minds. Then I'd go off to Croatia and [a crew member would] say, "Oh, this is the last time I'll see you on this show."

DAN WEISS: When it came time to shoot it there was so much pressure. We had gotten to it, which was great, but given where the show was at the time [in terms of its budget], it was a very complex thing to shoot and get right.

DAVID BRADLEY (*Walder Frey*): I liked the script not just because it was so appalling, but it had this vein of dark humor in it. There was Walder's welcoming speech he gave with the bread and the salt. He was so friendly and making everybody feel at home. I just knew underneath all that he could not wait to get his revenge.

RICHARD MADDEN: It was challenging to not hint at anything [in my performance] even though I know it's coming, especially with Catelyn knowing what the Freys are. We had to hint the Freys aren't good guys but hopefully kept the element of surprise.

MICHELLE FAIRLEY: By the end of the week, I was getting emotional. You know it's coming and it's calm and it's a wedding, but as the week progressed I was nervous and had to remain concentrated. But you have to remain [looking] fooled as well.

MICHAEL McELHATTON: I was in the makeup trailer, and there was another guy there who I thought was an extra. He introduced himself as Will. I asked who he was playing and he said he was one of the musicians, the drummer. I said, "Why'd they bring in an English musician when there are perfectly good local Irishmen who could play the bodhrán?"—which is the type of drum he was playing. Then I asked, "Are you in a band?" He said, "Yeah, I'm in a band." "You having any luck?" "Yeah, we're doing okay." You know the punch line for this. I asked what his band was called. He said, "We're called Coldplay," and I felt like such a dick.

A traditional way to direct the dinner sequence would be to gradually ratchet up a feeling of suspense and danger. Nutter took the opposite approach. The viewer was initially lulled into a relaxed ease. Edmure Tully was relieved to discover his mysterious Frey bride looked sweet and beautiful. Their wedding ceremony was lovely, and then there was the traditional bawdy "bedding" as the newlyweds were carried off to consummate their marriage. Robb and Catelyn, having clashed throughout the season, finally started to get along. Catelyn even warmed up to Talisa, who offered to name her baby Eddard. Robb, Catelyn, and Talisa were coming together as a new generation of the Stark family, feeling happy together for the first time . . . and the last.

DAVID BENIOFF: Robb and Catelyn had been through so much. They've been through the death of Ned. They had a major falling out after she released Jaime. They managed to get through that and work back into a loving relationship, and then they have all that taken away.

MICHAEL MCELHATTON: There was a panning shot, looking at the revelers, and David Nutter said, "Give me a smile!" I said, "This guy doesn't smile." He said, "Let's not give it away, let's take the audience somewhere else before we shock them," and he was absolutely right.

DAVID NUTTER: I wanted the tightest bond moment with our heroes before it began and to give the audience a sense of ease, that this is a happy ending, and give them some hope that everything is going to turn out well. I didn't want to make the audience feel like something bad was going to happen until the big switch.

Then one of Walder Frey's sons slowly closed the banquet hall's large wooden door. Suddenly, you got the feeling that something was not quite right.

DAVID NUTTER: It was all about touching it softly, not quite hard, so it could build up even more.

The band began to play the haunting chords of the Lannister anthem "The Rains of Castamere." The song, which was first introduced early in season two, recounts how Tywin Lannister led his army to murder every member of the rebellious House Reyne. The show had previously referenced the song five times—either played or sung on-screen, or discussed in the dialogue. So when Catelyn recognized the disturbing wrongness of the Freys' wedding band playing "The Rains of Castamere," so did the viewer.

Catelyn then looked to Bolton, who had a smug expression that read like, "*Yeah, that's right . . .*" She followed Bolton's eye line to his sleeve, tugged it up, and saw he was wearing protective chain mail hidden under his clothes.

CHRISTOPHER NEWMAN (*producer*): I noticed there was something animalistic about the way Michael looked at Catelyn during rehearsal. It reminded me of what Robert Shaw talks about in *Jaws* about how the shark's eyes roll up before it bites you. So I pointed that out to David Nutter, and he talked to Michael about doing it during the shot.

MICHAEL MCELHATTON: David had to drag that look out of me. Because it's quite theatrical, that half-smile glare down at her. David was like, "I don't want subtlety, I want melodrama."

DAVID BENIOFF: The sequence is all about Catelyn from the moment she pulls up Roose Bolton's sleeve to the moment she dies.

While Catelyn and Roose were exchanging glances, Walder Frey was giving a speech, announcing that he had a "wedding gift" for Talisa. What came next happened very quickly: Lothar Frey (Tom Brooke) marched up behind Talisa and repeatedly stabbed her.

OONA CHAPLIN: *Beat-beat-beat-beat*—which surprised me. It surprised me every time, with the gallons of blood coming out of my belly. It's quite a violent thing when somebody creeps up behind you and starts stabbing you. It was horrendous, very little acting required.

Robb looked profoundly stunned, unable to comprehend what just happened. Crossbows fired from the gallery and the Young Wolf was mortally wounded. He crawled to Talisa and saw her life fade away.

OONA CHAPLIN: It was so sad. I was heartbroken. I looked around at Richard and Michelle and the drummer for Coldplay and thought, "This is it, this is our last scene." My intention was to commit to the love of Richard—of Robb Stark, but really Richard, let's be honest.

DAVID NUTTER: The moment when Robb crawls over to Talisa, I remember talking to Richard about love and about relationships and honesty and how much she means to him, and he was really getting into it. He's such a tremendous actor and was hitting a home run. I remember hearing people crying, and it was the hair and makeup people. I'm a big believer that if a scene is not emotionally driving you as you're making it, how can you expect the audience to feel the same? I thought, "If we can make ourselves feel something, then this will translate."

DAVID BENIOFF: I turned to the script supervisor after one take where Richard was dying and I was like, "That was a good take." And she was just bawling. It's a bittersweet thing. You're making all these people sad. But on the other hand, that's the idea.

OONA CHAPLIN: I was actually crying while I was dead. The director had to come over: "Oona, you need to stop crying, dead people don't cry. You're dead, just be dead."

CHRISTOPHER NEWMAN: It's not a subtle scene. It's all anger and anguish. There is no way anybody could overact in that scene.

RICHARD MADDEN: Arya being so close to getting to Robb cut me up even more. With every episode Robb's been further and further from people he loves. For Arya to be so close, I think that's what really hurt, because that's what we've all wanted—to get the family back together—even if it was only one of us coming back. That's what made me really emotional about it.

DAVID BRADLEY: The fact that Walder stage-managed the whole thing, with the band and speech and the crossbows—he's a consummate actor, making sure nobody could guess what he was up to. To him, this was everything he'd meticulously planned coming to fruition. I had to make sure he was relishing it and enjoyed it.

DAVID BENIOFF: We're used to, in books and movies when a major character dies, we're used to a bittersweet final moment. The death speech. You don't get that here. There's no redemptive moment. There's just horror and slaughter. You want revenge so quickly, and you're deprived of that satisfaction.

Catelyn desperately tried to salvage something from the massacre. She begged for Robb's life, grabbed one of Frey's young wives, and held a knife to her throat.

MICHELLE FAIRLEY: At that point you've been living [a character] for three years. You know what drives this person; you have to watch her whole insides ripped to shreds watching her son be murdered. The woman was just grief stricken. But she didn't lose control. She knew she's dead, and in her mind she wanted to be dead and wanted to get revenge as well. Because of the way it's filmed you felt incredibly static, which is just powerful—the fact she stays rooted to her spot. Her grief had to be expressed in some shape and form, and that was vocally and through her face. It's brave and it's gutsy and "I don't give a flying fuck what happens to me."

GEORGE R. R. MARTIN: Catelyn has the moment there, to plead. There's also her murdering the hostage. [She's not a wife] Frey particularly values. So in the end her bluff is empty.

Bolton said, "The Lannisters send their regards," and plunged a knife into Robb's heart.

DAN WEISS: George gave [readers] a triumphant fuck-you death—but it's Robb Stark's death! Roose is the one that has the great one-liner before he puts the knife in his heart. It's got all the elements of a triumphant death, but it's completely flipped and it's the wrong side and happening to somebody you love.

Catelyn could have released Frey's wife, but she carried through on her threat, killing her.

MICHELLE FAIRLEY: I'd lost all my children and my husband. So what else did I have to live for? She came from a very honorable family. Her whole life has been about honor and doing the right thing. In some way she'd been held back by her sense of honor and duty. She constantly questioned her motives and actions. This was one where she didn't. "I'm not questioning this, I'm just doing it." I think that's incredibly liberating. Then she was standing there after like there was nothing left for her. She was dead already. She wanted it. She couldn't go on.

DAVID NUTTER: We organized it so Catelyn losing it at the end was the last scene we'd shoot. And we talked about how long she would stand there before the guy comes up and puts a knife in her throat. I told David Benioff, "I'll start it off so she kills Frey's wife and then she's in her moment of pure despair and starts to lose herself. I'll just hang there and wait until you nod your head and then I'll cue the guy to come in and cut her throat."

So I called "action." She took the one girl out and she's crying and crying. I look over at David Benioff. And she's still crying and losing it. Suddenly David nodded and the actor came in and cut her throat. The knife cut wasn't *exactly* the right positioning, it wasn't the right inch, but it looked so good.

RICHARD MADDEN: We were mentally exhausted. I cried my eyes out, completely, as did a lot of the crew and other actors. It was very emotional. The wrap party was that night, but I had to start filming another job the next day. So I washed my blood off and got on a plane.

DAN WEISS: We tried to call Michelle afterward. She wasn't answering. A week later she wrote an email saying, "Sorry, I haven't been able to talk to anybody about the show for the past week because I've been so shattered."

MICHELLE FAIRLEY: Dan had left me a voicemail, and I did try to ring him back. But by the end of the day I was a walking shell.

ALEX GRAVES: The way it worked out was that everybody walked out the door right afterward, and it was traumatizing. After that we made sure, like for Joffrey's death, that the actor would have more work after their death scene.

DAVID BENIOFF: It's weird to say, "Oh, it went great." Because we're not just killing characters, we're losing these actors who have been with us since the beginning. It's hard, because you love the actors.

DAVID NUTTER: I tend to beat myself up when making something, and I remember getting in my car to go back to my apartment and I said to myself, "That wasn't so bad." I felt good about it. No one knew the response would be so immense, but for a television director it was a wonderful feeling knowing how much I affected people in the process of telling a story. It was the best gift I could have ever had.

RICHARD MADDEN: David Nutter made it an operatic, epic sequence that just blew you away. The shocks you got in the book and subtleties from the book—those little details suddenly all pieced together in one big slamming action.

GEORGE R. R. MARTIN: They pulled it off correctly. They picked perhaps the most brutal scene I ever wrote and made it more brutal. They dialed it up to eleven.

DAN WEISS: It's not that nobody ever triumphs over adversity. Like Daenerys [unleashing her dragon] in the Plaza of Punishment is such a rousing "Fuck yeah!" moment. It's mixing up those moments with somebody making a horrible mistake and paying the worst possible price. If everything was gruesome and terrible all the time, you'd always know what was going to happen since it would always be the most gruesome and terrible thing. The range of different possibilities that play out makes it more real because that's what the world is like. Sometimes wonderful things happen, and sometimes horrible things happen.

MICHAEL LOMBARDO (*former HBO programming president*): What could have been just a bloodbath was an incredibly moving story about betrayal and a reminder to all of us enjoying the dragons and the ride that no one was safe and the traditional tropes of television were going to be violated.

OONA CHAPLIN: When I was there, I wasn't seeing everything. They killed his wolf! And Arya was there! All of this stuff was happening around it. And Michelle's scream. Then there's that silence. There is no music in the credits. It just sits in your belly. My heart was broken.

Madden pointed out that Talisa dying along with her husband wasn't just additional shock value but that her demise had a specific story-driven reason. "Because it's just a full stop to that train of the story of [Robb's] army," the actor told *Access Hollywood*. "I think it's more tragic that there's nothing left over from it, that there's no possibility that Talisa's in hiding and gonna have a baby and one day, that baby will take over as King in the North."

A subsequent scene revealed that Tywin Lannister orchestrated the killings, pulling Walder Frey's strings from the Red Keep. Tywin justified the murders by noting that the Red Wedding ended a civil war that would have cost many more lives had it continued.

DAVID BRADLEY: I didn't see Walder as an out-and-out villain. I saw him as a warlord, a powerful man who fought his way to the top. I imagined him as a bit of a street fighter when he was younger, and he took any rejection or betrayal personally. In his mind's eye, he had to avenge that snub. As far as he was concerned, in the wider world in which he lived—which is a very ruthless world—if he hadn't done anything about it, he would have been toast. It would have been seen as a weakness and exploited by his enemies.

DAN WEISS: One of the things that make these deaths so powerful is they're the machinations of other characters we know. In this case it's Tywin, a character we like in spite of ourselves. A monster doesn't come out of the woodwork and chop these people up. The monsters are our other characters, who aren't monsters but people with their own motivations and goals.

DAVID BENIOFF: Tywin wasn't torturing prostitutes for pleasure. He wasn't a sadist. He was ruthless, for sure, but there's an argument to be made that Westeros needs ruthlessness. I don't think of him as evil.

DAN WEISS: I would call him "lawful neutral."

GEORGE R. R. MARTIN: It was the hardest scene I've ever had to write. It's two-thirds of the way through the book, but I skipped over it when I came to it. So the entire book was done and there was still that one chapter left. Then I wrote it. It was like murdering two of your children.

When the book came out I got a lot of emails—and I still get them—saying, "I hate you, how could you do that, I'm never going to read your work again." Others say, "I threw the book across the room and a week later I picked it up again and it was the greatest thing I ever read." What can you say to someone who says they'll never read your book again? People read books for different reasons. I respect that. Some read for comfort. Some of my former readers have said their life is hard, their mother is sick, their dog died, and they read fiction to escape. They don't want to get hit in the mouth with something horrible. And you read that certain kind of fiction where the guy will always get the girl and the good guys win and it reaffirms to you that life is fair. We all want that at times. But that's not the kind of fiction I write, in most cases. It's certainly not what *Ice and Fire* is. It tries to be more realistic about what life is. It has joy, but it also has pain and fear. I think the best fiction captures life in all its light and darkness.

CHAPTER TWELVE

MUMMER'S FARCE

During the early seasons of *Game of Thrones*, the showrunners were known for pulling pranks on their cast. Sometimes an actor would play one of their own. Such behind-the-scenes hijinks are typically a sign of a close-knit group. That said, a comprehensive list of all *Thrones* set pranks will likely never be made public. "My 'funny prank stories' are not appropriate, and are maybe illegal," Jason Momoa said. "They will die with me and with the people I did them on."

DAVID BENIOFF (*showrunner*): Here's a minor prank we pulled during season one: We told Maisie and Sophie that since they were underage, they couldn't come to the pilot wrap party. So we told them they were going to have a special underage wrap party at McDonald's. They started crying.

DAN WEISS (*showrunner*): Then they came to the real wrap party and cried through that because they thought they might never see each other again.

The showrunners sent Kit Harington a fake script during season one for the scene where Jon Snow saves Commander Mormont from an undead wight. Only in this version, Snow threw burning drapes onto the creature and the flames engulfed them both.

"When the fire is finally out, we see by torchlight that all of Jon's hair has burnt down to the scalp," read the bogus script, according to the book *Inside HBO's Game of Thrones: Seasons 1 & 2*. "The skin on the top half of his face has been melted in the extreme heat, blistered and pustulant. Despite what must be the extreme agony of permanent disfigurement, Jon stands stoically by his master's side. Jon smiles, his teeth shining brightly in his destroyed face. Mormont, sickened, has to look away."

The twist had Harington believing he would play a gruesomely disfigured character for the rest of his time on the show and would have to spend hours getting prosthetic makeup applied each morning.

DAN WEISS: We told Kit that HBO was worried the Jon Snow storyline was "too Harry Potter," and they wanted to do something to make it darker. And they thought he was such a strong actor that he could handle it. We kept this up until we started laughing. He was a remarkably good sport about the whole thing.

In season two, Benioff and Weiss sent another fake script, this time to Alfie Allen. The season-finale script concluded with Bran Stark getting revenge on Theon Greyjoy for capturing his family's castle. "This is my Winterfell, not yours," Bran declared, and stabbed the traitorous Theon in the heart.

Except the prank didn't go quite as planned.

DAN WEISS: That one backfired because Alfie was in Ibiza and deep enough into whatever chill mode he was in.

ALFIE ALLEN (*Theon Greyjoy*): I thought it was cool. I went on a holiday, and David and Dan were all thinking I was going to call up going, "Hold on a minute, whoa-whoa-whoa!" But I just got on with it. Then they had to make it clear to me later on it was all a joke.

DAN WEISS: We had to go so far to try to get a rise out of him. "You're a *dead . . . naked . . . zombie.*" We just had to keep adding unpleasant adjectives to the word *zombie*.

Rose Leslie was pranked after the showrunners heard the actress was terrified of singing in public. The duo gave Leslie a script where Ygritte performed a lengthy song, "The Last of the Giants," from Martin's novels. The song includes lyrics such as, "*Oooooooh,* I am the last of the giants, so learn well the words of my song, for when I am gone the singing will fade, and the silence shall last long and long."

The showrunners even once pranked an actor who wasn't on *Game of Thrones.* Benioff and Weiss are friends with *It's Always Sunny in Philadelphia* creator and star Rob McElhenney, who recommended *Thrones* hire frequent *Sunny* director Matt Shakman. Despite Shakman lacking action experience, Benioff and Weiss took a chance on the director and gave him two ambitious season-seven episodes, including the battle-intensive "The Spoils of War."

DAN WEISS: We thought it would be funny if we told Rob that it was not working out with Matt and that he was a total disaster. He would feel so guilty because he recommended him. We went back and forth [on email] slowly, not throwing it out there all at once, asking questions like, "So when Matt's on set, how does he usually behave?" Rob was all, "*What-what-what's wrong?!*" We told him we're going to have to step in and take over the episode because it's turned into such a mess.

MATT SHAKMAN (*director*): I forgot about that! That was the darkest practical joke. Rob was legitimately tortured about it. He was so concerned for me and was like, "What can I do? Who can I talk to?" It went on for way too long.

DAN WEISS: When it got to the point where Rob was thinking of calling his agent, we took a picture of us, Kit, Emilia, and ten Dothraki all giving Matt the finger. We sent the photo to Rob, and it was beautiful.

Nikolaj Coster-Waldau (Jaime Lannister) decided that somebody should play a prank on the showrunners for a change. So after finishing primary filming on one of the midrun seasons—but before he was needed back on set for some critical reshoots—Coster-Waldau sent producers what Weiss dubbed an "Angry Actor Email."

DAN WEISS: He wrote how he was very upset that we were changing his hairstyle. He said he felt the need to own his hair because his hair was part of his character, and he was going to take it upon himself to get his own haircut that he felt best reflected Jaime Lannister as he saw him. He said he hoped we'd understand and that he'd send us a picture shortly.

Day went by, no picture. Another day, no picture. Finally, seventy hours later, he sent us a picture of him with this military buzz cut. He shaved all his hair off, and we had reshooting to do with him. We'd have to get a Jaime Lannister wig made at the last minute at tremendous expense. HBO's lawyers were calling his lawyers. Then he emailed back and told us the picture was from five years ago and he hadn't cut his hair at all.

Benioff and Weiss also played a modest prank on me during their interview for the book you're now holding. I tried to get the showrunners to reveal whether Jon Snow was, in fact, "the prince that was promised" (a.k.a. Azor Ahai, the reincarnated prophesied savior Melisandre was searching for throughout the series).

JAMES HIBBERD (author): So was Jon Snow—in the show at least—the prince that was promised?

DAN WEISS: Ask Kit.

DAVID BENIOFF: You should ask Kit.

DAN WEISS: Yeah. Kit knows.

Months later, during Kit Harington's interview . . .

JAMES HIBBERD: Finally, there's one question the D's said I should ask you: Was Jon Snow . . . the prince that was promised? . . . They said they told you.

KIT HARINGTON (*Jon Snow*): Did they? Fuck, I don't remember. No, wait. They didn't tell me shit! They're just taking the piss out of you and off-loading that question onto me.

(Harington, by the way, figured the prince that was promised was most likely Bran.)

The most elaborate prank was played on John Bradley during season six, when Samwell Tarly returned home with Gilly to meet his estranged family. Except it wasn't the showrunners who came up with this one.

DAN WEISS: Hannah Murray had long had the shittiest costumes on *Game of Thrones*; she'd been in a burlap sack for five years. She was so happy to finally get into a real piece of clothing. So Kit and Hannah thought it would be funny to play a joke on John and let him think he was going to get a new costume too.

HANNAH MURRAY (*Gilly*): Kit and I came up with the idea that John should have a new costume and it should be really stupid. We thought we'd tell him he had a new stupid costume and he'd be like, "Oh, no!" and that would be it. Then it became this bigger, more elaborate thing than we ever imagined.

Benioff and Weiss had the *Thrones* costume department create a gaudy outfit that made Bradley look like a Renaissance-fair fool and even staged a fitting session to help convince the actor that it was legit.

DAN WEISS: We thought it would be great to make the costume ludicrous but just believable enough to not know it was a gag, so he'd think he would be wearing this on-screen. It was all rental stuff, very Henry the Eighth, with Tudor bloomers and a massive codpiece.

JOHN BRADLEY (*Samwell Tarly*): I looked so bad and ridiculous, it was unbelievable. There was a huge vulgar codpiece—though flattering, to be sure. The reason I bought it is because we'd never seen Sam at home before, and [his parents think] he's an idiot. Maybe Sam dressed like an idiot before he came to Castle Black.

HANNAH MURRAY: He was talking about it all the time. "Have you seen my new costume? My hat has been made comically small." He was really annoyed. I had to keep going, "Oh, I'm sure it's fine." Eventually I went to David and was like, "Are we going to tell him this is a joke?" And David was all, "Oh, yeah, we probably should."

JOHN BRADLEY: You always think you're not going to fall for pranks. You always think, "I'll see through that," and I cannot believe I didn't see through it.

DAN WEISS: Near the end, pranks got difficult. Nobody trusts what you say anymore.

———◇———

CHAPTER THIRTEEN

"Go in Screaming"

G*ame of Thrones* broke many records during its eight seasons, but here's another: longest consecutive torture of a character in filmed entertainment. Theon Greyjoy was captured by Roose Bolton's bastard son, Ramsay, at the end of season two and didn't escape his clutches until the season-five finale. In between, nearly every time *Thrones* shifted to Theon's storyline, the traitorous former Stark family ward was enduring yet another novel form of physical torment or mental anguish at the hands of his sadistic keeper. Behind the scenes, Theon's pitch-black, years-long arc took its toll on actor Alfie Allen, who couldn't help but absorb at least some degree of his character's misery.

The storyline launched when Theon betrayed Robb Stark in season two. Theon seized Winterfell in a futile attempt to win the approval of his estranged father, Balon (Patrick Malahide). Young Bran and Rickon escaped, and Theon murdered two orphan boys for their corpses, preferring to trick his newly conquered subjects at Winterfell into believing he'd killed the Stark children rather than admit he lost such valuable hostages. Like Walder Frey, Theon feared that any perception of weakness would prove his downfall.

One constant thread in Martin's books is that achieving power is difficult, but maintaining power is much harder, perhaps even impossible, particularly without the ruler being corrupted. As King Robert said in Martin's *A Game of Thrones*, "Sitting on a throne is a thousand times harder than winning one." It's a lesson that Theon learned rather painfully.

DAN WEISS (*showrunner*): Theon is like Gollum in *The Lord of the Rings*. He's the most shadowy character. He's not good, but he's not really evil either. He's made lots of really bad, but also understandable, choices. He wanted the things we all want: He wanted to be taken seriously, he wanted to achieve things, he wanted his father to be proud of him. Yet those desires led him to do terrible things, and then he reaped Westeros karma. There's something very universal about Theon.

BRYAN COGMAN (*co-executive producer*): One of my favorite scenes I wrote was in season two, when Theon wrote a letter to Robb betraying his own father, then changed his mind and burned the letter. We weren't really sure if we could pull it off because it's a short scene with no dialogue. But then you get that camera on Alfie and everything you needed to know was behind those eyes.

DAVID BENIOFF (*showrunner*): Theon was caught in the ultimate no-win situation. He was going to betray his best friend or his family. People see him as a traitor, but if he had written that letter to Robb, his homeland would have thought of him as a traitor—not to excuse him for his wrongdoings.

ALFIE ALLEN (*Theon Greyjoy*): I think my character was severely misguided. He was just a boy, really. I think there was a nice guy down there. He just had no one teach him the ways of the world and tell him right from wrong. He'd observed it but not been told it. He was just trying to prove himself. I think that's a universal theme with anyone, whether people try to deny it or not. You're always looking for your parents' approval. Even if you're not looking for it, you kinda are.

As part of Ramsay's torture regimen, the Bastard of Bolton castrated Theon. It was a scene that even *Thrones* flinched from showing on-screen.

ALFIE ALLEN: I felt [the castration] was very appropriate because that's a huge change for any man to go through, but for Theon it was kind of his only weapon in the world of *Thrones*. He only had authority and power in the bedroom because he'd never had any decisions to make over his own life. To have that stripped away from him left him with nothing. But only [male fans] seem to mention it. No women ever mentioned it, which made me laugh.

The mutilation was like Jaime losing his sword hand—a sinful man being deprived of the part of him from which he wielded power over others, forcing him to reexamine his life and find new reservoirs of strength.

Theon's sister, Yara, received a box containing her brother's severed genitals that Ramsay sent to their father, Balon. The audience didn't see what was inside, just Yara's gravely disturbed expression. The box wasn't empty, though.

GEMMA WHELAN (*Yara Greyjoy*): The only thing I can say is that the props department did him proud. They definitely, um, filled the box.

Filming so many torture scenes had an effect on Allen, who tried to express the cumulative impact of Ramsay's abuse on his body when he was on-screen.

ALFIE ALLEN: I had to do more telling a story with my eyes than words. Since he had a nail driven through his foot, I added a bit of a limp. My posture in my back I tried to arch out and bring my shoulder blades back together. I wanted to replicate that feeling of being on the cross in a way. There's many times when it was tough, and if you were to ask me, "God, how much more can a character take?" I'd say, "I don't know."

DANIEL MINAHAN (*director*): Alfie would be screaming and then laughing. He'd have to scream and scream and scream. And then if he didn't laugh, then we would laugh because, you know, he's Alfie.

ALFIE ALLEN: [Ramsay Bolton actor Iwan Rheon and I] are really good friends and spent a helluva lot of time together. He beat me at pool many nights. When we're out people literally could not get their heads around the fact we're hanging out. We get these Belfast locals losing their minds over it.

DAVE HILL (*co-producer*): After Theon escaped, I asked Alfie how it felt to finally be free of Ramsay. He said: "You don't even understand. Those three seasons, after I was castrated and I had to play Reek, were really hard on me emotionally." He's friends with Iwan, and he said it would strain their relationship. After he had a day of playing Reek, they would go shoot pool and he couldn't beat him. They would weirdly slip back into their [on-camera] interaction, where Iwan would be a little bossy and Alfie would shrink back. His character started to bleed into his personal life.

ALFIE ALLEN: It definitely seeped into real life. It got you down. You had to use it. I'm not gonna lie, it was really hard. The character went through so many crazy changes. I always say Theon was one of the most human characters on the show. The Reek aspect amped up his pain and suffering, but for me as an actor it was great to tackle—excuse the pun.

As Theon suffered under Ramsay's control at the Dreadfort, Arya and the Hound were on a road trip that would conclude with some screaming as well. The duo was one of the show's most captivating odd-couple character pairings—the Hound helped teach Arya the savage ways of the world, while Arya inspired the Hound to rediscover some of his lost humanity.

DAN WEISS: Arya is a character who had the core of her life ripped out of her, and she existed in a very dark place for a young girl. She was driven largely by revenge and hate, and she had a great mentor in revenge and heartlessness in the Hound. They rubbed off on each other in ways that were unexpected.

MAISIE WILLIAMS (*Arya Stark*): She learned a lot from the Hound. She's like a sponge and heavily influenced by people around her. Being next to the Hound, she learned his brutal ways.

GEORGE R. R. MARTIN (*author, co–executive producer*): The chemistry between Maisie and Rory was brilliant. Arya and the Hound at the inn—"I'm going to have to eat every fucking chicken in this place!" I had a version of that scene in my books, but I didn't have those great lines.

Rory McCann said he struggled with playing the Hound during the show's early seasons, trying to find the right balance of fearsomeness and soul in a scarred warrior. One day, director David Nutter gave him a simple piece of advice that changed everything.

BRYAN COGMAN: David really unlocked something with Rory. He told him to channel Clint Eastwood. That he doesn't have to act scary—just give the flattest, simplest line read and it will speak volumes. There was a marked difference from then on in terms of how Rory approached the Hound.

RORY MCCANN (*Sandor "the Hound" Clegane*): The first couple years I was very nervous all the time, and then I found the character. I just look in the mirror and go, "Fuck, there's no reason to play scary, no wonder that little girl is frightened of me." Less is more.

McCann was also challenged by the Hound's heavy facial prosthetics, which were a never-ending struggle on the set. The actor spent hours in the makeup chair each morning before filming and had to wear the thick mask all day. The latex caused problems whether *Thrones* was shooting in a sweltering desert . . .

RORY MCCANN: You just got this pool of sweat underneath. And the buildup of sweat could split the prosthetic. And if it split there was a reservoir of sweat that came pouring out. A lot of shots have to be stopped just to squeeze all the sweat out and restart.

. . . or on a frozen tundra . . .

LIAM CUNNINGHAM (*Davos Seaworth*): Rory had terrible trouble in Iceland because the sweat underneath his prosthetic would turn to ice. His face got encased in latex. Which is not good. You could get gangrene from shit like that.

Playing the Hound's aloofness, however, came naturally for McCann. *Thrones* actors often hung out together after work, but McCann said that for many years he declined to socialize with the rest of the cast.

RORY MCCANN: I'm very close to being the Hound. I was doing a scene with Kristofer Hivju and he went to hug me as his character and I just said, "Don't touch me." I'm so like that at home. I'm not used to human touch. I'm a bit of a recluse. Before each season, I'd phone all my friends and tell them I don't want to speak or have any contact with anyone at all before starting the job. It was only in the final couple years I started to talk to people and go out to pubs and be with the actors. Before that I was the weirdo who's just in my room or in the gym or just back home saying, "Don't phone me until it's snowing."

McCann's lone-wolf tendencies had an unexpected impact on Williams, not entirely unlike how the Hound rubbed off on Arya.

MAISIE WILLIAMS: He would always chat with me about adventures he'd have in his life—buying a piece of land and living in a bunker—all these crazy things he'd do with his life. [During the early seasons] I was like, "Wow, that's crazy." Later I was like, "Oh, I bought a piece of land next to the sea," and I realized, "Wow, you've really shaped me quite a lot as a person." I've realized his way of life does seem really appealing, and I've learned a lot from him. I respect his friendship and loved working with him.

One of Williams's favorite moments in the show was after the Red Wedding, when the Hound tried to sell Arya to her aunt Lysa Arryn, only to discover Arryn had died too. Arya burst out laughing at the Hound's predicament and the absurdity of her own misfortunes.

MAISIE WILLIAMS: This whole time he'd been giving Arya such a hard time and he's so in control and being this tough guy and saying he's going to take me to my aunt in the Vale and going to get his money and "I don't care about you, I just want my money." And all of a sudden that happened and Arya completely loved it. Through laughter, she was saying, "*Now what are you going to do?*"

It was fascinating to see this little girl giggling in the sunlight. Laughing on command was the most difficult thing, and it was so weird to be able to laugh and joke around on set and not be told off for it.

Another revealing scene was when Arya stitched up the Hound's wound, and the exhausted Clegane gave some rare insight into his backstory. Some of the dialogue was originally intended for a season-one scene with Sansa, but producers had to cut the speech and give some of it to Littlefinger due to production trouble. Time made the monologue better. McCann delivered his lines with years of lived-in weariness, and instead of talking to a stranger, he was opening up to a young woman that he perhaps loved in his own way.

BRYAN COGMAN: The Hound snuck up on you as a major character. And even though you've heard other people talking about his origin story, just to hear him talk about it and give voice to it four seasons in, there was a vulnerability there that he allowed himself to do that for Arya. The whole monologue ends with the line, "You think you're on your own . . . ," and that's the most vulnerable we've ever seen him. Out of context, the line doesn't seem like much. But it was one of those simple, beautiful bits of dialogue that I don't think David and Dan got enough credit for as writers. A lot of the imitators of *Game of Thrones* try to do fantasy speak. In David and Dan's best episodes, there was a beautiful simplicity to their dialogue.

Arya's season-four road trip concluded when Brienne caught up to her and fought with the Hound. Brienne and the Hound both believed they were protecting Arya from the other. The vicious duel was shot in Iceland and pushed Gwendoline Christie and Rory McCann to their absolute limit.

GWENDOLINE CHRISTIE (*Brienne of Tarth*): I trained for six weeks. It was one of the fucking hardest things I've ever done in my life—fighting up hills, down hills, rolls, fighting on rock face with a sheer down drop. My hands were like tramp's feet, swollen. Rory McCann is an amazing actor and a very strong man, and that was a challenge—not just as actors, but as characters.

ALEX GRAVES (*director*): The idea was it would devolve into a street fight and be the ugliest fight we'd ever had on the show. I'd watch rehearsals and say, "What if he kicks her in the groin? What if she bites his ear off? And not just bite it off, but lock eyes with him and spit it out so he'd see it?" Gwen burst out laughing and couldn't wait to do it.

DAN WEISS: They're two people who by the time we got them together, you're rooting for both of them. Brienne, obviously, is a more moral character than the Hound, but I would hope you couldn't help but love the

Hound in spite of yourself. Here you got Achilles fighting Hector—there wasn't a good guy or a bad guy; it's two people you're both extremely invested in, and there's fascination and horror knowing one of them is inevitably going to get the worst of this situation.

GWENDOLINE CHRISTIE: I like it to be real. Rory and I might not be killing each other, but we were both making contact with those swords. We were quite serious about it. We are two people that really go for it in that situation. We wanted contact—rolling around in the dirt on a rock face with your hand bleeding. You're in pain and blood is pouring out of your mouth and you're falling over when you're meant to and falling when you're *not* meant to. You're on top of a mountain with this surreal landscape and your adrenaline is pumping and you've got what looks like blood everywhere and you're in pain and you're hitting the living daylights out of each other.

ALEX GRAVES: The way she ends up winning is by losing her mind and going totally psychotic.

GWENDOLINE CHRISTIE: You're genuinely scared, because you look into [McCann's] eyes and they *mean* it. It was frightening—that was one of the few times I've not had to do any acting. I was screaming, "Fuck you! Come on!" Blood everywhere, going insane. It was fucking mental. I lost it at points and would just go in screaming.

CHAPTER FOURTEEN

THE PURPLE WEDDING

There was something guiltily satisfying about watching the sadistic Joffrey Baratheon die over and over again.

It was September 2013, and the day was gorgeous, particularly by *Game of Thrones* filming standards. The production was set up on a shady hillside grove in Dubrovnik overlooking the deep-blue Adriatic Sea. Lannister flags fluttered in a light breeze. Long banquet tables were set with golden plates gleaming in the warm sun.

As the set was being readied for filming, cast members prepared in their own unique ways. Charles Dance slowly paced, the fearsome Lannister lord having a smoke. Sophie Turner grooved happily to some music. Nikolaj Coster-Waldau practiced his swordplay with an unsteady left hand. Natalie Dormer strolled through the grove looking focused, her lips moving, apparently running her lines. Newcomer to the series Pedro Pascal excitedly socialized, looking like a fan who couldn't believe his luck. Costumed extras playing the wedding guests were getting lunch at craft services (King's Landing elites mostly consist of wealthy older men partnered with young women—one of those subtleties you notice on set but seldom pick up when watching the show). And *Thrones'* legendary swordmaster, C. C. Smiff, whose credits include *Star Wars* films and *Gladiator,* decided to give a reporter a lesson in the basics of fighting with a broadsword. (When people ask my favorite moment from visiting the *Thrones* set over the years, this was it.)

Over in the video village tent (where producers watch monitors showing the camera feeds under a black canopy), executive producers David Benioff, Dan Weiss, and Carolyn Strauss looked gravely serious. They were taking advantage of the downtime by engaging in an epic Candy Crush battle on their phones. Meanwhile, Icelandic band Sigur Rós readied nearby to perform for King Joffrey, and admitted they were somewhat anxious about their cameo. "If they look nervous in front of a total sociopath, it's not the worst thing in the world," noted Weiss, wearing a "Don't Hassle the Joff" T-shirt.

For once, a show that was notoriously difficult to create was all running smoothly and easily, despite having to stage an incredibly complicated sequence.

Everybody was ready to kill the king.

For the first three seasons of *Game of Thrones,* Joffrey loomed large as the show's love-to-hate villain. The teen titan was an infuriating combination of spoiled petulance, cruel bullying, intellectual ineptitude, and utter cowardice. In a show packed with shades-of-gray characters, Joffrey was impressively devoid of any redeeming qualities (other than, perhaps, given his youth and upbringing, that he's arguably less responsible for his actions than an adult character would be).

GEORGE R. R. MARTIN (*author, co–executive producer*): Joffrey is a classic thirteen-year-old bully. Do you know many thirteen-year-old kids you'd like to give absolute power to? There's a cruelty in children, especially children of a certain age, that you see in junior high and middle school.

DAN WEISS (*showrunner*): Far more often than the evil alpha male, out to do evil for the sake of evil, bad things often come from people unfit to occupy positions of power. They don't have the moral fiber or leadership skills, but for some reason they find themselves sitting on the throne, and that's where things go horribly wrong.

Cersei Lannister had to watch her child evolve into an uncontrollable monster, and by season four she was suffering under his tyranny just like everybody else.

LENA HEADEY (*Cersei Lannister*): Joffrey was literally out of [Cersei's] control. She kept trying to be the soft, gentle mother with him, and he needed a good slap. It was so painful for her that it's such a big fuckup that the kid she loved so much was so out of hand and she has little to no control over him. Her honest state was fear, but it was covered by greed and pride. She was terrified of being found out by him.

I loved it [in season three] when she said, "If it weren't for my children, I'd have thrown myself from the highest window of the Red Keep." That also told me that Jaime wasn't the love of her life and her children were. She felt terribly fucking guilty that they're from that union, and she even talked to Tyrion about that—like, "I fucked my brother, now I have kids, and it's all going tits-up." Cersei really wished she were born a man. Her children were her sanity, so the more they crumbled, the more she did.

DAN WEISS: We were once at Comic-Con, and Samuel L. Jackson explained to us for five minutes why Joffrey absolutely, positively had to die and gave us all his reasons for wanting Joffrey dead.

In interviews over the years, the producers would take pains to point out that actor Jack Gleeson was vastly unlike Joffrey. The producers were partly concerned Gleeson might get mistreated for his role in real life, but mostly they marveled that such a young performer could so convincingly play such a loathsome psychopath.

DAN WEISS: Jack's soft-spoken. He's funny. He's decent to people. And yet he has this unfailing sense of what the most horrible person in the world would be like and how he would say a line, because he always gets it right.

When Gleeson got into character on set, the change was sometimes so abrupt and convincing, it left his costars unnerved.

ESMÉ BIANCO (*Ros*): Working with Jack was a total trip because he is like this very mild-mannered, sweet, soft-spoken guy. In between takes, when everyone else is on their phones, he sat there with a textbook studying theology and philosophy or something. Then you get on set with him. He's the only actor I have ever seen this with: I could actually see the moment, without him saying a word, that he became Joffrey. It was uncanny. Something changed in his eyes, and all of a sudden he went from being Jack to being Joffrey. It was so creepy. I have goose bumps now talking about it.

SOPHIE TURNER (*Sansa Stark*): Jack was such an insane actor. When he changed like that, he was a scary kid. But he wasn't like one of those Method actors that goes into a dark place. If he was one of those guys, he'd be horrible to work with.

JACK GLEESON (*Joffrey Baratheon*): Ninety percent of the time I was feeling what Joffrey would feel—glee or desire for attention or frustration or whatever. Then there's the 10 percent where through lack of focus or whatever you realize you're shouting at Sigur Rós and there's one thousand people looking at you and three cameras, and sometimes it became a bit mechanical. But that's fun as well, to take yourself out of it and appreciate it. But you wouldn't be able to work if you did that all the time; you have to focus on what the character thinks.

One of the most riveting Joffrey scenes was when Margaery Tyrell tried to find a way to connect with her betrothed in season three while he showed off his new crossbow. Margaery was skilled at discovering men's desires and fulfilling those desires. But she realized the king's tastes were far darker than she had ever imagined.

NATALIE DORMER (*Margaery Tyrell*): The crossbow scene was a high point in my experience because it was the first time Jack and I really got our teeth into, like, the dance of power between us, and I was really trying to work out if she was going to be able to control this psychopath.

DANIEL MINAHAN (*director*): That scene had all of these great turns as the power shifted back and forth between them. She would try one thing that wouldn't work. He would see through it. She would try another thing. He would try something, she would counter. It was really complex and beautiful.

Joffrey eventually used his crossbow to kill Ros, but not before he forced the sex worker to beat another woman with a scepter in one of the show's blackest moments.

ESMÉ BIANCO: That was the worst scene I had to shoot; it was horrible. It was massively uncomfortable. And that turned into a big controversy, because people thought I was doing something way worse than beating her with that scepter. I'm like, "How did you ever get there?" That reaction said more about the viewers than the show.

There were a few moments along the way where Gleeson was permitted to express some compassion. Joffrey was devastated when he saw his father, King Robert, on his deathbed, and there was a scene in season two in which Joffrey sincerely apologized to Sansa and kissed her.

JACK GLEESON: I was going to play that like I don't care. But Dan was like, "Try maybe to express a genuine love for Sansa that Joffrey actually has." That was an attempt to put some gray into the black. But overall, it was a pretty evil road.

And that road came to an end at a Croatian hillside park during the filming of season four's "The Lion and the Rose."

During rehearsal, Gleeson's politeness was on display as the cast sat along a banquet table on an elevated stage. All the characters were on one side of the table, with Joffrey in the center, a grouping reminiscent of Leonardo da Vinci's painting *The Last Supper* (and for Joffrey, of course, it was). As Gleeson read through Joffrey's taunts, Peter Dinklage got a kick out of tormenting the young actor for his character's behavior. "Uncle, where are you going?" Gleeson read. "You're my cupbearer, remember?" Then Dinklage joked: "God, you're such an asshole!" And when a few drops of prop wine fell onto Dinklage's iPad, Gleeson apologized, "Sorry, it's just a little dribble." Dinklage fired back, "What did you call me?!" Watching "Tyrion" make "Joffrey" look cowed and remorseful was amusingly surreal.

The dinner sequence also included a succession of character pairings amid the formalities of celebrating Joffrey's wedding to Margaery. For a curiously long time, nothing of importance occurred at the banquet, which paradoxically increased the tension.

ALEX GRAVES (*director*): This was a thirty-five-page scene. They've won the war against Robb Stark. Tyrion is celebrating his victory. Joffrey is turning into a man-king. Cersei's always got an edge to her, but she's really having a pretty good day. I had dwarfs and birds and cakes and pies, and nothing going wrong. I saw that as like one of the coolest challenges. There's a growing sense of dread and absolutely nothing showing it. You just keep presenting everything in such a way that's saying: "Nothing's wrong, nothing's wrong, nothing's wrong," which is unnerving.

DAN WEISS: The trick with any long sequence like that is that at a certain point people start to think, "I'm watching this, it's been fifteen minutes in one place, something momentous is going to happen." So one of the major tricks to pull off was to keep people in the moment with all the characters interacting with one another and not let them think about the bigger picture—why we've been at this wedding for fifteen minutes.

One of the party's diversions was Joffrey using his sword to smash open a giant pie filled with live birds. It was one of those complex and potentially hazardous stunts that nearly every other movie or TV show would have kicked down the line to CGI animators but *Thrones* producers insisted on doing it using practical effects. The "pie" was filled with twenty-one trained birds from Bosnia, which would be released with a hidden trapdoor. The scene caused a bit of concern, as nobody knew for certain what the birds would actually do when released.

"Live birds, what could go wrong?" Weiss deadpanned at the time.

"They could fly back to Bosnia," Benioff replied.

"They could attack Jack and peck his face off," Weiss countered.

When Joffrey struck the pie, the birds flew out perfectly. Gleeson looked a tad startled, but that was okay. A few prosthetic "dead" birds were added into the contraption to show viewers that some birds didn't survive. ("In a way, it's a metaphor for the show," Weiss noted.)

Another of the party's amusements was a play-within-the-play performance by jousting dwarfs that Joffrey orchestrated to humiliate Tyrion. The jaw of a twenty-foot-high lion's head opened, and five actors rushed out pretending to ride horses. In Martin's book, the dwarfs rode pigs, an idea the producers briefly considered.

GEORGE R. R. MARTIN: The producers couldn't find a pig that anybody could ride. I went on YouTube at one point and I found like seventeen videos of people riding pigs, but they all fall off after two seconds, and none had to hold a lance and go after each other.

DAN WEISS: It was not feasible, on a production level, to have a person riding a pig. We were told it was not fair to the pig.

GEORGE R. R. MARTIN: David and Dan came up with a brilliant conceit of bringing in dwarfs all representing the pretenders to the throne and having them fight each other. It accomplished the same purpose without having to deal with a pig.

For Dinklage, the dwarf joust—using little people for a mocking spectacle—made him "uncomfortable as an actor." But he added that such feelings were "good" because they helped his performance while he watched from the sidelines, wearing an expression of cold anger.

PETER DINKLAGE (*Tyrion Lannister*): I think actors get too comfortable. I like being uncomfortable as an actor because it keeps you alive. It is a true collaboration between Dave and Dan in terms of what works and what doesn't. If it doesn't work for me, they have this brilliant matter of convincing me it works, and nine times out of ten they're right.

As Joffrey's bullying humiliations increased, Tyrion walked a careful line: He was polite, yet maintained his dignity, refusing to play the fool. His resistance irritated Joffrey. The king always wanted total subservience, and his uncle wouldn't give him the satisfaction. The audience had long learned that any character defying Joffrey was playing a deadly game, and they began to suspect something horrible was going to happen to somebody—just not to Joffrey.

JACK GLEESON: Normal brides and grooms take control and go a bit crazy at their weddings. Joffrey is already controlling and crazy, so this was just fanning the flames of his petulance.

DAVID BENIOFF: He's like the bridezilla. Weddings bring out the worst in a lot of people, and this is supposed to be a showcase of his power. His sigil is everywhere. He's wearing his finest clothes. He invited the most powerful people. And, of course, it all goes terribly wrong.

ALEX GRAVES: Things start to get weird, and you assume they're going to get weird with Joffrey the way they always have—somebody is going to be the victim of Joffrey. He's an unstable character in our minds. He's like Joe Pesci in *Goodfellas*. You have no idea what he's going to do. Is this going to be the death of Tyrion? Is this gonna be the death of Sansa? It doesn't occur to you that the strongest guy in the room is the one who's gonna get it.

Then Margaery jumped up with the show's most hilarious non sequitur: "Look, the pie!"

The viewer was relieved and thought the arrival of the enormous pastry might deescalate the tension. For a few moments, it did. Then Joffrey once again started into Tyrion. And ate pie. And gulped wine. And then . . . began to choke.

Joffrey clutched his throat, convulsed, and collapsed, a tyrant reduced to a terrified boy.

Originally, Joffrey's death was going to be even more graphic. Martin's script for the episode was unearthed by *Vanity Fair*'s Joanna Robinson, who noted the young king was initially supposed to slash his own face during his death throes.

Joffrey's death was perhaps Martin's most ingenious twist. While the Red Wedding is considered the show's most shocking moment, this scene—the one fans dubbed "the Purple Wedding" (because purple is associated with royalty)—is arguably more surprising. In a tale that had firmly established its unpredictability and disruption of traditional storytelling patterns, the last thing a *Thrones* viewer expected after a brutal massacre at a wedding was another major character's death at yet another wedding. And the method of Joffrey's death (poisoned, and without a clear culprit) denied fans the usual satisfaction of seeing a hero enacting justice upon a villain.

GEORGE R. R. MARTIN: I based it a little on the death of Eustace, the son of King Stephen of England [who reigned during the twelfth century].

Stephen had usurped the crown from his cousin, the empress Maude. They fought a long civil war. Their anarchy was going to be passed onto the second generation, because Maude had a son and Stephen had a son. But Eustace choked to death at a feast. People are still debating one thousand years later: Did he choke to death, or was he poisoned? Because by removing Eustace, it brought about a peace that ended the English civil war.

Eustace's death was accepted [as accidental], and I think that's what the murderers here were hoping for—that the whole realm would see Joffrey choke to death on a piece of pie or something. What they didn't count on was Cersei's immediate assumption that it was murder. Cersei wasn't fooled for a second.

DAVID BENIOFF: There's something wonderful, reading the book, the way Joffrey dies, because it's completely unexpected. There's no hero coming back to vanquish the evil king. He's not killed really as an act of vengeance. He's killed for purely political reasons.

DAN WEISS: There's something anticlimactic about it. The standard move would be to give you a sense of release, a sense of happiness. The idea that somehow the moral calculus of the world has been made right and this person who's had it coming for so long has finally gotten what he deserved.

DAVID BENIOFF: It's a character you've despised for so long and wanted to see him killed. Yet what you're seeing is a young man, still a boy, really, choke to death—which is a horrible thing to witness. Even if it's a character you hate, it's almost impossible to block out that thing inside of you when somebody suffers terribly. We didn't want this to be a stand-up-and-clap moment so much as a horrible death of a horrible person.

GEORGE R. R. MARTIN: There's a moment there where he knows that he's dying and he can't get a breath and looking at his mother and at the other people in the hall with just terror and appeal in his eyes—"Help me, Mommy." So I didn't want it to be entirely, "Hey-ho, the witch is dead." I wanted perhaps more complex feelings on the part of the audience. I don't know that we should be cheering deaths in real life. We don't want thirteen-year-old bullies to be put to death; sometimes people do regret their actions. But Joffrey will never get that chance, so we don't know what he would have become. Probably nothing good, but still. . . .

The episode ended with Cersei accusing Tyrion of killing her son and having him arrested. Yet there was another twist that took place off camera: Gleeson publicly revealed on the set that day that he was quitting acting.

JACK GLEESON: The answer isn't interesting or long-winded. I've been acting since age eight. I just stopped enjoying it as much as I did. It was the prospect of doing it for a living whereas up until then it was always something I did for recreation with my friends or in the summer for fun. [Acting as a career] changes your relationship with it. It's not like I hate it; it's just not what I want to do. I also found it slightly uncomfortable to see my face on a bus or a poster. I like just being known by my friends and family.

GEORGE R. R. MARTIN: I felt a little guilty that he quit acting. I hope that playing Joffrey didn't make him want to retire from the profession, because he did have quite a gift for it.

ESMÉ BIANCO: I saw him recently, and yeah, he's not worked since. It's sad in a sense, because he's an amazing actor. At the same time, I'm like, you do you. Just do one outstanding role everybody is going to remember you for, then say, "Next . . ."

That was supposed to be the end of Gleeson's acting story—and this chapter. Then there was another unexpected turn of events. Just as this book was being completed, Gleeson, now twenty-seven, emerged from retirement and signed on to a six-episode BBC comedy titled *Out of Her Mind*. It will mark his first filmed role since *Thrones*. A return of the king.

CHAPTER FIFTEEN

TRIAL AND TRIBULATIONS

Tyrion Lannister drank, and he knew things, but he was perhaps most adept at getting himself captured. The Lannister was held captive six times on *Game of Thrones* by different aggrieved parties. In season one, Tyrion was held prisoner by Catelyn Stark and then Lysa Arryn. In season five, he was apprehended by Ser Jorah, then again by slave traders. And in the final season, he was locked up by Daenerys Targaryen. "I'm very well-acquainted with the prop guys who have to handcuff me every ten minutes," Peter Dinklage once quipped on set.

Yet Tyrion's finest prisoner storyline was in season four, when he was falsely blamed for Joffrey's murder. The arc was *Thrones* at its best: George R. R. Martin's gripping plot dynamics combined with some of the show's finest writing and performances. There were shocking twists, scenes intimate and epic, and a story driven by the well-established rival agendas of compelling characters.

The quieter moments included a succession of players visiting Tyrion in his cell. The scenes leaned into season one's accidental discovery of the power of "two-handers." Dinklage's favorite of these was one of the most unusual scenes in the show. In a speech penned by showrunners David Benioff and Dan Weiss, Tyrion reminisced to Jaime about a "simple" cousin's predilection for smashing beetles and how he became obsessed with trying to understand the boy's madness. This was Tyrion mourning humanity's capacity for unfathomable and nonsensical cruelty.

"His face was like the page of a book written in a language I didn't understand, but he wasn't mindless, he had his reasons," Tyrion said. "And I became possessed with knowing what they were. . . . I had to know because it was horrible, that all these beetles should be dying for no reason. . . . In my dreams, I found myself standing on a beach made of beetle husks stretching as far as the eye can see. I woke up, crying, weeping for their shattered little bodies."

PETER DINKLAGE (*Tyrion Lannister*): Many of those scenes in the jail cell defined all these different relationships in Tyrion's life. I loved the scene with Nikolaj when we're talking about our cousin. There's so much in the show that's necessary to push the story forward because everybody is just trying to stay alive. I loved the lines about the cousin being a bit thick and smashing the beetles just because. It was about something from their past. It's like he's in shock. He doesn't know why he's telling that story, and he just wants to know what it was about and what life is about. It had such an abstract non–fucking–King's Landing feel to it. It was such a breath of fresh air. I loved that monologue. Whether I serviced it or not is a matter of opinion.

While Tyrion awaited his fate down in the dreary black cells, Tommen (Dean-Charles Chapman) got to know Margaery Tyrell up in his posh Red Keep bedchamber.

Tyrell had set her sights on wooing the realm's newly crowned boy-king, but during one scene, her flirtations were interrupted by Tommen's cat, Ser Pounce. In George R. R. Martin's novels, the young king has three black kittens (Ser Pounce, Boots, and Lady Whiskers). Co–executive producer Bryan Cogman thought it would be fun to have one of the cats make a quick cameo.

BRYAN COGMAN (*co–executive producer*): Ser Pounce wasn't in the outline. I said, "Dan, I'm getting Ser Pounce into the show!"

The idea was simple: Tommen is in bed. Margaery sits beside him by candlelight. The romantic tension rises. Suddenly Ser Pounce leaps from the floor to the bed—pounces, if you will. Then Tommen says a line ("That's Ser Pounce!") and Margaery pets the cat as they continue to chat.

All the cat had to do was jump up to the bed and then stay relatively still.

BRYAN COGMAN: Ser Pounce was supposed to be a little dainty kitten. And then this giant-ass cat showed up. And then the cat wouldn't do anything.

For take after take, the team could not convince the cat to jump onto the bed on cue. Eventually, an off-screen crew member had to toss the cat up from the floor.

BRYAN COGMAN: We never got the shot! You never see a shot of him jumping on the bed. He just appears on the bed. We never got the shot of him *pouncing*. To be fair, cats aren't famous for taking direction.

Then the cat wouldn't stay still. Dormer had to firmly hold him while delivering her lines.

NATALIE DORMER (*Margaery Tyrell*): That cat was a real diva. It was upstaging us at any given moment. We were all pulling out our hair. The cat would not do what it was supposed to short of pinning it down to the bed. We got one take that was halfway passable, and that was the one we used.

BRYAN COGMAN: Natalie Dormer punched me in the arm at lunch— playfully, I should add. "Why the fuck is this cat a Sumo wrestler?"

But this is one of the weird things about *Game of Thrones*: Ser Pounce then became an Internet sensation, and for no reason that I can state; the cat doesn't do anything.

The showrunners jokingly came up with an off-screen fate for Ser Pounce after Tommen committed suicide in season six.

DAVID BENIOFF (*showrunner*): Obviously Cersei hated the name "Ser Pounce" so much she could not allow him to survive. So she came up with her most diabolical [execution]. Ser Pounce's death was so horrible we couldn't even put it on the air.

DAN WEISS (*showrunner*): If you buy a super-extended, super-charged *Game of Thrones* box set, "The Death of Ser Pounce" will be in there. Just one whole episode devoted to the death of Ser Pounce.

Cogman added that despite the on-set hassle, he's rather proud of the scene, and noted that even the seeming randomness of Ser Pounce's cameo had a purpose.

BRYAN COGMAN: Ser Pounce is a great symbol of Tommen's innocence, and it's an organic way to get Tommen to talk about Joffrey and their complicated relationship. But there's a reason you never saw Ser Pounce again.

But eventually the royal family in King's Landing had to turn to the far more serious matter of Tyrion's trial for regicide.

The episode "The Laws of Gods and Men" was the *Thrones* version of a traditional courtroom drama, with Tyrion accused of a crime that the audience knew he did not commit. Tyrion endured a procession of witnesses making accusations. Each claim was a kernel of truth stripped of its proper context and spun into damning evidence of his seeming guilt.

GEORGE R. R. MARTIN (*author, co–executive producer*): Something I've tried to make a point of through the whole series is that decisions have consequences. One of Tyrion's problems has been his big mouth. He said things since the beginning of the series, kind of veiled threats to Cersei, "Someday I'm going to get you for this, someday your joy is going to turn to ashes in your mouth." All those declarations came back in a major way to make him look really guilty.

Adding to the intrigue was that Margaery and Olenna Tyrell knew Tyrion was innocent.

BRYAN COGMAN: Natalie was so much fun to watch. We know that Margaery knows who the murderer is, but she's putting on airs, and Natalie is doing all of that behind her eyes.

NATALIE DORMER: I mean, that's all you can do. The beauty of it is in the cut. So many of the editors on the show are the unsung heroes, and that scene is a great example of how strong the editing is. The average Joe doesn't always understand how imperative that is—the cutting of all the looks together.

Even Cersei didn't fully believe her brother was guilty.

LENA HEADEY (*Cersei Lannister*): Cersei's obviously disliked him since the beginning, since she holds him responsible for the death of their mother. She also believed—she didn't *really* believe it but was happy to believe it because she could hate him more—that he murdered Joffrey.

As for Tywin, the stone-faced patriarch didn't know whether his son was guilty or not, actor Charles Dance told HBO's *Making Game of Thrones*. "He isn't entirely sure who is responsible but a scapegoat has to be found," Dance said. For Tywin, the trial was more about manipulating Jaime into agreeing to quit the Kingsguard as part of their backroom plea deal in exchange for letting Tyrion live out the rest of his days at Castle Black.

The trial's showstopper moment came when Tyrion's secret mistress, Shae, who he thought had safely fled Westeros, testified against him. Shae revealed their intimate moments and accused Tyrion of plotting with Sansa to kill Joffrey.

BRYAN COGMAN: Every previous interaction with Tyrion and Shae was building to that moment in the courtroom.

GEORGE R. R. MARTIN: There were several actors who improved on their characters from the books, and I wish I could go back and write them better. The most conspicuous change was Sibel Kekilli playing Shae. The Shae in the books is a gold-digger camp follower. I have a certain amount of sympathy for her. She was probably abused or put into sexual service at a young age, and has been traveling around with the army. Tyrion picked her up. She's using her sexuality for advancement and has no real affection for him. But the way David and Dan wrote her, and the way Sibel played her, is a character with far more depth, who had genuine feelings for Tyrion. My Shae would have never turned down the bag of diamonds that Varys offered her to leave.

SIBEL KEKILLI (Shae): Our split-up scene was hard. Tyrion told her, "You're a whore, just go away." As Sibel Kekilli, I was feeling like Shae has to understand what's going on. So I was struggling with it. I talked to Dan and David: "This is not my Shae; she has to get why Tyrion is behaving like this." But I had to do what's in the script. It was really hard to understand that scene, but I loved it. The trial was heartbreaking. I tried to put all of Shae's humiliation into that moment to show her pain. It didn't work. I think the fans hated Shae.

Tyrion was devastated by Shae's damning testimony. Despite having agreed to the deal with his father to plead guilty, something inside him snapped.

BRYAN COGMAN: The Shae moment triggers what's been building up inside him his entire life. He was going to take Tywin's deal and go quietly. Now he'd rather die than give him that. But before he dies, he's going to tell them all what he really thinks of them. He sticks it to his father, to Cersei, and to the crowd.

In a speech adapted by Cogman, Tyrion raged: "I am guilty of a far more monstrous crime. I am guilty of being a dwarf. . . . I've been on trial for that my entire life. . . . I did not kill Joffrey, but I wish that I had. Watching your vicious bastard die gave me more relief than a thousand lying whores. . . . I wish I had enough poison for the whole pack of you!"

And if you thought Dinklage's speech in the episode was searing, his first take on the material was even more volcanic.

NIKOLAJ COSTER-WALDAU (*Jaime Lannister*): Peter went big for the first take of giving his speech at the trial. He "did it to the room," if you will. They picked the take [for the episode] where he brought it down for the close-ups. But his first take was so raw, it was beautiful. All the hair stood up on your body, and you're like, "This is amazing."

BRYAN COGMAN: The thing about Peter is there's probably fifteen takes that we didn't use that we could have slotted in and have an equally incredible and entirely different version of the same scene. The take they ended up using is not too over-the-top. I keep coming back to how piercing his gaze is throughout that speech; he's just stabbing daggers into every person he's talking to.

PETER DINKLAGE: I served on jury duty a while back for a case that went on awhile, and it wasn't dissimilar, because we had a whole week to shoot and I was up on that podium for like a week. It was a chance for Tyrion—without any bullshit, without any humor—to tell everybody [what he thought of them]. People say things about others in this show, down corridors and in bedrooms, and this was Tyrion's moment to pull back that curtain and pull the ripcord on the whole Lannister legacy, and especially expose his father, things that have been stuffed down deep inside of him. He's always dealt with things with humor and wit, but this time, enough's enough. It would have been fine until the love of his life was brought into it. He would have taken the deal.

Instead, Tyrion chose trial by combat, and Prince Oberyn Martell volunteered to serve as his champion. The Red Viper had been introduced in the season-four premiere along with his seductive paramour, Ellaria Sand. All season Martell had daringly antagonized the Lannisters, seeking vengeance against them and their murderous knight Ser Gregor Clegane for their war crimes against his family decades earlier. The fight would give the prince a chance to get his confession and revenge.

PEDRO PASCAL (*Oberyn Martell*): I was a true audience member of the show. When the audition came around, it had seemed unattainable. I got seventeen pages of sides and it was full of spoilers, so I was really upset the season was spoiled for me. So I put myself on tape and sent it in. I was really surprised when I heard back, and it gradually grew from there. Dan and David wrote this really generous email talking about the character and were very articulate, and it made a lot of sense to me.

DAVID BENIOFF: That was a role we were nervous about casting, as Oberyn embodies so many characteristics. He's a favorite character from the books. He's sexy and he's got the swagger, yet he's smart. He loves his family, and he's sexual in all sorts of ways. And Pedro is just phenomenal.

PEDRO PASCAL: When the casting announcement was made, it scared the shit out of me. It was like, "The guys love him, the girls love him, he's the most amazing human being in the world!" I was like, "Ahhh, thanks a lot. Set the bar a little higher."

SIBEL KEKILLI: Actors who joined in the later seasons were nervous. Pedro Pascal was so nervous on set. I was taking care of him: "Hey, come on, we're all a team here, we're going to have a drink and you can join us."

DAVID BENIOFF: The scene where Pedro tells Tyrion [he'll fight for him against the Mountain] is the first scene Pedro had to shoot. It was just intense pressure for a guy who hasn't been on the show before and he's coming over and doing a brand-new character and his first scene is a seven-minute scene opposite Peter Dinklage.

DAN WEISS: "Welcome to the show, here's your costume, now summarize the emotional apotheosis of your character—go!" He did a brilliant job of encapsulating everything about that character with no tricks or bells or whistles. He was so nervous about it, he wanted so badly to get it right. It took a long time to convince him that he had gotten it more than right. He thought we were being nice. He didn't know us yet.

The "Mountain and the Viper" fight was filmed at a seaside amphitheater in Dubrovnik. But first, some obstacles needed to be cleared.

ALEX GRAVES (director): When we scouted the amphitheater, there were all these yachts out front. So we needed to make a deal to make sure the yachts weren't there when we filmed. They all backed off a quarter mile so they wouldn't be in the shot. Everyone agreed to do it—except one person.

Multiple people working on *Thrones* insisted this person was, in fact, actor Bruce Willis, and that the *Die Hard* star not only refused to move his yacht but attempted to disrupt filming by piloting the boat back and forth in front of the amphitheater once shooting was under way. Crew members called it an act of "yacht rage." But the actor's presence in Croatia during the time was not confirmed.

ALEX GRAVES: [The yacht] circled trying to say, "Fuck you, I'm in your shot," a couple of times and we were all laughing because we were aimed away from the water at that time anyway.

BERNADETTE CAULFIELD (*executive producer*): I think that's been blown up a little bit more than it probably really was. We never actually *saw* Bruce.

The fight sequence was shot over three days, with Icelandic strongman Hafþór Björnsson having stepped into the role of Ser Gregor "the Mountain" Clegane. On the set, it's surreal to watch Björnsson stomp around, especially when he's costumed in armor that gives him even greater bulk and height. You feel slightly dizzy and confused, as if you're somehow looking at a special effect that's been rendered into real life; a human version of the show's supersized direwolves.

HAFÞÓR BJÖRNSSON (*Gregor "the Mountain" Clegane, seasons 4–8*): People hire me based on being a good, hardworking guy who happens to be six foot nine and 450 pounds, and they trust me to stay true to the script whilst adding my own personal touches.

RORY McCANN (*Sandor "the Hound" Clegane*): One time Hafþór ordered chicken and they brought him two breasts of chicken. He just looked up and said: "No, *a* chicken. Not just chicken. A chicken." Then he'd be eating a couple hours later again. He's a beast.

For Martel to take on such a fearsome opponent, the stunt team created a unique style of fighting for the Red Viper unlike anything previously seen in the show.

ALEX GRAVES: I wanted to see somebody airborne and moving and spinning musically, like in a dance, to convey the Sinatra-esque style of the character. The style is meant to give the audience the impression he could win against this gigantic opponent. Because when you look at the Mountain you figure he's going to kill him. And Pedro was such a spectacularly likable personality and such a smooth operator, you could put some doubt in the audience's mind.

PEDRO PASCAL: It was really intense. We were in the arena that was exposed to sunlight for the entire day, and I was covered in armor and flying around like a wasp. Just flying around this [huge] guy, who literally had a sword that went from the ground to my chin.

HAFÞÓR BJÖRNSSON: Working with Pedro Pascal was great; he's a good guy, and we had some good times between takes. But shooting was extremely difficult, both physically and mentally demanding. Going over everything again and again in full armor and high temperatures. Tensions were running high during the most intense filming, when the actors and most everyone were working sixteen to eighteen hours per day. All the training with swordmaster C. C. Smiff—several weeks, in fact—really paid off. I think the audience doesn't really realize how much work went into making *Game of Thrones*.

ALEX GRAVES: We wanted to misdirect the audience step by step. So throughout the training, I would go over and say, "Can you kick him there?" if it seemed like the Mountain or the Viper was doing too well.

DAN WEISS: It's not just people hacking at each other with spears and swords; it's the culmination of Oberyn's twenty years of anger and hatred and thirst for vengeance coming to a head in this amazing set piece.

For a couple of tense moments, Oberyn appeared to defeat his rival. The Mountain, severely wounded, collapsed to the stone floor. Instead of finishing him off, however, Oberyn insisted on trying to get the Mountain to confess his sins against the Martell family. Victory at hand, Oberyn was distracted by Ellaria's proud smile for just one second.

DAN WEISS: It's a very classic tragic-flaw situation, the character who can't leave well enough alone. He can't help poking the hornet's nest. He does it with great amusement throughout the season. He finally does it to the wrong person at the wrong time. The results left a big giant mess on the floor of our set.

PEDRO PASCAL: He got too close and was delivered by his own passions. Because ultimately, it is about defeating this man who raped and killed his sister, but before he can do that, before he can end this man's life, he needed a confession. He needed to hear it.

The Mountain swept Oberyn's leg, climbed on top of him, and then he . . . well, you saw what happened.

ALEX GRAVES: Everybody says, "Oh my God, the shot where his head explodes!" You actually don't see the head explode. It's a sound effect, but what you do see is the split second before it exploded. And a lot went into building the head that could be pressed and begin to cave in. We had tubes for blood and everything. At first, we forgot to add bone, and he started to squeeze and the whole head caved in.

HAFÞÓR BJÖRNSSON: The VFX and prosthetics team did such a great job that it felt in a way like I was actually crushing someone's head in.

INDIRA VARMA (*Ellaria Sand*): He was doing so brilliantly in the fight. It was all going his way, and he just lost it, didn't he?

ALEX GRAVES: Then after the Mountain fell back we laid different types of meat over the stunt actor's face. You're so far away in the show, you don't know it's meat. It's just all so horrifying.

PEDRO PASCAL: Interestingly, I had this great conversation with Lena Headey about Oberyn's journey. Even though it ends badly, he still hears the confession, you know? I don't even need to go on after that once it's been said out loud. And the ecstasy of achieving that, even though it's being achieved in the instance of my demise.

It seemed as though Tyrion was fated for execution once again. Then Jaime, in keeping with his lifelong devotion to looking out for his younger brother, freed him from the black cells. But just like Oberyn, Tyrion could not leave well enough alone. He had unfinished business with his father. And he discovered Tywin was not alone.

GEORGE R. R. MARTIN: Sometimes people just get pushed too far. Sometimes people break. I think Tyrion reached that point. He'd been through hell, faced death over and over again and been betrayed, as he sees it, by all the people that he's tried to take care of and tried to win the approval of. He'd been trying to win his father's approval all his life and, despite his misgivings, fell in love with Shae.

SIBEL KEKILLI: This girl is in the bed with the father. And Tyrion came in this room, and Shae has to say, "My lion!" I refused to shoot it. "Please don't do this."

ALEX GRAVES: It was very hard to kill Shae. I don't think any sequence has left me so exhausted.

GEORGE R. R. MARTIN: [Tyrion is] strangling her slowly, and she's fighting, trying to get free. He could let go at any time. But his anger and his sense of betrayal is so strong that he doesn't stop until it's done. That's probably the blackest deed that he's ever done.

ALEX GRAVES: The way Tyrion ends up after he's killed her is the worst part of the scene in that he's kind of hanging off the chain he uses to choke her. He was meant to kill her on the bed. But we were rehearsing, and Peter threw himself off the bed and held on to the chain even though he landed on the side of the bed. He said, "What if I just keep going from here?" Peter came off the bed and just kept pulling. So he was killing her without having to face her and it was awful, and we were going for awful.

SIBEL KEKILLI: People keep asking me: "Did Shae love Tyrion?" For me it was clear. She loved Tyrion. If she didn't she would have left him when he lost his power or when Varys offered her money. He married another girl. She loved Sansa. In the end it was too much pain.

My explanation is that of course she knew all the power games between the family. But she's a lowborn and didn't have the power. She didn't have any choice. She had to be with someone who would protect her. Tywin and Cersei somehow forced her—"You have to help us or you're going to die." So what's the next step for a lowborn girl in that situation? She can be a prostitute, or she can be a lover to this powerful guy, and that would be Tywin.

Tyrion, armed with a crossbow, surprised his father on the toilet. Even when confronted by the son he thought was in prison, the stern Lannister patriarch was almost entirely unflappable.

ALEX GRAVES: I remember trying to find a piece of wall because I wanted that shot of Tyrion walking to the bathroom. You couldn't just cut to the next thing right after Shae's murder. I wanted the drama of six seconds of him walking to the next thing with the crossbow. People were like, "With all the money being spent on this show, why does Graves need a freaking wall?" Because you *need* it.

Tywin called Shae a "whore." Despite having just murdered Shae, Tyrion warned his father not to disrespect her by saying "that word again. . . ."

GEORGE R. R. MARTIN: Lord Tywin was convinced that since he didn't love Tyrion, no one could love Tyrion. Shae's obviously some lower-class girl who's just trying to get the dwarf into bed because he was a Lannister so she could become a lady and have money and live in a castle— basically the equivalent of being a whore. She's just fucking him for possession of status. Tywin is trying to teach Tyrion a lesson in that regard, and so he keeps using the word "whore," which is like pouring salt into his wound. Tyrion tells him, "Don't say that word again," and he says that word again. At that moment, Tyrion's finger pushed on the trigger.

PETER DINKLAGE: Tyrion is grief-stricken about what he just did, and Tywin doesn't give a shit . . . that's the finger that fires.

Martin added that Tywin was killed not just because of his words in the moment, and his dreadful treatment of his son in general, but due to something quite specific he had taught Tyrion many years before.

GEORGE R. R. MARTIN: It's very much Lord Tywin's philosophy that you don't make threats and then fail to carry them out. That's an important thing he drilled into Tyrion since his youth. You threaten someone and then they defy you, and you don't carry out your threat, who's going to believe your threats?

PETER DINKLAGE: I loved working with Charles Dance. I loved their relationship too, as horrible as it was. It's so loving in a way within a fucked-up relationship. God, I sound like somebody who was abused and says it's their own fault! I just loved how Charlie played it. He respected Tyrion, but he just couldn't help it.

CHARLES DANCE (*Tywin Lannister*): Tyrion was a continuous reminder, as far as Tywin is concerned, of the one area he's failed in. Especially in fifteenth-, sixteenth-century Europe, any imperfection—whether it's dwarfism, being blind, a child born unperfected—ideally, you smother them, get rid of them, put them in a bucket. He let Tyrion live. To his astonishment, Tyrion is the brightest of his three children, the whiniest, and the cleverest, and that's a continual [annoyance]. The little shit shouldn't possess all these qualities. Those are the qualities that I would admire in him if he weren't a dwarf, but the fact that he's a dwarf is a continual reminder of his failure.

It's horrible. But I'm not one of these actors that tries to find the good in a character. If a character is a shit, he's a shit and you play him full-on as a shit. Don't try and make him nice. Peter is extraordinary. I just would have loved to play some scenes with him where I don't treat him like shit, you know?

CHAPTER SIXTEEN

THE BIGGEST SHOW IN THE WORLD

G ame of Thrones wasn't an overnight success, nor did any particular episode or season cause the series to explode into the phenomenon it became. The rise of Thrones was gradual yet unceasing. It wasn't entirely unlike the growth of Daenerys's dragons—each year Thrones and its fandom got bigger and wilder, until one day it ruled the world.

By the end of season four, Thrones was HBO's most popular show of all time, with nearly twenty million US viewers watching each week across all the network's platforms and tens of millions more viewing around the globe. Thrones had also earned the dubious honor of becoming the world's most illegally downloaded series (by one estimate, the season-eight premiere was illicitly viewed by fifty-four million people).

Awards piled up too. Thrones would eventually take home fifty-nine Primetime Emmy awards, the most ever given to a drama or comedy series, including four wins for best drama and an equal number for Dinklage in the Outstanding Supporting Actor category.

Merchandising took off as well, with HBO approving dozens of official products. There were Thrones craft beers, wines, bobbleheads, mugs, figurines, games, and so many T-shirts (even Ser Pounce had his own shirt). Composer Ramin Djawadi launched the Game of Thrones Live Concert Experience, a spectacular global touring show that combined a live orchestra performance and special effects. Terms like *khaleesi, the Red Wedding, winter is coming,* and *Dothraki* became everyday references. Parents named their newborns after characters, such as Arya and Daenerys.

For any city where *Thrones* was filmed, the show was a godsend of revenue and tourism. Dubrovnik became so overrun with *Thrones* fans, the King's Landing stand-in started limiting visitors to its ancient walls in 2017, while a report from Northern Ireland in 2018 calculated that *Thrones* delivered $40 million a year in local tourism dollars.

The show's creators and cast, most of whom had little to no experience with being a celebrity, were given a crash course in the perks and detriments of fame.

PILOU ASBÆK (*Euron Greyjoy*): I'd acted for fifteen years in Denmark and in international productions. I'd worked with Morgan Freeman, Scarlett Johansson, Kirsten Dunst—big-ass stars. It wasn't until I joined *Thrones* that people were like, "Fuck yeah, bro, we love you."

I was at the Chilean airport, and one of the customs people looked at me and goes, "Greyjoy?" Then they closed the border at the airport in Santiago so we could take photos. For fifteen minutes no one could enter their country! I was like, "Holy fucking shit, this is massive." I couldn't imagine how it was for Kit or Nikolaj. It was the biggest show in the world.

Such fan encounters were almost always positive, the actors said.

LIAM CUNNINGHAM (*Davos Seaworth*): People were always happy to see Davos. He could do no wrong, and people confused me with him. It's fantastic to walk around and get that reaction.

KRISTIAN NAIRN (*Hodor*): People don't believe you're real; they see you as the character. You get *Hodor*s yelled. But *Thrones* fans tend to be respectful. Everyone is super chill, even the slightly annoying ones.

JACK GLEESON (*Joffrey Baratheon*): Most people separate the character and the person. Nobody ever said a mean thing to me. People would say, "Are you okay? I hear you get bullied on the street."

GEMMA WHELAN (*Yara Greyjoy*): It's so, so rare that I'm recognized, but when I am it's really nice. They say I've made their day, but I think they've made *my* day! It works both ways.

ESMÉ BIANCO (*Ros*): I had a woman come up to me at a convention and tell me she's a sex worker. She said she'd never watched a TV show or film where she felt somebody playing a prostitute had represented her—"You didn't play Ros as a prostitute, you played this amazing woman, you played a person." When I have days when I want to quit the industry, I remember that woman.

But some fan encounters were a bit odd, uncomfortable, or, occasionally, frightening.

MARK ADDY (*Robert Baratheon*): A guy showed me a tattoo of King Robert he had done on his shoulder. It's a picture of me on his shoulder. I'm all: "That's there forever! What are you doing?!"

HAFÞÓR BJÖRNSSON (*Gregor "the Mountain" Clegane, seasons 4–8*): I get a lot of requests by fans asking if I will squeeze their eyes; that's very popular. Or pick them up over my head. I don't lift everyone, usually just girls. And sometimes I have had to say no because if I'm going to lift one person, then so many others are going to ask. You have to try to be fair to everyone, you know.

NIKOLAJ COSTER-WALDAU (*Jaime Lannister*): A fan stayed in Belfast for three months hoping to meet us. She finally did at the hotel bar. So we gave her autographs and pictures. Very sweet girl, but I was just going, "Holy shit, am I the only one disturbed by this?" I asked her why she did it. She said this was on her bucket list. Well, thank God you finally met us so you can go home!

OWEN TEALE (*Alliser Thorne*): A guy came up to me once when I was with my wife and said, "Would you do me a favor? Would you call me a bastard into my phone?" I said, "Don't be silly," and my wife said, "Oh, go on!" I grabbed his phone and said, "You fucking bastard." He was so excited.

GEORGE R. R. MARTIN (*author, co–executive producer*): At Comic-Con we'd do a group signing and there would be ten of us at a table and each one of us would sign the poster. You'd sign it and then slide it down to the next person. At one of these, I was sitting next to Lena Headey and I started to slide the poster to Lena, and the woman whose poster it was said to her, "No! I don't want *you*! You're evil!" Lena just looked stunned.

At another signing, a guy asked if he could cut off a piece of my beard. I said no and resumed signing. The son of a bitch got a pair of scissors and snuck up around behind me and tried to get some of my hair. My assistant at the time, Ty Franck, who is half of the writing team James S. A. Corey, wrestled him and took the scissors away.

CHARLES DANCE (*Tywin Lannister*): At times, it can get a little intrusive, especially if you're quietly having a dinner somewhere with a forkful of food in your mouth and someone comes up and just suddenly someone pulls out a phone and clicks. Am I behind a piece of glass? Am I an animal in a zoo?

MAISIE WILLIAMS (*Arya Stark*): It's easy to rely on other people and become like, "How do I make coffee?" I look at Lena Headey; I admire her lifestyle. She's a fantastic actress. She goes to the award shows and does the famous things but still lives a very normal life. I don't want people to follow me everywhere. I want to live anonymously, and that's the one thing I miss—being anonymous.

SOPHIE TURNER (*Sansa Stark*): I had a burning desire to work at Starbucks. The standard nine-to-five routine was really appealing to me. Because acting is so unpredictable, except when working on *Thrones*. I wanted to keep acting for the rest of my life but maybe with a random Starbucks job thrown in.

EMILIA CLARKE (*Daenerys Targaryen*): I didn't feel equipped as a human being to handle the success or the failure of how the show was viewed by people outside of the show, and that ended up having a profound effect on my character. I became so much more invested in her because I couldn't look anywhere else for a long time. I was always expecting everyone to turn against her, because fame and success and whether your show does well or not, that's all fickle as fuck. It's all going to change as the wind blows. People change their minds. And if you measure your self-worth by all that, then you're screwed. So I just became even more obsessive. Like, "What is Daenerys?"

Just because an actor got recognized, however, it didn't necessarily mean the fan knew which character they played.

JOE DEMPSIE (*Gendry*): There's been numerous occasions where someone would say, "You're in *Game of Thrones*, aren't you?" And I'd be like: "Yeah." They're like, "Yeah, you're the clumsy dude!" [Meaning Podrick, played by Daniel Portman.] "No, but he's great."

KIT HARINGTON (*Jon Snow*): So many times I was told I look like Jon Snow, and then I said I was Jon Snow and then they said: "No, he's taller."

CONLETH HILL (*Varys*): A lot of people think I'm security or a wine waiter. It's great because when my hair grows back in I'm not recognized, so I don't get tortured the way some of the better-known actors are.

PILOU ASBÆK: I had a meeting with producers on a very big film. We sat down, and they were so uninterested in all the things I had to say. After twenty minutes they ask, "So what have you done?" And I say, "I've done *Game of Thrones*"—this was before season six was released. And one goes: "No, fuck you, man! I knew it! You're fucking amazing!" They went from zero to too much interest. "You are a chameleon! Dude, tell me one thing and be honest: How was it to do the scene where you got your dick cut off?" They thought I was Alfie Allen. This was the worst meeting in the history of meetings. I just went, "That was very tough, but I'm a professional and I'm going to keep it as a secret." I went out of the meeting and called Alfie and went, "If you get this villain role in this movie it's because of me."

Saying an iconic line on the show in particular became a double-edged sword. Just ask Rose Leslie, who immortalized Ygritte's recurring taunt, "You know nothing, Jon Snow."

ROSE LESLIE (*Ygritte*): It's a lovely thing that fans are so passionate. But those five words are all they want to hear. And I put on an accent on the show, so when I say, "You know nothing, Jon Snow," in my own voice, you get a furrowed brow, and they're like, "That doesn't sound like Ygritte." Then I have to go into the accent, and it's a long, boring process for the fan and I'm sure they walk away wishing they hadn't asked me because it's such a kerfuffle.

Sophie Turner had a rougher time than most during the show's first couple of seasons. In Martin's books, Sansa is initially meant to be a frustrating character, a shallow and immature contrast to her brave and capable sister, Arya. Sansa believed in the tales of noble knights, chivalrous princes, and happily ever after—the fantasy tropes that Martin's story-line cruelly overthrows.

SOPHIE TURNER: At first it came as a shock because people didn't like Sansa. I thought I was being personally attacked but knew I wasn't. A lot of fans would recognize me and go: "I kind of hate you." I'm all, "Cool, well, you've just made this sufficiently awkward." [And once], me and Maisie were in line and they were all [to me], "You're my least favorite," [and then, indicating Williams,] "You're my favorite." I couldn't take it personally because people hated [Sansa] in the book. I suppose if they hated her on-screen, I was kind of doing justice to her.

MAISIE WILLIAMS: People constantly compared us—this character compared to that character—when we're two completely different girls playing two completely different characters.

The showrunners likewise wrestled with how best to interact with fans. The duo had an encounter when filming the show's first season that gave them a reason to mistrust outsiders.

DAN WEISS (*showrunner*): We were in Malta reshooting Dany's wedding. Some Russian kid comes up and asked if he could come on the set. He was very nice and decent, if maybe a little off. I was like, "Sure." Nobody gave a shit then. The show didn't exist. I figured the kid walked all this way out here, he found this place, he cares.

Later, he posted photos online of everything he'd seen plus a blistering critique, saying here is everything we were doing wrong and that we needed to hire him because he was the only one who could make it right. I've thought about that kid many times.

Benioff and Weiss later made a vow to stop reading online commentary about the show (or try to, anyway). Being a showrunner requires trusting your instincts to make countless decisions. The duo were increasingly wary of being influenced by a rising tide of voices from fans and the media, who regularly second-guessed their every move.

DAVID BENIOFF (*showrunner*): You can get lost in this world of online *Thrones* commentary if you're not careful, and we both felt a lot saner after we stopped doing that. There might be nine positive comments but if the tenth one is negative, then that's the one you'll remember, that's what sticks in your head. You want to have an argument with that person—"Well, here's why this happened. . . ." You start having an argument in your mind, and you realize you're losing your mind. You're having an internal argument with somebody named DragonQueen42—you're never going to win that argument.

DAN WEISS: Even the positive stuff. You read five, six, seven of those and you get the feeling people love what you're doing. It gives you a little pleasure hit each time you click on a comment, and before you know it, you're like a coke-addicted lab monkey clicking-clicking-clicking. I don't want to be a coke-addicted lab monkey. It completely confounds the normal creative process. It's an all-or-nothing thing. Either you're listening or you're not listening.

Many cast members likewise decided to minimize reading about themselves online, with an unusually large percentage of the show's cast opting against having social media accounts at a time when online fan outreach was increasingly common (and even required by some networks and studios).

PETER DINKLAGE (*Tyrion Lannister*): I'm sort of a private person. The less you know about an actor, the more serious you'll take them because they will disappear a little bit. Nowadays, there's so much information about everybody that it's hard to see the performance when you know what they had for dinner last night. You want to keep some mystery.

For female cast members, the Internet was especially perilous.

EMILIA CLARKE: Bright-eyed and bushy-tailed, I looked on the Internet [after the first season] and then stopped. You can read lots of lovely things and the one nasty thing forever stays in your mind. You go to bed thinking about the person who thinks that your bum is too big or whatever. Later, I read an actor's interview who said, "If you ever hear an actor say they don't google themselves, they're lying." I don't google myself! One minute I'm engaged to James Franco, the next I'm in a love triangle with my best friend and my gay best friend.

ESMÉ BIANCO: I learned my lesson pretty quickly and stopped looking. I think I've read pretty much every negative thing that can be said. People can be horrible, and it can be devastating. It can start to affect people's performances when you're getting this feedback as you go along. I made a conscious decision that I didn't need to know what everybody thought, that if I wasn't doing my job, then the producers would tell me.

Many *Game of Thrones* insiders said the most intense fan experiences were not online or at any convention but when the production first went to Spain to shoot portions of season five. The production wasn't prepared for the extraordinary passion of Spanish fans. A local casting call resulted in eighty-six thousand emails and crashed the casting office's servers. Outside the cast's Seville hotel, a crowd of hundreds stood vigil, all day and night, hoping for a glimpse of the *Thrones* cast.

DAVID BENIOFF: We have never worked in a place where the passion for the series ran so high. You couldn't walk down the street with a cast member, even a minor cast member, without being mobbed—a friendly mob.

JESSICA HENWICK (*Nymeria Sand*): We were shooting at the Alcázar palace. It's got a fence going all the way around it, and we had covered it in plastic sheets so that you couldn't see into the set. I remember looking over the set and seeing this fire that was getting bigger and bigger. I realized people on the street were setting fire to the plastic sheets to make holes so that they could look through them.

LIAM CUNNINGHAM: The fans in Spain broke into the hotel. They had to bring in the police because they were pushing the gates down. You'd come out at five A.M. and there were people out there—four or five hundred people. Peter tried to leave his room and they were running down the fucking corridor.

PETER DINKLAGE: They're all so sweet on an individual basis. You multiply it by hundreds, it gets a little intimidating. I don't like crowds, but the love and support is so sweet. When you're part of something this big, it's not about us as individuals; the hysteria is about the universe that was created. It's like when the Beatles used to play, fans didn't even want to hear the music, it was all about John, Paul, George, and Ringo. I didn't just compare the Beatles to *Game of Thrones,* by the way.

LIAM CUNNINGHAM: At one point I ran out of underwear and there was an H&M across the street. Big Steve—our ex-cop [security guard] from Northern Ireland—jumps up and goes, "I'll come with you." I said, "You're not coming with me to buy fucking underwear." He wouldn't take no for an answer. So I'm buying underwear and I look up and Steve is holding back a crowd of people trying to get at me.

Harington was especially an object of obsession, with the Spanish crowds screaming "Kit"—which sounded a bit like "Keet," so his costars began teasingly calling him "Keith." Coster-Waldau was also a target; the chiseled Dane was stalked by a group of girls wearing Burger King crowns and had to change his hotel.

KEISHA CASTLE-HUGHES (*Obara Sand*): I went out and was talking to one of them and told them, "Nikolaj's not staying here." They all looked at me like I was an insane person and went, "Well, we *know* he is." And I went, "Oh, that's creepy."

JESSICA HENWICK: They would say, "Slay me, Kingslayer!"

NIKOLAJ COSTER-WALDAU: I made the mistake of going to the gym, and it became crazy. People would come up, "We've been looking for you for two days!"

Some of *Thrones'* biggest fans were famous themselves, and one in particular was given special access to the show. President Barack Obama would hit up HBO chief Richard Plepler for advance copies of *Thrones* episodes, even top secret season finales. And he got them.

RICHARD PLEPLER (*former co-president and CEO of HBO*): Obama was a huge fan of the show. One time, I was at a state dinner and I was going through the receiving line and he said: "I need my episodes." Later, as we were leaving, I heard him call out to me. I was excited; I thought he wanted my thoughts on something. But he said, "And don't forget: I need those last two episodes." I said, "I promise you, Mr. President, you will get your episodes."

Obama's successor also wanted something from *Thrones,* though President Donald Trump's interactions with the company were more combative. Trump repeatedly tweeted memes touting his administration with a font used on the show's marketing material while making declarations like "Sanctions Are Coming" (referring to Iran). HBO coolly replied with a statement: "We would prefer our trademark not be misappropriated for political purposes."

Protecting the show's assets was an enormous and often impossible task, and Trump was the least of the network's concerns. As the show's storylines left behind the published material from Martin's books, outsiders made increasingly sophisticated efforts to infiltrate the production and post spoilers online. The most damaging leak was in 2015, when the unfinished first four episodes of season five were posted on BitTorrent from DVD screeners that HBO had sent to members of the media. The leaker was not a critic ("The screeners were sent to someone who no longer worked at a place and they were left on a desk and somebody took them off the desk," Benioff explained), but the leak marked the beginning of the end of physical copies of media being distributed before a show's release—not just at HBO, but at studios worldwide.

DAVID BENIOFF: That was a huge deal. It was four episodes. You think of all the hours of work from all the people who work on the show and the millions of dollars it cost. Having these half-made episodes air long before they were supposed to was really disappointing. We didn't have harsh words for HBO so much as we asked, "How do we try to prevent this from happening again?"

MICHAEL LOMBARDO (*former HBO programming president*)**:** It's one of those moments where the good news was that we had a show people were desperate to steal. The bad news is we were now in a different world. Everyone realized at that moment—not just with *Game of Thrones*—that things had changed. It required a whole rethink. The number of people that were allowed access to content changed dramatically at that point.

Then there was the extraordinary drama of the Great HBO Hack of 2017, which played out like something from a high-tech thriller. A hacker social-engineered access to one HBO employee's email account and managed to download a claimed 1.5 terabytes of stolen data. The infiltrator, who called himself "Little Finger," threatened to leak the company's assets if he wasn't sent $6 million in Bitcoin.

"The greatest leak of cyber space era is happening," wrote the hacker in emails sent to the media. "What's its name? Oh I forget to tell. It's HBO and Game of Thrones . . . !!!"

HBO enlisted the FBI while the network's internal security team scrambled to figure out what material had been compromised. Luckily for *Thrones,* the hacker did not obtain actual episodes but had to settle for some scripts along with episodes of other titles, such as *Ballers, Curb Your Enthusiasm,* and *Room 104.*

In 2019, the FBI charged former Iranian military contractor Behzad Mesri with the cyberattack. US Attorney Joon Kim announced to reporters: "Winter has come for Behzad Mesri." It was never clear if HBO paid any of the ransom, but for a tense period of time at the network, nobody knew if their private communications might have been compromised and what assets might suddenly spring up online.

MICHAEL LOMBARDO: It was Armageddon. There was a moment where every company felt exposed in a way they've never contemplated before. We were still thinking that somehow what you submitted digitally to one person was private and that this was this secure system. People were looking at their emails and paranoia seeped in. It was a wake-up call that there were bad people out there. You somehow thought that because you were in the entertainment world, you were safe. You realize modern culture has become international and you're exposed on a much bigger scale.

On the show's sets in in Northern Ireland and Spain, paparazzi were going to increasingly extreme lengths to penetrate *Thrones'* on-the-ground security. The production had to continually ramp up its countermeasures to keep pace. The Northern Ireland sets were designated by the government as no-fly zones. Perimeters were expanded and heavily patrolled. A sensitive set in Spain was literally guarded by the country's military, which established a roadblock miles away.

DAN WEISS: There was a guy who hiked eighteen hours on foot in the middle of the La Mancha desert to take pictures, and another guy in Northern Ireland who crawled through the mud and did his own little private commando mission.

BERNADETTE CAULFIELD (*executive producer*): There were times when even I couldn't get on the set because I didn't have my badge, because I had told them, "Whoever comes through here, they have to have a badge." Then I'd have to do the sad walk across the street to go get it.

Even within a guarded perimeter, measures had to be taken to prevent somebody from seeing something they shouldn't. Printed scripts were largely banished from use in the latter seasons. Every character was given a code name on any production documents. Cast trailers had numbers on their doors rather than character names, so an interloper couldn't tell which actors were in a scene together.

SOPHIE TURNER: We had like this app where everything disappeared after twenty-four hours; it was like Snapchat for scripts. And we all had code names, which is highly confusing when you needed to remember who was who.

Spoiler photos sometimes leaked anyway. The show's security team would then use forensic analysis to track down precisely where and when the picture was taken. One aerial shot of a King's Landing set in Northern Ireland leaked online during filming of season eight, and analysts determined it had been taken from a specific window at the *Titanic* museum blocks away. The crew then took steps to seal off that particular line of sight.

The most devastating photo leak came during the filming of season eight, when an image of Jon Snow killing Daenerys was posted on Reddit by a day-player crew member.

BERNADETTE CAULFIELD: A lot of times, the person will send it to the girlfriend and then the girlfriend sends it to somebody else, and then the "somebody else" realizes how valuable it is and puts it out there. But sometimes people are lying. So sometimes people will get fired whether they're lying or not. Because if you don't reprimand somebody properly, others will think, "Oh, it's not really a problem, then." If anything, the crew would get more upset if we didn't do it—"Why did this person not get fired when we're all following the rules?" Because everyone else works so hard to keep information from getting out. So we were put in the position where we had to let people go unless what they did was really benign.

After the finale photo leaked, the producers put out misleading images to try to generate confusion online. Cast members were even flown to sets where their characters weren't actually filming to throw off any spies. The only thing the production did not do was shoot alternate endings to the show, despite reports claiming otherwise.

DAN WEISS: We didn't shoot other endings because that would have been an insane waste of time and money. But we had a lot of fake images and shots. We staged Jon Snow bowing down to Cersei on a set we knew people would be taking pictures of.

DAVID BENIOFF: We had a zombie giant walking through King's Landing; we had the Night King at King's Landing.

DAN WEISS: It was all about putting enough fake things out there that looked real. Sadly, at a time when truth is disappearing from the world, the best way to fight truth was putting out lots of plausible falsehoods. Just drown the truth in bullshit.

Ultimately, the spoiler leaks and fandom obsession were luxury problems. It meant *Thrones* was drawing the interest of perhaps hundreds of millions of fans. The show's cast was boosted to stardom, and crew members gained an invaluable credit on their résumés. The success of *Thrones* was also a financial windfall for thousands of people who profited either directly from the production or, far more often, indirectly—from restaurateur in Belfast to tour operators in Croatia to hotel owners in Spain to entrepreneurs who launched tie-in products.

And yet . . .

BRYAN COGMAN: It's hard to remember, but for a long time we were the underdog. We didn't win the [best drama] Emmy until season five. We were this strange little upstart that people kept talking about. Being the biggest show, for me, was a double-edged sword. To see the Bud Light ad in the Super Bowl and the White Walker Oreos . . . that's all fine. I'm not saying we shouldn't have enjoyed it. But at the same time, there was a feeling of . . . I remember when we were a company that was just trying to put on a show.

CHAPTER SEVENTEEN

THE FORKS IN THE ROAD

George R. R. Martin sat at a tucked-away table at his favorite restaurant in Santa Fe, a modest family-owned spot where green chili enchiladas and taco plates are ordered by their number. Even though he was out of sight from the main dining room, *Thrones* fans still managed to find him and ask for a photo. With his fluffy snow-white beard, suspenders, and ever-present fisherman's cap, Martin looks a bit like a literary character himself, as the author admits.

"When we did the first season, Sean Bean was the only well-known actor in the cast, but I was a bestselling author," Martin said. "So HBO used me in a lot of their early publicity, and my picture got out there and I became well-known. I guess my appearance is rather distinctive. Then I discovered you can't turn that off. Like, I can't go into a bookstore anymore, which is one of my favorite pleasures in life. I used to spend a whole day browsing around and leave with many books under my arm. Now I'm there five minutes and somebody asks for an autograph or a photo and pretty soon I have a circle of people around me. You gain a lot and lose things too."

Martin pointed across the dining room to an even more secluded nook. *Right over there,* he said, was where he'd sat with David Benioff, Dan Weiss, and Bryan Cogman back in 2013 and revealed his long-held secret ending for *A Song of Ice and Fire*. By that time it was clear to Martin that the show would have major divergences from his novels.

"During the pilot reshoot, I visited the set on the isle of Malta and met some of the new actors," Martin recalled. "There was some crisis that occurred. The director called David and Dan over, and they were having some discussion about ten feet away about how to handle it. And that was when I realized my baby wasn't entirely my baby anymore, because I wasn't part of that discussion. The director was talking to Dan and Dave. Nobody was saying, 'George, come over and tell us your opinion.'

"I didn't throw a tantrum or anything," Martin added calmly. "I just came to the realization: I gave my baby up for adoption and now there is a parent-teacher conference and I'm not invited."

Another early sign of the show's autonomy was when the producers decided to have King Joffrey order Ser Ilyn Payne to cut out the singer Marillion's tongue in season one (in the books, the victim is a different minstrel). "George was none too pleased because in the books Marillion ends up being the patsy for Lysa Arryn's murder, which happened in season four," Bryan Cogman said. "David and Dan's reasoning was it's better television to have this minstrel whose tongue is ripped out be the minstrel that we'd spend the season with and that we'd figure out Lysa's murder when we got to it, and we did."

Martin's fifth *A Song of Ice and Fire* novel, the 1,040-page *A Dance with Dragons,* was published in 2011, the same year *Thrones* debuted. Martin still had two more books planned, *The Winds of Winter* and *A Dream of Spring.* Given that *Dragons* took six years to write, fans worried from the start that the HBO series was going to outpace the books. "Finish the book, George!" became an Internet rallying cry. A few years into the series, executives at the network grew nervous as well. "I finally understood fans' fear, which I didn't a couple of years before," Michael Lombardo said during production of season three. "What if the storytelling catches up to the books? Let's all hope and pray that's not going to be a problem."

Fandom and network angst paled in comparison to Martin's own concern. The author posted dismayed updates on his blog detailing his struggle to complete *Winds*. He attributed the setbacks to a mix of factors—the complexity of the story, his perfectionism, and the distractions and opportunities that came along with being part of the HBO series. "On Tuesday, I think it's the greatest thing I've ever done," Martin said. "On Wednesday, I think it's all garbage and I should throw it all in the fire and start again."

DAN WEISS (*showrunner*): We just did the math on how many seasons we got, how many the story could shoulder and service, and we realized we were going to outstrip the books. So we sat down with him in Santa Fe for three days and dug as deep as we could into what he had in mind for the future of the series through the end.

BRYAN COGMAN (*co–executive producer*): I can't even describe that meeting. It was like learning the meaning of life. Like God was coming down and telling you the future. We knew at that point that we were going to catch up. So it was learning a lot of these secrets and then in your mind figuring out, "What of that will work in the context of our show?"

GEORGE R. R. MARTIN (*author, co–executive producer*): It wasn't easy for me. I didn't want to give away my books. It's not easy to talk about the end of my books. Every character has a different end. I told them who would be on the Iron Throne, and I told them some big twists like Hodor and "hold the door," and Stannis's decision to burn his daughter. We didn't get to everybody by any means. Especially the minor characters, who may have very different endings.

DAN WEISS: What makes the books so great is that George doesn't make meticulous blueprints for every beat of this story, then fill in the blanks by dutifully going from A to B to C, fleshing out an outline. George didn't have ultra-detailed versions of the last hundred pages of his story figured out.

DAVID BENIOFF (*showrunner*): George often used the metaphor of being a gardener instead of an architect. He plants the seeds and watches them grow. Even if we wanted to be gardeners, we couldn't. We had to plan out entire seasons. We had to write a detailed outline and provide that to production. Writing a novel is a solo endeavor, and television is a team sport. I'm horribly mixing my metaphors, but the basic point is George was a gardener, and we had to be architects to plan out the seasons meticulously so they get shot and were ready in time. It's just a fundamental difference between writing novels and TV series.

GEORGE R. R. MARTIN: David warned me: "We're catching up." I said: "I know you are." But at that time I still thought they wouldn't catch up. I thought I'd stay ahead.

Martin was confident he could finish his saga before the end of *Thrones* because he'd made an assumption about how the showrunners would use his already published fourth and fifth *A Song of Ice and Fire* books. The show's first two seasons were based on the author's first two novels, *A Game of Thrones* and *A Clash of Kings*. Seasons three and four were based on the fan-favorite 992-page *A Storm of Swords*.

Martin's next two titles, *A Feast for Crows* and *A Dance with Dragons*, were a combined 1,824 pages. So the author believed that was more than enough to keep the show occupied for several more years. But the new books also added many new characters and storylines, particularly set in Dorne and the Iron Islands. There were so many added threads that the books had an unusual format—covering the same chronological period while focusing on different characters.

GEORGE R. R. MARTIN: In *The Lord of the Rings*, everything begins in the Shire with Bilbo's birthday party, and then the four hobbits set off and they pick up Strider and Gimli and Legolas, and then they start to split up and go their separate ways. That was the same structure I used. It all begins in Winterfell with everybody except Dany. They split up and split further and further. Everything is getting wider, and it's always been my intent to curve back at the end. It's the same structure as the show, but David and Dan made the turn much sooner and didn't introduce some of my new characters, like Arianne Martell and Quentyn Martell.

Martin considered his new characters essential. The showrunners felt their show had to stay focused on its existing cast and maintain the momentum of its established storylines. By season five, *Thrones* was bursting at the seams with up to thirty series regulars and darting between eight stories set in different locations—Daenerys fighting an uprising in Meereen, Cersei struggling with the Faith Militant in King's Landing, Sansa dealing with Ramsay at Winterfell, Brienne traveling in the North, Arya training at the House of Black and White, Jon navigating his newfound leadership duties at Castle Black, Stannis and Ser Davos marching their army south, and Jaime trying to rescue Myrcella in Dorne.

That's a lot of story. So much, in fact, that *Thrones* was occasionally leaving major characters out of certain episodes, or gave them just a few minutes of screen time, even though series regulars are paid for every episode produced whether they're used or not. One major arc—Bran's journey to becoming the Three-Eyed Raven—was sidelined for the entire fifth season. The Hound was likewise benched that year. Asking an actor to take a year off is always risky or expensive, as they need to be kept under contract lest they get snatched up by other projects. Plus, all those storylines meant that *Thrones* had grown from filming with two units to occasionally using four (dubbed Wolf, Dragon, Raven, and White Walker). Having four units shooting an ambitious fantasy television series at the same time in different locations was a madcap juggling act that was very tough on the crew and made it more difficult for the producers to maintain quality.

In other words, adding even more characters and locations to *Thrones*, from a practical storytelling and production standpoint, seemed totally impossible . . . though, to be fair, making a "totally impossible" adaptation was always part of the deal. Martin made it clear from the outset that he was was writing a story that was shattering storytelling conventions, so it's perhaps not surprising that the author would continue to find new ways of doing so.

DAVID BENIOFF: We didn't want to do a ten-year adaptation of the books. We didn't want to spend four years with Dany in Meereen. If we were to remain entirely faithful to *A Feast for Crows,* half the characters—the most popular characters—would be absent from the screen. There would be no Tyrion, no Dany, no Arya, no Jon Snow. It's always been about adapting the series as a whole and following the map George laid out for us and the major milestones but not necessarily each of the stops along the way. It's an adaptation. It had to adapt in order to survive.

GEORGE R. R. MARTIN: I thought *Feast for Crows* and *Dance with Dragons* would be recombined, because you can't separate them the way I did in the books, and I thought there were three seasons there. At the very least, two seasons. But they got through it all in one season because they eliminated so much. They really started taking shortcuts and cutting things. They eliminated Lady Stoneheart and Quentyn Martell and his voyage across the world and Tyrion's journey where he goes to Pentos and hooks up with Magister Illyrio, and then he crosses the hills and meets up with Jon Connington and Aegon on the river and they make the long journey down the river to Volantis and they encounter Jorah Mormont, who takes him prisoner—they skipped over that.

DAVID BENIOFF: We don't get bonus points for being strictly faithful to the books. It doesn't give us anything extra. For every decision, if there's a fork in the road and the fork to the left is strictly adhering to the books and to the right is what's better for the series, we're always going to take that path to the right.

GEORGE R. R. MARTIN: So I thought I had three years to get out the next book, and suddenly I was racing to get it out before season five. I realized season five was supposed to come out in April [of 2015], and my publisher said, "If we get it in by the end of the year, we can rush it out in March." I said, "Okay, I can still get this one book out before the next season." When it became clear I wasn't going to have it done by the end of the year, it really took a lot of wind out of my sails. Suddenly, they were ahead of me. I should have gotten the last two books out sooner.

The producers attempted to represent some of Martin's new characters. The show introduced the Sand Snakes in Dorne and added Euron Greyjoy in the Iron Islands. But the jettisoned character fans clamored to see the most was one who had only a couple of cryptic appearances in the books—Lady Stoneheart. At the end of *A Storm of Swords,* Catelyn Stark was resurrected from her Red Wedding fate as a silent undead specter of vengeance. The reveal is one of the most shocking moments in the books. The character also appears in one more subsequent chapter, but her purpose to readers is not yet clear.

GEORGE R. R. MARTIN: Lady Stoneheart has a role in the books. Whether it's sufficient or interesting enough . . . I think it is or I wouldn't have put her in. One of the things I wanted to show with her is that the death she suffered changes you.

DAVID BENIOFF: There was never really much debate about [including Lady Stoneheart]. There is that one great scene.

DAN WEISS: *That* was the only debate. The scene where she first shows up is one of the best "holy shit" moments in the books. I think that scene is where the public response came from. But then . . .

DAVID BENIOFF: We can't go into detail. Part of the reason we didn't want to put it in had to do with things coming up in George's books that we don't want to spoil [by discussing them]. Part of it too was we knew we had Jon Snow's resurrection coming up. Too many resurrections start to diminish the impact of characters' dying. We wanted to keep our powder dry for that. And Catelyn's last moment was so fantastic, and Michelle is such a great actress, to bring her back as a zombie who doesn't speak felt like diminishing returns.

Another popular mythological aspect of the books that was pared back was the direwolves, which play a larger role in Martin's novels. The issue with the direwolves wasn't a storytelling problem, or a lack of interest by the writers, but purely a technical challenge. Once the wolves became larger than ordinary wolves, the show struggled to find ways to portray them in a convincing manner. After using dogs in the first season, the production subsequently filmed real wolves and used CG to make them larger. Even so, there was a degree of uncanniness to their shots that became difficult to disguise.

DAN WEISS: We did some testing, and at a certain point they look unreal. We reached a nice balance with them.

DAVID BENIOFF: With dragons you get some leeway. You don't say, "Well, that doesn't look like a real dragon." And dragons are easier to animate since they don't have fur.

DAN WEISS: With a wolf you have a million years of evolution telling you what they're supposed to act like.

BRYAN COGMAN: The show had constraints and the wolves were very challenging to pull off in a way that looked good.

So what, then, did the direwolves mean? Their fates seemed loosely connected to that of each Stark. Jon Snow's direwolf was Ghost, which was appropriate for a man who rose from the dead. Bran's direwolf was Summer, the opposite of the supernatural winter force that Bran was destined to confront. Sansa's direwolf, Lady, was killed by the Lannisters and then she was ensnared by them as well. Robb Stark's Grey Wind was trapped and shot with crossbows just like his master. Rickon Stark's Shaggydog was slain by men loyal to Ramsay Bolton, then the boy died by Ramsay's arrow shortly thereafter. And Arya's Nymeria was chased into the wild, where she found her strength and independence. ("That's not you," Arya told Nymeria when she was reunited with her wolf in season seven, echoing her own line—"That's not me"—to her father in season one.)

BRYAN COGMAN: [Arya and Nymeria are] lone wolves. They can't go back to the way things were. It was also a foreshadow for what Arya was going to encounter when she reunited with her family.

MAISIE WILLIAMS (*Arya Stark*): Nymeria has created her own world and created her own pack and wasn't ready to be Arya's pet. To be someone's pet would reverse everything she's learned. So they just regard each other and go their separate ways.

BRYAN COGMAN: The direwolves were supposed to mean more than they ended up meaning. A lot of plans for the direwolves ended up not coming to fruition. Even in the first season, there were a lot of direwolf scenes we had to cut even though we were just using dogs because the dogs couldn't execute the scenes; it would just take too long.

That aside, I think the direwolves represent the spirit of the North and the soul of House Stark and the soul of those characters. It's no accident Lady was killed and Sansa was left on her own, and it was no accident that Grey Wind was put in a cage, and it was no accident Nymeria found her independence and went her own way. But we never really wanted to lean too heavily into the spirit-animal trope of it all. And certainly in the books, the direwolves function in a different way. Arya and

Jon are wargs in the books, and Sansa and Robb would have been except their wolves died—I don't know that for a fact, but I assume so.

After season four, Martin decided to stop writing scripts for *Thrones*. He told the producers he needed to focus on finishing his novels.

DAVID BENIOFF: It wasn't a contentious thing, it wasn't a screaming match. He just felt like he needed to prioritize the book, and that made sense to us.

The showrunners had to figure out how best to use what they knew of Martin's master plan to plot their remaining hours, and they emphasized the silver lining of their show surpassing the books.

DAN WEISS: We chose to see it as a great thing on both sides. There's this amazing world George has created, and now there are two different versions out there. There's no reason we can see why you can't be thrilled and surprised and dismayed by both of these two different versions of this world.

Ultimately, Martin and the showrunners are passionate creatives grappling with a staggeringly complex tale in two very different mediums. Despite their occasional disagreements, each side is respectful of the other, even in private. Benioff and Weiss never fail to express the magnitude of their respect for Martin's writing, while Martin is grateful for the show and says the showrunners did a great job overall despite aspects that he wishes were different.

DAVID BENIOFF: We don't always agree on everything in the series, but we have a great relationship with him.

GEORGE R. R. MARTIN: One thing David and Dan did really right, that I couldn't have done if I was the showrunner, is the vast majority of our Emmys are for below the line—costuming, set decoration, stunt work, and so on. They put together an incredible team of craftsmen, and some of them were new to the industry or without a lot of credits. If it were me, I would have done what most people would have done and picked people I've worked with before who are competent. But would they have been the extraordinary people David and Dan found?

Martin's comment brings up a frequent point made by those interviewed for this book. Several cast and crew members emphasized that Benioff and Weiss never received enough public credit for their hands-on involvement with the nonwriting aspects of the production, from supervising filming to overseeing decisions made by a variety of departments. The showrunners received praise (and criticism) for story elements, but few outsiders realize how many other facets of the *Thrones* production likewise bore their fingerprints.

DEBORAH RILEY (*production designer*): David and Dan don't get the credit they deserve for being the leaders that they are. They gathered a team of workaholic perfectionists who they trusted with their work. We all were allowed to get on with our jobs, but it was always their vision that we were trying to fulfill. They would have to approve everything; we wouldn't put anything on set they had not seen. So the sheer volume of work they were presented with that they would have to comment on and provide advice about was phenomenal. I cannot bear to have them criticized.

SIBEL KEKILLI (*Shae*): Dan and David took really good care of us. They'd invited us to their house in Belfast to have Thanksgiving dinner with their families. They'd take two actors to dinner one night, then another two actors to dinner the next night. They really tried to make sure we had a good time when we had days off.

LENA HEADEY (*Cersei Lannister*): David and Dan were always there. They were there 24/7. They didn't just leave and sit in an office. They were there.

But for Martin, being creatively involved with *Game of Thrones*—and commenting on it publicly—became increasingly difficult after season five. How can an author talk about, for instance, the Battle of the Bastards when he likely has his own very different, yet still unpublished, version of the same battle in his mind?

DAN WEISS: The differences between the show and the books became difficult to track in parallel. It's almost like George was in a weird science fiction movie trying to keep two similar-but-different universes in his mind at the same time.

GEORGE R. R. MARTIN: It's been an incredible ride, and almost all of it has been great. The show is the end for a lot of people. It's not the end for me. I'm still deeply in it. I better live a long time, because I have a lot of work left to do.

CHAPTER EIGHTEEN

A DETOUR TO DORNE

Not all of Martin's new characters from *A Feast for Crows* and *A Dance with Dragons* were left only on the page. Producers added Dorne to the show as a new location and introduced Oberyn Martell's trio of bastard daughters, the Sand Snakes, who sought vengeance for their father's death. Even just adding the Sand Snakes, however, required some concessions. In the books, there are eight Sand Snakes. The show originally planned to introduce four and ended up with three—Obara, Nymeria, and Tyene. Oberyn's paramour Ellaria Sand was similarly combined with another character to serve as Tyene's mother. The result would be one of *Thrones'* most unique storylines, but one that garnered mixed reactions and sometimes struggled to feel like an organic part of the show.

BRYAN COGMAN (*co–executive producer*): Dorne was always tricky. When you read the book, it's essentially a spin-off within the book. It's really compelling. It's really interesting. But it's an entirely new cast of characters, and it only really links up with the main storyline through Myrcella. For a long time, I didn't think we were going to do it. Season five is not the time when you normally introduce twenty-five new characters.

DAVID BENIOFF (*showrunner*): There weren't a lot of ways to cram it in. But it's such an important place. Of all the places in Westeros you'd ever want to settle, the Dornish seem to have it figured out in terms of their approach to life. And Indira Varma, once you have someone of her caliber, you're doubling down on that casting strength.

BRYAN COGMAN: I proposed that Jaime would be a good way in. You take one of our main characters and use that person as an audience surrogate into this new world and that might be a way that we can do a version of Dorne that fits in our framework and, frankly, within the time and budgetary constraints of the show.

Another advantage of adding Dorne was it gave the show an organic way to add more diverse actors to its cast. One longtime criticism of *Thrones* was that its core players were overwhelmingly white. It was a point that was raised more frequently during the show's latter seasons, as Hollywood studios were increasingly urged to make on- and off-camera diversity a greater priority.

Casting director Nina Gold explained the team's initial thinking to *Vanity Fair*'s Joanna Robinson: "Even though these are fantasy worlds, there are tribes, families, and dynasties. Once you've put one mark on the canvas for the Targaryens or the Starks, you really owe it to . . . the authenticity of trying to make them a family somehow. In the books, the Targaryens are these white, white people with silver hair and violet eyes. The Starks are kind of rough, like Northern English people. The Lannisters are golden, aren't they? We really believed we were doing it like the books, basically."

Jessica Henwick (Nymeria Sand), Keisha Castle-Hughes (Obara Sand), and Rosabell Laurenti Sellers (Tyene Sand) were cast as the Sand Snakes. Each of the actresses came from a different ethnic background and adopted her own twist on the Latin-inspired accent Pascal had created for Prince Oberyn. The trio trained for months to learn fighting and weapon skills.

JESSICA HENWICK (*Nymeria Sand*): Originally David and Dan planned to have Obara, Tyene, Nymeria, and Sarella—they wanted four sisters. Then they realized during casting that was going to be too many to introduce during a short period of time. When I auditioned they were thinking of cutting Nymeria and I was like, "*Nooooo*," because as a fan that was the one I wanted. I auditioned two or three times, and Sarella, unfortunately, was lost.

KEISHA CASTLE-HUGHES (*Obara Sand*): I knew that season there would be a call for brown actors. My people, if you will, just kept pushing and annoying [casting director Nina Gold]. As soon as I got the part, we started training. A lot of my training was in the martial arts of wushu. It was maybe about five months of lead-up.

JESSICA HENWICK: My whip was a really scary weapon because you're just as likely to injure yourself. I hit myself so many times. I hit Rosabell; I hit my younger sister across her cheek.

DAVE HILL: I remember them at dinner the night before we first shot the Sand Snakes. The girls were so excited. They'd been inventing backstories for themselves, and they were running them by David and Dan and me, and David was making up some of it on the spot. They were super thrilled.

INDIRA VARMA (*Ellaria Sand*): It was great to be inventing our own country, not just being visitors in King's Landing. The previous season I felt like I was a guest in someone else's show.

The Sand Snakes were introduced in a scene with Ellaria as they plotted how to best avenge Oberyn's death. They also tortured a ship's captain buried up to his neck in the sand with scorpions on his head to get information about Jaime Lannister coming to Dorne.

JESSICA HENWICK: It was a trial by fire from day one. Straightaway there's a real actor buried up to his neck in the sand, real scorpions on his head, real whip, real camera, real crew—let's go. I had to knock the bucket off the head of this guy with my whip. The crew got out riot shields to protect themselves. I remember the scorpion handler coming up to me and being like, "Please don't kill my babies."

INDIRA VARMA: I was so anxious about the scorpions I kept forgetting my lines.

DAVID BENIOFF: It was fun watching them together because they're three half sisters and constantly fighting, but it's the kind of family that if anyone else, like an outsider, comes in, they all band together and unify.

KEISHA CASTLE-HUGHES: It was interesting because I felt like the Sand Snakes moved as a unit. We didn't really have individual storylines.

MARK MYLOD (director): It felt fine. They're really good actors. But it was not the kick-ass introduction to such important characters in the novel that I wanted it to be. If I'm being honest, it was difficult to find the characters beyond the "kick-ass." I was trying to find a sense of family, which is massively key to all the show's characters. The balance between the intimate and the epic is exactly what's so brilliant about *Game of Thrones*. We'd always been successful at creating those bonds so the audience could latch on to those relationships. It didn't feel to me like it was gelling.

JESSICA HENWICK: It was always acknowledged that it was going to be very hard to give each of us a storyline. They had to introduce three characters all at once and differentiate them. When you're limited to an introduction of two lines per character, and there's four characters in the scene during our introduction, it's hard to create a lasting impression. You kind of have to shove a character down the audience's throat, and *Game of Thrones'* success is in its multifaceted characters.

One element from that debut scene was changed in post-production. A leaked set photo revealed that Obara's original breastplate armor had nipples. Costume designer Michele Clapton later admitted to *New York* magazine that the *Batman Forever*–like design was "slightly cheesy" and a mistake due to the structured molds that were used and weren't noticed until filming was already under way. Ironically, one expression from Martin's novels is "like nipples on a breastplate," meaning that something is useless. Thanks to some CGI, the nipples were, um, tweaked.

Even so, critics struggled with the Dorne scenes. "Every time we flash to beautiful Dorne, they're just angrily trying to get revenge for Oberyn with no space for nuance or surprise, so it ends up feeling as if we're watching the same scene again and again," wrote *The Washington Post*'s Travis M. Andrews. One scene singled out in particular was a fight at the House Martell palace, the Water Gardens. The setup was that Jaime and Bronn were infiltrating the palace seeking to kidnap/rescue Myrcella (Nell Tiger Free) when they were attacked by the Sand Snakes. In any other series, the sequence would have been perfectly suitable. But *Thrones* had set a very high bar for its fight scenes.

BRYAN COGMAN: The Water Gardens fight, as I conceived it, happened at night. That's when you would sneak into a palace to steal someone. You'd do it at night.

DAVE HILL: It was a perfect storm. We had this gorgeous location, the Alcázar palace, but we weren't allowed to shoot there at night. So we couldn't have night infiltration, when you'd logically do it. But at least we could have a cool fight during the day, where you can see everything. Then we lost our stunt people a few days before, so we had to make do with what the actors had learned up until that point and cut around it. The Water Gardens fight was supposed to be much more elaborate. I remember Jeremy at the time not being happy with it.

JEREMY PODESWA (*director*): I actually don't remember that. I do remember we thought we were going to be using the doubles a lot more than we did. The actresses were great. They had worked really hard and had become really proficient, so we used the doubles as little as possible.

JESSICA HENWICK: I was going back and forth every two days to do fight training. They always said, "You're going to do most of [the fight] yourself."

JEREMY PODESWA: The only "perfect storm" I remember was that we literally had a storm in the middle of it. A total deluge. The actors were getting drenched, and nothing matched. Finally [Bernadette Caulfield] was like, "Okay, stop," because it just became so ridiculous. It was one of the rare times where we had to stop shooting and Bernie admitted defeat in the face of an uncontrollable act of God.

JESSICA HENWICK: It was definitely drizzling? I don't remember it pouring. . . .

Producers originally planned more Dorne scenes in season five but later cut down the storyline.

DAVE HILL: We thought it would be a fun adventure, but it fell prey to all the other storylines. Once we realized how long Daznak's Pit and "Hardhome" were going to take to shoot, we realized one storyline had to be cut down a bit.

The Dorne thread was quickly tied up early in season six, with each of Oberyn's children and Ellaria meeting various tragic fates (which are discussed in more detail later). But for the producers, the fan reaction to the Dorne scenes seemed to confirm what they'd initially suspected: It's extremely difficult for a television show to add several cars onto a moving train that's already halfway to its destination.

DAVID BENIOFF: There are times I'm watching shows, or even reading books, where I'm wondering, "Why are we spending time with these characters we don't really know or care about when I want to be with that person instead?" The big lesson was there are characters who mean so much to us and that's who we want to spend time with. It's their journeys we're most curious about seeing where they go.

DAN WEISS: In a book you can branch out into a whole different world. But if you do that in television, for whatever reason, a different set of rules apply. I'm sure it would have been fascinating to build out a proper Dorne, but the time it would take would come at the expense of what we needed to cover.

BRYAN COGMAN: There's a lot of great work in those Dorne sequences, and I think the way it all resolves—particularly in the scene with Lena and Indira in the prison cell—is very interesting and messy and compelling. Ultimately, it was hard to make it feel like something other than an offshoot. It was a lesson in how much you can expand a TV show.

JESSICA HENWICK: It was definitely a frustrating feeling, like there's so much potential here, and a lot of the stuff that we shot didn't make the final cut. It was hard. But overall, given the size of the character, I've been very happy with how it came out. It was still so worth it.

CHAPTER NINETEEN

RUNNING ON FAITH

G ame of Thrones didn't really do "themes." The writers thought about their show in terms of individual characters and story-lines, and there were so many of each scattered across Westeros and Essos that the idea of trying to tie a bunch of threads together to form some kind of unifying idea was unworkable and, arguably, unnecessary.

But season five had a theme.

"A major theme of that season was the old world colliding with the new and these fundamentalist thinkers vying for power," Bryan Cogman said. "The Sparrows were fundamentalists. . . . The Sons of the Harpy were fundamentalists who turn to terror tactics to oust an occupier. . . . Members of the Night's Watch who objected to Jon Snow trying to bring the Wildlings from Hardhome are fundamentalists."

Melisandre too was a religious fundamentalist, one whose faith had devastating consequences. And Arya wrestled with the cultlike ortho-doxy of the House of Black and White.

Fans often think season five had a theme too, only a different one: Season five was "the dark one," the season with some of the show's grim-mest and most disturbing subject matter, where popular characters suf-fered horribly. The dive into darkness wasn't an accident and followed classic story structure. The most dire moment for a traditional hero, when all seems lost, is always at the end of act two of three. Season five

Ygritte and Jon Snow face off.

Ygritte falls at Castle Black in the arms of Jon Snow.

Bran's direwolf, Summer, and Jojen Reed (Thomas Brodie-Sangster).

Theon Greyjoy's torment begins.

Robb Stark (Richard Madden) and Talisa Stark (Oona Chaplin) in love.

Robb grieves for Talisa
at the Red Wedding.

Catelyn Stark (Michelle Fairley) makes a desperate final attempt to save her son.

Margaery Tyrell (Natalie Dormer) learns about crossbows
and a king thanks to Joffrey Baratheon.

Brienne of Tarth (Gwendoline Christie) squares off with
Jaime Lannister (Nikolaj Coster-Waldau) on a bridge.

Ros (Esmé Bianco) in service.

Theon (Alfie Allen) gives his tormentor
Ramsay Bolton (Iwan Rheon) a close shave.

Oberyn "the Red Viper" Martell (Pedro Pascal) fights
Ser Gregor "the Mountain" Clegane (Hafþór Björnsson).

Emilia Clarke gets some shade on the set of season four.

Isaac Hempstead Wright on the move in Northern Ireland.

Sandor "the Hound" Clegane (Rory McCann) fights Brienne.

Margaery Tyrell and King Joffrey at the Purple Wedding.

Joffrey struggles for breath.

Obara Sand (Keisha Castle-Hughes)
takes a stand.

Tyene Sand (Rosabell Laurenti Sellers) prepares to get stabby.

Sansa Stark (Sophie Turner) prepares to marry Ramsay Bolton
in "Unbowed, Unbent, Unbroken."

Sansa and Ramsay on their wedding night.

Shireen Baratheon (Kerry Ingram) resists her fate.

Nymeria Sand (Jessica Henwick) whips a prisoner into submission.

Tyene Sand and Ellaria Sand (Indira Varma) in their final moment.

Shae (Sibel Kekilli) takes the stand against Tyrion.

Tyrion Lannister on trial.

A completed post-effects shot of the village of Hardhome with its stockade
border wall in the aftermath of the Army of the Dead attack.

A closer look at Hardhome.

The Night King (Richard Brake) raises the dead at Hardhome.

likewise concluded roughly two-thirds of the way through
(A final act typically has the hero, having learned from t
rising to conquer their greatest challenge or succumbing to
just as *Thrones*' major characters did in the final three seaso

"We knew in the writing and execution that season five w
est and most troubling season," Cogman said. "We put our
through hell, but it's a very carefully thought-out hell. Seaso
meant to break a lot of these characters down."

In King's Landing, Cersei thought she could use the pow
Sparrows to the crown's advantage. Then their leader, the High
(Jonathan Pryce), turned the tables.

GEORGE R. R. MARTIN (*author, co-executive producer*): The Sp
are my version of the medieval Catholic Church, with a fantasy
Instead of the Trinity—the father, the son, and the holy ghost—you
the Seven, one god with seven aspects. In the Middle Ages you had
ods where you had very worldly and corrupt popes and bishops who w
not spiritual but were politicians. They were playing their own version
the game of thrones.

Having the legendary Pryce on set occasionally knocked the show'
producers and directors onto their heels.

MARK MYLOD (*director*): I was a massive fan of the show, but I didn't
have the résumé that would really support me being a director on it. I just
really wanted to work with those writers and characters. On my first day,
I turned up in Dubrovnik to join a location scout with all the department
heads. I stood up on one of those ancient walls in Old Town with everybody waiting for me to say what to do, and I had no idea what was expected of me. I just felt absolute bloody blind terror. I just had to pull
stuff out of my butt to pretend like I knew what I was talking about. Then
my first take was of Jonathan as the High Sparrow, and it was his first big
scene with Lena.

DAVE HILL (*co-producer*): During rehearsal, Jonathan asked to change some words. Usually on *Thrones* our response to actors who ask to do that is, "No." We've thought about those words. No changing, no improvising, no adding to them. And Jonathan was making changes. I turned to Bryan: "That's not what the line is. . . ." And Bryan glared at me. It was the closest he ever came to murdering me. Bryan went, "If you think I'm going to tell Jonathan Pryce he can't cut words on his first day on our set, you're crazy."

MARK MYLOD: I love working with actors and directing them. But after Jonathan's first take I didn't have a single piece of direction, not one idea, apart from my jaw open on the floor at the absolute perfection of his first take, literally down to the movements of his feet. It was almost embarrassing how good he was.

DAVE HILL: Mark came up to the monitors: "Am I crazy, or did he just nail everything in that whole thing?" Nope, you're totally right. Even Lena was a little nervous around Jonathan.

NATALIE DORMER (*Margaery Tyrell*): Jonathan Pryce was the best sparring partner any actor could ever hope to have. He has such an affable, self-deprecating, charismatic manner about him. The way Jonathan played the character came across so sincere. It was "Who's bluffing who?" He's not like any other man Margaery has had to handle, where she could just throw her sensuality at him or use their greed or ego against them. The High Sparrow indulges none of these things.

Handling Pryce was a cakewalk, however, compared to the show's *other* intractable British silver-screen legend.

MARK MYLOD: I was also terrified of Diana Rigg, because my very first scene with her I asked her to do a very minor thing. Like, "Would it make sense if you close the door and walk a few paces before this moment?"

She came back with some rebuttal about why she wanted to do it another way and then said: "Thank you! Go away!" I became a five-year-old boy. I could feel myself blushing and creeping back to my monitor, stripped of any kind of dignity or authority. So I enjoyed killing her later on.

JESSICA HENWICK (*Nymeria Sand*): Have you been hearing Diana Rigg stories? We had a scene. She walked onto the set, and she went, "I'm ready now!" A cameraman came over and went, "Well, okay, but we haven't finished setting up." She interrupted him and said, "Roll the cameras!" And she just started doing her lines. She did two takes, and then the guy came over and was like, "Great, now we're going to do a close-up." And she just stood up and she went, "I'm done!"

Now, she can't walk fast. She has to be helped. So basically we just sat there and watched as Diana Rigg effectively did her own version of storming off the set, but it was at 0.1 miles per hour. She cracked me up. I loved her.

NATALIE DORMER: When you have someone who has that many accolades, you just shut up and watch. She had a very dry sense of humor and was aware of the parody of herself. Sometimes I think she was mischievous to see what she could get away with.

EMILIA CLARKE (*Daenerys Targaryen*): I only had one scene with her and was very blessed to have had that. Like with Peter, it was watching an acting master class. I kept thinking: "Okay, not my line yet, I'm not just watching you—really! I'm acting *with* you. . . ."

DAVE HILL: When Miguel Sapochnik was directing Pryce and Rigg, they were kind of just fucking with him. I went to Miguel with a little performance note and he goes, "I've got Jonathan Pryce and an English dame on my hands right now, sit down, I have to deal with this." They were batting him back and forth like a ball of yarn between two cats.

The High Sparrow was aided by the heartless Septa Unella (Hannah Waddingham), his devout servant, who tortured Cersei, urging her to "confess."

HANNAH WADDINGHAM (*Septa Unella*): The director, Miguel Sapochnik—he's a very intense man—he would come out from behind the camera and try to get me to do as little as possible; like, [I have the] the widest smile and most overactive face. He said, "Trust me, the *least* you do will be more terrifying." He'd squeeze his cheeks together with his hands, going, "*Less! Less!*" and by the third or fourth time he did it, I was like, "Dude, seriously. I can't do any less. You should have gotten a white dinner plate in a wimple." But, of course, he was right. I was doing the least I've ever done, and it spoke the most.

There was also one scene where I may have given Lena an extra whack on the head with the spoon. The spoon was rubber, but still. You can see it in the show, when her jaw tenses and she looks up at me, like: *I'm gonna get you after this.* And, of course, she did, but it's nothing you can print. It added a little something. We've been great pals ever since.

Across the Narrow Sea, Daenerys was on a winning streak. She conquered Slaver's Bay, sacked Astapor, liberated Yunkai, and invaded Meereen, where she took residence in an eight-hundred-foot pyramid. Once again on *Thrones,* ruling proved far trickier than conquest. The harder Daenerys tried to reform the cities' slave-based traditions, the more they rebelled against her.

One of Daenerys's losses was particularly distressing. Her trusted protector and advisor Ser Barristan Selmy (Ian McElhinney) was slain by the terror group Sons of the Harpy. Daenerys took the loss hard. Actor Ian McElhinney took it hard as well. Selmy is still alive in Martin's books, and McElhinney naturally assumed his character would continue further into the show. "I gave [Benioff and Weiss] some arguments of my own why I thought Barristan was kind of important in Daenerys's story, important enough that he should stay in Daenerys's story," the actor told *HuffPost*.

IAN MCELHINNEY (*Barristan Selmy*): It proves you should probably not read the books [if you're an actor on the show]. I was disappointed. But you have to accept—as I accepted—that the demands of TV are different than the demands of book writing. With TV there's a pressure to create a number of high points. One of the big things about this series—it's true in the books and even more true in the series—is the surprise element, the shocks. They had to keep that up because people expect that. You can't predict anything, but what you can predict is that there will be surprises.

The writers killed off Ser Barristan partly to create a vacancy among Daenerys's advisors. Three episodes later, Tyrion joined up with the Breaker of Chains (a meetup that has not yet happened in Martin's books). McElhinney was pleased, however, that Ser Barristan at least went down with his sword in hand.

IAN MCELHINNEY: He had to be seen fighting. He'd been talked about as the greatest knight who ever was, so he had to fight. So that's great that he did.

Interestingly, when asked his favorite Ser Barristan scene, McElhinney said it was from the show's first season, when Joffrey unfairly fired the legendary knight from the Kingsguard. It's rather fitting—and a credit to the show's spot-on casting—that an actor who protested his dismissal in real life liked best the scene where his character was dismissed, took off his armor, threw it on the ground, and stormed off.

McElhinney's reaction wasn't entirely unique either. Benioff and Weiss say actors largely took their "death calls" well, but occasionally a cast member was clearly disappointed by the news.

DAVID BENIOFF (*showrunner*): Most of the time actors kind of knew when their time was up. Once we were ahead of the books and making those phone calls, some actors were stoic about it—"Oh, that's cool." Some were a little upset.

DAN WEISS (*showrunner*): I won't name the actor, but there was one who protested vociferously.

DAVID BENIOFF: One person argued with us on the phone for a half hour and then wrote a long letter why it was a mistake and still talks about it on whatever dumb forums he's on. But most people are great even when they're disappointed.

Back in Westeros, Stannis marched his army toward Winterfell and was beset by a crippling winter storm that threatened to trap and starve tens of thousands of his men. The uptight would-be king; his wife, Selyse; and his mistress, Melisandre, were fundamentalists of the worst kind, fanatics who burned so-called heretics. But what happens when you're a true believer in the Lord of Light and are told the only way to change the weather and save your army is to sacrifice your own daughter to your god?

DAVE HILL: There are a lot of people claiming to know the gods' will and claiming to speak for god or gods. We like playing with the idea that the gods, if they exist, maybe have their own agenda and ulterior motives. Humans can glimpse them, but you can't really ascribe human notions and actions and consequence to gods—that's what makes them gods.

CARICE VAN HOUTEN (*Melisandre*): I thought, "This is the end of my sympathy point." I knew my days as a friendly character were over. I knew the audience was going to hate me from then on. They didn't like me in the first place, but that was really pushing it, and rightfully so. But at the same time I thought it was so bold and cruel and epic, even though it was awful.

LIAM CUNNINGHAM (*Davos Seaworth*): When I read the script, I thought, "You've got to be fucking kidding me." But it's genius dramatically. When Stannis tells Davos to [leave their camp for Castle Black], you know you're not getting that information for a very fucking good reason. I've had shouts from people on the street, "Why didn't you stay?!" and I shout, "I tried!"

CARICE VAN HOUTEN: I don't know how to play evil. The only thing I can do is play that this is for the greater good and my methods are not . . . *friendly,* and to think there's something even worse out there and that I'm actually doing people a favor. If I thought about it too much I don't know if I could do it, so I just had to go into a completely different zone.

Stannis couldn't bring himself to tell his angelic young daughter, Shireen (Kerry Ingram), what he was going to do to her. So in the next scene, guards slowly led a confused Shireen through a crowd of soldiers. At first, the girl seemed uncertain of where she was going and why. Then she saw the funeral pyre and realized: Her own father had condemned her to die. Shireen called to her parents, begging them to save her.

Stannis killing his daughter was one of the most agonizing scenes in *Thrones* and one of the moments Martin had told the producers he was planning for *The Winds of Winter* (though the book version of the scene will play out a bit differently).

DAVID NUTTER (*director*): A lot of the screaming was ad-libbed. When Shireen is screaming and crying for her mother, we got that on location [rather than looping it in later] to add the emotional resonance. When the mother finally realizes how awful this is, it's so powerful.

CARICE VAN HOUTEN: The girl was so sweet and cute, and we had fun behind the scenes. Another moment where you're like, "What kind of job is this?"

LIAM CUNNINGHAM: There's an old saying in Hollywood: "Don't work with children or animals." I found the opposite. Kids play for a living, that's their job, and most of us, when we grow up, we put play to one side. Kids are experts at it. Kerry Ingram was incredibly impressive. She has this inner contentment about her, like an old soul. A lot of us aim for things. She's not aiming. She walks on, and there's just 100 percent truth when she speaks.

DAVE HILL: It was harder for the adults than it was for Kerry. She had bubbly kid energy. But Bryan refused to watch. He was like, "No, I have kids of my own. I cannot watch him burn a child." While Stephen was like, "This is pretty rough, guys, even for *Game of Thrones*."

After the brutal sacrifice came the gut-punch twist: The winter storm let up, but Stannis's wife, Selyse, committed suicide and half of his army used the easing of the weather as a chance to desert him. The sacrifice of Shireen might have technically worked, but it had unintended consequences that left Stannis even worse off than before: mostly abandoned and entirely damned.

CARICE VAN HOUTEN: The moment I liked the most was after we had just burned Shireen. I think this is going to help us, it's going to save us, and the snow is melting and she thinks it worked. Then someone comes up and says that it's all gone to hell. I really loved the silent acting of thinking, "*Oh, fuck!*" and to show that with one look. My whole world is upside down. Those few human moments is what I'm better at, but I cannot complain because that's not the character.

DAN WEISS: It's impossible for us to see [Shireen's death] through any other lens than how we view fanaticism. People who watch *Game of Thrones* don't see the world through the same lens as Melisandre and Stannis. To the characters, magic works and is real. That's something that's fun about the genre as a whole; because you see the magic with your own eyes, it gives you a window into the heads of people who do and believe crazy things on faith. I can't really get my head around how those people operate in our own world. But fantasy is a cockeyed window into the heads of people who would do something terrible for an irrational reason.

On the subject of prophecy, the showrunners were in lockstep with Martin's books, where magic is never to be trusted. Cersei was haunted by the witch Maggy the Frog declaring her children would perish and that she would be overthrown by a "younger and more beautiful" queen. But like in the story of Oedipus, Cersei brought about her fate only by desperately trying so hard to avoid it.

Melisandre was wrong about Stannis being "the prince that was promised," and very wrong about sacrificing Shireen. But in season two, the Red Woman burned three leeches, plump with Gendry's royal blood, and told Stannis her spell would bring about the deaths of three usurpers to his claim to the Iron Throne. It was a bold storytelling move to correctly tell viewers that two major characters, Robb Stark and Joffrey Baratheon (along with Balon Greyjoy), were going to be killed in advance. Yet fans were still shocked by those twists because the show had made clear that magic was unreliable. Even now, it remains uncertain if Melisandre's sorcery had anything to do with their fates.

GEORGE R. R. MARTIN: You're supposed to debate that. Melisandre wanted everyone to think that the spell she did with the leeches killed the three kings, but there is another explanation: Her ability to see the future through the flames showed her that the kings were going to die because of the machinations of other characters. Seeing their deaths were coming, she just staged this demonstration to take credit for their deaths.

Martin pointed out that even his use of prophecies had a medieval-history precedent.

GEORGE R. R. MARTIN: It happened in the War of the Roses. One of the lords [Somerset] was prophesied that he would die at [Windsor Castle]. So he always made pains to avoid that castle. But then in the First Battle of St. Albans, he was wounded and died outside a pub that had that castle on its pub sign. You have to look at prophecies carefully and look at the weasel wording.

Later in season five, Jon Snow witnessed some genuine dark magic. The newly elevated lord commander took a band of Night's Watch brothers to rescue a group of Wildlings at a fishing village called Hardhome. The group was overrun by the Night King and his army of undead wights, and the living had to frantically scramble to escape.

To direct the episode, producers initially reached out to Neil Marshall, who had helmed the battles at Blackwater and Castle Black, but he wasn't available. ("My biggest regret," Marshall said, "is that I turned down 'Hardhome.'") So the production took a chance on a newcomer to the show, a director who would evolve *Thrones'* style and raise the bar for action sequences in television and, perhaps, cinema as well.

DAVE HILL: It was trial by fire for Miguel Sapochnik. It was: "Here's our biggest action sequence for season five. We all love it. You don't know all the actors or the crew. Make your magic happen." But Miguel is a super prepper. He came in with a plan of attack. It was all hands on deck for that month, and it came out even better than what we had on the page.

MIGUEL SAPOCHNIK (*director*): In the first draft of "Hardhome," the battle took place on a huge beach with the wights descending from the top of the beach down to the shoreline over the course of the entire fight. But because it's an ambush, the Wildlings are unprepared. We figured that it would only take the wights about forty seconds, running at full pelt, to cover that distance. Adding to the challenge was the simple fact that it was wights versus ninety-five thousand Wildlings, which made seeing much of this on-screen too expensive.

So we started looking for some obstacle to slow down the wights. My first idea was to stem their flow by forcing them through a naturally occurring bottleneck between two cliffs. Eventually we came up with a staked fence that surrounded part of the encampment. It was also a way to avoid seeing beyond a certain point and hiding what we couldn't afford to dress or populate.

[What viewers saw] was essentially a microcosm of the action that we could control and point the camera in almost any direction. We were able to reduce the overall scale of the battle, focus on the massacre aspect, and see a lot less but feel a lot more. The most successful and frightening monster is the one you cannot see.

The production built a stockade wall that was eighteen feet high and three hundred feet long to delay the Army of the Dead. For the wights, prosthetics supervisor Barrie Gower explained to *Making Game of Thrones* that costumed background actors were costumed three different ways: "Super fresh" (those who looked recently killed and wore a minor amount of makeup and prosthetics), "mid-decomps" (those who appeared as if they'd been dead for about six months), and "green screen" (actors who wore green bodysuits with a minimal amount of ragged clothing and were made to look skeletal with CGI during post-production). Sapochnik pitted the groups of wights against the Wildlings during frantic shots, declaring on set, "When I call action, I want you to take them down."

But as usual for shooting *Thrones* battles, the weather gods decided the filming of "Hardhome" would be a perfect time to deliver a massive storm that made everything harder.

DAVE HILL: The rain was coming in *sideways*. It was coming right through the tents. But the rain doesn't really read on the screen. When you see all them running you don't realize it's pouring. They all ran up and down the quarry, over slippery rocks and mud. They had to run up and down over and over and over again.

KIT HARINGTON (*Jon Snow*): It was chaos. Joyous chaos. The weather helped [the performances]. A lot of people remember Battle of the Bastards, but for me Hardhome was the battle I loved the most. I loved shooting it. Story-wise, it was fantastic.

MIGUEL SAPOCHNIK: What impressed me most about Kit is that he thinks his way through the action scenes in the same way he thinks his way through a dialogue scene. He finds time to play the beats in between the action. That episode was endless for him, but he never complained and was always willing to go the extra mile, do the extra take, and put his all into it. I don't know any other actor who works that hard, and it shows in the finished product.

CHRISTOPHER NEWMAN (*producer*): Kit is slight of build but enormously strong. You had to be careful with him because he never says "stop," so you could wear him out. You don't want to drive your leading man into the ground. And we were still worried about the state of his ankle because he wouldn't say anything if it was bothering him. Kit is like Jon Snow in real life. He's the actor who never gives up. And that's a good role model to have for all the other actors and the crew.

DAVE HILL: We had some extras who were Dublin based. They would get picked up at one A.M. and get bused all the way to the north coast to get dressed as Wildlings. They would then lie down on these rocks, with the water washing over them from the rain, and stay there—for *hours*. They'd get home at ten P.M. and then get up again at one A.M. to do it all over again. God bless the Irish.

During the fighting, Jon Snow discovered, to his amazement, that his Valyrian-steel sword could kill White Walkers, a fact that would be key later on. But the big villain of the piece was the Night King. The supernatural leader of the White Walkers and the Army of the Dead was first introduced in season four. During a flashback we'd learned the Children of the Forest had created the Night King thousands of years ago to fight their enemies, the invading First Men, and now, with winter finally arriving, he was leading his legions south to invade Westeros. The Night King was a character-design home run—a striking, stoic, blue-eyed specter of wintry death that quickly became the show's most popular original addition to Martin's mythology.

DAN WEISS: It was almost logical as you went back in time, as you create the prehistory for all this. We've seen what the White Walkers do, we've seen how they perpetuate themselves and created the wights. If you're going backward, well, they made these things . . . so what made them?

We also liked the implication that they weren't some kind of cosmic evil that had been around since the beginning of time, but that the White Walkers had a history—that something that seems legendary and mythological and permanent *wasn't*. They had a historical cause that was comprehensible, just like the way the wars we're seeing are comprehensible. They're the result of people, or beings, with motivations we can understand.

DAVID BENIOFF: I don't think of him as evil; I think of him as Death. And that's what he wants—for all of us. It's why he was created, and that's what he's after.

The Night King was played by actor Richard Brake in seasons four and five, and then Slovak actor and stuntman Vladímir Furdík took over for seasons six through eight. Furdík also played the White Walker that Jon Snow killed in "Hardhome."

VLADÍMIR FURDÍK (*the Night King, seasons 6–8*): Somebody made him the Night King. Nobody knows who he was before—a soldier or part of [nobility]. He never wanted to be the Night King. I think he wants revenge.

The producers decided to keep the character utterly silent, continuing what they had learned after initially wanting the White Walkers to speak during the scrapped pilot.

DAVID BENIOFF: What's he going to say? Anything the Night King says diminishes him.

VLADÍMIR FURDÍK: Every director had a different vision of how to play him. Dan and David wanted him to be like a cold man. Some of the directors wanted to show that there's some human in him. Many times they asked me, "Don't blink your eyes." This was very difficult.

The final shot of "Hardhome" was one of the show's most iconic: The Night King stands on the beach. Jon Snow and the surviving Wildlings were slowly escaping in rowboats. The Night King locked eyes with Jon, raised his arms, and all the slaughtered Wildlings were resurrected to join his Army of the Dead. At that moment, Jon Snow fully understood the Night King's seemingly insurmountable power—and that Westeros was facing a threat that could annihilate them all.

MIGUEL SAPOCHNIK: The silent ending in that moment came from a happy mistake. Someone forgot to extend the music track over that part of the rough cut, and I found it much more powerful without music. All these things are a process. As much as it would be nice to start at the end, it's the process that brings out the best in an idea.

DAVE HILL: It was funny to see that become a meme. In the script we thought of it as the Night King being the conductor of a symphony, raising his hands and raising the dead. But on-screen it came off like, "Come at me, bro."

MIGUEL SAPOCHNIK: Seeing an emoji of the Night King raising his arms was probably the most famous I've ever felt about my work.

KIT HARINGTON: I remember looking back at that beach with the Night King standing there and all the wights are standing up. The camera was behind us on a wide shot, so I was looking at it as [the viewer] would see it—from the front of the boat back at the beach. I'm one of the few people who got to experience that. And it was glorious.

CHAPTER TWENTY

"SHAME . . . SHAME . . . SHAME . . ."

Lena Headey looked so ghastly that you wanted to call for help.

Her hair was shorn ragged, her eyes red rimmed, her pale skin was scabbed and smeared with what looked like blood and pieces of . . . well, hopefully that was only mud?

Yet Headey was happily munching on pizza as Peter Dinklage and Conleth Hill led a chorus of cast and crew singing "Happy Birthday" to the actress.

It was October 2014 in Dubrovnik, and Headey was enjoying a birthday party unlike any other: a cheerful celebration in a production tent between filming scenes in Old Town, followed by taking a long trudge through ancient streets while five hundred bystanders screamed vile obscenities at her.

"Aside from being covered in shit, a girl doesn't want for more," Headey quipped.

The "Walk of Shame" was a gripping sequence adapted from Martin's *A Dance with Dragons*. Modern use of the term stems from college campus slang for a person walking home the morning after sex while still wearing clothes from the previous night out. But Martin's usage was based off the punishment of King Edward IV's mistress Jane Shore in the fifteenth century. After Edward's death in 1483, the king's brother took the throne and charged Shore with conspiracy, accusing her of "sorcery" and "witchcraft." Shore was forced to endure a penance walk through London wearing only a thin white undergarment while the crowd "shamed" her.

LENA HEADEY (*Cersei Lannister*): George told me they used to do it to women in the Middle Ages. Well, they do it *now*. They take women out and stone them to death. Fucking terrifying. I can't even imagine people wanting your blood. Cersei has done wrong, but I don't think anyone deserved that treatment.

GEORGE R. R. MARTIN (*author, co—executive producer*): It was a punishment directed at women to break their pride, and Cersei is defined by her pride.

Shooting the season-five sequence was a major challenge to pull off in the middle of a popular tourist destination. During the planning phase, a Dubrovnik church tried to block the Walk of Shame from filming, citing a city policy against "public displays of sexuality." Producers still managed to get permission but had to switch a key scene to a different location within Old Town. The religious protest was ironic given the sequence's striking similarity to one of the most iconic biblical stories: the Walk of Shame plays like a gender-swapped version of Jesus being forced to walk to his crucifixion through the streets of Jerusalem while he's abused by a screaming crowd.

Another production issue was far trickier to solve. Headey informed the producers she did not want to appear nude and suggested Cersei perform the penance partly clothed instead. In Martin's book, Cersei was stripped naked, and the producers likewise believed nudity was essential to the sequence.

DAVID BENIOFF (*showrunner*): They're trying to shame her. They're trying to humiliate her as much as they possibly can. It's supposed to be like a scene from a nightmare. And the nightmare is you're walking naked in front of a city of people. It's a common anxiety dream to be naked in front of people. I don't think it's as common that you're in your pajamas in front of people. It's much more horrific if they've just completely dehumanized you and taken off all your clothes and you have nothing to hide behind.

LENA HEADEY: I chose not to be naked for many reasons. [After the episode aired] some people thought I was less of an actress because I didn't get my tits out. That was really a bit shocking. I've done nudity. I'm not averse to it. But I'm a very emotional actor, and I get really driven by that. In order to do my job, I allow myself to be really vulnerable. I don't know any other way to do my job. Things really affect me. The thought of being naked for three days and trying to contain her in the way she would be . . . I think I would feel very angry. I didn't want to be angry. I don't think Cersei would be angry. I film every year and I have kids and it was just too much on top of that.

The production came up with a solution: Headey would perform the walk while wearing the plain Jane Shore–like shift, and they would cast another actress as her body double to perform the same walk nude and then merge the two actors with CGI—put Headey's head on another actor's body, stitching them together like a naked Frankenstein's monster.

The production put out a casting call, and roughly one thousand actresses applied for the role.

DAVID NUTTER (director): The most difficult thing was to find an actress who could look like Lena but also knew how to copy Lena's emotional state. I had to almost have a psychological therapy session with the actors. I said, "This is going to be a three-day event, and you have to be prepared for the fact that it's very probable somebody will get a shot of this from the crowd and you'll be trending as the most important thing online. Can you handle that?"

Seven finalists were flown to Belfast for final auditions. Nutter and the producers gave the role to a newcomer, Rebecca Van Cleave.

DAVID NUTTER: Rebecca was the only actress to do the audition with her underwear on; everybody else did it naked. But she had this quality that matched Lena, especially where her shoulders and neck were concerned.

REBECCA VAN CLEAVE (*Cersei's body double*): It was the most comfortable casting I've ever had, considering.

LENA HEADEY: Rebecca is a great actress, and she was aware of what it was. It was a long process trying to find somebody who got what it means physically to be there. But people assume I picked her. Like I was in the casting and I demanded to have a hot body. In reality I said, "If somebody will do this, I have no choice about it, whatever you decide. If somebody is brave enough to do it, I applaud it." I had no judgment in that or desire to be involved. I wanted to clear that up, because as a woman that drives me mad—the thought I'm in a room going, "Nope! Nope!"

To prepare for the scene, Headey and Van Cleave walked Cersei's path through Old Town, discussing precisely how the character would feel and move as each stage unfolded.

DAVID NUTTER: I wanted to make Lena and Rebecca feel like a team. So the day before shooting we went to the location and walked through it, so they had a great tag team as to what they were doing.

LENA HEADEY: It was as helpful for her as she was for me. She was very cool and brave. It takes a lot to walk through the crowd naked for three days in a row with the crowd braying at you. I didn't phone it in; I was there for three days with Rebecca.

The costume department fashioned a pubic wig, or "merkin," for Van Cleave, which became a source of backstage amusement.

REBECCA VAN CLEAVE: It was hilarious dealing with the merkin and everything that came with it. On the first day the costume girls gave me a fake mustache instead of the merkin to wear, which was great. And a lot of bits of food got stuck in the merkin, so before every take we'd be like, "Check! . . . No, there's a bit of bread in there." Lena decided to name it "rice catcher."

BERNADETTE CAULFIELD (*executive producer*): We're shooting it in a city where you're surrounded by walls that looked down on our Walk of Shame. We covered most of [the view lines] with umbrellas. That was our biggest challenge. We wanted to protect her, and we wanted to make sure just everybody behaved and was respectful of the situation, and we didn't want to offend anybody. We left very little exposed, so to speak.

The scene began with Cersei and Septa Unella at the top of Old Town's famed Jesuit Stairs, which were used as the steps of the Sept of Baelor. The High Sparrow had led Cersei to believe she was being released from imprisonment after she "confessed" her sins, then revealed she would also have to perform a nude penance walk to get back home. From the stairs, Cersei could see her sanctuary of the Red Keep in the distance, but she would first have to trek through the bowels of a city full of people who despised her.

LENA HEADEY: She's been beaten and starved and humiliated. She thinks when she comes out and confesses that this is it. Even when she was on her knees she's partly lying. She thinks she's good to go. She has no idea what's coming when she walks out to the steps, or when they shave her hair off like Aslan.

REBECCA VAN CLEAVE: The first time I took off the robe there was all this anticipation building up to it. But it's such an emotional experience for Cersei, you almost check out of the fact that you're nude. You're so in touch with the scene and what you're going for.

Along the way, Cersei was escorted by the cruel Septa Unella, who rang a bell and chanted a word that served as chastisement for Cersei as well as a command to the wild crowd: *"Shame . . . shame . . . shame . . ."*

HANNAH WADDINGHAM (*Septa Unella*): This is something Unella does all the time. She's taken a vow of silence [except for saying *confess* and *shame*], and her only function is to make people confess and then to rally the crowds to make people feel as low as they can feel so they can atone for their behavior. Then there are the times when I'm saying it more into Cersei's ear; that's really a worm getting inside her head. Everybody thinks she's evil. I think she's a simple person.

Time and time again, Headey and Van Cleave took turns walking the path as extras screamed every conceivable obscenity.

REBECCA VAN CLEAVE: We've been playing tag team—"You're it!"—and trying to make light of the fact we're all covered in everything and going through this together. Moments when I got all kinds of stuff thrown at me, with the chamber pots being [thrown out on her], and you realize, "This is all a bit much!"

HANNAH WADDINGHAM: That poor young girl had never done any naked work. When [the AD] shouted "cut," she wasn't standing there as Cersei, she was standing there as a naked woman. So I would battle my way through the crowd and wrap my habit around her until the costume department could get to her, because you'd have this load of guys just staring.

DAVID NUTTER: What was important there was to really sell the hate. The villagers, their disdain of her, as well as to make it violent. Sometimes Rebecca would be walking, and the background actors would have this look of awe. The first AD came up to them and said, "If you act like this, I'm going to have to take you off the set! Haven't any of you ever seen a pussy before? Let it go!"

LENA HEADEY: It's not hard when people are screaming at you and you look like shit and you're being fucking humiliated [to express] how that would feel. I did what I thought she would do emotionally. And wonderful Rebecca was able to contain herself and be naked. She found it very difficult, obviously. It's not a natural thing to do.

DAVID BENIOFF: Some of those shots we got, some of those close-ups, Lena had to go to a dark place to get the right emotion. It's incredibly compelling, yet you almost want to turn away because you're looking at someone who's suffering.

DAVID NUTTER: I wanted to give her a little empathy because she's still a mother who will do anything for her kids.

LENA HEADEY: I can maybe do two or three scenes if I'm—[*suddenly Headey looked utterly anguished, then snapped back to appearing calm and composed*]—and then my truth is finished. I fucking hate "lying" in a scene.

At one point, a man in the crowd dropped his pants and screamed at Cersei, "I'm a Lannister, suck me off!" The moment prompted a brief sidebar discussion among the director and producers. The actor was circumcised; was that a problem? Are men in Westeros cut or not? Benioff decided it didn't matter (worst-case scenario, the man's penis could be digitally fixed later).

As the march continued, Cersei's stern composure began to crack and crumble. Tears flowed; she was a royal despot at her lowest moment. Cersei's murderous crimes were selfish and evil, yet her punishment felt wrong too.

Once the Red Keep was finally in sight, Cersei stumbled. It was the point on set at which the crowd, so successfully riled up, had reached its maximum intensity.

HANNAH WADDINGHAM: At that point David Nutter had gotten the supporting performers to really be goading us, even me, who's supposed to be stoic. Lena was bashed into, I was bashed into. Lena and I were quite shaken and in tears. The aggression . . .

David said to me, "Maybe you could help her up?" But because I had got so into the zone by then, I was like, "The best thing I can do is *not* help her up." As a woman, let her get up herself and I'll be smirking at her as if to say, "This is what you get for being dirty and incestuous and this is how you atone for your behavior."

At last, Cersei crossed the bridge into the sanctuary of the Red Keep. The Mountain picked her up. Cersei was shamed and starved, abused and humiliated, yet not broken. Alyssa Rosenberg for *The Washington Post* wrote: "*Game of Thrones* has used nudity casually in previous seasons, but [season five was] a marked improvement, and this scene of shame and humiliation is a real high point for the series. In the march, Cersei's whole body is exposed on occasion, but in a way that makes those of us watching at home complicit in the violence the Faith is doing to her. When un-named characters, both men and women—in one of the rare cases of equal opportunity nudity on cable television—expose themselves to Cersei, it's assaultive to her and to us. This is nakedness as violence towards a character we know, if not love, rather than lovingly photographed nudity, presented for the consumption of both corrupted characters like the former High Septon (Paul Bentley) and those of us watching at home."

DAVID BENIOFF: What was really impressive about what David Nutter did with the scene is you feel what it would be like for this to happen to you. Obviously you, the viewer, are not standing in the street being pelted with shit and tomatoes and eggs and everything else, but he's letting you feel it. A lot of the shots are first person. You feel quite viscerally the horror of that moment. And once you've been inside a character's skin, it's very hard to loathe them.

REBECCA VAN CLEAVE: It was one of the scariest, most wonderful experiences I could have imagined. I never in a million years would have thought I would be in Dubrovnik surrounded by hundreds of crew members and extras throwing food, but it was an amazing and gratifying experience. It helped me; I feel stronger than ever now.

LENA HEADEY: The thing about Cersei is she's never going to be fully broken. There's something in her that's vengeful and angry and survivalist. You can break every bone in her body, but if there's one left, she will fix it.

CHAPTER TWENTY-ONE

ROMANCE DIES

The Walk of Shame generated scrutiny and debate, but it wasn't the most controversial scene in *Game of Thrones*. Nor was Shireen getting burned alive, the Red Wedding, Theon's mutilation, or the death of Ned Stark. The show's most controversial scene was (at least, by the subjective standards of media and fandom uproar) Sansa and Ramsay Bolton's wedding night.

Arranged marriages are the norm in Westeros (as well as in many countries of the world today). Parents typically brokered unions between their children to gain money and power. Even Ned Stark and Catelyn Tully had an arranged marriage, with Catelyn gradually growing to love her husband.

So in season five, in an effort to consolidate his alliance with the Boltons, Littlefinger arranged a marriage between Sansa and Ramsay (he claimed Sansa wasn't legitimately married to Tyrion since their union wasn't consummated). The master manipulator persuaded Sansa that uniting the Stark and Bolton houses would be the best way for her family to regain Winterfell and protect her from the Lannisters, who still falsely blamed her for Joffrey's death.

There was just one problem: Ramsay was a psychopath. And despite Littlefinger's "knowledge is power" proclamation, Baelish was unaware of Ramsay's nature when he made the deal.

The result provoked a fierce debate over whether the arc was right from a story and character perspective, as well as whether it was handled in an appropriate way.

In Martin's book, Ramsay's wedding night is more shudderingly explicit (Theon is forced to participate), but the bride is someone else. Ramsay marries Sansa's friend Jeyne Poole after Littlefinger managed to trick him into believing she was the long-missing Arya Stark.

GEORGE R. R. MARTIN (*author, co–executive producer*): Jeyne Poole was included in the pilot—she's shown giggling next to Sansa—but she's never seen or referred to again. I actually wrote Jeyne into "The Pointy End," my first script, when Arya killed the stableboy. I had some stuff with Jeyne running to Sansa being all hysterical and dialogue in the council chamber with Littlefinger saying, "Give her to me, I'll make sure she doesn't cause any trouble." That was dropped.

DAVID BENIOFF (*showrunner*): Sansa is a character we care about almost more than any other. We really wanted Sansa to play a major part in that season. If we were going to stay absolutely faithful to the book, it was going to be very hard to do that. There was a subplot we loved from the books, but it was a character not involved in the show.

GEORGE R. R. MARTIN: I was trying to set up Jeyne for her future role as the false Arya. The real Arya has escaped and is presumed dead. But this girl has been in Littlefinger's control for years, and he's been training her. She knows Winterfell, has the proper northern accent, and can pose as Arya. Who the hell knows what a little girl you met two years ago looks like? When you're a lord visiting Winterfell, are you going to pay attention to the little kids running around? So she can pull off the impersonation. Not having Jeyne, they used Sansa for that. Is that better or worse? You can make your decision there. Oddly, I never got pushback for that in the book because nobody cared about Jeyne Poole that much. They care about Sansa.

Thrones producers say Martin's reasoning—that fans cared about Sansa, not Jeyne Poole—was also why they chose Sansa to marry Ramsay instead.

BRYAN COGMAN (*co–executive producer*): You have this storyline with Ramsay. Do you have one of your leading ladies—who is an incredibly talented actor we've followed for five years and viewers love and adore—do it? Or do you bring in a new character to do it? You use the character the audience is invested in.

GEORGE R. R. MARTIN: My Littlefinger would have never turned Sansa over to Ramsay. Never. He's obsessed with her. Half the time he thinks she's the daughter he never had—that he wishes he had, if he'd married Catelyn. And half the time he thinks she is Catelyn, and he wants her for himself. He's not going to give her to somebody who would do bad things to her. That's going to be very different in the books.

BRYAN COGMAN: Our Littlefinger is a bit more brazen than the backroom dealer in the books—not to say that one is better than the other. And Ramsay's not known everywhere as a psycho. Littlefinger doesn't have that intelligence on him. He just knows the Boltons are scary and creepy and not to be fully trusted.

DAVID BENIOFF: The interesting thing about Littlefinger is he seems to have almost no weaknesses aside from his affection for Sansa. He's been obsessed with her. You could see he's got an unhealthy interest in her since that early episode at the joust. But as much as Littlefinger might care for Sansa, he cares for nothing more than power and sees this as an opportunity to gain more power for himself.

ALFIE ALLEN (*Theon Greyjoy*): There's a common theme with both [Sansa and Theon's] storylines of leaving Winterfell and having these delusions of grandeur about where they'd end up. Theon thought he was going to become prince of the ironborn, and Sansa thought she would end up queen. Then they both ended up together back at Winterfell.

The show's writers, along with director Jeremy Podeswa, discussed how best to handle Sansa's wedding night. On the production's schedule breakdown the scene was called "Romance Dies."

BRYAN COGMAN: The way we work is that David and Dan choose the episodes they want to write, and [Dave Hill and I] get the pick of the rest. I could have had poor Dave write it, but I felt a responsibility to Sophie. I felt and feel protective of her. I wanted to make sure it was sensitively handled, and I knew I would be the producer on set if I wrote it.

So originally the pitch in the room was that Ramsay takes her arm and we just shut the door. I made the argument that if we don't at least take it a bit further and stay with her and Theon's point of view a bit longer and get the enormity of the horror of what's about to happen, then we're doing a disservice to the story and to the subject matter.

JEREMY PODESWA (*director*): None of us went into that sequence lightly. We fully understood that the audience had so much invested in Sansa and saw her grow up on this show. This was something that would be shocking and upsetting, and we were all aware of that.

When filming season five, Turner was excited about the scene, as it represented a dramatic turn for her character and provided an acting challenge. "Alex Graves was saying, 'You get a love interest,'" she said at the time. "So I get the scripts and I was so excited and I was flicking through and then I was like, 'Aw, are you kidding me?!' I thought the love interest was going to be Jaime Lannister or somebody who would take care of me. Then I found out it was Ramsay and I'm back at Winterfell. I love the fact she's back home reclaiming what's hers. At the same time, she's being held prisoner in her own home. I felt so bad for her, but I also felt excited because it was so sick, and being reunited with Theon too, and seeing how their relationship plays out. I think it's going to be the most challenging season for me so far just because it's so emotional.

"I like getting my teeth into scenes," Turner added. "There are scenes that are quite emotional and quite terrifying and uncomfortable, but I love doing them. If you can start with the uncomfortable and make the audience feel like that, that's great."

The filming of the sequence, at least, did not have the darkly intense mood backstage that one might have expected.

MICHAEL MCELHATTON (*Roose Bolton*): The wedding in the snow. Alfie was sniffing and dribbling and crying, and Sophie was practically crying and shaking, and I'm gloating and smiling. It was so Machiavellian, so dark, and so horrific, what we were doing to Alfie and Sophie, that it just tipped into laughter on a number of occasions.

JEREMY PODESWA: We were very careful in the way it was shot, and we were very careful in making sure that Sophie was comfortable with everything. She understood the complexity of what was happening and the horror of it, but she was never in a situation where she was made uncomfortable.

ALFIE ALLEN: I knew there was going to be a huge reaction to it, and I thought that everyone involved did a fantastic job. It was a horrible day to shoot. Iwan was having a real tough time with it. But Jeremy Podeswa smashed it. Sophie was amazing, and the way she handled it was admirable. It was pretty light in between takes.

For the bedroom scene, Ramsay bent Sansa over the bed and tore the back of her dress. Then the camera cut to an emotionally wrecked Theon for a protracted moment as he was forced to watch. The filmmakers wanted and expected an emotional reaction from viewers, but they were stunned when the episode generated an unprecedented amount of uproar.

JEREMY PODESWA: We were all taken aback by the reaction. We knew people would be upset but not so specifically in the way that manifested. From the reaction you would imagine the scene was explicit and insensitive. You see virtually nothing. You see the beginning of something about to happen and then we cut away. It was unthinkable to actually show what was happening.

Focusing on Theon's face for the scene's final twenty seconds as Sansa's cries are heard off camera was specifically cited as promoting "the male gaze," a term used to describe art that focuses on a man's perspective while women are portrayed as objects. "Encouraging the viewers to feel sympathy for Greyjoy rather than the young woman being violently raped was a woefully misguided choice," Nina Bahadur wrote in *Self*. The filmmakers thought cutting to Theon was the least exploitative, yet still dramatic and visual, way to convey the horror of what Sansa was experiencing.

BRYAN COGMAN: What's always bothered me about any criticism of David and Dan is a presumption of bad faith on their part—the idea that David and Dan, or I or George, or any of us, are playing fast and loose with these characters that we love and have lived with and lost sleep over a hell of a lot more than anyone else has.

One of the main reasons we cut over to Theon was so it would *not* be graphic. Then that was criticized. I understood that criticism when thinking about it. I still understand our reasons for doing it.

JEREMY PODESWA: I understand the issue around the male gaze—that we're away from Sansa's experience in that moment and with Theon. The intention was to be as sensitive as possible. I think from a storytelling point of view it was very strong. And I think from a performance point of view it was very strong.

The filmmakers also wondered if there would have been less protest had viewers known the rest of Sansa's journey in advance, just as book readers had known about the Red Wedding and other traumatic twists. Martin's readers often defended tragic story moves online after they aired in the show because they had a clear sense of how such events fueled the story moving forward. Producers say the lady of Winterfell's triumphant turn in the later seasons was always the show's secret plan (and not, as some speculated, a reaction to the wedding-night uproar).

BRYAN COGMAN: We knew where we were going with Theon and Sansa for the next three, four seasons. The viewer didn't know that. And the nature of a lot of criticism these days is reactive. You write something as you're experiencing it for the first time and then you publish. Once you have experienced the full arc, the reasoning behind that scene made more sense.

DAVID BENIOFF: That was the thing that was slightly frustrating, was the idea we were responding to the criticism and beefed up the female roles—that's blatantly untrue. We can take criticism, and certainly we've gotten our share of it. But what happened later was not a response.

SOPHIE TURNER (*Sansa Stark*): Everybody was just sympathetic. I had more "You're my favorite character" than ever before, which is amazing, because before I used to get, "You're my least favorite character."

Critics of the scene counter that the victorious outcome of Sansa's storyline didn't address their primary concerns. Actress Jessica Chastain made headlines by tweeting about the scene, "Rape is not a tool to make a character stronger. A woman doesn't need to be victimized in order to become a butterfly." While *Slate*'s Inkoo Kang wrote, "There was something brashly truthful about season one's reminder that royal wombs have historically always been currency and the dehumanization of the women attached to them considered collateral damage, as well as season two's candor-via-Cersei during the Battle of the Blackwater that women's bodies are considered spoils in wartime. . . . In its inspirational or sympathetic modes for its female characters, *Game of Thrones* could be powerful storytelling. But sexual assault is a storyline (or spectacle) that the show's never gotten right—because rape, or the threat thereof, is used as an instrument to get from Point A to Point B, rather than an event deserving its own focal point."

BRYAN COGMAN: For many, the scene will never work and they'll never like it. But the scene led to a larger cultural conversation that I think was very important.

That broader discussion focused on the depiction of violence against women in Hollywood productions in general, as well as on *Thrones* in particular. It was a topic that had circled the show ever since Daenerys's wedding night in the series premiere. It was likewise a growing topic in media circles, as TV critics increasingly called dramas out for showing sexual violence in ways they felt were exploitative or unnecessary. "Martin, Benioff, and Weiss could conjure dragons, but not a world in which men could be the targets of female desire," wrote *Esquire*'s Gabrielle Bruney in 2019. "They brought White Walkers to terrifying life, but couldn't consider sexual assault as anything more than a provocative plot point. This failure has thrown a pall over seven seasons of otherwise great television, and it's a sin that threatens to limit the show's watchability in future years, as audiences tolerate less and less chauvinism in their entertainment."

Thrones insiders felt one reason their show received such criticism was, ironically, because they had so successfully created and evolved so many strong female characters in the first place. Daenerys, Cersei, Brienne, Arya, and Sansa had all become pop culture icons with their own dedicated and protective fandoms. Each was fully realized and nothing like the other, as well as unlike any other characters on TV.

MICHAEL LOMBARDO (*former HBO programming president*): **Dan and David have never been two people who pushed nudity or sexual content**

to titillate or increase viewers. This was also a show that had more kick-ass, unique female characters than anywhere in the television landscape. So I think the reaction struck us as, "Oh, could we be more mindful of this? Let's learn from this and ask hard questions." I think it was partly because the show became so successful and widely watched that it began to draw viewers who came to the show for great drama and it didn't feel right to them, and I understand that. It was wounding and at the same time started a conversation that we continue to have about how we deal with nudity and sex on-screen.

Many of the scenes that provoked controversy also stemmed from a fundamental challenge faced by *Thrones*' writers—how to balance an authentic depiction of savage medieval times with the ideals of a modern television audience. How much should *Game of Thrones* reflect our world versus a fantasy realm based on Europe's Dark Ages, with all its accompanying historical horrors, which Martin sought to illuminate? Other dramas in warlike settings, such as Starz's *Outlander*, have wrestled with the same issue. Turner told *Rolling Stone* in 2019 that she thought "the backlash [to the scene] was wrong" given that the show was staying true to its medieval inspiration. Several of her costars similarly said that *Thrones* was sometimes unfairly criticized for the handling of its female characters.

GWENDOLINE CHRISTIE (*Brienne of Tarth*): A lot of this show is inspired by actual historical events, and that's what's occurring with the women. Women have been treated appallingly in history. Men have too. Human beings have. The show shines a light on women with an exploration of female characters that has rarely been approached before, and I applaud that. Yes, those scenes are difficult, and they should be difficult.

EMILIA CLARKE (*Daenerys Targaryen*): It pained me to hear people taking *Game of Thrones* out of context and doing an antifeminist spin. It showed the range that happened to women and depicted real scenarios.

Ultimately it showed that women are not only equal but have a huge amount of strength. *Game of Thrones* showed women in so many different stages of development, from having zero power or rights to women who are queens and are literally unstoppable.

NATALIE DORMER (*Margaery Tyrell*): The female characters are three-dimensional, fleshed out, often antiheroines as well as heroines. They are as complex and contradictory as the men are. In characterization, yes, *Game of Thrones* is completely feminist. What might occasionally be lost sight of is there's a lot of the darker elements of human nature in the real world. Physical violence, misogyny, and rape are not fantastic issues. The reason *Thrones* is such a strong show is because it's so real. If you want pure escapism, that's fine, but then you probably should not be watching *Game of Thrones*.

MAISIE WILLIAMS (*Arya Stark*): It's always been a constant debate because women are treated badly on the show, but it's the same as the boys and the girls and the men and the animals. I get it that people don't want to watch scenes like that. But that's the show we've made. . . . I get upset when animals get slaughtered. People are like, "But this is worse than that!" and I never understood that. I think everybody's allowed to be upset about what they're upset by.

Though Martin wasn't on board with season five's changes to Sansa's storyline, the author has long defended the inclusion of sexual violence in *A Song of Ice and Fire* as a necessary story element.

GEORGE R. R. MARTIN: The books reflect a patriarchal society based on the Middle Ages. The Middle Ages were not a time of sexual egalitarianism. It divided people into three classes, and they had strong ideas about the roles of women. One of the charges against Joan of Arc that got her burned at the stake was that she wore men's clothing—that was not a small thing back then. There were, of course, strong and competent women, but that didn't change the nature of the society they were in.

There are people who will say to this: "Well, he's not writing history, he's writing fantasy, he put in dragons, he should have made an egalitarian society." But just because you put in dragons doesn't mean you can put in anything you want. I wanted my books to be strongly grounded in history and show what medieval society was like. I was also reacting to what a lot of fantasy was like. They do what I call the Disneyland Middle Ages—princes and princesses and knights in shining armor—but they didn't want real consideration of what those societies meant and how they functioned.

To be nonsexist, does that mean you need to portray an egalitarian society? That's not our history. That's something for science fiction. Even twenty-first-century America isn't egalitarian. There are still barriers against women.

And then there's the whole issue of sexual violence. But if you're going to write about war—which I'm writing about, and which is what almost all epic fantasy is about—and you just want the cool battles and heroes killing a lot of orcs and don't portray [sexual violence], there's something fundamentally dishonest about that. Rape, unfortunately, is part of war today. It's not a strong testament to the human race, but I don't think we should pretend it doesn't exist. I want to portray struggle. Drama comes out of conflict. If you portray a utopia, you probably wrote a pretty boring book.

CHAPTER TWENTY-TWO

PLAYING DEAD

George R. R. Martin's *A Dance with Dragons* revealed the surprising death of Jon Snow. The Night's Watch lord commander was betrayed and assassinated by a contingent of his own men after he let thousands of Wildlings south of the Wall to protect them from the onset of winter. Just like Ned Stark, Jon Snow was killed because he stayed true to his humanity.

But since Martin's readers did not yet know whether Jon Snow was going to remain dead in the books when it came time for *Game of Thrones* to stage his assassination in the season-five finale, the show's producers decided to keep the character's season-six resurrection a secret.

That sounds simple, right? Yet convincing the world that the leading man on TV's most popular series was really gone required an elaborate two-year deception that went to exorbitant lengths even by *Thrones* standards and put Kit Harington under around-the-clock pressure.

The first stage was planning Jon Snow's death scene. When the lord commander is stabbed by his men, one after another, like Julius Caesar, how definitive should the character's fate appear?

BRYAN COGMAN (*co–executive producer*): It seemed cheap to have it end with, "Is he dead or isn't he?" You could have done a *Princess Bride* thing—he's "mostly dead." But the show has a precedent for the Lord of

Light resurrecting a dead person before. So if we were going to kill him, we were going to really kill him. The decision was made to make that explicitly clear. So if anyone asked if he's dead, saying "He's dead" was not really a lie.

DAN WEISS (*showrunner*): To anyone watching the scene, it's not ambiguous what happens. His pupils dilate as life leaves his body, which apparently is what happens.

The season-five scripts were sent to the cast with Jon Snow dying in the final scene: *"The brothers retreat, leaving Jon to die alone on the ground, bleeding out,"* read the script. *"The light goes out of his eyes as we fade on season five."*

When Harington read those words, he thought the producers might be really killing off his character. But he had been fooled into believing a fake scene was real before, back in season one. He wasn't going to give the showrunners the satisfaction of calling them up all worried.

KIT HARINGTON (*Jon Snow*): I never ask them anything. And I think they left me hanging for a bit just to see if I would ask. I was with the whole cast, doing the pessimistic thing, saying, "I really think this is it, I think I'm dead, it's been a good ride." They were like, "No, fuck off, you're not." And then we started theorizing. The main point that people seemed to circle back to, and I agreed with them on this, is why would there be this whole arc about his mother if that was never going to be relevant information because he died before finding out?

OWEN TEALE (*Alliser Thorne*): I thought, "I'm loving this because they're pushing my character." I thought, "They're either going to really invest in Thorne and he's going to take over Castle Black, or it will mean his end." I liked either of those options. I remember thinking that I hoped Jon really was dead, because if you play the card of the magic too much, then the credibility of the whole thing drops a little.

A few days into filming season five, Harington was working at the Castle Black set when David Benioff and Dan Weiss asked him to go for a walk.

KIT HARINGTON: I got quite nervous. It could have been the walk that said, "Yeah, listen, dude, you're dead, you're not in next season." Or, "You're going to take a season off, but you might be this or might be that." I didn't know if I'd be recast as a CGI wolf, and I'd just be a voice-over, and I thought that would be really shit. Or I would be dead as a zombie guy, and that would be shit as well. I didn't know what.

Checking over their shoulders, David said: "You are now going to know this. Me and Dan, we know this. About three of the producers know this. And George knows this. Now you're going to know this. And you can't tell anybody. Not your mom, not your dad, not your family—not anybody. *You can't tell anybody.*"

I'm like, "Okay."

"You are back next season; you are alive. Melisandre brings you back, and you've got a shitload to do next season. You have a really heavy season."

Dan turned to David and said, "He's going to tell Rose, isn't he?" So she was allowed to know.

At first, Harington was relieved and elated. Then reality set in. His castmates had seen him walking with the showrunners and would assume Jon Snow's death had been discussed. All of a sudden, Harington had two acting jobs on *Game of Thrones:* one while he was playing Jon Snow in front of the cameras and another when he was offstage playing a dejected actor.

KIT HARINGTON: I went back into the room with all the Night's Watch guys. Going in, knowing this thing—they had all seen me go on this walk—I had to say, "Yeah, I'm dead." I had to lie to all my friends. I felt really wrong about it. I had to lie to a lot of close friends and cast members and crew I'm family with, and I don't like lying.

KRISTOFER HIVJU (*Tormund Giantsbane*): I was shocked when I read the scripts. Like, "Oh my God." Then Kit was like, "This is my last year, I'm going to do different projects." He was so definite. He was lying so good to everyone.

KIT HARINGTON: Sophie Turner, bless her, wrote me a really long letter about how much she loved working with me. That made me chuckle. She bought it hook, line, and sinker.

SOPHIE TURNER (*Sansa Stark*): He took me aside on a night out and was like, "Look, this is it, I'm done." And I think he genuinely thought that? I don't know if he was bullshitting me or not. He probably was, knowing him.

KRISTOFER HIVJU: I remember Maisie was like: "Tell me: Are you lying?" He said: "I'm sorry, I'm dead, I'm out of this, this is my last season." So I was very unsure.

DAVID BENIOFF (*showrunner*): Even Emilia called him, and he was keeping up the pretense.

KIT HARINGTON: Liam Cunningham didn't believe it, though. He told me to fuck off from the start.

LIAM CUNNINGHAM (*Davos Seaworth*): Yeah, I told him to fuck right off. "You don't need to tell me the truth, but fuck off." I just didn't see them doing two Ned Starks. He was much too valuable. I never doubted for a moment he'd be back.

When it came time to film Jon Snow's murder, the deception continued on the set. Even the finale's director, David Nutter, didn't know Jon Snow was coming back. After wrapping his "final" scene, Harington was put in the supremely awkward position of having to give a farewell speech to the cast and crew.

KIT HARINGTON: Genuinely no one knew at the end of season five. They had all been told I was dead. David Nutter told the crew, "This is Kit's last season," and I had to do a fake goodbye speech. I couldn't do a big weepy "I love you all, this has been amazing." I said, "It's been great, guys, thank you," and I got the fuck out. So I gave the game away there a bit. Some of them bought it, some of them didn't.

DAVID NUTTER (*director*): He told the crew how much he cared about them and how much he would miss them. How this was really his first major job as an actor, and he gained so many relationships and friends. He said how much he cared about them and how that part of his life would now be an empty part. It was very powerful.

KIT HARINGTON: It was like being at your own funeral. It was awful. It was the worst acting I've ever done, and that's saying something.

After the finale was shot, Harington decided there were a few people he felt morally obligated to let in on the secret. When an actor leaves a TV show, his career move can impact many others in their orbit.

KIT HARINGTON: At first I thought I would find it fun—this will be a fun game. The more it went on, the more I felt like I was betraying people. So I did end up letting people in slowly. Because what you're saying to your friends and family is: "I'm out of a job next year and I'm looking for new work." It's like saying to your mum and dad, financially, this is where the money stops from *Thrones*. So my mum, dad, and brother, I told them what the deal is. "I am still in *Thrones*, but don't tell anyone."

Harington's inner circle included some of the actors playing his Night's Watch brothers.

KIT HARINGTON: There are a lot of storylines that revolve around Jon. He's a central figure. If you're turning to other people whose storylines depend on yours and saying, "I'm not in it," you're telling them they're not in it too, and I wasn't comfortable with that. "Are you saying we're not coming back to the Wall?" I had to be honest with some people who were friends and say, "It's not what it seems, I can't tell you what it is, but it's not what it seems." They weren't prying, but at the same time, this is people's jobs that they love.

When the season-five finale aired in June 2015, a new phase of the Jon Snow ruse began. Until then, producers and Harington only had to keep the character's return a secret from *Thrones'* cast and crew. Now, somehow, they had to keep it a secret from the world.

MICHAEL LOMBARDO (*former HBO programming president*): It's one thing [for producers to ask to keep a character's return a secret] hypothetically before the world has experienced it. You go, "Okay, we can do that. We've killed off main characters on other shows." But the death of Jon Snow resonated. I wasn't in a meeting, at a dinner party, without people asking me about Jon Snow. It was very challenging to navigate the landscape, to be honest and forthright with friends and people I respect who were desperate to hope or hear that Jon Snow might be coming back.

At the Television Critics Association's press tour in Beverly Hills that summer, Lombardo was put in the uncomfortable position of maintaining the deception while onstage at a media event facing 150 reporters. A critic asked if Jon Snow was really dead—but not if the character was coming back.

LIAM CUNNINGHAM: Everyone fucking asked the wrong question: "Is Jon Snow dead?" Yes, he's dead.

MICHAEL LOMBARDO: I was enormously relieved. That's the answer I gave. "He's dead." And when we pick up [in season six], he's really dead.

DAVID NUTTER: I was at a photo opportunity with President Obama at [sitcom producer] Chuck Lorre's house after the finale aired. Obama turned to me and asked: "You didn't kill Jon Snow, did you?" I said, "Jon Snow is deader than dead."

The show's cast and crew were officially let in on the secret once the scripts were sent out for season six. But how could Harington work on a TV set for months, often outdoors, without his return being revealed to the public?

DAVID BENIOFF: "Jon Snow" never appeared in any of the [season-six] scripts. It was now "LC," standing for "lord commander."

KIT HARINGTON: No one was allowed to say "Jon Snow" on set, ever; everyone had to refer to me as "LC."

CARICE VAN HOUTEN (*Melisandre*): There were many jokes on set about his code name. Some people made it into "Little Clit."

BERNADETTE CAULFIELD (*executive producer*): There were a couple of us in a meeting, and David Benioff said, "When LC goes to—Why am I using that? I know who he is!" We created our own worlds of hiding from ourselves.

And Harington was encouraged to stay hidden as much as possible while filming in Belfast.

LIAM CUNNINGHAM: Kit wasn't able do anything. It was a nightmare for him.

KIT HARINGTON: I was put in a different apartment [instead of the cast hotel]. But I'd go stir-crazy if I stayed in all the time. I went out for meals with the cast. It's not life or death.

CARICE VAN HOUTEN: It was dangerous to have dinner with Kit anywhere. The guy has to eat. But we tried to hide him.

Set security was also ramped up, but one paparazzo got a photo of Harington filming during the Battle of the Bastards.

DAVID BENIOFF: Honestly, we were hoping [the finale] would air and we'd get a few weeks of uncertainty out of it. The fact it went on as long as it did was a pleasant surprise.

DAN WEISS: If you looked online you could see Kit in a field with a sword in his hand surrounded by three hundred extras and you're going to say he's probably not dead, unless this was a weirdly expensive flashback sequence to a battle Jon was never in. But the vast majority of people don't troll around online looking for things that are going to fuck up their viewing experience.

There was, however, a second matter that needed to be handled. Before season six began filming, Harington had appeared on *Late Night with Seth Meyers,* where he playfully griped about always having to film on sets in Northern Ireland instead of, say, the warmer climates of Croatia or Spain, like many of the show's other cast members.

Asked what he would tell a traveler going to Belfast, Harington replied, "It's wonderful for two or three days," and joked the city has a "wonderfully depressing tourist board." Then he dug deeper. "They celebrate three things: Having the most bombed hotel in Europe, which is great. They built the *Titanic,* which is a ship that sunk on its maiden voyage. And now they have *Game of Thrones,* the most depressing TV show in history."

Harington was far from alone when it came to envying members of the show's cast and crew working on the Spain and Croatia sets, where filming was far easier and the after-hours parties were more lively. Still, Harington's interview didn't go over well with the show's fiercely proud Northern Ireland crew.

KIT HARINGTON: I'm kind of a bumbling English buffoon at times. I'll put myself down and be pessimistic about a situation. That's something I need to improve on. But on a talk show, you walk out and own the situation—"This is me, this is what I'm selling." I'm not a natural salesman; I tend to put things down.

BERNADETTE CAULFIELD: Kit did not mean anything by that. This was a talk-show setup and, "Tell us a funny story about what it's like being in Belfast." Is it the most cosmopolitan city in the world? It's not London, but we all loved it, and we loved the people of Belfast, and people there are very proud of their city. When it's dissed, it's like a fuck-you. So as soon as that aired, I'm like, "We need to show Belfast that we love them."

Caulfield had T-shirts made for the crew that declared, "You Know Shite All, Jon Snow," on one side and then "GoT Loves Belfast" on the other.

BERNADETTE CAULFIELD: [The crew] got over it. Kit has hung around Belfast more than anybody else and really loved staying in town.

So Jon Snow was coming back to life. But when, exactly? The writers debated how long to keep their hero dead before his inevitable resurrection by Melisandre using her oft-unreliable powers granted through the Lord of Light.

DAVE HILL (co-producer): There was some talk about putting [the resurrection] at the end of the first episode of season six because it's such a great premiere ender. But Bryan made a great point, that we really want to milk Jon Snow's death, otherwise he's only been dead for fifty minutes. At the same time, his body would start to decompose, and story-wise we had a lot of pressing action that took place with him that season, so we didn't just want him lying on a table for three episodes. Plus, Kit probably would have murdered us.

KIT HARINGTON: It was such an easy two episodes. I loved it. I'm in a warm room, which is unusual for me. I'm lying down for a week's worth of shooting. Though I actually fell asleep and woke up in the middle of a scene. You know how terrifying it is when you wake up when you don't know where you are? Imagine waking up in *Game of Thrones* world; it's like a nightmare.

JEREMY PODESWA (*director*): We knew something had happened there; it was quite funny.

KIT HARINGTON: I also had to lie buck naked on the table. It's very weird, like a teenage boy's wet dream. You're lying there naked and Carice van Houten is washing you.

CARICE VAN HOUTEN: It took forever to resurrect him. Forever! It was such an important scene; we shot it from so many angles. I washed Little Clit's body fifty times. There would be a lot of people who would be very jealous, including my mother and sister. I was joking about that—"If only my mother could see this"—and he loved that.

JEREMY PODESWA: It was very important to me that up until the last second, you don't really know if he's going to come back to life or not. The sequence has a kind of protracted tension within it, through this whole long ceremony, whether it's going to work or not. There are people there who are doubting Melisandre, and she is doubting herself. Is this going to show the limits of her powers?

CARICE VAN HOUTEN: I was going through a difficult time in my private life, and it was really hard. It was hard to remember my lines in Valyrian. I made up the lines at some point, just putting letters behind each other.

Eventually, Melisandre gave up. The sorceress and Ser Davos defeatedly left the room. Suddenly, Jon Snow returned to life with a shocked gasp.

JEREMY PODESWA: That was a combination of him like a baby being reborn and a drowning person coming up out of being underwater for air.

CARICE VAN HOUTEN: I brought Jon Snow back to life and all of a sudden, fans went from "Die, bitch, die" to "Will you marry me?" Such a huge difference from being a complete bad guy to America's sweetheart.

JEREMY PODESWA: Watching people on YouTube react to the scene was one of the more satisfying things I've experienced. People were jumping off their chair, screaming and flipping out.

Jon Snow then executed his traitorous would-be assassins and quit the Night's Watch. He was finally free to pursue his own destiny.

KIT HARINGTON: He was done with it. He'd seen the other side, seen what's there, and comes back and realizes he needs to live his life and get out of there: "This place betrayed me and everything I stood for has changed." He's also had to kill a child, and that's what really does it—he kills Olly, the underage kid, and can't see the point in being up there anymore. At the heart of it he knows by staying at the Wall he can't help the kingdoms. "I'm going to die here if I stay here, I'm going to die very quickly." Then he gets brought around to a different mission.

CHAPTER TWENTY-THREE

THE PACK SURVIVES

If season five had the darkest storylines for *Game of Thrones* characters, the next year had perhaps the most triumphant. Season six depicted a succession of victories for the Starks, Targaryens, and Lannisters alike. Jon Snow and Sansa Stark defeated Ramsay Bolton. Arya broke free of the repressive House of Black and White. Bran became the Three-Eyed Raven. Daenerys ditched Meereen and set sail for Westeros. And Cersei crushed the Faith Militant. All gained personal or political power as the show edged toward its planned final two seasons.

In Braavos, Arya was locked in a battle of wits with the Waif (Faye Marsay) while she learned the mystical skills of becoming an assassin with the Faceless Men in order to avenge her loved ones. Yet Arya rebelled against the order's mandate to sever ties to her past and truly become No One. "I don't think she ever believed she could give everything up," Williams said. "She tried. She really tried."

As part of her training, Arya was temporarily blinded, an effect that presented a real-life challenge for Williams. While the production could have used CGI to cloud Arya's eyes, the actress—just as she'd opted for the tougher decision to play her character left-handed like in George R. R. Martin's books—volunteered for the less expensive and more convincing method of wearing thick full-eye contact lenses.

MAISIE WILLIAMS (*Arya Stark*): Then I realized they were the most painful things ever. I hate saying that because I hate hearing people complain. Hearing about Jennifer Lawrence and her [thick blue body paint for playing Mystique in *X-Men*], I remember thinking, "That can't hurt." Now I'm like, "Holy shit, I'm sorry I ever felt like that, because these little things in your eyes are so thick and they're the most painful ever." I didn't anticipate they'd get so sore after such little time.

Williams and Marsay had several sparring scenes as part of Arya's training, which fostered some behind-the-scenes competitiveness.

MAISIE WILLIAMS: [Marsay and I] spurred each other on. I had a bit of pride. I've done some sword fighting before. But she had to be better than me, and every time she'd be getting it right and I'd be getting it wrong, I'd be like, "Hang on, I'm going to lose, but Arya still needs to get good." And every time I was doing well, she was like, "Yeah, but I have to look the best." So it was a healthy way to train.

JEREMY PODESWA (*director*): They're both young and agile and incredibly athletic. For Maisie, because she's meant to be doing it blind, she was absolutely remarkable and tireless about wanting to make it look right.

Arya and the Waif's increasingly combative relationship came to a head after Arya refused to carry out an assassination. The result was an intense chase scene through Braavosi city streets that ended with Arya getting repeatedly stabbed.

MAISIE WILLIAMS: We wanted people to think this could be the end. Arya hasn't been emotional in a long time, and we wanted to bring the emotion. It's the first time she's not going to make it, and it's scary. She ends people's lives like there's no tomorrow, but when it's finally happening to her she's petrified of dying. She's got so much more to do. And just the sheer anger—the Waif? Really? Of all the people!

Staging the chase included a discussion about Arya's abilities. How much of a super-assassin is Arya Stark, exactly? Arya had her ever-evolving kill list (from which she would personally cross off only three names—Meryn Trant, Polliver, and Walder Frey). But Williams always preferred to keep her character grounded.

MAISIE WILLIAMS: I wanted it to look like she was struggling, so there were a lot of times I was like, "I don't want to do that." In the latter seasons, I took control a bit more because I knew Arya better than a lot of the directors. I'd ask, "Why would she run over *here*? She'd just duck under here and just get out. It doesn't look quite as cinematic, but you'll have to find something else if you want cinematic." I felt awful because the job of the stunt guys is to make everything look as crazy and cool as possible. But you want to be happy with the work you've done.

BRYAN COGMAN (*co–executive producer*): It was always a struggle in the writing and in the shooting of the Arya scenes: How much ninja warrior versus how much humanity? The idea was that Arya was losing her sense of self, but Maisie was adamant about preserving her humanity. And she really appreciated the final season because Arya eventually found a way to balance both.

MAISIE WILLIAMS: We did so many different takes of emerging out of the water the first time she was stabbed. I had been to a music festival, so I hadn't slept the whole weekend. I was jumping in the Irish Sea for a million different takes. It was a totally manic day. We wanted it to be real frantic and panicked, but she's also a fighter. There's this constant spectrum of how petrified Arya needs to look.

Arya outwitted the Waif by luring her into a pitch-black room, where all those blind training sessions gave Arya a much-needed edge. Killing the Waif served as Arya's unsanctioned graduation from the House of Black and White.

MARK MYLOD (*director*): I got some stick from some of the fans for some of [the chase sequence]. I never managed to get the right energy into the shooting of that. It was functional but wasn't great. But I loved what was written in the script in terms of Maisie's character using the weapon of her blindness, turning her weakness into a strength against the Waif. I thought that worked well.

Back in Westeros, Arya's brother Bran had been carried and dragged by Hodor up and down the continent, season after season, which was particularly arduous for Kristian Nairn given his back injury.

ISAAC HEMPSTEAD WRIGHT (*Bran Stark*): Bran's mode of transport changed over the years. First it was a sled, then a wheelbarrow, then a [backpack]. It sounds so spoiled to complain about being literally wheeled around all day, but the wheelbarrow was a bit of a nightmare.

KRISTIAN NAIRN (*Hodor*): No matter what they did, it never got easier. People think the sleigh was easy, but it was a proper sleigh, and I wasn't on ice or snow but grass and terrain. The easiest was having him on my back, and I think he would have stayed there if he hadn't kept growing. It had gotten ridiculous, where his legs were almost dragging on the ground.

Then Bran underwent a major transformation when he became the Three-Eyed Raven, a wizard who could potentially see all past and future events (well, sort of). But it wouldn't be *Game of Thrones* if Bran gaining power wasn't accompanied by a tragic loss. The moment of Bran's transformation was paired with one of the saddest deaths in the show, when Hodor perished as he was helping Bran escape an attack by the Night King and the Army of the Dead.

KRISTIAN NAIRN: With *Game of Thrones* nothing is ever certain, and that I made it that far was pretty good. Ned Stark only made it to episode nine! I couldn't have asked for a better goodbye.

While taking refuge in a cave, Bran used his seer powers to travel into the past and saw Hodor as a young boy, then named Willis. In the present, the Army of the Dead attacked, and Hodor was ordered to "hold the door" to allow Bran and Meera Reed (Ellie Kendrick) to escape. While back in his vision, Willis had an epileptic-like fit, repeating "hold the door" over and over. Gradually, the phrase morphed into just one word: "Hodor," which became the name everybody called him. Hodor spent years loyally looking after Bran, saving him countless times and keeping him safe, and all the while it was Bran who was inadvertently responsible for his friend's mental debilitation.

Martin conceived of Hodor's backstory when writing the first book in his saga, and it was one of the ideas he told the show's producers about during their season-three meeting in Santa Fe.

GEORGE R. R. MARTIN (*author, co–executive producer*): It's an obscenity to go into somebody's mind. So Bran may be responsible for Hodor's simplicity, due to going into his mind so powerfully that it rippled back through time. The explanation of Bran's powers, the whole question of time and causality—can we affect the past? Is time a river you can only sail one way or an ocean that can be affected wherever you drop into it? These are issues I want to explore in the book, but it's harder to explain in a show.

ISAAC HEMPSTEAD WRIGHT: We learned how sad it is, what Hodor has become. He really is a vulnerable soul, who had such potential to live a happy life. Through Bran's selfish actions, not picking up that I should get out of the dream, and going to the White Walker vision in the first place, I've screwed him over. Then he sacrifices himself— you've been through all this and still you're having to do this! It's mortifying. Bran would be nowhere without him. It encapsulates the *Game of Thrones* world; the nice guys who deserve looking after don't always get it.

KRISTIAN NAIRN: My favorite part is it tied up the question of why Hodor is Hodor. Why does he say the word *hodor*? It's incredibly sad. The minute you finally learn something about Hodor, they kill him!

Martin said the "hold the door" scene in a forthcoming book will play out a bit differently than in the show.

GEORGE R. R. MARTIN: I thought they executed it very well, but there are going to be differences in the book. They did it very physical—"hold the door" with Hodor's strength. In the book, Hodor has stolen one of the old swords from the crypt. Bran has been warging into Hodor and practicing with his body, because Bran had been trained in swordplay. So telling Hodor to "hold the door" is more like "hold this pass"—defend it when enemies are coming—and Hodor is fighting and killing them. A little different, but same idea.

Thrones opted to have Hodor use his strength to block the door as he was agonizingly stabbed by the wights' skeletal bones—which helped communicate the concept of "hold the door" in a literal way.

DAVE HILL (*co-producer*): For our purpose, holding the door is visually better, especially because we have so much fighting.

KRISTIAN NAIRN: I had tears in my eyes watching it. I don't see myself on-screen; I see Hodor. I always talk about him in the third person. I just saw the character die, and it was very sad.

ISAAC HEMPSTEAD WRIGHT: Of course, Bran was just a warg the whole time. There were a couple times I literally fell asleep shooting it, just lying on a comfy sled.

KRISTIAN NAIRN: There were rumors of bringing Hodor back as a White Walker, and that would have been awesome, but I'm so happy with the storyline. I like [that] they left a bit of mystery there. We don't know what happened to him.

DAN WEISS (*showrunner*): *Hodor* is the one word you can say to somebody and immediately evoke the show or the books. He'd just been quietly there in Bran's storyline, being lovable while delivering the hell out of many, many *hodor*s.

KRISTIAN NAIRN: There was a *hodor* I really like where Meera and I are talking about sausages. This guy loves his sausages, clearly, and bacon. His face lit up, and he started talking about food. I also enjoyed the *hodor* in season three with Osha. She's complaining about having to build the camp, and he did this "Why you telling me?"–type *hodor*. That was a fun one. I can't believe I can actually isolate two *hodor*s from all those times.

Another character that, like Bran, spent a lengthy stretch of time off camera was the Hound. The weary Clegane brother was revealed to have survived his fight with Brienne and joined a pacifist religious community led by Brother Ray (Ian McShane), who lent the Hound insights such as: "Violence is a disease. You don't cure a disease by spreading it to more people."

The sequence was a rare stand-alone mini-story—"that *Witness* sub-movie," as Mylod called it—within the larger *Thrones* narrative. It was also a glimpse of the type of storytelling the series might have regularly included if the show had continued long beyond season eight.

BRYAN COGMAN: It was my favorite week on *Game of Thrones* because it was a beautiful little three-act play shot out at Cairncastle. We'd done episodes mainly about one thing before, but they were action episodes. Here you have this New Age sept led by a man with a painful history of violence. He's found his own flock trying to rebuild their lives. Brother Ray has this wonderful philosophy that I wish more characters had: "I don't know if my god is the real god, but I just know we need to believe in something greater than ourselves." He sees Sandor as a candidate. He recognizes in Sandor a bit of himself. The Hound, apart from being grateful, started to open up to the first and only friend he's ever had.

The scenes have a light touch, a gentleness and humanity and humor that you don't find on the show. It very much on purpose doesn't really feel like *Game of Thrones,* tonally, until the end, when the raiders ride in and everyone gets slaughtered. In some ways, it sticks out. Some people had trouble with that episode because it doesn't feel like an episode of *Game of Thrones.* I like it for that reason.

Fans wondered why the group's leader had such an un-Westerosi name. When the episode was scripted, "Brother Ray" was secretly a nod to the writers' first choice to play the role, actor Ray Winstone.

BRYAN COGMAN: Ray is a blend of a few characters in George's book. We thought it would be interesting if it was a Hound-esque bruiser sort of guy, so Ray Winstone was the guy we were thinking about. I'm sure overtures were made to Ray Winstone. I was the one who thought of Ian McShane, and I'll be proud of that to the day I die.

MARK MYLOD: Ian McShane was a force of nature. He's gone down in *Game of Thrones* crew folklore as being the person who most improved the catering. His lunch was brought up to him and he disliked his burger so he kicked it and it went flying, and had a few choice words of what he thought of the burger. The burger whacked into Rory [McCann], who was enjoying his burger and had no complaints. But a few days later we had a new caterer who was brilliant. So thanks, Ian.

Even more famously, McShane was accused by fans of spoiling the Hound's return to the show during an interview. The actor then dismissed *Thrones* altogether as a show about "tits and dragons."

MARK MYLOD: I was surprised by that. I think he was being defensive because he was accused of giving away spoilers. A typical Ian-style defense is defense through attack. I never took it personally.

Down at King's Landing, Cersei reclaimed control of the city in a most spectacular fashion in the sixth-season finale. The queen regent didn't simply kill her Faith Militant enemies; she blew up their entire house of worship—along with the imprisoned Margaery and Loras Tyrell for good measure.

FINN JONES (*Loras Tyrell*): I got scripts for one through nine and read them all and thought, "Cool, cool, cool, this is good, I only got episode ten to come." I felt really positive—"There's only one more." Then it was the evening before we got together for the table read and they were holding back episode ten. I was like, "Why didn't I see episode ten yet? That's really weird. It's five P.M. and we're doing it tomorrow, why haven't I received it?" And just as I was saying that I got a call from David and Dan. As I'm picking up, I'm staying positive, thinking maybe they're checking in to say hi. And they were just like . . . [*dead silence*]. And I was like, "Ah, God no! I was so close to season seven!"

NATALIE DORMER (*Margaery Tyrell*): I preempted the phone call because in true Natalie Dormer style I tried to fit a million and one projects in a single year. I requested David and Dan release me early the previous year so I could do something. They were like, "We weren't going to tell you this for a few more months, but we're not going to release you now, so you can't do that job you really want to do and we're really sorry about that. But on the bright side, we are going to release you proper in the not-so-distant future."

DAN WEISS: Except we'd forgotten to tell Jonathan Pryce that he dies too. We were at the read-through and Bryan is reading the stage directions: "The High Sparrow is engulfed in green flames . . . ," and Jonathan goes, "*Nooooooo!*" His reaction to being told he was going to die played out in front of sixty people.

The finale opened with a poetic sequence that showed all the King's Landing players preparing for Cersei's long-awaited trial at the Sept of Baelor—or, in Cersei's case, preparing *not* to go to the trial and instead to go to war. Ramin Djawadi's striking score for the sequence marked the first time the piano had ever been used in the show, a choice that cued the viewer that something unique was about to occur.

DAVE HILL: The idea of opening the episode with everyone getting ready for the trial was director Miguel Sapochnik's idea, to spend a lot of time putting on the armor and the bracelets. The original temp score he put in was real close to what we ended up going with. David and Dan told Ramin, "Something like this temp score."

At the sept, Loras submitted to further humiliation as the High Sparrow ordered the cult's seven-pointed star carved into his forehead.

FINN JONES: The character was wild and desperate. He's been in a cell a month or two months, no toilet, he's having to shit, piss, eat, and drink in a little tiny space with no light, away from his family, not knowing what's going on. He's scared and doubting himself. All he knew was his sister, who he's relied on and has always been by his side. He was just begging her to help him. He wasn't Ser Loras, the gleaming Knight of Flowers, who all the girls want to marry and all the dudes want to be, anymore.

Margaery began to insist that something was wrong. If Cersei wasn't at the sept for her trial, there had to be a very good reason.

NATALIE DORMER: The reason it all goes tits-up is because Margaery wasn't in control of the battle against Cersei. She had to hand the reins over to the High Sparrow, and Cersei outplayed him. Margaery is a victim of the High Sparrow's incompetence. He underestimated Cersei, and that's something Margaery Tyrell would never do.

Margaery became one of the show's most tragic characters. She had everything required to win the game of thrones—a powerful family led by a cunning matriarch in Olenna Tyrell, multiple opportunities to become queen, a whip-smart mind, and an ability to read people and situations and act accordingly. Margaery was also a kind person, though not foolishly so. Her fatal flaw was something that was entirely out of her control: Margaery was spectacularly unlucky.

NATALIE DORMER: I am given a moment of some vindication at the very end, which was the perfect way for Margaery to leave the show. She's given a platform to say that she was right, as she always is. I was very grateful for those last lines. She knows. She worked it out before anybody else has, as she always does. They gave me that beautiful exit where I'm like, "Oh, c'mon, guys, catch up," and then *shebang*.

BRYAN COGMAN: Natalie originally had one more line of dialogue that was cut in the edit. She said to the high septon: "You fool, she beat you." That was Natalie's original last line, and then it all blew up. I suspect it was deemed unnecessary because it's implied. Natalie is as good as anyone alive at conveying an unnecessary bit of dialogue.

In the catacombs below the sept, Lancel Lannister desperately tried to prevent the catastrophe. His legs disabled, Lancel crawled along the floor attempting to reach Cersei's hidden wildfire stash before it ignited.

EUGENE MICHAEL SIMON (*Lancel Lannister*): That catacomb corridor was just as long as it looks, about thirty meters, no CGI. And bats live down there so it's covered in batshit. I was crawling all that way, over and over, and I was determined not to move even a toe below the waist because [Lancel's] spinal cord had been severed. By the end, I was so exhausted I was literally frothing at the mouth and the ground was covered in blood, shit, sweat, and a few tears.

They put petroleum on top of the "wildfire." When the fire went off, it burned off my eyebrows and I could smell my own burnt hair. [Director Miguel Sapochnik] told me, "When the fire goes I want you to have this minuscule breath, almost childlike, like, *Oh no.*" Lancel is a pretty broken person at the end. But he really did not want to die and really did not want Cersei to win.

Cersei's power play was the final straw for her sensitive son, Tommen. The young king was betrayed by his mother; lost his wife, Margaery; and was stripped of all authority. In a chilling scene, Tommen maneuvered about his chambers, numb and defeated. The king momentarily walked out of frame while the camera held on a window, waiting for him to return. When he did, he stepped onto the ledge without hesitation and fell face-forward in a suicidal plunge.

DAVE HILL: That was in the script. You don't know why the shot is holding on the window even though the character is gone. Right on the other side of that window was a bunch of cardboard boxes. Dean, being a teenager and invincible, did take after take falling face-first. The hardest part was overcoming that natural human instinct to move your hands or turn your face.

Cersei also got her revenge on her Walk of Shame and prison tormenter, Septa Unella. But what viewers saw on-screen was not the show's original plan.

LENA HEADEY (*Cersei Lannister*): It was so filthy. I don't think people will be able to help going, "Yes!" It's so depraved. It was meant to be worse, but they couldn't do it. That was the tame version.

Originally, Hannah Waddingham said, Unella "was going to be raped by the Mountain." Except nobody had told Waddingham her scene had changed until she was on the set and tied to a table. And the substituted "tame version" ended up being a rather torturous experience—quite literally.

HANNAH WADDINGHAM (*Septa Unella*): They instead decided to have her waterboarded. But I didn't know that until I was lying on the torture table. All I knew was I had been given a wetsuit top in my trailer. So I put it on going, "I don't know what this is for, but hey-ho."

So David Benioff and Dan Weiss come up to me while I'm strapped to the table. They go, "Look, the script said, 'Cersei empties the remainder of her glass of red wine into Unella's face to wake her up.' But fans are going to be expecting more brutality toward Unella, so it needs to be a full carafe of wine."

We then spent the whole day with me being waterboarded. I'm not exaggerating when I say that—other than childbirth—it was the worst day of my life. The wine was going in my face for seven or eight hours while they were getting every pass under the sun. It was basically like drowning while the rest of your body is dry. One of the crew came up and was like, "Hannah, are you all right? Because we are actually waterboarding you." And I'm all, "*You don't have to tell me that!*"

LENA HEADEY: I loved shooting that. Hannah is a joy. It didn't feel so great endlessly drowning her in wine, but we had a laugh.

HANNAH WADDINGHAM: Thank God I love David and Dan, and I'm so thankful for the opportunity, but it was hideous. It literally gave me claustrophobia. I had bruises all over and lost my voice from screaming.

Lena kept going, "I'm *so* sorry." I was like, "Wow . . . I've been *Throne*d."

CHAPTER TWENTY-FOUR

THE MAGNIFICENT "BASTARDS"

K it Harington took his shirt off.

The actor had been getting beat up on set all day as Jon Snow fighting the Bolton army and was muddied and battered. Finally, he was able to strip out of his grimy costume. Liam Cunningham, eyeing the chisel-chested Harington strolling across the production's base camp, quipped, "He's just doing that to annoy the rest of us!" Even out of his costume, there was plenty that still needed cleaning. That night Harington took a photo of his bathtub full of black water after his soak.

Sophie Turner had some *Thrones*-mandated grubbiness as well. Sansa Stark had been away from the comforts of a proper castle for so long that the actress was told not to wash her hair during certain season-five filming periods. "It is the most amazing feeling to have a shower after you go a week and you have [artificial] snow, and mud, and horse shit, and all these disgusting things in your hair," Turner said.

Hygiene challenges were, of course, the easier parts of staging "The Battle of the Bastards," or "BoB." The clash among northern houses, led by Jon Snow against Ramsay Bolton, marked the biggest battle yet on *Thrones*. The episode is a favorite of critics and fans, and it went on to win six Emmy awards—tying for the most of any episode of television ever. "Possibly the best episode of television in history," wrote *The*

Independent's Anthony Cody. "I was genuinely left awe-struck." "BoB" also marked the drama's first proper field battle, a style of warfare the show had long avoided due to its logistical difficulties and high cost.

MIGUEL SAPOCHNIK (*director*): After "Hardhome," there were a lot of happy campers in the *Game of Thrones* offices. But there was also a sense that we somehow had to make "BoB" bigger and better. I personally felt the pressure and tried to quash it as quickly as possible by using as my mantra this response: "Let's just make it the best we can."

At first, the director watched battle footage from war movies, trying to figure out the best way to show the action.

MIGUEL SAPOCHNIK: I watched every field battle I could find, and footage of real ones too, looking for patterns—what works, what doesn't, what takes you out of the moment, what keeps you locked in. The big reference was Akira Kurosawa's *Ran*.

Interestingly, one of the things I noticed is that the staging of these battles through the years has changed dramatically. Back in the day, you'd see these huge aerial shots of horse charges, and there were two big differences. First, it was all real—no CGI or digital replication. And second, often when the horses would go down, you could tell they got really hurt. Nowadays you'd never get away with that, and nor would you want to.

Also, the more I watched these scenes, the more I felt like those aerial shots that are so synonymous with a charge scene kind of take you out of the moment. That is to say, you experience the moment as an objective observer in all its glory with no sense of danger from the inevitable impact of hundreds of huge stampeding animals. I was interested in what it must feel like to be on the ground when that shit happens. Absolute terror? A moment of clarity? What goes through your head when you are right in the thick of it? That said, at some point you need to put all the research down and tell a good story.

The most prized resource for a director filming an episode isn't money, exactly, but the amount of filming time that money buys you. How many days of shooting will you have to get the coverage you need? Sapochnik read the original "BoB" outline and requested twenty-eight days for the battle sequence. The producers countered with twelve days. After a negotiation and a search for ways to make each shot more efficient, the production settled on twenty-five days.

That was a perhaps unprecedented commitment for a mere sequence within an episode of television, and yet, as usual, it wasn't enough. A production team can create a schedule, but once you add animals, rain, and unexpected obstacles, the plan is quickly trampled. Each morning during filming, Sapochnik would walk to the top of a hill, survey his battlefield like a general, and "try and figure out whether the plan for the day was still solid."

MIGUEL SAPOCHNIK: Then everything would change according to the weather. The best-laid plans would fly out the window and we would have to improvise. Being so well planned, and at the same time being ready to throw it all out, was really the tip of the iceberg. We battled time, the elements, fatigue, and ourselves.

For starters, there was the terrain of the location, called Saintfield.

CHRISTOPHER NEWMAN (*producer*): It looks like you're going out to a field and having a battle, but there's a lot more to it when you have a soft, undulating field. The trick was making it friendly for man and beast, and that takes a lot of time and money. Because the minute you put them on something that's not hard tarmac, they sink. Then it rained for the first three days, which turned everything really slick and muddy, and it never recovered.

The field was also slightly bowl shaped, which made it even more of a muddy soup. During filming, 160 tons of gravel were laid down by hand using shovels and wheelbarrows (it would have been far easier to use machines, but they would have left tracks in the field that would be seen on camera). If you stepped off a gravel-laid path, you would quickly get stuck. Tug your leg, and your boot was slurped right off your foot.

As getting on and off set required trudging up a steep, slippery hill, Sapochnik only allowed himself a single once-a-day pee break (which, perhaps, ranks as the resolute director's most impressive feat of endurance).

The field also had to be dressed with mock corpses, of the human and horse variety.

DEBORAH RILEY (*production designer*): It was a huge job. You can buy a prop body, but then you need to make prop costumes as well. And make sure all the prop horses were wearing the appropriate prop saddlery. It was something like $4,000 for each prop dead horse. And then of course it rained; then all the bodies became waterlogged and we had to shift them around the battlefield. It was a lot of lugging these heavy things around.

And then there were all the challenges with the horses. . . .

MIGUEL SAPOCHNIK: With horses, everything takes about 50 percent longer. Horses also get bored and spooked, and some perform better than others. They also need an entire separate field to rest in. Oh, and they shit and piss all the time.

In fact, one of the hardest scenes to shoot was the parley [meeting between Jon and Ramsay] prior to the actual battle. Getting a bunch of horses to just stand there all day and do nothing is much harder than getting them to run around. They would fart and pee a lot, often in the middle of Kit's lines.

LIAM CUNNINGHAM (*Davos Seaworth*): I nearly got killed during the Battle of the Bastards. I'm reasonably handy on a horse. I'm sitting on the horse and they had this very expensive crane with what they call a "Russian head" on it. They came in like *this* [swooping across toward him], but the horse wanted to play with its mates and ride off, and he jumped two feet to the left and the camera went straight over where my head was. I could have been decapitated, but I ducked. A bunch of people ran up horrified. You couldn't blame anyone. It was just one of those horsey things.

MIGUEL SAPOCHNIK: And every time we charged the horses it took twenty-five minutes to reset all the fake snow on the field and rub out the previous horseshoe prints. So how many times can we afford to charge the horses each day knowing we need time for a reset that's ten times longer than the actual shot? Another thing was: How do we make five hundred extras look like eight thousand when shooting in a field and there's just nowhere to hide your shortfall? It became like a bonkers math equation.

The horse breaks allowed for some team members to likewise have bouts of downtime during filming. During one such intermission, several of the actors sat in the green room tent playing the classic board game Risk (appropriately, "The World Conquest Game," as its description reads). Turner sang pop songs. The reserved Aidan Gillen found a quiet spot to read a David Foster Wallace novel. And the producers watched playback on monitors in the video village tent, as spiders from an adjacent hillside crawled through the flaps and fell onto them.

The writers based Jon Snow and Davos Seaworth's initial strategy to defeat Ramsay on the legendary battle between the Romans and Hannibal of Carthage. Hannibal allowed the much larger Roman army to push forward, absorbed their initial attack, then sent part of his forces around the sides of the battle to the rear, enveloping the Romans in a chokehold.

After their parley, however, Ramsay surprised Jon Snow. Instead of charging, Ramsay advanced just one of his pawns, a captive Rickon Stark (Art Parkinson). He ordered the youngest Stark brother to run across the field toward Jon, then fired arrows at the fleeing boy, trying to spur Jon Snow into foolishly charging and scrapping his original strategy. Of course, Jon did exactly what Ramsay wanted.

MIGUEL SAPOCHNIK: A key thing for David and Dan was they wanted to make sure we could see the way Ramsay ensnares Jon the same way Davos had planned to defeat the Bolton army.

KIT HARINGTON (*Jon Snow*): He doesn't have much choice. The guy's just killed his younger brother. He knows what he's doing by charging in, but he doesn't care. Jon is not afraid of death. He'll do what is right over what's safe 100 percent of the time, and that's why we like him. In that moment, his rage gets the better of him. The Starks are always fighting with their balls and not their heads.

IWAN RHEON (*Ramsay Bolton*): Jon Snow's the antithesis of Ramsay. They're almost a yin and yang. They both come from such a similar place, yet they're so different. And even though they're enemies, they've both risen so far as bastards, which is almost incomprehensible, and now they're both here facing each other. They couldn't be any more different yet more similar.

Despite Jon Snow's heroic effort, Rickon was felled by one of Ramsay's arrows. The youngest Stark, whom the producers once briefly considered leaving out of the show entirely, only spoke a handful of lines throughout the series.

Jon's move also left him exposed, the House Stark king suddenly vulnerable to Ramsay's thousands of charging frontline pawns. Davos ordered Jon's men to rush into battle to back up their commander. Soon Jon was engulfed by the chaos, and the camera followed him on a minute-long "one-shot"—a single take of Jon Snow hacking and ducking and staggering through a blizzard of wartime mayhem and carnage.

KIT HARINGTON: I can pick up a fourteen-beat fight very quickly. That was important, because everything would change once we got out there; it just naturally does. It's like a dance. If you get it just right, it's the difference between an epic moment and "all right." I want it always to be right, and I want to sell it. I don't want the editor to have to cut around a swing or a parry. I like whole movements. The hard bit was letting it go when Miguel said we needed to move on. The hardest thing is when they said, "It'll do." If I could have another take, I wanted it.

DAVID BENIOFF (*showrunner*): It's become such a trend in action scenes to have them all chopped up into quarter-second shots to make everyone look superfast and superhuman. You can fake it, but we're so good at picking up fakery on-screen. There was something about watching Kit do a sixty-second take where he's doing all the moves and he's just so fucking good at it.

DAN WEISS (*showrunner*): He might actually be of serious value in a medieval army.

KIT HARINGTON: The one-shot was a lot of rehearsal. There are three cuts, but it was all one shot. We had gotten the shape of it and rehearsed it for a couple weeks before. It was the longest "one-up," as we called it, we'd done. Then you add horses into anything and it has to be pinpoint accurate.

But I will forever look at that shot and see the faults. Just little bits I could have done better with the sword. It's always going to irritate me. I loved it, and to everyone else it looked good, I guess, but to me there's always going to be bits I could have done better. I think that will be the case with all of it.

Jon's forces ended up pinned between a growing pile of corpses and the Bolton army with its Roman legion–inspired wall of shields and spears. Bryan Cogman dubbed it the *Game of Thrones* version of the trash compacter scene from *Star Wars*.

MIGUEL SAPOCHNIK: The Bolton shield wall was a production-friendly way to emulate a "double-envelopment pincer move" [flanking an enemy on two sides] without using horses as originally scripted, and also as a way to avoid seeing horizons on the field and therefore having to dress fewer dead bodies or stage background fights too deep because we didn't have the money. I also really liked the visual of a wall of Bolton red-and-white crosses on the shields. It felt very fascistic and graphic.

DAVE HILL (co-producer): One reason the battle looked so good is we hired a military drillmaster, and he took the soldiers before the season and trained them and molded them into separate units so they each had their own fighting style. The Boltons and the Wildlings and northern men all trained separately. Then when filming was over they even had separate wrap parties.

Between takes, the drill instructor would call out soldiers who weren't quite perfect. "Who's new on shields?" he yelled after a shot where the Bolton lineup looked insufficiently congruent. "No one! That was shit! The shields should not move!"

DAVE HILL: The stunt coordinator also had to keep pulling Kristofer back because Kristofer loved the fight scenes. He'd get really into it. "No, Kristofer! You need to hold back a little bit!"

KRISTOFER HIVJU (Tormund Giantsbane): It's like doing a heavy metal rock concert with a guitar exchanged with a sword, and your singing is exchanged for screaming. It's real adrenaline, five hundred people to dress up like wild people with swords and screaming and fighting. For a modern man to do this stuff, it's catharsis.

Filming the battle was controlled chaos. But Sapochnik's ability to adapt to the ever-shifting circumstances on the ground was put to a critical test when he realized he wasn't going to have enough time to shoot a key sequence. The result was a very rare instance when the meticulous production, where thousands of cast and crew members are always following an intricately detailed months-long plan, went entirely "off book"—working without a script.

MIGUEL SAPOCHNIK: I realized we just could not complete a sequence as planned. Consistent rain had turned the field into a bog nine inches deep with mud so thick that things were slowing down, and morale with it. The crew were a tough bunch, but when the wind and rain is blowing in your face thirteen hours a day for weeks on end, and it's literally a game of death to walk up the hill to grab a drink or use the loo because it's so slippery, everyone gets a bit down.

DAVE HILL: There was a part in the script where Jon was going to run up the body pile and he and Tormund would stand up there with a 360-degree view of how the battle was progressing. But to do that, you'd have to keep re-dressing that entire field.

MIGUEL SAPOCHNIK: On the body pile, Jon was going to survey the carnage, unaware that a horseman with a spear had locked on to him. As Jon watches his men perish, we were going to have an "all is lost" moment. The horseman charges up the body pile toward Jon. At the last minute, the pile of bodies explodes and the giant Wun Wun bursts through, coming between the horseman and Jon and punching the horse, knocking it back down and saving Jon in the process.

DAVE HILL: Miguel was like, "I need three extra days to do it." The production didn't have three extra days.

MIGUEL SAPOCHNIK: I wrote a long email to David, Dan, and the other producers to suggest an alternative that I thought we could achieve in the remaining time, but that would mean going off book. I finished the email and waited for the response, which I fully expected to be a chastisement and general reaming for even suggesting it. Dan and David like their scripts executed the way they wrote them, and with good reason. And if we were going to do this we needed to employ the idea first thing the next day. I hadn't even worked out exactly how to do it, I just knew we needed a Plan B.

DAVE HILL: Miguel wrote, "What if Jon gets knocked out and kept getting run over and it's this suffocating, claustrophobic scene? 'This is how he's going to die, being trampled by his own men.'"

MIGUEL SAPOCHNIK: Not fifteen minutes later, I got a ping on the email. David and Dan said it sucked not to be able to finish as scripted but they also understood the crunch we were in and they trusted me and to have at it. That's a kind of trust you can't buy. It felt like a privilege to have been given that kind of support to go into uncharted territory by the producers during such a high-stakes game.

Once again, a creative pivot to an unexpected problem resulted in a classic *Game of Thrones* moment.

KIT HARINGTON: It was a last-minute genius choice by Miguel and worked a lot better than what we had planned. It's not fun being trampled on by a ton's worth of Northern Irishmen. But it felt right.

MIGUEL SAPOCHNIK: No VFX, no fighting, just Kit giving a stellar performance and a crazy top shot as he pushes his way back out.

KIT HARINGTON: I've always loved the overhead shot [of Jon clawing his way up through a mass of soldiers] because it echoes Daenerys when she's held aloft at the end of season five with all of them calling her

"Mother." It's the opposite for Jon having to fight his way out instead of being held aloft, which says a lot about their stories.

CHRISTOPHER NEWMAN: It's perhaps the burden of being the most moral character in the show that Jon Snow has to fight everything.

BRYAN COGMAN (*co–executive producer*): I always thought that Jon feels like he's living on borrowed time, that he's not supposed to be here and that following his death and resurrection, he doesn't deserve it. He says to Melisandre the night before the battle, "If I fall, don't bring me back." I think part of him for the rest of the series wanted to die, and events that transpired don't make him feel any better about it. So that moment where he's being kind of swallowed up by the crush of bodies and pulls himself out is very powerful.

In general, I don't think Kit gets enough credit for the subtlety of his performance post-resurrection. There's this lazy criticism—"He's exactly the same as he was before"—but that's not true. If you watch closely, he's doing very subtle and sophisticated work. Jon's just not the type of guy who's going to talk about it. If anything, he finds coming back almost . . . shameful.

KIT HARINGTON: There's a brilliant line when Melisandre asks, "What did you see?" He says, "Nothing, there was nothing at all." That cuts right to our deepest fear, that there's nothing after death. That was the most important line in the whole season for me. He realized something about his life now. He has to live it because that's all there is. The Battle of the Bastards was him wanting to go to sleep and then he pulls through and gets his focus back.

Jon Snow and his allies were rescued at the last minute by the timely arrival of the Knights of the Vale—thanks to Sansa having secretly sent a raven to Littlefinger requesting his help. Yet the fight wasn't over. Ramsay fled to Winterfell and was pursued by Jon Snow.

DAVE HILL: The smallest detail can be much more difficult than you ever thought. You know the scene where Jon charged Ramsay in the courtyard? It was scripted that Jon picked a shield off the ground and charged Ramsay, catching his arrows on the shield. Then you're shooting it and have to figure out which shield it should be. Is it a Wildling shield? A Bolton shield? A Stark shield? A Glover shield? A Mazin shield? They're all different shapes. They all have different hand guards. We had to try all of them to figure out what could Kit get quick enough around his arm that would give him enough protection, but also be able to explain—in our minds—why it was there.

After grabbing the shield (it was from House Mormont, as it turned out), Jon finally got his hands on Ramsay, knocked him down to the ground, and savagely pounded his smug, hateful face.

DAVE HILL: Jon Snow would be the most exhausted man on earth after that battle. So how do we sell that he's exhausted, that he's been driven by pure adrenaline and rage and now he's going to beat Ramsay to death—but then stops when he sees Sansa and realizes Ramsay is not his to kill? Conveying his exhaustion, rage, lack of control—and then adding control—was tricky. You could think, "Oh, it's just one dude punching another dude." But we're still trying to tell a story in that moment.

MIGUEL SAPOCHNIK: We spent an entire day beating Ramsay. It was a little surreal. Kit and I discussed how that moment should feel like an empty victory for Jon. His character takes a nosedive into darkness this season in some respects. His faith in humanity is fractured and fragile. He's tired of fighting and living, and yet he cannot seem to die, and so in a way he's lost.

KIT HARINGTON: He's beating on Ramsay and he's killing Ramsay and he just doesn't care. At the end we should be more terrified of Jon because he's not him anymore, he's like this machine pummeling bread.

DAVE HILL: Kit was supposed to be pulling his punches, but at the end of the day, Iwan was like, "Yeah, he got me a few times." He put a few bruises on Iwan.

MIGUEL SAPOCHNIK: There's this weird moment when Iwan stops scrunching up his face to receive the blows and just lets himself relax into it. On camera it looks like we've used some sort of digital effect to make his face change, but it's all real. It's kind of disturbing.

SOPHIE TURNER (*Sansa Stark*): I was loving the idea of Kit killing Ramsay. Then I was like, "No, Sansa needs her first kill, and it has to be Ramsay." When he says, "He's yours," I'm like, "*Yes.*"

Jon turned Ramsay over to Sansa. The Bastard of Bolton was tied up in the kennels with his beloved killer hounds, which he'd been starving in anticipation of having enemies to feed to them. Instead, Sansa let her former tormenter get devoured by his own beasts. The move was foreshadowed by Ramsay's father, Roose, who had warned him, "If you acquire a reputation as a mad dog, you'll be treated as a mad dog—taken out back and slaughtered for pig feed."

IWAN RHEON: I got the call, and Dan and David joked, "Isn't it great Ramsay ends up on the Iron Throne?" I said, "He's dead, isn't he?" It was right he went down, because where else could he go? It's justified. And Jon Snow needed to win because otherwise there was no hope left in the world. But it is interesting because it isn't fair—without the Knights of the Vale, it would have been over [for Jon Snow and his army]. Then Ramsay still thought he'd won. He was so arrogant and self-assured he thought he'd still be fine, until the last.

MIGUEL SAPOCHNIK: It wasn't fun for Iwan. He spent the night tied to a chair, covered in sticky fake blood and surrounded by dogs that were really quite scary in real life. We also didn't know whether it was his last day on set or not, which was disconcerting for him too after so many years.

DAVE HILL: Dogs are hard to make vicious. And because of health and safety we could never have Iwan in the cage with the dogs when they attack. But it all cut together beautifully.

Originally the scene was meant to be even more gruesome, showing Ramsay's flesh being ripped off his face, *Variety* reported.

IWAN RHEON: I feel really lucky he got a proper send-off. It's a gruesome death, and it's so ironic as he's been banging on about those hounds. And it leaves Sansa in an interesting place as a character. He's saying, "I'm inside you." [*Rheon shudders.*] It's horrible, but he probably has done some damage. He's got in her head, and he's probably broken her in some way.

SOPHIE TURNER: He just gets under her skin, and that he violated her in such a terrible way, she can never get that part of her back again. He's imprinted in her mentally and physically.

MIGUEL SAPOCHNIK: I must admit I kind of wanted to make people start to feel for Ramsay [during his death scene] in that wonderful way *Thrones* turns these things on their head. But David and Dan were clear: They didn't want anyone to sympathize with Ramsay Bolton. In a way I agree; that was not a time to be morally ambiguous. Ramsay needed to die, and horribly. That was what the audience had been waiting to see.

The most effective moment for me was the sound of a squealing pig you hear from Ramsay in the background as Sansa walked away. Apparently that's what happens when you rip someone's windpipe open while they're still alive and gasping for air.

There's also the moment where she turns to leave, stops, and leans back in, lingering a moment longer. That's my favorite shot of my episodes that year.

DAVE HILL: That smile Sophie gave as she walked away was all her. That wasn't in the script. We saw it in one of her takes, and David and Dan were like, "Oh, *that's* great. . . ."

MIGUEL SAPOCHNIK: "The Battle of the Bastards" was all about the journey back to life at the eleventh hour, rediscovering the desire to live. Looking back, it seemed like an insurmountable task . . . then season eight happened.

CHAPTER TWENTY-FIVE

ALL SHOWS MUST DIE

When is the right time to end a story?

For TV networks, the answer is usually simple: A show ends when it is no longer sufficiently profitable. Networks run a show until its ratings sink below what a new series would likely deliver. The quality of a program's content is often irrelevant so long as it isn't controversial and its Nielsen ratings stay above a certain number—critics could slam CBS's *Two and a Half Men* all day, so long as it kept delivering fifteen million viewers a week. When a show slips below the red line, it's abruptly yanked off the air or quietly shut down between seasons. Producers and cast are fired the same as any other corporate employees—no advance warning, no poignant goodbyes, you're done.

That's how TV shows end. Usually. There were always exceptions. Megahits with hefty cultural influence, such as *M*A*S*H, Cheers, Hill Street Blues, Friends*, and *Seinfeld*, had such massive ratings and acclaim that their producers were granted time to craft a legit finale. But even those endings typically consisted of one or two conclusive-feeling episodes tacked on to an otherwise regular season.

Things began to change with the rise of heavily serialized dramas in the early 2000s. Shows like *Lost, The Shield, The Wire, Battlestar Galactica*, and *The Sopranos* demanded producers plan in advance not just episodes but entire seasons—better yet, multiple seasons—with tightly woven narratives and a fleshed-out final arc. When one of these kinds of shows was prematurely canceled and its fans were denied closure (like with NBC's *Hannibal,* ABC's *Lois and Clark,* and TNT's *Southland*), they would justifiably howl.

Well-planned endings for serialized TV shows also started to make financial sense due to a growing after-market on home video, and, later, on streaming services. The previous TV afterlife of programs' retiring to daytime syndication, where episodes were watched casually and sporadically, was being replaced by fans' bingeing a show from start to finish, and perhaps even buying a copy of the show to own. And if a studio is selling "the complete series" of a title on Blu-ray or on Amazon Prime, the show had better feel, well, complete. In the on-demand age, networks and producers grappled with a new problem: When is the right time to end a story . . . *creatively?*

Dubrovnik, Croatia, 2011: On the season-two set, the *Game of Thrones* showrunners were asked: "How long is *Game of Thrones?*"

"We went into this with the potentially overambitious notion that to get to the end, we would have seventy or eighty or however many hours," showrunner Dan Weiss said.

Weiss called this idea "overambitious" because when *Thrones* debuted, seven seasons was considered a very long and successful run for a cable TV drama. As David Benioff said a couple of years later: "To start on a show and say your goal is seven seasons is the height of lunacy."

Belfast, Northern Ireland, 2012: The showrunners had given more thought to *Thrones'* ideal length. The biggest problem, they figured, was the battles, particularly the climactic spectacle Martin had envisioned for the final season. They didn't see any way they could possibly pull off a proper ending for *A Song of Ice and Fire* on a TV budget. So when asked, "How long is *Game of Thrones?*" the producers once again said around seventy hours, but with a twist.

"The worlds get so big, the battles get so massive. In our dream, we do three seasons after this one and then [*Thrones*] movies," showrunner David Benioff said.

Weiss added: "It's what we're working toward in a perfect world. If everything works, we end up in the best of both worlds—epic fantasy story but the level of investment in those characters that is impossible in a movie."

HBO shot down that plan rather quickly (as in, literally within hours of our conversation after I asked the network for a comment). Programming chief Michael Lombardo said he told the producers, "Guys, I have to remind you, that's not our business." HBO's model is to serve its subscribers, not to tell paying customers to go to a movie theater to see how the network's own show wraps up. So Benioff and Weiss went back to their far more difficult Plan B—make *Thrones* so popular that HBO would feel obligated to bankroll a big-budget final season. As actor Harry Lloyd (Viserys Targaryen) put it: "*Game of Thrones* had to become the biggest fucking TV show in the world so they could make it."

Dubrovnik, Croatia, 2013: On the set of season four, the producers were asked the question once again.

"Seven seasons is the plan," Benioff affirmed. "Season four is right down the middle, the pivot point. Seven gods, seven kingdoms, seven seasons—it feels right to us."

If the producers' replies to this question are starting to feel repetitive, that's the point. Many have speculated *Thrones* concluded with season eight at the height of its popularity because the show's writers wanted to move on to lucrative new opportunities or had grown exhausted by the production's labor-intensive demands. But Benioff and Weiss always envisioned *Thrones* as lasting roughly seventy hours (which it ultimately did, nearly exactly). "That people would give credence to the idea that they rushed it because they wanted to go off and do another show just makes you realize how little people understand the level of commitment this show had for everybody," producer Christopher Newman said.

Which isn't to say other factors didn't weigh into the showrunners' decision. Here's one that likely did: Fox's *The X-Files* was derided for airing too many seasons, running an increasingly incoherent mythology into the ground. ABC's *Lost* had introduced so many compelling mysteries that it became impossible for any final season to tie them all together satisfactorily. *Battlestar Galactica* had an impressive run out of the gate, then creatively stumbled in its latter half. As of this writing, AMC's *The Walking Dead*—for years, the only series to beat *Thrones* among young viewers in the United States—is staggering into a tenth season long after most of its original cast (and its audience) has left.

But then there was *Breaking Bad*. Benioff and Weiss revered the AMC crime drama. *Breaking Bad* concluded in 2013 after only sixty-two episodes with a final arc that was praised by critics and fans alike. Even *Breaking Bad*'s endgame, however, wasn't entirely a creative decision.

It's difficult to imagine now, but *Breaking Bad* was not a ratings success its first four years. Critics loved the show, and that was worth something, but episodes averaged fewer than two million viewers. The show's future was once so much in doubt that creator Vince Gilligan wrote his season-four finale to potentially serve as a series ender. After it aired, AMC wanted to wrap up *Breaking Bad* with a shortened fifth-and-final season, while studio Sony lobbied for two more seasons. Their protracted negotiation went down to the wire, and a compromise was struck in 2011. *Breaking Bad* would conclude with sixteen episodes for season five that would be aired across two years. "As Vince would say, you don't want to be the last person at the party," star Aaron Paul said at the time.

Then something happened that nobody expected. With *Breaking Bad*'s old episodes addicting new viewers on Netflix, the ratings for its final season on AMC surged from two million viewers to ten million, stunning the television industry (and, especially, AMC).

It's fair to say that if *Breaking Bad* had delivered those kinds of numbers before its final-season negotiations, even Saul Goodman couldn't have convinced AMC to end the show.

For the makers of *Game of Thrones*, how these other acclaimed serialized genre dramas had ended—as well as their experiment with adding the Dorne storyline—all seemed to point to the same conclusion: The big trap was trying to tell too much story and being forced to stay on the air too long. Weiss often quoted a line from writer David Mamet: "Doing a movie or a play is like running a marathon. Doing a television show is like running until you die." The showrunners didn't want to die, or to inadvertently kill their show. "Would I have watched another two seasons of *Breaking Bad*? Of course," Weiss told *Vanity Fair*. "The fact that I would easily have watched much, much more than I got made the ending so much more poignant and stronger and better for me."

Having *Thrones* run for nine or ten seasons looked to Benioff and Weiss like an obvious mistake when they could instead ramp up the spectacle and finish strong.

After all, nobody had ever accused a hit drama series of intentionally ending too soon.

DAVID BENIOFF: We didn't want to become a show that outstayed its welcome. Part of what we love about these books, and the show, is this sense of momentum and building toward something. If we tried to turn it into a ten-season show, we'd strangle the golden goose. We wanted to stop when the people working on it and watching it wish we had [kept going] a little bit longer. There's the old adage of "Always leave them wanting more," but also when you stop wanting to be there—that's when things fall apart.

BRYAN COGMAN (*co–executive producer*): There are White Walkers and dragons, and once they come together the story has to go where it goes. There's probably a world where we could have milked this thing for another eight seasons, and that would have been very lucrative for all of us, but at a certain point the guys just really wanted to go out on a good high place. The characters are all meeting for a reason, and that's because shit's going down, and so the shit has to go down.

There was yet another potential concern as well. It was becoming difficult (and expensive) for *Thrones* to hold the show's cast together as other Hollywood studios eagerly sought to grab its stars for their tentpole films. The production always tried to accommodate cast members when they wanted to make something else—Emilia Clarke and Gwendoline Christie had appeared in *Star Wars* movies, and Sophie Turner, Maisie Williams, and Peter Dinklage were cast in *X-Men* films. ("Are they still making those?" Dinklage wryly asked Turner on the *Thrones* set when she told him that she was going to play Jean Grey.) But making *Thrones* still took up the bulk of the year for the core cast, eliminating their ability to accept many other opportunities. And ever since Clarke had had her brain surgery and Harington had shattered his ankle, the showrunners had been aware that the odds of successfully keeping such a large and popular cast together until the very end of the series were slim. They counted themselves fortunate to have come so far with so many intact. Every additional season, and every cast contract renewal, meant betting on another roll of a couple dozen dice.

Benioff and Weiss deciding to end *Thrones* was not a conclusion made lightly, however, and it came with a significant degree of mournfulness. One night around four A.M. during the filming of season six in the Spanish desert, the showrunners sat in a tent and discussed their feelings about wrapping things up. They were waiting for their crew to finish prepping the village of Vaes Dothrak for the scene where Daenerys burns it down. With no immediate duties, they opened a bottle of bourbon and grew introspective.

DAVID BENIOFF: You end up spending a shitload of time away from your family and friends. Well, I don't have any friends left. Theoretically, if I had friends left. You instead spend time with your colleagues, and I'm truly fond of all of them. If you're going to spend years working on one show, you better really love the people. And we love the show too, which isn't always the case. You always work hard on things, even stuff that turns out poorly, and you always put everything you got into it. To spend time on a show that people respond to all over the world is incredibly gratifying. You don't want to fuck it up and you're scared about whatever comes next, because it's 99 percent likely to be anticlimactic after *Game of Thrones*.

DAN WEISS: I just think about how bizarre it will be to not be doing this anymore, because it becomes the water you swim in. It becomes every minute of every day, 365 days a year, this show is on your mind or in your life. After it's done, it will be like reentering some weird universe where I don't even know how people act there anymore.

DAVID BENIOFF: Even on a basic level, I'm sitting here in a tent in the desert, and if I want a chocolate bar, somebody will get you a chocolate bar. That's not normal. And just on a writing level I'll think, "It would be fun if Tyrion makes a joke about that, maybe not this season but maybe next season. . . ." You have characters you love and you're immersed in the stories and you can come up with ideas for them, and a few months later, these incredible actors will be saying those things. That's such a rare gift for a screenwriter.

DAN WEISS: If ten years ago somebody had given me a chance to write a ticket, I wouldn't have been crazy enough to write a ticket to something this great. When I'm seventy-five years old, I'm going to be saying [*affecting a quivering, elderly voice*], "You know, it would be great if Tyrion said . . . Ah, goddamn it!"

And making *Game of Thrones* wasn't just creatively and financially fulfilling, it was occasionally incredibly fun. There were times when their work ended and the partying began.

DAVID BENIOFF: The cast and crew love to party. It was a hard-drinking, hard-partying group, and we had some really great times.

The show's end-of-season wrap parties held at Dubrovnik's EastWest Beach Club were as epic as anything on the screen. A crew member once passed out naked locked out of their hotel and then had to walk to the front desk to ask for a key. ("Do you have ID?" the clerk asked.) Another woke up, also naked, at the top of a Croatia hotel's water slide and found himself being kicked in the ribs by an annoyed eight-year-old.

Still, by season five, Benioff and Weiss had a plan to end their show. But convincing themselves was one thing; convincing HBO was another entirely. It was pretty ironic. *Thrones* had to become the biggest show in the world in order to secure a budget that could pull off its cinematic storytelling and epic battles. Yet its success also created tens of millions of fans who didn't want the story to end and a network that didn't want to risk losing licensing revenue and subscribers. *Thrones* wasn't just a TV show; it was a network's most lucrative product, one that parent company Time Warner heralded in its quarterly Wall Street conference calls (by one estimate, *Thrones* had generated more than a billion dollars of revenue for HBO). The writers were at risk of being trapped by their own success.

One bit of leverage in the showrunners' corner was HBO's brand within the television industry. The network had painstakingly cultivated a reputation as an island of creative freedom where top filmmakers were trusted to call their own shots. Still, it's difficult to dream of a hypothetical scenario that would put HBO's creator-friendliness to a tougher test than this one. Would HBO really cut off the largest revenue stream it'd ever had because a couple of writers said they wanted to quit telling a story about fire-breathing dragons and supersized wolves?

MICHAEL LOMBARDO (*former HBO programming president*): It's not often creators come in and say, "I see the end." It happened with David Chase on *The Sopranos* and Alan Ball on *Six Feet Under*. But this was on a bigger scale. I pushed back hard. The question was: Are we going to get over this? If you have showrunners who aren't devoted to the journey, you're going to feel it.

DAVID BENIOFF: They knew we were looking at seven seasons for a while, then ultimately eight. HBO would have been happy for the show to keep going, or to have more episodes in the final season.

DAN WEISS: "How about season ten?"

MICHAEL LOMBARDO: They said, "We can do it with season six and then thirteen hours, then we think we're done." I'm all, "Thirteen hours? Where did you come up with that? Why couldn't it be two seasons of ten?" We pushed, we cajoled. I tried to think of financial incentives. They were dug in. Honestly, it was hard after the books ended.

DAN WEISS: When we gave them the final outline, that helped. They were able to see why taking this and stretching it into another ten episodes would ruin this and make something that's ideally powerful and affecting feel drawn out.

DAVID BENIOFF: It would have meant a lot more money for them. But once [CEO Richard Plepler] realized that we didn't want to, he never pushed it. That was their philosophy the whole way through.

Ultimately, HBO agreed that *Game of Thrones* would conclude with season eight. The show's budget escalated to more than $15 million per episode for its final year (with five of the show's leads earning more than $1 million per episode). Whether one views HBO's decision as right or wrong, it's highly unlikely any other major media company would have agreed to honor a writer's request to end a phenomenon like *Game of Thrones* at the summit of its popularity (or, in this era of perpetual franchises, ever will again).

DAN WEISS: To their credit, HBO [said], "We'll give you the resources to make this what it needs to be, and if what it needs to be is summer-tentpole-size spectacle in places, then that's what it will be."

LIAM CUNNINGHAM (*Davos Seaworth*): I hadn't come across one soul who's said they were happy it was coming to an end, but it had to.

PETER DINKLAGE (*Tyrion Lannister*): A lot of shows stay on television too long. You could see it become a version of what it used to be and trying to recapture that. Like guys who go hang out at their former high schools too much. No decision should ever be made just because something is making a lot of money. David and Dan were smart enough, and HBO was smart enough, to not just go, "Well, everybody's getting rich, let's keep going." No, no, no. That's the *worst* thing you can do with something creative like this.

MICHAEL LOMBARDO: It was painful. But one thing I learned about Dan and David was when they were coming from a position of principle. And part of trusting the creative is supporting them when they think a show should end. You don't want to become a network producing episodes that the creators do not believe are integral to the storytelling. The idea of pushing them to a place where they're not excited about the journey felt like the wrong way to end this. And the idea of continuing with other writers would never be considered. The hallmarks of this show are not just the action and CGI and the dragons. People respond to the storytelling. It's so authentic, the characters are so well crafted. Once you lose that, you never get it back.

So if we're true to who we say we are, and we just keep going, then we're doing what other networks have done. Nobody wanted that. However unhappy we were from a business standpoint, it was part of the journey of HBO. Did I hope they would change their mind? Sure. But they didn't. Ultimately, I think we did the right thing and they did the right thing.

CHAPTER TWENTY-SIX

SHIPPING OUT

Fewer episodes, but bigger and, hopefully, better—that was the strategy going into season seven. For the first time, *Game of Thrones* had to make only seven episodes instead of its usual ten. The reduced count came with behind-the-scenes benefits. Making fewer hours allowed *Thrones* to save money on some things (such as cast salaries, which are paid per episode) and spend more on others (such as visual effects). Season seven took roughly six months to film, the same as previous years, yet every element was labored on with more care. "What we normally spent in ten episodes we spent shooting seven," as actor John Bradley put it.

In addition, the show's storyline brought more main characters together for longer stretches than ever before, and many actors were getting an unprecedented amount of screen time. "Before, if you put all your scenes together, it wouldn't amount to very much," Kit Harington said. "Now everybody left was left with more to do." And given that making *Thrones* can be grueling, much of the cast found themselves working harder and longer. "You would think fewer episodes meant less work," Nikolaj Coster-Waldau said, "but it was actually more intense than before."

DAVID BENIOFF (*showrunner*): We imagined the penultimate season would ramp into the final season with less action and more conversations, and we told [producer Bernadette Caulfield] that. Then we started planning and realized all the conflicts that were about to occur.

DAN WEISS (*showrunner*): We handed Bernie the schedule, and she was like, "What the fuck, this isn't going to be relaxing, this is going to kill everybody just like last year."

In the season premiere, Daenerys returned home to Westeros and climbed the ancient stone steps to take the throne of her ancestors at Dragonstone. There she met a delegation from Winterfell led by Jon Snow, as the King in the North attempted to convince the invading Dragon Queen to focus on the impending threat from the Army of the Dead. Finally, fire and ice had come together, and there was a tremendous amount of pressure to get their long-awaited meeting just right—particularly since the characters were destined to become lovers by the end of the season.

EMILIA CLARKE (*Daenerys Targaryen*): Kit and I are very close. So acting opposite him in the beginning was very difficult because we just giggled our way through it. Our entire friendship had been *not* acting together. Both of us were going, "Ahhh, what are you doing on *my* set?!"

KIT HARINGTON (*Jon Snow*): We were both kind of freaking out. With a movie you meet the other actor for the first time and you develop that chemistry over that time. But if you've known somebody for seven years and shared this incredible journey in your own lives together and watched their character on-screen for seven years, it's a unique experience to be in, and you know the world is watching.

DAVID BENIOFF: That scene wasn't so much about instant chemistry, it's about two monarchs coming together and the conflict between them. So it's fun that there *wasn't* chemistry. He's annoying and she's annoying, and somehow we've got to try and make peace.

EMILIA CLARKE: It felt like the Battle of the Stares.

KIT HARINGTON: You gotta take yourself out of the mind-set of the viewer. As far as Jon knows he's just meeting this queen he's heard about and trying to negotiate with her. He's not meeting the Daenerys who the audience has been watching. That helps with the surprise of it. He walks into the room and doesn't expect to see such a beautiful young woman of similar age to him. Any young man's reaction is going to be, "*Okay . . .*" But he puts that aside because he has to.

BRYAN COGMAN (*co–executive producer*): That was a seven-page dialogue scene where they just stay put and talk. I think people are so used to the excellence of our cast that they take that for granted. If you really pick apart the last two seasons, we were just as devoted to character and dialogue and human moments as we'd ever been.

LIAM CUNNINGHAM (*Davos Seaworth*): There's a streak in Benioff that's willful. He likes to stir the shit. When we first meet Daenerys, Benioff and [director Mark Mylod] wanted Davos to have a crush on Missandei. And I fought them. "I'm not fucking doing it." It's the only thing I ever stood up to them on. The woman is a goddess, but with Davos's history with Lyanna Mormont and Shireen, you can't have him getting the hots for a young woman. I'm not 100 percent sure David wasn't just doing it to annoy me. "You're not undoing my hard work engendering the sympathy of the audience to have him be a perv."

Over a succession of scenes at Dragonstone, Daenerys and Jon warmed to each other, while Clarke and Harington found it easier to perform together as well.

EMILIA CLARKE: After we eased into it, Kit became the one person who I truly felt like I'd met my match with. As actors we spoke exactly the same language, as opposed to being like, *How can I . . . ? Do you need me to . . . ?* It became the easiest thing in the world. Working with Kit was like sliding on your favorite jacket.

KIT HARINGTON: I would ask, "What's the sexual tension in this scene?" and she would be like, "Stop talking about sexual tension!"

EMILIA CLARKE: Then Jon decides to go off and fight the White Walkers, she's like: "Why don't I want you to go? Why don't I want you to—don't fall for him, don't do it!" There was a battle going on in herself.

As Daenerys and Jon Snow were trying to resist each other, Grey Worm and Missandei were giving in to their passions and had their first love scene.

JACOB ANDERSON (*Grey Worm*): When I first auditioned, the role's description said Grey Worm and Missandei were siblings. So [their romance] was definitely a surprise. I wondered if this was going to be another incestuous situation. I'm just glad they didn't suddenly reveal they were related.

NATHALIE EMMANUEL (*Missandei*): You're like, "Okay, I'm getting naked." And that was really strange for Jacob and me, because we'd danced around that scenario and we'd become good mates and now we got to be naked around each other. It was fine and done really respectfully. But whether you've done it many times or none at all, it's a big deal. You feel like you're giving something quite vulnerable, and yes, it's hard. It helped to feel vulnerable and exposed in that scene, so it was good to use that energy, and it made it better.

Before filming, Jacob Anderson asked Benioff and Weiss a question fans had long wondered: When Grey Worm was mutilated as part of his indoctrination into the Unsullied, which of his parts were removed, exactly?

JACOB ANDERSON: I'm not sure they really knew. I'm pretty sure they hadn't decided when I asked. It seemed they were having a bit of debate about it while they were answering the question. Not that it matters in the end.

For whatever it's worth, Anderson said their answer was: "He still has the pillar, not the stones."

For a show that had become somewhat notorious for its graphic content, the Missandei–and–Grey Worm coupling was the most widely praised sex scene in the show.

NATHALIE EMMANUEL: It was kind of beautiful. These two have always hidden behind their duty. And there's something unique about it because of Grey Worm's situation. There's a real sense of trust there. This is a really big deal for him, and Missandei knows that and doesn't really care. She just loves him, and that intimacy they've shared comes to a head.

JACOB ANDERSON: There was something really lovely and sweet about those two characters finally saying things to each other that they hadn't been empowered to say before. But the main reason I'm proud of it is it felt like something I haven't ever seen on TV. They were two people of color and one of them is a man in a show where people are always talking about their dicks. He has a physical disability and is accepted by this person that he loves. Whether intentional or not, the scene felt like it said something about masculinity and how bodies are seen.

The scene was also a relief for Emmanuel and Anderson after spending so many filming days over the years standing rigidly at attention beside Daenerys while she held court.

JACOB ANDERSON: The stuff in audience halls was always intense because I had to stand really, really still through sometimes ten pages of dialogue. A lot of the time I was just trying to not move and not lose my mind through fourteen hours of standing still. I'd get a bit delirious.

As Missandei and Grey Worm consummated their relationship, Daenerys dispatched a fleet led by Theon, Yara, Ellaria, and the Sand Snakes to attack King's Landing. Their ships were ambushed by Cersei's forces during an intense sea battle the likes of which the show never could have pulled off during season two's "Blackwater." The frenzied sequence was also an opportunity to showcase the legendary Iron Islands pirate culture in action, as demonstrated by Euron Greyjoy (Pilou Asbæk).

Asbæk first joined the *Thrones* team as Theon and Yara's mad uncle in season six (oddly enough, the Danish actor had once worked as Coster-Waldau's nanny). His character didn't make much of an initial impression, and the producers cut some of Euron's early material. For a while, it seemed that Euron—like the Sand Snakes—was destined to become another latecomer struggling to stand out amid a sprawling cast of fan favorites. As the production prepared for season seven, Asbæk pushed to give his character a makeover.

PILOU ASBÆK (*Euron Greyjoy*): It's weird to be a fan of something and then to be a part of it. I watched every second of the first five seasons. It's like seeing a beautiful girl in class for five years and then one day you talk to her and end up kissing her and then all of a sudden you're married and then you're in an old relationship and you try to make it work as best you can.

When I did season six, I had some great lines at the [Iron Islands' leader-selecting ceremony, the kingsmoot] that they took away. He was talking to Yara and had twenty more lines where he was being ruthless. He was doing a comedy show for the Iron Islands. Dan and David said, "This is too much."

So I had an idea for season seven. I said, "What if we made him a bit more like a rock star, where you don't know if he's going to kill you or fuck you?" The costume designer was totally into that and made his outfit more rock star–ish.

And that's how Euron Greyjoy went from looking like just another grumpy, scraggly ironborn brute to a darkly charming leather-and-guyliner-wearing buccaneer.

JEREMY PODESWA (*director*): Pilou had strong ideas about Euron being really dangerous but also having this kind of sexy-funny veneer. The script suggested that, but Pilou brought a lot more. It was a great example of how characters are never just one thing on the show.

MARK MYLOD (*director*): I was worried about losing Ramsay because he was such a great baddie, just like people were worried about losing Joffrey in season four. With Euron, we got a new great baddie, but in a totally different way. It was "big," but it worked. Pilou managed to make it real, which is difficult to do.

PILOU ASBÆK: When I was talking to Cersei and Jaime in the throne room, I said, "So here I am with a thousand ships and two good hands." Dan and David came up and said, "Take away 'two good hands,' it's too much." Because I had more confidence in season seven and felt like I belonged more, I went, "Guys, don't take it. I know exactly how to be this. He's gotta be charming, he's gotta be arrogant, he's gotta look Jaime right in the eye and say it with the biggest fucking smile—because he's an idiot and a prick, and that's what I like about the character." They said, "Let's try it out." We did it, and then they said, "We're so fucking happy you insisted on that."

DAN WEISS: We really haven't had somebody in the show who has a kind of rock-star swagger, who just doesn't give a shit. Everyone else in this world cares very deeply, whether they're awful, wonderful, or, like most of them, somewhere in between. To have somebody traipse onto the stage with the swagger and attitude that Euron had was a lot of fun because it lets air into the room. There aren't many people who could do that convincingly.

Which brings us back to that sea battle. Just before Euron attacked Daenerys's fleet, Theon watched as his sister, Yara, made out with Ellaria. It was a scene that underwent a couple of changes at the last minute.

GEMMA WHELAN (*Yara Greyjoy*): Originally in that scene it was meant to be Ellaria kissing Alfie—a different dynamic. Then it was changed to Theon, once again, watching.

INDIRA VARMA (*Ellaria Sand*): In the script, Yara invited Theon to join them, saying, "He might not have the tackle but I'm sure he can give pleasure." They had to change it because there's so many eunuchs in the series that they've already used that line on someone else! So there was a little rewrite.

GEMMA WHELAN: Indira and I are quite fearless. It wasn't directed that we would kiss. It was just meant to be a suggestion. But it just seemed like something we should do. So we led it, very much so, and then it became much more sexual than we anticipated. But it just felt right. Who wouldn't want to kiss Indira? I mean, come on! Yara looked at Theon as if to say, *Well, a girl's gotta do what a girl's gotta do.* And then things go tits-up, to use an appropriate expression.

The boat was violently jolted by Euron's attack. But Whelan had previously injured her back during filming, so a stuntwoman briefly stepped in to play Yara for the impact shot.

INDIRA VARMA: So I had to start kissing this poor stunt double, and she was so terrified! It was quite funny, bless her. I don't think she'd ever been put in that situation before. She's used to falling over and being attacked and all the rest of it, but to be kissed by an actress was a bit beyond her.

Euron's boat the *Silence* latched on to its target. Three of the ship's defenders were whip-snapping Nymeria, spear-stabbing Obara, and dagger-throwing Tyene. It was the beginning of the Sand Snakes' final appearances on the show, but Nymeria almost didn't come back at all. After shooting *Thrones* season six, actress Jessica Henwick was snatched up by Marvel's *Iron Fist* (an example of why *Thrones* producers were wary of adding more actors than they could afford to keep on a constant payroll). Marvel agreed to lend Henwick to *Thrones* for just two weeks of filming during her December holiday break. While her time on season seven was brief, and the sea battle was staged on the show's mundane-looking parking lot ship set, Henwick said the experience was "the most insane set [she'd] ever been on."

MARK MYLOD: You read it on the page and think, "Oh great, a water battle!" Then you have to shoot in a car park in Northern Ireland. There's no book you can read on how to direct a sea battle; you can only watch other sea battles. So you try to find your way through it. Euron had such a messy viciousness to him that that seemed like a good way into the treatment of the fight—make it really nasty, the opposite of ordered and nice. We also took a little influence from the style of *Mad Max: Fury Road*.

GEMMA WHELAN: We rehearsed our fights in a tidy tent, very slowly, no costumes, and it was all very easy. Then you got on set and there was fire everywhere—real pyrotechnics going off and embers being fired on us. You're wearing a heavy costume, everything's wet and moving, and there were all these stuntmen. You didn't have to do any acting because it was terrifying. You just had to remember your badass face.

JESSICA HENWICK (*Nymeria Sand*): It was a clusterfuck. It was more intense on set than on-screen. Normally there's a lot of CGI [when filming action scenes] and you watch it on-screen and you see a massive, epic battle, but when you're filming it's all quite tame. The *Thrones* audience couldn't feel the heat on their face from the pyrotechnics going off, or feel the wave machine trying to knock us off our feet, or the sweat dripping off our faces.

MARK MYLOD: It was slightly torturous. After every shot we needed to let the boat cool to a certain temperature. So it was, "Light the torches, go water, and go action!" You get thirty seconds of action, then you have to cut. Then you extinguish all the fire, take down the water, refill the water tanks, and let the boat cool down. Everything was so methodical, it was difficult to get momentum going. It took a lot of patience on very cold nights. But the Sand Snakes actors were brilliant at latching on to that physical work.

JESSICA HENWICK: Obara's stunt double's wig caught on fire—wigs are full of hairspray and highly flammable. At least three crew members fell through the floor because some of it was balsa wood so you could smash through it, but it wasn't marked off, so occasionally you'd just hear this yelp as another crew member fell through.

PILOU ASBÆK: Whenever I would [hold back during the fighting], there was a guy who would come down and go, "Why the fuck you faking it? I got three hundred guys standing behind you giving three hundred percent and you're standing in front of the camera fucking faking it!" So you couldn't fake it. I was almost breaking ribs on those guys.

Euron viciously turned the Sand Snakes' own weapons against them, spearing Obara and strangling Nymeria with her whip.

JESSICA HENWICK: There was an accident when Pilou almost freaking choked me out with my own whip. Then they were shoving me onto a forklift and hoisting me up there [for Nymeria's death shot]. It was cold, windy, and I don't do well with heights. They wanted to tie me there and put pressure around my neck. As soon as they put it on I was like, "Get it off, get it off, get it off!" Even just the slightest pressure around my neck was really awful.

For a few moments amid the fighting, Theon finally found his heroism. But faced with Euron holding Yara hostage, his "Reek" alter ego was once again triggered, and Theon jumped off the ship. It was arguably a wise decision, as Euron would have surely killed Theon, yet the move felt like it was inspired more by cowardice than strategy.

BRYAN COGMAN: Trauma runs deep. Even though Theon acquits himself in the battle, Reek resurfaces when he comes up against Euron. And a huge, expansive fight scene shrunk into one that's very personal.

PILOU ASBÆK: Honestly? I don't think Euron gave a shit. For Euron his main focus is power, and Theon doesn't have any. Yara and Theon are nothing to him. They're not a concern. I think he was just keeping Yara for fun.

The finished sequence was a uniquely frenetic set piece. Like just about every action scene on the show, the sea battle had its own style and told a character-driven story while still feeling like part of the *Thrones* world.

MARK MYLOD: I'm very proud of the sequence, and the special effects guys did an excellent job of making it not feel like a car park, giving the whole thing texture and making you feel like you're really at sea.

Euron captured Ellaria and her daughter, Tyene, and took them back to King's Landing. Then Cersei got revenge for her daughter Myrcella's murder in one of the most devious ways possible: poisoning Tyene while forcing a chained and gagged Ellaria to watch, unable to comfort her dying daughter. Ellaria and Tyene's desperate agony, combined with Cersei's slightly conflicted gloating, made for a deeply disturbing sequence.

INDIRA VARMA: What I love about that scene is you're reading it, and from one sentence to the next you don't know what's going to happen—how Cersei is going to treat her victim. I just thought the delivery of that information was so clever. Especially since the kiss [of death] comes before the information.

MARK MYLOD: The most obvious thing would be for Cersei to just bathe in her revenge. But there's almost this self-loathing about her character—that she was giving in to this, and on some level hated herself, but was doing it anyway.

Lena always made that left-field choice. She always played the black notes on the keyboard and surprised you with her choices, they were so smart and almost counterintuitive. She never played her character like a baddie but a character trying to do the right thing from her point of view.

INDIRA VARMA: It was a lot of blood and snot and sweat and tears. Rosabell [Laurenti Sellers] and I had to be shackled. They very kindly put some felt inside the handcuffs so we didn't get bruised and battered, though we ended up [bruised] anyway because your acting takes over. The shackles kept coming off, so they had to tighten them, and then we couldn't get them off.

Ellaria hasn't had quite the screen time, so people are inevitably more invested in Cersei. But obviously, nobody wants to see somebody's child killed in front of them. It's every parent's worst nightmare, beyond worst nightmare. It was quite a challenge from an acting perspective to be interesting with no lines. It was fun trying to play anger, resentment, and impotence in that situation but still wanting to fight. At what point do you give up wanting to fight? It's a parental instinct where you just want to keep fighting for your child.

Daenerys dispatched yet another fleet to the Lannister homestead of Casterly Rock to seize the Lannister fortress. But Jaime had already taken his forces and departed to attack Daenerys's allies at the Tyrell seat of Highgarden. Jaime was using the same ploy Robb Stark used on him at the Battle of the Whispering Wood.

At Highgarden, Jaime personally executed Olenna by commanding the Queen of Thorns to drink poison. The unruffled Olenna still got the last word by revealing she had been the one who'd arranged Joffrey's assassination. "Tell Cersei," Olenna said in one of the show's all-time best final lines. "I want her to know it was me."

NIKOLAJ COSTER-WALDAU (*Jaime Lannister*): Finally, Jaime got something right. He was this man who you'd heard so much about, but you'd never seen him do anything that worked. Here he succeeded in a clever outmaneuvering of Daenerys, and then he's up against this powerhouse, Olenna Tyrell. She was like Cersei, just from our point of view she's on the good side. She goes out with bite.

MARK MYLOD: Nikolaj walked into this scene with all the power in the world. He just decimated this army, he's a god, a conquering hero, and yet this little old lady takes him apart him in fifteen seconds. She takes every bit of power from him even though she's dead. That's so *Game of Thrones* to me. And Nikolaj's directness and not milking the moment—yet showing the underlying humanity that's been growing in him—was so brilliant.

NIKOLAJ COSTER-WALDAU: Jaime Lannister finally kills a major character—and it's a grandmother with poison! He was trying to be nice about it, but he's still killing her. She's an old lady, but has to go. She got the final word and it was devastating. She was never going to beg.

And Diana Rigg did an amazing job. It was fun to be there when we wrapped and the showrunners came out and said a few words. She had a huge impact on the show.

DAN WEISS: Olenna was probably the only character to win her own death scene.

MARK MYLOD: My one regret was there was some confusion over how we wanted that scene to end. I wanted to end by stealing a shot from *The Godfather*. So when Nikolaj leaves you can still see Lady Olenna through the cracked doorway as the camera pulls back. The door ended up being built in a different spot, which was a heartbreaker at the time.

Having looted some spoils of war from Highgarden, Jaime led a Lannister army wagon train back toward King's Landing. But an enraged Daenerys was finished playing nice and ambushed the Lannister forces with her Dothraki bloodriders and dragons. Finally, we saw the nuclear potential of Daenerys's full-grown children with a sequence that set an industry record for the number of stuntmen set on fire.

DAVID BENIOFF: Our stunt coordinator really wanted to get in the Guinness book of world records for that.

ROWLEY IRLAM (*stunt coordinator*): We had seventy-three fire burns, and that itself is a record. No film or TV show has ever done that in a whole show, let alone in one sequence. We also set twenty people on fire at one time, which was also a record. In *Saving Private Ryan* they had thirteen on a beach, and on *Braveheart* they had eighteen partial burns. Because of the nature of our attacking animals, we had the liberty to expand on that.

As you might expect, setting a person on fire and then watching them burn for a while is a rather tense business. Each stuntperson is covered with fire-resistant clothes, a cooling gel, and a mask, but the process is still dangerous. Once aflame, a stuntperson has to hold their breath until the shot is complete and all the flames are extinguished. Even a shot lasting just thirty seconds can feel like an eternity when you're engulfed in flames, unable to see, and weighed down by heavy protective gear and a costume, all while running around waving your arms.

ROWLEY IRLAM: It's totally different than going underwater in your bathtub and counting the seconds in your head. If somebody bumps you and you breathe in by accident, you will breathe in flame. The most dangerous thing is reignition. There's a good minute of everybody staying down afterward as you're still very flammable at this point.

Getting a unique performance out of each stuntperson is also difficult, because when a person is on fire, their focus is pretty strongly fixated on not dying. Back in season one, a scene at Castle Black required setting a stuntperson on fire when Jon Snow threw a lantern onto a wight, except the take originally didn't go as planned.

DANIEL MINAHAN (*director*): We had to figure out what does a wight do when it burns, and wanted to avoid the zombie trope. The one thing I knew I *didn't* want was for him to run around and wave his arms—because that's what people always do when they're in a burn. So we rehearsed with the stuntperson, "This is what you we want you to do." We got everything ready with the mask and the chemical on him, and then we threw the fire on him. And what did he do? He ran around and waved his arms!

One victim of Daenerys's dragons in the Loot Train attack may have been a character who wasn't shown on camera during the sequence. Earlier in season seven, pop singer Ed Sheeran had a cameo as a singing Lannister soldier. Later, season eight would include a curiously specific throwaway line of dialogue describing the fate of a Lannister soldier named "Eddie," "a ginger" who "came back with his face burnt right off"—"he's got no eyelids now"—following the Loot Train dragon attack. The showrunners never revealed whether the dialogue referred to Sheeran's character, who was the object of considerable discussion when the season aired.

JEREMY PODESWA: One thing that *Game of Thrones* never did was stunt casting. Everybody in the world wanted to be on *Game of Thrones,* and Dan and David never rose to that bait. With Ed Sheeran, it didn't feel like a weird thing to anybody on the show because Maisie knew him, he's in the UK, we needed somebody who could sing, it was a small part, and he had acted before. Then when he got there he was the loveliest, most grounded guy you could ever meet. It was really cold, and we were out in the wilderness all day long. He didn't run back to his trailer. He sat down with all the extras playing the Lannister army and was happy to be there. And he did a lovely job. If he wasn't Ed Sheeran, pop star, nobody would have ever batted an eye at the person playing that role.

Daenerys's firebombing attack also sparked a debate between the showrunners, one they say is a typical example of their occasional disputes.

DAVID BENIOFF: There was a long argument over when the dragons fly over the Dothraki. Should their horses be afraid? And Dan is like, "You know they've been with her for a long while. . . ."

DAN WEISS: Why would they be afraid?

DAVID BENIOFF: Because they're horses and they're fucking dumb and dragons are big and scary. So we spent like an hour on that.

DAN WEISS: An hour discussing literally four seconds of film that probably will happen when most people are looking at their watch or checking their messages.

(The Dothraki horses, by the way, were fearless.)

Just four episodes into season seven, the Martell and Tyrell families had been wiped out and the Lannister forces had been attacked during an epic sequence that normally would have served as a season's climactic battle. Behind the scenes there was some debate about the show's quickening narrative urgency.

NIKOLAJ COSTER-WALDAU: I had been lulled into a different pace. Everything was happening quicker than I was used to. Storylines met and clashed, and it was very surprising—"Already? Now? What?!" A lot of things that normally took a season took one episode.

KIT HARINGTON: *Thrones* had been a plodding, slow machine, and it was turning into a classic drama, like a thriller. I was worried about that, if I'm honest. "Will changing what *Thrones* is work?" Because it was so different than what everybody is used to.

DAVID BENIOFF: For a long time we'd been talking about "the wars to come." Well, the war was pretty much there. So it was really about trying to find a way to make the storytelling work without feeling like we're rushing it and give characters their due.

DAN WEISS: It's urgency from *within* the story that drove the pace rather than any external decision. It wasn't "Let's make things move faster." Things were moving faster because in the world of these characters the war that they'd been waiting for was upon them, the conflicts that have been building the previous six years were upon them, and those facts gave them a sense of urgency that made them move faster.

BRYAN COGMAN: We made a choice to "just get on with it" that season. You can sit at home and do the math for how long it took boats to get from point A and point B and whatever that was, yeah, that's what it was. There was always something everybody had got to graft on to, and I guess that outrage was better than others.

The epicenter of the pacing debate was "Beyond the Wall," the visually spectacular sixth episode of the seventh season, following Jon Snow as he led an expedition with Tormund, Beric (Richard Dormer), Gendry, the Hound, Jorah, and Thoros (Paul Kaye) to capture a wight in order to obtain proof of the Army of the Dead's existence.

On the set in 2016, Alan Taylor directed the bulk of the sequence in a Northern Ireland quarry that had been dressed to match a real-life location in Iceland. The set's "frozen lake" looked unnervingly real; when you stepped on the "ice" you expected your foot to slide right out from under you.

The actors trudged across the set against paper "snow" getting blasted into their faces from a trio of giant fans. It might not have been Iceland, but the set was still freezing. "You can tell when people are really cold; they get this *look*," said co-producer Dave Hill, noting the ruddy, braced expression on the faces of the cast.

Between takes, the actors coughed up paper, rubbed their eyes, and made jokes about getting "white lung" from the fake snow. Harington attempted to crack up Joe Dempsie before one shot as they prepared to look deadly serious on camera. "I'm gonna tickle your balls later," Harington intoned gravely. "I'm going to reach under and give them a little tap."

The group then came under attack by an undead polar bear, a creature the showrunners had wanted to wedge somewhere into their tale since season four. Taylor had the actors circle up for a cinematic *Magnificent Seven* shot where the reluctant band of brothers began to work together for the first time. "It should feel like a shark attack on dry land," Taylor said. The director infused the scene with a sense of dread that the bear could strike from any direction (though on set, the creature was simply a stuntman pulling a green sled).

The trip beyond the Wall was a solution to a puzzling creative problem: How do you get the Night King and his Army of the Dead south of a seven-hundred-foot ice wall that was constructed eight thousand years ago specifically to keep them out?

DAN WEISS: We were talking about breaching the Wall and trying to figure out what pieces we already had on the board without introducing new deus ex machina pieces. What was in the world already that could conceivably knock down the Wall? Just getting the Night King past the Wall didn't do it; just getting the White Walkers past didn't do it. You needed to get an army of a hundred thousand dead men past the Wall, which means a giant hole. We were racking our brains as to what could do that. Then we realized there would be something massive in the show—they weren't massive at the time we thought of this—and that was the dragons. But getting a dragon north of the Wall was tricky.

There were other benefits to the plan as well. If the Night King captured a dragon, it would boost his formidability and make the seemingly unstoppable Daenerys more vulnerable going into the final season.

So when Jon Snow's group got trapped by the Army of the Dead on the frozen lake, Gendry ran to get help from Daenerys back at East-watch, who then flew her dragons to the rescue. While the Mother of Dragons saved Jon Snow along with most of his men, Viserion was killed by the Night King, who transformed the beast into a creature who would serve the forces of death.

The action was rivetingly shot yet nonetheless drew complaints over the practicalities of the rescue and how fast Daenerys arrived on the scene.

DAVE HILL (co-producer): You obviously don't want any criticism of any kind. But with all the things we were balancing to set things up for season eight, sometimes we had to speed things up within episodes. We had a lot of time cuts that the vast majority watching didn't catch. Sometimes when moving pieces around, you're going to cheat a little bit.

ALAN TAYLOR (director): I thought we were covered by the fact that in the North it's this eternal twilight up there. It was never clear on how much time was passing up there. So I thought we had wiggle room for saying what the timeline was. That turned out to not be the case for most of the audience, who had a very clear idea of what they thought the timeline was and that we weren't sticking to it.

So my first response was to be glib and say, "Um, you know, we have a show where giant lizards the size of 747s are flying around and you're concerned about the airspeed velocity of a raven." I thought I was pointing out the absurdity. On the other hand, it's absolutely true that people love the show because they think they can depend on us to be accurate about the airspeed of a raven. It's the underlying realism that is critical to the suspension of disbelief in the big thing. I learned a lesson about that. That was chastening.

KIT HARINGTON: There were natural problems. I could see them going north of the Wall to get proof, because having that proof was important and there's only one way to get it. And a fantasy is a fantasy at the end of the day, and there are things that have to happen which are not in a real world. But we drew people into the fact that it's a very real fantasy in earlier seasons. You do trick an audience a bit if you say, "The dragon flew this far back. . . ." Some of the timings of things, some of the speed at which people met, it was difficult. But it was also necessary to get us to the end point.

The surviving heroes sailed back to the Seven Kingdoms. During the voyage, Jon Snow knocked on Daenerys Targaryen's cabin door and they wordlessly acknowledged their undeniable mutual attraction. In the passageway, Tyrion could hear what was going on in the cabin and looked rather grave. The scene was intercut with Samwell at the Citadel discovering evidence that revealed Jon's parents were Ned Stark's sister, Lyanna Stark, and Daenerys's older brother Rhaegar Targaryen. The show's biggest mystery, the one Martin had quizzed Benioff and Weiss about over lunch all those years ago, was finally solved. Jon Snow was Daenerys's nephew and the true heir to the Iron Throne.

PETER DINKLAGE (*Tyrion Lannister*): "Keep it down over there, I'm try-ing to get some sleep!" No, ah, it was complicated. Like a lot of things with Tyrion, it was professional and personal. Obviously he had feelings for Daenerys. He loved her, or thought he did. She was awe-inspiring. He was questioning that because he didn't have a good track record falling in love. There was jealousy wrapped up in there. And he loved Jon Snow too; they're the two he had the most in common with, in a way—outsiders in their own families who refused to follow the path their family had taken. He was wondering how smart of a move [their coupling was], be-cause passion and politics don't mix well, and he knew the two getting together could be very dangerous.

JEREMY PODESWA: That was an interesting scene because Kit and Emilia are really good friends and they're having to do something friends don't normally do. But they're also actors and know they had to do it. For them it was goofy fun. But at the same time they were very aware of not wanting to cross a boundary with each other or make the other uncom-fortable. So they asked me to be really specific about how we were going to shoot it. "How are we going to do this, exactly? What's going to be shown, exactly?"

Also, from a storytelling point of view, that Dany and Jon are making love is a huge thing. So I felt very strongly they need to stop in the middle of it and have a moment where they're just looking at each other. It's a moment of, "Should we be doing this? Is this a terrible idea? Is this a good idea?" And then decide, "This force is greater than us and we can't not do it." And that gave the scene an extra loaded quality. That there was something going on that had a sense of epic fatality or inevitability about it. We didn't know yet what it was, but we knew there was a force bigger than both of them, and they couldn't stop it.

CHAPTER TWENTY-SEVEN

A SORT OF HOMECOMING

G *ame of Thrones* began with the Starks at Winterfell, and a reunion was always destined for the show's final arc. But when making an intense fantasy drama where the stakes are typically life and death, what do you do with a family of heroes after you bring them together to hang out in a castle for an entire season? How do you maintain the show's usual level of intrigue? The solution was to focus on all the ways each Stark had evolved since season one, and then throw in a scheming Littlefinger.

"When people move apart, they grow apart, and this is a fantasy exaggeration of that," showrunner Dan Weiss said. "Bran's entire personality has been altered to the point where it's hard for any human to relate to him, even his sisters, but is there anything left of him in there? How much is Arya Stark of Winterfell, and how much is the Faceless Men? Sansa has undergone her training, for good or for ill, under Littlefinger's supervision. How much of his Machiavellian quality has rubbed off on her?

"You would think a family reunion among three siblings who all thought the others were dead should be unalloyed joy—and it was, to an extent. But there was a lot of tension and anxiety under the surface because we didn't know how they were going to relate to each other now that they were under the same roof."

SOPHIE TURNER (*Sansa Stark*): I was so overwhelmed by the Starks meeting again. I was sitting in the corner on the set of something else scrolling on my phone [reading the scripts] going, "Aahhhhh!" Then I rang Maisie up. "Can you believe it? We have so many episodes together!"

BRYAN COGMAN (*co-executive producer*): Sansa and Arya were never close and never particularly liked each other and have been through so much. Now they had more in common than either was probably willing to recognize.

SOPHIE TURNER: Our first scene together was our reunion scene. We fucked up so many times.

MAISIE WILLIAMS (*Arya Stark*): It was the weirdest thing. We were both embarrassed to do our thing in front of each other. It took a few hours for us to get serious.

SOPHIE TURNER: We couldn't keep a straight face. Our relationship is so close, but it's only that fun side, never the business side. But apparently it works? I was nervous. It's like performing for your mom; when somebody is watching, you don't do it quite as well. But in the long run it benefited us because we could be free with each other in our acting. We were not afraid to "go there" because we feel so comfortable with each other.

When family members reunite in the real world, it's difficult to not fall back into habitual patterns and assumptions, and so it was on *Game of Thrones*. Sansa still thought Arya was reckless and unskilled, and Arya still believed her older sister was ambitious and naive, each underestimating the other.

SOPHIE TURNER: Arya still saw Sansa as the snooty, prissy child that she was before she left for King's Landing. They didn't really talk about what they've gone through, they never really had that communication before, and then when it was vital to do it, they don't have that [ability to communicate] and they can't understand each other.

MAISIE WILLIAMS: If Arya had gone through what Sansa's gone through, she'd be dead. And if Sansa had gone through what Arya's gone through, she'd be dead. They're both very good at handling what they've been put under. If either had switched roles, they wouldn't last.

Littlefinger tried to play Arya and Sansa against each other, revealing a letter Sansa was forced by Cersei to write in season two urging Robb Stark to swear fealty to King Joffrey during the War of the Five Kings. The letter made it seem like Sansa had betrayed Robb, and it caused Arya to question her sister's loyalty.

AIDAN GILLEN (*Littlefinger*): It was pretty obvious what my game was there. At the same time my character was becoming quite aware that Sansa was becoming as bright as me and as wary of my manipulations. They used each other, they enjoyed each other and kept a lot from each other. With carefully laid plans there's always a bit of risk involved. I think he liked that. He put himself on the line like a good gambler.

Petyr Baelish had previously spotted Arya in season two when she was working incognito as Tywin Lannister's cupbearer at Harrenhal. So Littlefinger had some sense that she was not to be underestimated.

AIDAN GILLEN: Arya's a character I was wary of. I wasn't fully aware of her capabilities, of her drive, but I had an idea. It was unclear if he recognized Arya or not [at Harrenhal], but I have my own thoughts on that: Yes, I did recognize her, I just didn't say anything or do anything about it.

Turner later noted that she struggled with the idea that Littlefinger could have manipulated Sansa and Arya to be at each other's throats to such a life-threatening degree.

SOPHIE TURNER: It was basically all fighting and suspicion and scheming. It didn't feel very natural.

BRYAN COGMAN: It was very tricky to work out, and the tone was difficult to strike that season. But the girls did fantastic.

Alan Taylor worked with Williams and Turner in the first two seasons, then came back and saw how they had evolved as actors by season seven.

ALAN TAYLOR (*director*): In the first season they were basically kids. Then I came back, and I did a scene with the two of them where it's pages of dialogue, there's a power struggle between them and they're circling each other. They were still cracking up and singing songs and goofing around. But when we would do take after take, their eyes would start to glisten at exactly the same beat in the scene. It wasn't crying, it was the emotion pressing up. And it wasn't a onetime thing. It was literally every time we got to that moment with both of them. I thought it was beautiful how much they'd grown as actors

As for Bran Stark, his transformation into the Three-Eyed Raven meant reinventing the character, and it required actor Isaac Hempstead Wright to become more conscious of his performance.

ISAAC HEMPSTEAD WRIGHT (*Bran Stark*): The first few years I'd be lying if I said I had any great understanding of the craft of creating a character. I was just reading the lines they gave me and listening to the director. And that worked for Bran because he was just a kid. I was mostly around adding bits to the story here and there. It wasn't until season seven that I really had to transform myself and I realized, "Okay, I have to really do something with this," and I got into it. Before then I was just happily going along, enjoying the experience.

BRYAN COGMAN: It's what [Meera Reed] says to Bran: "You died in that cave." The bighearted innocent boy died with Hodor. Now there was something else. He's still Bran and wanted to do good, but he became something larger. Our nickname for him was "Dr. Bran-hattan."

Wright developed an intense, all-knowing stare for the Three-Eyed Raven. When on camera, the nearsighted actor would forgo wearing glasses or contacts, leaving him "completely blind," as Wright explained on *Jimmy Kimmel Live!* So while it seemed like Bran was staring straight into a character's soul, in fact, the Three-Eyed Raven couldn't see at all.

ISAAC HEMPSTEAD WRIGHT: Getting to creep everybody out was cool. Now he was the focus of any scene he was in because he was so weird.

SOPHIE TURNER: He's very stare-y. It made Sansa quite uncomfortable. Sansa's motive was to stay alive and survive. She wants everything to be exactly as it was before, and when everybody came back she was so excited and then Bran was completely different, and same with Arya. She was losing her childhood bit by bit, and it gave her a bit of an identity crisis. "Why the fuck am I here, then?"

The writers wanted to be careful, however, with Bran's abilities. Having a character who knew the past and the future could add all sorts of plot holes and get fans asking "But then why couldn't he . . . ?" questions about the story.

BRYAN COGMAN: You don't want to lean heavily on the time travel or it becomes a crutch. The way we worked around that—and it's built into the storyline—is because his cave was breached by the Night King, it's the classic *Empire Strikes Back* trope—"incomplete is your training." Bran had all the information but lacked the tools to sift through it. So it came in fits and starts.

DAN WEISS (*showrunner*): One of the things we loved about *Game of Thrones* from the very beginning was, it's not a world where magic was the primary driver of the story. It's a world where human psychology and behavior and desire are drivers of the story, and we tried very hard to make sure it stayed that way because those are a lot more relatable to the vast majority of the audience than magic powers—as much fun as those are.

One chunk of data the Three-Eyed Raven successfully downloaded was insight into Littlefinger's betrayal of Ned Stark, as well as Baelish's chat with Varys where he proclaimed: "Chaos isn't a pit. Chaos is a ladder. Many who try to climb it fail and never get to try again. The fall breaks them. And some are given a chance to climb, but they refuse; they cling to the realm or the gods or love. Illusions. Only the ladder is real. The climb is all there is."

Weiss wrote the "chaos is a ladder" speech back in season one and tried to get it into two previous Littlefinger scenes before the lines finally found an appropriate home in season three.

DAVID BENIOFF (*showrunner*): That was cut twice. We kept trying to get it in.

DAN WEISS: We filmed it once in another scene and it wasn't working, so we had to cut bait on it. By the third time it came around, David must have thought, "Dude, c'mon, it's just four words, just let them die."

AIDAN GILLEN: I remember shooting the [original "chaos is a ladder"] scene quite well; working with Conleth Hill is always interesting and dangerous and fun. But it was really in a post-production ADR session that the scene ratcheted up a notch. I've always liked dubbing sessions because at the very least you replicate what you've done already but there's also an opportunity to finesse the tone of the scene. When I saw the cut—especially that it cut back to Sansa as she watched the ships sail—I knew it needed more intensity and pointedness. Producer Frank Doelger was supervising that session, and he indulged me with time to play around. The line became the Petyr Baelish mantra. That and "Pimpin' ain't easy."

ISAAC HEMPSTEAD WRIGHT: Getting to say Littlefinger's line back to him was one of my favorite moments. It's such an iconic line, and watching him get freaked out was so cool.

AIDAN GILLEN: When Bran told him "chaos is a ladder," that's when the ground started to shift beneath my feet. At that point I knew the things I'd done in private are not necessarily private.

Littlefinger's scheme backfired, with the Starks uniting to uncover his plot. They summoned Baelish to the great hall, where they served as his judge (Sansa), jury (Bran), and executioner (Arya). The twist also meant the departure of Gillen, who generously bought the *Thrones* crew seventy bottles of whiskey each year.

DAVID BENIOFF: Littlefinger became a much different character than we initially imagined. Aidan's one of these guys who's able to change things in ways that are strange and beguiling, to the betterment of the character. Relatively speaking, he's a minor character if you look at his screen time. But the fact that Littlefinger looms so large when people talk about the show and when we think about the show, it's really a credit to him. Every scene he's in, he manages to make you think about Littlefinger. And scenes where he's at the center, like in his final scene, he's completely mesmerizing.

CONLETH HILL (*Varys*): It would have been great to have had one more meeting with Varys and Littlefinger. I think they tried to make that work and couldn't. And I was bummed not to have any reaction to him dying, if he was my nemesis. After [season six], I felt like I dropped off the edge a bit.

DAVID BENIOFF: Diana Rigg was so true to her character in the end, and Littlefinger was true to his character in the end—in his own cowardly, horrible way. It was one of the harder death calls we had to make, but he fucked with the wrong girls.

SOPHIE TURNER: That's my favorite scene, because it showed the power of these two sisters and how together they're more powerful than apart. It's a liberating moment for Sansa when she realizes she doesn't need him anymore. It felt amazing for the character. She's finally free of this manipulating, overbearing presence. It's never been an easy relationship. She's always had qualms about him. It's like a graduation. In order for her family to be a strong unit, she had to get rid of him. At the same time, it was bittersweet because he'd been a friend to her; he'd put her into shitty situations, but he'd pulled her out of situations too. And Aidan killed it. It was the first time you saw him get emotional.

JEREMY PODESWA (director): The twists in the scene are very strong. There's a great amount of satisfaction seeing the Stark kids come together, and it's a vindication for Sansa, who Littlefinger basically sold to Ramsay. It's also moving and surprisingly powerful to see Littlefinger have the tables turned on him. He's the one who's always been able to manipulate every situation. He's a character you love to hate that you now have some empathy for because he's a guy fighting for his life. It was one of my favorite scenes I've done on the show and was for Aidan too—even though he had a hard time leaving. He probably had one of the most satisfying endings of any character.

Gillen pointed out the full-circle perfection of Littlefinger's death. The character's overambitious rise to power was fueled by the moment, decades earlier, when Ned Stark's brother Brandon defeated him while dueling for Catelyn Stark's hand. Brandon left Littlefinger with a cut along his torso as a reminder of his defeat, a scar Baelish forever kept hidden by wearing high-necked tunics. Then Catelyn's daughter condemned him to die while Brandon's namesake nephew, Bran, provided the evidence leading to his doom—including the dagger Baelish once gave to an assassin to use when he tried to kill Bran in season one.

AIDAN GILLEN: As soon as he walked into that room and Arya produced the dagger, he knew the game was up. It was an emotional farewell and a humiliating position to be in. He was back in the position that had been a driver for him—the rejection of Catelyn Stark, the humiliation by Brandon Stark.

There had to be more feelings for Sansa than I let on. But I don't want to say too much about that. I want to preserve that. I don't want to lay my cards on the table.

---◇---

CHAPTER TWENTY-EIGHT

WALKS AND TALKS

G ame of Thrones actors had no idea how their storylines were going to end. So when a date was set for a read-through of the final six episodes in October 2017, the cast grew anxious. The production was preparing to send them a secure link to the top secret scripts. At last they would know the conclusion of the story they had spent a decade telling the world.

"As the seasons have gone on, we've all thought: How's it going to end?" Peter Dinklage said. "Who's going to be alive? If you die, how do you die? It can drive you mad."

And the cast weren't the only ones who were nervous.

DAVID BENIOFF (*showrunner*): We knew when our script coordinator sent the scripts out to the cast. We knew exactly what minute they sent them. Then you're just waiting for the actors to email.

DAN WEISS (*showrunner*): When you've been working on something for ten years, knowing you're writing the last episodes is harder because there's a lot more weight and pressure on those scenes. "Is a line right?" seems more important. On the other hand, the motivations behind the scenes are things you've been thinking about for five years, so the foundations in your mind are stronger for what you're putting on paper.

JOE DEMPSIE (*Gendry*): The scripts came the Thursday before the Sunday of the read-through. I was just idly checking my emails at the gym and then they were there.

EMILIA CLARKE (*Daenerys Targaryen*): I was on a plane coming back from a holiday, and I had this little tiny break between *Star Wars* and *Game of Thrones* and I thought, "I bet when I'm on my break they're going to send me the fucking scripts and I'll have to read them and feel sad." I did the whole holiday, and as soon as I landed in Heathrow, *boop*, they're there, perfect. I turned to my best mate who I was with and was like, "Oh my God!" and completely flipped out. "I gotta go! I gotta go!" And they're like, "You got to get your bags!"

JOE DEMPSIE: Everybody's WhatsApp [the cast's private group chat] sparked to life: "*They're here!*" Everybody was saying, "Don't ruin anything for me!" But Jacob admitted he checked episode six first to see if he survived.

JACOB ANDERSON (*Grey Worm*): I had a certain level of suspicion. It's the end and you're going to find out the fates of everyone in the show. "What's mine? Where am I gonna be?" And I didn't really want it to end. This is the first time the scripts arrived that I didn't want to read them because then I would have to accept that it's over.

PETER DINKLAGE (*Tyrion Lannister*): This was the first time ever that I didn't skip to the end [to see if Tyrion survived].

ISAAC HEMPSTEAD WRIGHT (*Bran Stark*): At first I genuinely thought it was a joke script, that David and Dan sent one to everyone with their own character ending up on the Iron Throne. Yeah, good one. Then I realized it was real. I just wanted to shout, "King, motherfuckers!" in the street.

LIAM CUNNINGHAM (*Davos Seaworth*): I was in New York, and the fucking things wouldn't open—the double extra security! Everybody thought I was a Luddite that I couldn't open them. Later I got to Belfast and went, "Here you go!" and they couldn't open it either. So it wasn't my fault.

MAISIE WILLIAMS (*Arya Stark*): I hadn't realized we received them. I was hanging out with friends having time off and Sophie was like, "Have you read them?" She said, "Whatever you do, you have to skip to *this* episode, *this* scene first." It was the Arya-and-Gendry scene.

SOPHIE TURNER (*Sansa Stark*): I did! I'm all, "Read it, this is awesome," and she was very happy with that. We always end up spoiling it for each other.

Gwendoline Christie and Nikolaj Coster-Waldau were also surprised that their characters hooked up in the final season.

GWENDOLINE CHRISTIE (*Brienne of Tarth*): I received a text from Nikolaj just laughing. I sent back a being-sick emoji. How modern.

As the showrunners continued to watch their email and wait, several cast members felt abruptly inspired to take long walks.

DAN WEISS: Why aren't they writing?! Does that mean they like it? Does that mean they hate it?

DAVID BENIOFF: Sophie was the first one to write, so she got credit for racing through all six scripts in like an hour or something.

SOPHIE TURNER: You have so many expectations of what it's going to be and how it's going to end. I'd thought up a hundred different scenarios of what will happen. When you're actually reading it, and partly because David and Dan are pranksters, you're thinking, "This can't be true! Is this the way it really ends? *Oh my God oh my God oh my God.*"

EMILIA CLARKE: This is going to sound really sad, but how I hope a mega-fan approaches watching the final season is how I approached reading the final season. I was like, okay, I got myself situated, I got my cup of tea—I had to physically prepare the space—and then read them. The effect it had on me was profound. I left the house and took my keys and phone and walked back with blisters on my feet because I walked for hours.

SOPHIE TURNER: Afterward I felt numb and I had to take a walk for hours and hours. And I cried a lot. It wasn't anything in particular, just that it came to an end. But I thought it was an awesome way to end the show.

GWENDOLINE CHRISTIE: If you're lucky enough to get to season eight, you expect to die on the first page. The very worst-case scenario is dying off-screen. Every couple of pages I kept thinking I was dead. It's an emotional thing; I put my heart and soul into this project and had thrown myself into it physically as well, which had been incredibly challenging. There were also a few times reading them that I blushed very intensely. It was a powerful emotion to read some of the things that were occurring. I had to go for a very long walk, and I had lots of questions.

The cast also felt the weight like never before of knowing spoilers. They held the pop culture nuclear codes that the world wanted access to, and they were worried about saying the wrong thing—even to each other.

JOE DEMPSIE: There were moments where you didn't trust yourself to have that in your brain. You were in possession of something millions of people wanted to know. It was such a bizarre feeling, like being a spy and having a briefcase full of secrets.

EMILIA CLARKE: People would say, "Hey, dude, what's up?" "Nothing, what's up with you?" "Done any good reading lately? . . ." Then you got paranoid about putting anything in text form.

Actors who discovered their characters did not survive to the very end had varied reactions to their fates.

IAIN GLEN (*Jorah Mormont*): For eight years, you go, "*Please-please . . .*" You just want to stay in the party, you just want to stay on board. This was the season to [get killed off], if you're going to go. It's a heroic and satisfying demise [for Ser Jorah]. Dan and David were sweetly nervous about everyone's reaction, and their instinct is you'll be upset if you go. So the first thing I did was I emailed them and told them how much I loved the scripts.

CONLETH HILL (*Varys*): At the time, nothing could console me. I kept thinking, "What'd I do wrong?" You couldn't help feeling that you failed in some way, that you hadn't lived up to some expectation that you didn't know about. I don't think anybody who hasn't been through it can identify with it. They think, "What's all the fuss about? We're all finishing anyway." But you take it personally; you can't help it. With a bit of perspective, you go, "Oh, it's a great way to go, it's noble and for the good." With hindsight, I'm okay, but I really was inconsolable.

DAVE HILL (*co-producer*): Of course, some actors were like, "I wanted to be king or queen at the end," or would want a ten-page monologue for their character. But they all received it well.

And then there was Kit Harington's reaction—or lack thereof.

KIT HARINGTON (*Jon Snow*): Emilia and I sat next to each other on the plane on the way to Belfast. I told her I hadn't read them.

EMILIA CLARKE: Oh, God. That literally sums up Kit and my friendship. *"Boy! Would you?! Seriously? You're just not? . . ."*

KIT HARINGTON: What's the point of reading it to myself in my own head when I can listen to the [rest of the cast at the table read] do it and find out with my friends?

DAN WEISS: "Kit's not writing us. . . . Fuck. Does he hate it? If he hates it does that mean we got it wrong?" We spent a lot of time thinking about his character.

Then we saw him on the day of the table read. We said: "So?"

KIT HARINGTON: I walked into the room going, "I haven't read it, don't tell me. . . ."

DAN WEISS: He was like: "I want to experience it the first time in this room." Which was a huge relief, because if he had read it and hadn't said anything, that probably meant at the very least he felt strong ambivalence.

KIT HARINGTON: I became a kind of litmus test, because they were looking to my reactions to things. It made the day really fun.

PETER DINKLAGE: I should have thought of doing that too, because it was such a visceral experience.

MAISIE WILLIAMS: Before the table read, everybody was talking about episode three. Miguel was like, "Have you read the script yet?" And I was like, "No." And he's like, "Oh, I can't tell you." And I was like, "Are we fighting the wights? So does [the Night King] die? Who kills him? What happens?" And no one would say anything. Why is no one saying it?

Over the course of two days, the *Game of Thrones* cast read through the season-eight scripts in a conference room.

CARICE VAN HOUTEN (*Melisandre*): It's like coming back to school. You're seeing all your friends again. This was coming back for the last time. When different cast members met their demise, everybody cheered each other and showed love and applauded. When somebody had their final moments, the whole room would erupt to show support for that person.

KIT HARINGTON: When Arya dropped the Night King and plunged in the dagger, it got a huge fucking cheer.

RORY McCANN (*Sandor "the Hound" Clegane*): It was quite emotional. You're seeing deaths and all happening in front of you and seeing people get upset. When the so-called Clegane Bowl started, I brought a trumpet with me and blew it right before I said one of my last lines.

Then the cast got to the most pivotal moment in the final season: Jon Snow putting a knife through the heart of his lover, Daenerys Targaryen. The series-finale script reads:

Standing before the Iron Throne, Dany steps forward and kisses the man she loves. A perfect kiss, an expression of pure love and passion.
    We push in on them until we're tight on their faces—their eyes closed, his hand behind her head, her hand on his cheek.
    Dany's eyes open suddenly as she draws a sharp breath. Jon's eyes open as well, already filling with tears. For a moment, neither moves, as if moving will make this real.

In a wider angle, we see Jon with his hand still on the hilt of the dagger he just lodged in Dany's heart. Her strength leaves her and she collapses to the marble; he keeps her in his arms as she falls, kneeling down to the floor beside her.

He looks down at what he's done. Terrible. And necessary. He hopes for one last moment with her.

KIT HARINGTON: Emilia sat opposite at the table. I was reading it. I looked at her and there was a moment of, *"No, no . . . ,"* and she was going [*nods sadly*].

Harington can be seen in HBO's documentary *Game of Thrones: The Last Watch* pushing away from the table, tearing up, and covering his mouth with his hand.

MAISIE WILLIAMS: He looked up, and Emilia was, like, nodding, and he had a little tear. Honestly, it was a relief. Everything you've been waiting for is finally coming to an end, and it felt right. I saved episode six for the read-through, so I didn't know the end either.

KIT HARINGTON: I cried at two points. One was the scene with Jon and Dany, which I found very emotional, and then again at the very end. Every season, you read at the end of the last script, "End of Season 1" or "End of Season 2." This read, "End of Game of Thrones." And you go, "Fuck, okay, it's really happening."

CHAPTER TWENTY-NINE

THE LONGEST NIGHT

Winterfell's courtyard was covered with snow, dirt, and blood. Wood logs burned in fire pits, throwing off heat and smoke. Stiff corpses bearing all manner of gruesome mortal injuries lay in crumpled piles. From the castle walls, the Stark banners hung limply.

I mounted the slippery stairs and walked along the castle's creaking ramparts, passing through cramped battlements. Near the top of the main gate, there were gaps in the parapet wall offering a dizzying view of the battlefield stretched out below. On the field were hulking trebuchets, deep trenches lined with wood stakes, and hundreds of uniformed men preparing to fight. My breath was icy. The freezing rain had begun again. Somewhere an assistant director yelled for extras to reset on their marks: "This is not a tea party, c'mon!"

Ser Davos walked past. "I signed up for a character piece," he sighed.

During the first season of *Game of Thrones*, a Winterfell set was constructed in the middle of a sheep field. The castle was impressive, but in 2017, the production rebuilt it at nearly three times its original size for the final season and the great battle between the living and the dead. You could now wander in any direction on the grounds and maintain the illusion that you were at the Stark home. It was the ultimate medieval fantasy playground, young George R. R. Martin's turtle castle brought to life.

DEBORAH RILEY (*production designer*): Part of expanding Winterfell was being able to show spaces that had never been shown before. We never understood where the food came from, where the beer came from, where the bread came from—all of those back-of-the-house activities. I was actually able to understand it more as a living, breathing castle.

But had anybody understood in season one where the show would be heading, Winterfell would have been put in a different spot and not a boggy sheep farm. Just making it so soldiers could run back and forth, let alone bringing in machinery, without being knee-deep in mud, was a huge ordeal.

Closer to Belfast, there was another enormous *Thrones* set that reconstructed several streets in the Old Town of Dubrovnik. That was built for the *other* final-season battle, the one set in King's Landing, and it was impressive in a different way—a mini-maze of cobblestone streets that looked precisely like their Croatian counterparts. It was necessary to make a meticulous copy of an existing city because, as showrunner Dan Weiss pointed out, "we cannot blow up Dubrovnik."

The showrunners had long imagined these two battles for the show's final season: one war against the dead, and another where the survivors turned on each other. Both were unthinkable on the show's previous budget and schedule. The production also spent nine months filming six episodes instead of the six months they normally took to shoot ten episodes. To put that in context, principal photography on most Hollywood films typically takes around three or four months.

When you factored in the amount of time the *Thrones* team spent filming the final season, the intensity of staging the action scenes, the global pressure to deliver a satisfying ending, and the show's brutal outdoor working conditions, the obstacles faced by the show's cast and crew during season eight were, as Nikolaj Coster-Waldau put it, "unheard of."

"A scene that would have been a one-day shoot two years ago was a five-day shoot," Kit Harington said. "They wanted to get it right. They wanted to shoot it every single way so they had options. And because it was the finale, after eight seasons most scenes are emotional. Consistently having to have your emotions that high, it became fucking exhausting."

The production's biggest challenge—not just for season eight, but throughout the entire show—was the episode titled "The Long Night." The threat of the White Walkers had been teased since the pilot's opening scene. Everybody working on *Thrones* knew the Winterfell battle had to pay off years of anticipation.

DAVID BENIOFF (*showrunner*): We've been building toward this since the very beginning, and it's the living against the dead, and you couldn't do that in a twelve-minute sequence.

DAN WEISS (*showrunner*): The idea from the beginning was there were all of these squabbles going on that seemed so important and global and earth-shattering and were happening against the backdrop of much larger and more momentous events that very few—people who lived on the fringes of the political world—knew about. It always was the overarching structure of the series that these things in the far east and far north would come together and decide the fate of everybody in the middle.

Typical battle episodes on *Thrones* would contain about fifteen minutes or so of calm-before-the-storm discussion scenes before all hell broke loose. In season eight, the writers devoted an entire episode to the characters' preparing for battle, Bryan Cogman's playlike "A Knight of the Seven Kingdoms" (we'll discuss some of the major moments from that episode later). That way, "The Long Night" could hit the ground running with arguably the longest consecutive battle sequence ever filmed—an eighty-two-minute episode consisting entirely of various types of action sequences (by comparison, the famed Omaha Beach assault that opened *Saving Private Ryan* was twenty-seven minutes, and the battle of Helm's Deep in *The Two Towers* was forty minutes). To lead the project, producers brought back "Hardhome" and "Battle of the Bastards" veteran Miguel Sapochnik.

MIGUEL SAPOCHNIK (*director*): There was a bit of trepidation because there was now this expectation that you have to beat yourself, which I loathe.

DAVID BENIOFF: Having the largest battle doesn't sound very exciting. It sounds pretty boring. Part of our challenge—and really Miguel's challenge—was how to keep that compelling. If it's just humans hacking and slashing at wights for fifty-five minutes, it was going to quickly become dull.

MIGUEL SAPOCHNIK: At some point you exhaust an audience. I watched *The Two Towers*, and it's actually three different battles in three different places intercut. I was trying to get a sense of when do you tire out. It felt like the only way to really approach that stuff properly was to take every sequence and ask yourself: "Why, as an audience member, would I care to keep watching?"

The battle's not-so-secret weapon was the show's ensemble of beloved characters. The team figured if the episode focused on fan favorites having different kinds of battle adventures, then a variety of character-driven stories would pull the audience through all the requisite hack-and-slash.

DAN WEISS: The action is driven by character, not by how many swords and spears you can swing around. We've been lucky enough we've had seventy-plus hours of showing who everybody is. There were so many individual stories you bring to that situation.

DAVE HILL (*co-producer*): Most battles are the last fifteen minutes of a movie for a reason. People lose interest. So we'd have a big field battle. Then we'd have Arya in a haunted-house sequence in the library. We'd have Tyrion and Sansa in the crypt, which would become like a horror movie. We have Dany and Jon on the dragons. Each story had different textures so it wouldn't just be the same thing.

MIGUEL SAPOCHNIK: The process of whittling down the script took a lot longer this time because David and Dan wanted to keep everything. We all wanted everything but were up against the reality of what we could achieve. And one of the things I found interesting was the less action—the *less* fighting—you can have in a sequence, the better. And we switched genres from suspense to horror to action to drama, and that way we're not stuck in killing upon killing, because everybody gets desensitized and it doesn't mean anything.

The original production plan for "The Long Night" was to break up filming into small segments, which would require fewer cast and crew members to be on the set at any given time. But that would make the filmmaking heavily structured and limit Sapochnik's ability to improvise or to have as many shots that included large groups of cast members. As Sapochnik had learned on "Hardhome" and "Battle of the Bastards," nothing ever goes precisely according to plan—especially when filming outdoors in hostile weather—so it was essential that he could quickly pivot in response to changing circumstances.

MIGUEL SAPOCHNIK: We built this massive new part of Winterfell and thought, "We'll film this part *here* and this *there*," and basically broke it into so many pieces it would be like a Marvel movie, with never any flow

Davos Seaworth (Liam Cunningham) mourns Jon Snow as Ghost sleeps.

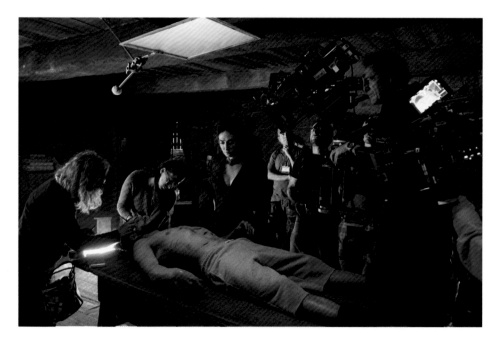

Carice van Houten and Kit Harington prepare for the resurrection scene.

The return of Jon Snow.

Grey Worm (Jacob Anderson) and Missandei (Nathalie Emmanuel)
share a couple of tender moments.

Sophie Turner and Alfie Allen share a laugh between shots in season six.

The "Queen of Thorns"
Olenna Tyrell (Diana Rigg).

Hodor (Kristian Nairn) holds the door.

Free Folk giant Wun Weg Wun Dar Wun (Ian Whyte) among Jon Snow's line of troops
at the Battle of the Bastards.

Jon Snow takes on the Bolton army at the Battle of the Bastards.

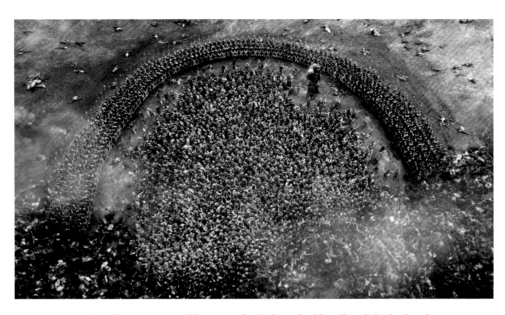

Jon Snow's army trapped between the Bolton shield wall and the body pile.

Jon Snow struggles up toward the light during the Battle of the Bastards.

Kit Harington checks his last take during the battle filming.

Peter Dinklage peers at a "dragon" on a cliff on the set in Spain.

Jaime Lannister charges a dragon.

Daenerys Targaryen, meet Jon Snow.

Drogon lays waste to the Lannister army.

Pilou Asbæk plays Euron Greyjoy on a rampage
during the filming of the "Stormborn" sea battle.

Isaac Hempstead Wright, Maisie Williams,
and Sophie Turner perform at Winterfell's weirwood tree.

Joe Dempsie, Rory McCann, Kristofer Hivju, Kit Harington, Richard Dormer, and Paul Kaye take a rest while shooting "Beyond the Wall."

Filming the "Beyond the Wall" wight attack on a mock frozen lake in Northern Ireland.

Daenerys fights alongside Ser Jorah Mormont (Iain Glen) during "The Long Night."

Emilia Clarke intently rides the dragon rig (aka "the Green Turtle")
in the motion-capture suite.

Arya is throttled by the Night King a moment before she passes the dagger to her right hand.

Cersei and Jaime Lannister spend their final moments together.

The throne room in ruins while filming "The Iron Throne."

Filming the series finale, "The Iron Throne."

King Bran I the Broken along with Arya and Sansa.

The final *Game of Thrones* panel at Comic-Con 2019.

or improvisation. Even on *Star Wars,* they build certain parts of the set and then add huge elements of green screen. Everything would be broken into little morsels to be put back together. And that makes sense. There's an efficiency to that. But there's something that you lose when doing it that way, and you lose the spontaneity of being able to move the camera anywhere. And I was walking around the set thinking, "This is really cool, I can walk around and find angles I would never have found beforehand."

So Sapochnik suggested an alternative schedule that would include eleven weeks of consecutive night shoots.

MIGUEL SAPOCHNIK: I turned to producers and said, "I know it's shitty and going to be cold. I don't want to do eleven weeks of night shoots, and no one else does. But if we continue the way we're going, we're going to lose what makes *Game of Thrones* cool—that it feels real, even though it's supernatural and we have dragons."

Thrones had filmed plenty of nighttime action sequences over the years, but the rain-drenched battles for the Battle of the Blackwater and the Battle of Castle Black had taken about three weeks each. To the producers' knowledge, no movie or show had ever attempted a filming schedule like this before.

LIAM CUNNINGHAM (*Davos Seaworth*): They brought us into a tent and broke the news to us. They ran through the episode's pre-viz—a slightly animated storyboard in visual form. We saw this extraordinary series of images. Miguel was saying we're going to do this over fifty-five nights, and there was a lot of people looking at each other. There were those of us who were on "Battle of the Bastards," which was less than half of what this was attempting, and during the day. I immediately thought, "Fucking hell. This is a nightmare. It's like a deliberate attempt to fuck the whole thing up." On paper, it's madness. But they wanted everybody to be aware of the shit they would put us in so nobody could say they didn't know.

DAVE HILL: Miguel sent out an email to all the cast: "Please get on a night schedule ahead of time, because you're going to be so tired and wet and cold you need to give yourself every advantage you can."

GWENDOLINE CHRISTIE (*Brienne of Tarth*): I requested a meeting with Miguel. It was very important to me that we saw Jaime and Brienne's relationship expressed throughout the battle. That what we should see is this relationship has been going on and building for a long time, and they're in a rare situation where they can completely trust and depend on each other. You take that complicated and solid relationship and take that into brutal, mind-blowing, apocalyptic war. Does it break them apart or force them closer together?

MAISIE WILLIAMS (*Arya Stark*): I had skipped the battle every year, which is bizarre since Arya's the one who's been training the most. Then Miguel called me a year before and said: "Start training now, because it's going to be really hard." And I said, "*Yeah, yeah . . .*"

The episode would include the death of several characters, such as Theon Greyjoy, who finally had a selfless and heroic moment when trying to protect Bran from the Night King. . . .

BRYAN COGMAN: It was difficult for Alfie because there was a degree of physical stunt work and effects and things that were out of his control. And for him to have to play his final moments amidst all that chaos and craziness was tremendously challenging for him. I remember the night we shot it, and it was just one of those things you had to do in addition to a bunch of other things. It's only when it came together and you see beautiful subtlety and anguish in his performance, but also that kind of catharsis that Theon's finally at peace going out protecting Bran. For all the talk of redemption arcs, fulfilled or not, his was certainly fulfilled.

. . . and Jorah Mormont, who died protecting Daenerys from the Army of the Dead.

IAIN GLEN (*Jorah Mormont*): You either conclude as a character, or you get to the end of the whole thing and people try to project forward of what's the future of your character that you'll never know. I was happy to conclude. He would absolutely sacrifice his life for her to succeed. In a way, he was given the conclusion he wanted.

DAVE HILL: For a long time we wanted Ser Jorah there at the Wall in the very end—the three coming out of the tunnel [in the series finale] were to be Jon, Jorah, and Tormund. But the amount of logic we'd have had to bend to get Jorah up to the Wall and get him to leave Dany's side right before [her tragic turn]—there's no way to do that blithely, and Jorah should have the noble death he craved defending the woman he loves.

Another casualty was young Lyanna Mormont. Actress Bella Ramsey was originally only cast for a single episode in season six, but she was such a ferocious scene stealer, the showrunners kept bringing her back. (Ramsey's favorite of her character's feisty lines: "I don't care if he is a bastard, Ned Stark's blood runs through his veins!")

BRYAN COGMAN: Bella's first scene could've been a disaster. It could have easily ended up on the cutting-room floor if some cute kid actor came in. But she was utterly credible. And at one point Kit blew a line and she fed it to him because she had memorized every line in the scene.

MARK MYLOD (*director*): Kit was all, "I wished I'd learned my lines better. I'm being shown up!" It was one of those times when you called "cut" and there was a spontaneous round of applause.

In "The Long Night," Lyanna faced off against a zombie giant. She was crushed in his fist, yet still managed to take him down by stabbing him in the eye.

BELLA RAMSEY (*Lyanna Mormont*): There was one thing Miguel said to me that I don't think I'll ever forget. I wasn't sure if she would be really scared or just a slight bit of scared. We tried it several ways. He said, "It's like someone removed her fear gene." And that was a really great bit of direction. Her story maybe had the potential to grow, but she was going to go at some point because everyone does, and the way she went was the best way she could have. I wanted to either end up on the Iron Throne or have a really good death. So I'm happy.

Melisandre perished as well. The Red Woman returned to help defeat the forces of darkness, then stripped off her necklace granting eternal youth and walked into the sunrise, her body decomposing, to join the piles of dead.

CARICE VAN HOUTEN (*Melisandre*): She saved the day, so she's a bit of a hero in the end, which is cool, because for a long time she was hated. In a very bombastic orchestra piece, I was happy to be the soft piano notes at the end. We finally know what she came for, and it's the end of her journey—I can go now, my work's done. I tried to play it with tiredness but with relief.

Sometimes a character's last line, even a simple one, can be the toughest to say. Once you speak those words, you will never again play a role that you've lived for so many years.

CARICE VAN HOUTEN: I wasn't able to nail my last sentence. I say to Liam: "You don't have to kill me because I'll be dead before dawn." I got a bit cranky. I feel like I'd done sixty takes of that line. I couldn't nail it. I don't know why.

Perhaps most crucially, the Night King also fell. Arya dispatched the White Walker leader with her Valyrian-steel dagger, which was introduced in the show's first season when an assassin used it to attack Bran Stark. The dagger passed to Catelyn, then to Littlefinger, then to Bran, and then to Arya (who also used it to kill Littlefinger in season seven). Given that the Night King is not in Martin's books, the manner of his death was a major climactic decision that was left to the showrunners. They initially considered several hero candidates to take out the story's biggest villain.

DAVID BENIOFF: It had to be somebody with believable access to Valyrian steel. We didn't want it to be Jon because he's always saving the day. We talked about the Hound at one point, but we wanted his big thing to be Clegane Bowl. Ultimately it wouldn't have felt right if it was Jon or Brienne or the Hound.

DAN WEISS: Then we put in Sam's book from the Citadel how dragonglass had found its way into the design of implements when people didn't even know what they were working with, and there's a picture of Arya's dagger.

DAVID BENIOFF: That dagger had been set up from the very beginning, and we knew Arya was going to get it at the end of season seven to kill Littlefinger. It had to be Arya. It goes back to the whole "not today" thing.

DAN WEISS: "What do you say to the god of death?" Well, the Night King is the closest embodiment of the god of death.

There was also a prescient line uttered by Arya in season two: "Anyone can be killed."

MIGUEL SAPOCHNIK: I was going to have this sequence before she kills him showing each character in the story fighting their way to the final moment. I was going to shoot it so that we begin to intercut between them and they all begin to become the same character. I was interested in the idea they're all the children of these kings who are all fated to become this role—including the Night King. He's the product of something that went wrong with the Children of the Forest. It would culminate with all the characters having the same composition. But we cut that.

Once we pared it back, I thought, "Hmm, if I see Arya running I know she's going to do something." So it was about almost losing her from the story and then have her as a surprise. We're pinning all our hopes on Jon being the guy going to do it, because he's always the guy. So we make him a continuous shot. I want the audience to think: "Jon's gonna do it, Jon's gonna do it . . . ," and then he *fails*. He fails at the very last minute.

DAN WEISS: We wanted to show there were overwhelming numbers and how nobody through sheer hack-and-slash could do it. The obstacle between them and the Night King was insurmountable—unless you had something magical going for you on your side, which Arya did. She's a person the Night King wouldn't be thinking about, and ideally the audience wouldn't be thinking about her at the moment either.

MAISIE WILLIAMS: It was so unbelievably exciting. But I immediately thought that everybody would hate it and that she doesn't deserve it. I told my boyfriend, and he was like, "Mmm, should be Jon though, really, shouldn't it?" And that didn't give me a lot of confidence. The hardest thing is in any series you build up a villain that's so impossible to defeat and then you defeat them. Some hundred-pound girl comes in and stabs him. It has to be intelligently done.

Williams's perception of the twist changed after she shot her scene with van Houten in which Melisandre reminded Arya what she told her in season three: "I see a darkness in you. And in that darkness, eyes staring back at me. Brown eyes. Blue eyes. Green eyes. Eyes you'll shut forever. We will meet again." The scene suggested Arya was fated to destroy the Night King, though the order of the eye colors was changed to conclude with "blue eyes" when Melisandre repeated the line.

CARICE VAN HOUTEN: I felt like that guy in the movie who gives the main character one last push to do it, like in a football game.

MAISIE WILLIAMS: We were shooting the bit with Melisandre, and she brings it back to everything Arya's been working for over these past six seasons. It all comes down to this one very moment. So then I was like, "Fuck you, Jon, I get it."

So Melisandre not only gave Arya the confidence to attack the Night King but also convinced Williams that her character could pull it off. Of course, whether Arya was truly destined to destroy the Night King or Melisandre simply encouraged the right person at the right time is—as with all prophecies on *Thrones*—left unclear. But thousands of years ago, the Children of the Forest created the demon by piercing a captive man in the heart with dragonglass, and the young Stark managed to stab him in roughly the same place. The Night King was unmade as he was made.

KIT HARINGTON (*Jon Snow*): I thought it was gonna be me! But I like it because it gives Arya's training a purpose. It's much better how she does it. It will frustrate some audience members that he's hunting the Night King and you're expecting this epic fight and it never happens, but that's kind of *Thrones*.

ISAAC HEMPSTEAD WRIGHT (*Bran Stark*): That moment before when Bran sees the Night King is about to attack him—my reading of that was that Bran should look at him with pity because he knows how this guy was created. He's not a monster; he's a weapon who's gone badly wrong. He's an innocent man with a piece of glass plunged in his heart. And we ended up playing it like that. "I'm sorry this happened to you."

There were also dragons and giants and Jon Snow's direwolf, Ghost, in the battle as well. But the producers ruled out adding the fabled ice spiders that Old Nan had hauntingly described in season one when telling the legend of the Long Night.

DAN WEISS: "Big as hounds." Didn't we talk about that for thirty seconds? Sounds good. Looks good on a metal album cover. But once they start moving, what does an ice spider look like? Probably doesn't look great.

Even with all of Sapochnik's warnings, the episode's schedule was far tougher than any of the cast or crew had anticipated. Filming started with two weeks of night shoots in December. Then there were a couple more weeks of scattered night shoots at the start of the year. Then came fifty-five night shoots in a row. And finally, there was about two months of daytime filming inside a studio.

Those fifty-five nights sandwiched in the middle of an already demanding schedule became like a real-life version of an eternal soul-crushing supernatural winter. The production had the added misfortune of getting slammed by two "polar vortex" storms, dubbed "the Beast from the East" in the press, as if White Walkers had literally arrived on the set. The storms brought extreme low temperatures with weather that local reports said felt as low as nineteen degrees Fahrenheit. "One night we were supposed to film Jorah defending Dany by a flaming trebuchet, and we had to call it off because it got so cold that the gas fire bars wouldn't light," Dave Hill recalled.

The cold blast combined with freezing rain, gusting wind, and an intensively physical and technical job that stretched from early evenings to the mornings. The *Thrones* crew prided themselves on being resilient, but the "The Long Night" very nearly broke them. The cast had to become actor-athletes, enduring week after week of physical endurance challenges while continuing to give their usual acclaimed performances.

IAIN GLEN: I don't think people can comprehend what eleven weeks of continuous night shoots does to the human body and brain. It destroys your system and your thinking. We just had to get so wet and so dirty and so cold and do it again and again that it really was the hardest thing in all eight seasons for all departments. You kind of try and retain a gallows humor, but it was absolutely brutal.

In storytelling terms, it made sense because of who they were up against. But it was a real test. It completely fucked your body clock. You have no life outside it. On day shoots you'll go have a meal in the evening and do a bit of something. On nights those down hours are removed. You get to sleep at seven in the morning and then you get up in the midday and can't really do anything. It was the most unpleasant experience in all of *Thrones*.

JACOB ANDERSON (*Grey Worm*): Grey Worm doesn't say much, so I had to put a lot of feeling and expression into how he fought. You're trying to keep all the meaning in your face yet also remember the technical details—then do that twenty times.

JOE DEMPSIE (*Gendry*): Every night there was a tipping point around two A.M. where everybody started behaving a little bit weird.

GWENDOLINE CHRISTIE: It was utter madness. It's the crew I felt for. They were the ones who were truly at the face of brutal suffering when it came to the relentlessness of the schedule.

RORY McCANN (*Sandor "the Hound" Clegane*): Everybody prays they never have to do that again. You could recognize crew members [during the day] who were on it because they looked gray.

LIAM CUNNINGHAM: It wasn't an exercise in creativity. It was a lesson in discipline. Not getting tired, not getting bored—if you get bored you take your eye off the ball and you mess it up.

MAISIE WILLIAMS: Nothing could prepare you for how physically draining it was. It was night after night and again and again, and it just didn't stop. And you can't get sick. You have to look out for yourself because there's so much to do that nobody else is going to. You get wet and then at four A.M. the wind comes and your leather outfit is soaking and you just have to keep going. It's bizarre because when you see the movies it looks so glamorous. And there are times when it is. But there are times when it goes the other way so far that it's not even recognizable as the same industry. There are moments you're just broken as a human and just want to cry.

CHRISTOPHER NEWMAN (*producer*): It was just the unremitting nature of every day knowing that you're going to be working in the cold until five in the morning. You're fighting your brain and trying to take it one step at a time. The person you admire the most is the director, because he can't take it one step at a time and default to simply doing his job. He's the one building a jigsaw puzzle without the box to look at.

DAVE HILL: I don't know how Miguel did it, because I was not sane, and I didn't have to be fixing things every second of every day. You became a shell of a person.

IAIN GLEN: How Miguel managed to hold it together is beyond my comprehension.

RORY MCCANN: There are some directors who don't speak much, and if you're doing your job there are no words. Sometimes younger actors do a scene and there's a feeling of "want" on their face: "Did I do good?" And some directors, there's not a word from them, not even a nod. He's not thinking about you, but his other fifty jobs.

But with Miguel, even when you think you're not in a scene much, he'd go to every actor and go, "Do you know where you are?" You're in the middle of a battle and he came up and went: "Why are you here?" *Why am I here?* . . . It gets you thinking. Then he'll go to another actor and go: "What are you fighting for?" *I'm fighting for life. I'm fighting for good.*

JOHN BRADLEY (*Samwell Tarly*): Miguel was very keen on making us think about it in terms of our own narrative all the way through. "What is going on with your character when the camera is not on you? We may not have shown you for ten minutes, but something has happened to you in those ten minutes—you've been constantly fighting, or you've been running, or you've been hiding. How has your story through the fight developed? You have to hold it in your mind, what's happened to you since we saw you last." He's got such a forensic sense of detail, the way he can hold the points of view of each of these characters in his head and know what each individual beat means to them.

MIGUEL SAPOCHNIK: Stuff I've done previously was generally from Jon's perspective. Here I had twenty-four cast members and everyone would like it to be their scene. So that was complicated, because I find the best battle sequences are when you have a strong point of view. Here the point of view was objective even when you made it subjective, going from one person's story to another, because you're cutting back and forth, so it all becomes objective whether you want it to or not. I kept thinking, "Whose story am I telling right now? And what restrictions does that place on me that become a good thing?"

At one point on set after the night shoots, Sapochnik was darting between supervising three different units filming at the same time: a scene capturing fire-trench action, another with Daenerys on her dragon rig, and still another of field battle action. Yet even Sapochnik, who also directed the final season's fifth episode, "The Bells," reached his limit.

BERNADETTE CAULFIELD (*executive producer*): Miguel originally wanted to direct episodes three, four, and five. I said, "That's crazy, we're going to have a tough enough time having you do two episodes." Then he kept yelling, "I was supposed to have a bigger break [between episodes]!" But all I remember was him saying, "I don't want anybody else to do the other battle."

DEBORAH RILEY: He was *so* exhausted. I was trying to get Miguel to focus on making decisions for "The Bells" while he was shooting "The Long Night" and he couldn't.

The punishing delirium of making "The Long Night" was compounded by director David Nutter simultaneously shooting episode four, "The Last of the Starks," which *also* used the Winterfell set. So the *Thrones* team wasn't just working nights but running twenty-four hours a day, with many essential crew members tasked with servicing both day and night units. Some crew members were clocking up to forty thousand steps on their pedometers, walking roughly twenty miles every day.

DEBORAH RILEY: All you ever hear about is the crew shooting at night, but we were working on two episodes at once. For people like me, I had to service both. We would have to turn the whole set over to Miguel in the afternoon, then at four A.M. we would start receiving emails about how it was all going to change for David Nutter. You're always trying to stay ahead of a moving train, and there were times I felt like the train was running over the top of us. Season eight sucked every piece of energy that we had.

CHRISTOPHER NEWMAN: It was like fighting a battle. It's sheer force of will that you're telling people, "This is what we're doing." The minute people doubt that you know what you're doing, you are sunk. You can't have, for instance, a stunt coordinator roll his eyes at what he has to do. No weakness at any level, so everybody below you just follows you. The minute they feel your resolve is not up to it, that spreads like cancer.

Amid the exhaustion, every decision mattered. Here's an example of the level of detail that went into just a few swings of a sword. During a "Long Night" shot, Samwell Tarly was fighting wights. Watching the scene on set, I said to Cogman, "Sam looks like a badass." Cogman looked perturbed. "You hear what he just said?" Cogman said to the other producers. "That's the problem. Sam's not supposed to look like a badass."

Bradley was asked to adjust for a second take to appear a bit more confused and uncertain. Now he skittered back as each wight attacked. After another take, Weiss tweaked Bradley's performance further. "He's always facing the right direction for each attack, like he's anticipating it," Weiss noted, and reminded Bradley that Sam doesn't know where the next wight will come from. Then it all came together, and Bradley looked precisely like a terrified novice action hero reacting to an unpredictable onslaught of wights.

JOHN BRADLEY: You get carried away sometimes when doing these huge fight sequences. You can see yourself [on the monitor] and want to make yourself look as good as possible. Miguel kept having to say to me: "Remember your character, he's not that good at this. I know that you want to show you're quite good at this, you want to show you're better than Sam is at this. But you have to play him because that's what's going to be truthful. So stop being so good!" You never look as good as you think you do anyway. You always think a scene is going to be a game-changer. Then you watch it and it's just you.

There was, however, one actor who actually *liked* the night shoots—unlike every other person interviewed for this book.

You can probably guess who it was.

KRISTOFER HIVJU (*Tormund Giantsbane*): I enjoyed the night shoots! It's a special atmosphere. It's cold and dark, and you have almost a thousand people every day staying up at night to make this happen. You have people just being bodies for twelve hours. It was magical. I killed so many zombies. I was dreaming about killing zombies.

Not every actor in "The Long Night" had the same grueling schedule. Performers whose characters were in Winterfell's crypts, like Peter Dinklage, Nathalie Emmanuel, and Sophie Turner, were spared the worst of it.

SOPHIE TURNER (*Sansa Stark*): I only had two night shoots. It wouldn't have been in Sansa's nature, really, [to have been fighting]. But I wanted to work with the stunt guys so much—they're an Emmy-award-winning stunt team—and the only time I worked with them was when I was being slapped or beaten, which wasn't so fun. Then again, if I did have stunts, I'd probably have had to do seventy night shoots, so it probably worked out.

When filming scenes inside the studio, the cast was kept far warmer. But generating the episode's "fog of war"—a blinding blizzard of mist cast by the Night King—required either fog machines or CGI. Naturally, *Thrones* opted for real smoke, which meant burning paraffin and fish oil inside the studio. But as they inhaled smoke day after day, crew members began coughing up fish wax. Face-covering breathing masks multiplied on set. At least one crew member was taken to the hospital for an asthma attack. The studio hangar's massive doors were opened periodically to clear the air, and red-eyed crew members poured outside into the Belfast rain and cold seeking relief from the "comfort" of the studio.

One of the studio rooms was the motion-capture suite (or "mo-co"). There, Harington and Clarke took turns on the dragon rig, which looked like a large green mechanical bull that tilted and swiveled against a green screen. There Sapochnik tried to find ways to add more storytelling into what actors called the show's most monotonous on-camera task, and what one director dubbed "Emilia's own mini theme park roller coaster."

MIGUEL SAPOCHNIK: You put an actor on a rotating buck and you blast them with wind and they're on a green-screen set, so the last thing they're thinking is they have to do a performance. My focus was on getting a performance from the actors so their story continues even though they're on a dragon.

KIT HARINGTON: I was slightly pissed off I was on a dragon. It stopped me from fighting in a crowd. In some ways, as Jon does, I wanted to get back down on the ground. The fact he can fly a dragon means he has to, but his place is down there amongst the sword swingers.

MIGUEL SAPOCHNIK: I pitched the idea of designing shots that felt like they could have actually been shot in real life, and [I looked at] footage of World War II Supermarine Spitfires in action. I also pushed for the idea of allowing the dragons to constantly break frame. That is to say, frame shots slightly smaller than the actual dragon is so that it felt more like wildlife "on the fly" photography. The dragons should be so big and fast that it's hard to keep up with them.

As Williams pointed out, the cast and crew didn't have the luxury of getting sick. But, of course, some got sick anyway.

EMILIA CLARKE (*Daenerys Targaryen*): Mo-co was called "the infirmary" because everybody got sick with a most intense flu. Everybody in the room was fucked. I was incredibly ill on the back of the dragon. So I'm being thrown around on the back of this dragon going "*Aaaaahhhh-chew!*"

Then the dragon started to malfunction a bit and you'd just try to hold on. I like to say that Kit broke it.

"The Long Night" almost certainly ranks as the most filming hours ever dedicated to a single episode of television. After shooting was complete, there was a massive feeling of accomplishment among the *Thrones* team, though some said it took them six months to fully recover from filming. Crew members proudly donned "I Survived the Long Night" jackets.

MAISIE WILLIAMS: The sense of achievement after a day on set is unlike anything else. [Even on] one of those really tough days, you know it's going to be part of something so iconic and it will look amazing. The hard work pays off on this show.

IAIN GLEN: You had an absolute fucked bunch of actors, but on-screen it looks horrible and dirty and dark and cold. Without getting too Method about it, it bleeds onto the screen.

DAVID BENIOFF: Maybe my proudest moment from this show was when screening "The Long Night" at the Mann's Chinese Theatre. When Arya gets the Night King, the whole theater erupted. I was sitting next to my wife and her best friend, Sarah Paulson. My wife was grabbing my arm, and Sarah was screaming. I'll never forget that feeling.

The critical reaction to the episode was quite positive, if less effusive than the team had hoped. "'The Long Night' certainly lived up to being the show's biggest rumble yet, and it was extremely effective," wrote *Empire*'s James White. "We felt the emotional impact of those who died, cheered at various near-misses, and watched as the conflict evolved between skirmishes, grand conflicts, and some true horror stalking the halls."

Many viewers at home, however, struggled with the episode's intentional dimness, which was used to literally dramatize a long night. The issue was likely made more noticeable when the episode first aired due to video compression (some cable providers significantly reduce content resolution, particularly during peak usage). Subsequent viewing of the episode, especially on Blu-ray and on properly calibrated TVs, show the episode's action clearly. But it's also fair to say that fans shouldn't need the highest-quality video stream, or to change their TV settings, in order to watch their favorite show.

Game of Thrones insiders point out the production has always used "source lighting," meaning lighting that's justified with a visible illumination source in the scene (such as sunlight, moonlight, candles, or torches). Many previous dark scenes in the show were lit the exact same way as the shots in "The Long Night," but there were never so many in one episode before.

BRYAN COGMAN: There's a famous story about the director of photography for *The Lord of the Rings*. Sean Astin asked him about a scene [in Shelob's lair], "Where's the light coming from?" And he said: "The same place as the music." Perfectly valid answer. And if you watch *The Two Towers,* there's light coming from everywhere; the battle is lit up like a Christmas tree. And that's fine; I'm not dissing it. But that was never *Game of Thrones*. You write a battle at night, then this is how you light it.

Another complaint was about the length of the final season; some wished *Thrones* had filmed more episodes to further flesh out the story's final arcs. Those who work on the show insisted they could not have shot additional hours for season eight, especially after making "The Long Night." Each year, the *Thrones* team pushed their limits. In the final season, they reached them.

CAROLYN STRAUSS (*former programming president at HBO; executive producer*): People are like, "Well, they should've done more." The truth of the matter is it took so long to make the episodes that we made, I don't know how it would have been physically possible. There are a lot of factors that go into making this, practical ones and storytelling ones. These guys did a masterful job of considering all those questions.

Could the show have made a ninth season instead of more episodes for season eight? In addition to the showrunners' belief that there wasn't enough story for another round, some claimed delivering the spectacle of season eight was only possible because the cast and crew knew it was the finale.

BERNADETTE CAULFIELD: Several of our hero team players were like, "I almost quit." People were willing to go that extra mile for season eight only because they knew it was the final season and they knew it had to be spectacular.

NIKOLAJ COSTER-WALDAU: If that hadn't been the last season, there would have been a mutiny halfway through the night shoots.

BERNADETTE CAULFIELD: David and Dan did not hold back. They wrote the biggest that they could. We tried to reduce some things, and David and Dan and Miguel were like, "Nope, we need it." Every department was stretched beyond where we should have stretched them. Like, we had two visual effects teams—which we never had before—working seven days a week for a year trying to keep up with the shot list. Everybody said: "I never want to do that again." It was the hardest thing all of us have ever done. It was definitely the maximum we could do.

NIKOLAJ COSTER-WALDAU: George R. R. Martin, back in the day, said that this would be impossible. And there we were, shooting it.

CHAPTER THIRTY

THE THINGS WE LOVE
DESTROY US

Daenerys Stormborn of the House Targaryen, after years of struggle and hard-earned lessons in leadership and love, returned to Westeros with her Unsullied and Dothraki armies. She forged critical alliances with the Starks, Greyjoys, and Tyrells. At the Battle of Winterfell, Daenerys helped lead the victorious effort to destroy the Night King and his Army of the Dead.

Daenerys then took her forces south to King's Landing. Riding the fearsome Drogon, the Mother of Dragons blasted the city's battlements and terrified the City Watch and Golden Company mercenaries. The city's defensive forces surrendered, and Daenerys's soldiers seized control of the capital. Daenerys took her rightful place on the Iron Throne with Tyrion Lannister as her loyal and trusted Hand.

In the ensuing days, Daenerys I Targaryen, First of Her Name, ordered Cersei Lannister executed for treason at the ruins of the Sept of Baelor. Cersei's punishment took place at the same spot where Ned Stark had been unjustly killed many years before. The surviving Starks bore witness to her fate. Jaime Lannister, given his thorny history of heroism and brutality, was sentenced to serve the remainder of his days in the Night's Watch. Sansa Stark was granted permission to rule the North as an independent kingdom.

As for Jon Snow, his Targaryen ancestry was kept a closely guarded secret for the good of the realm. Daenerys formally legitimized him as Jon Stark, and they were married in a beautiful ceremony by the sea.

While she never did produce children (of the human kind, anyway), Daenerys peacefully ruled Westeros for decades with her loyal and courageous husband by her side.

If only.

For seven seasons, Daenerys seemed destined for that sort of hero's-journey ending. It's the linear road a typical fantasy story would take. But since *Game of Thrones* was anything but typical, Daenerys on the Iron Throne was not meant to be. Martin often let readers see hopeful glimpses of a safe and comforting path ahead for his characters, then he'd veer in an unexpected direction—somewhere darker, more perilous, and more aligned with the complexities of human nature. As Ramsay Bolton put it: "If you think this has a happy ending, you haven't been paying attention."

When Emilia Clarke received the final-season scripts detailing Daenerys's descent into madness and mass murder, the revelation went off like a nuclear detonation in her mind. Clarke had formed a particularly strong bond with her *Thrones* avatar. When she went through her health struggles, she drew strength from her character. Then, when on the set, she channeled the resilience she gained from overcoming her personal obstacles back into Daenerys.

EMILIA CLARKE (*Daenerys Targaryen*): I cried when I read the scripts. It was a fucking struggle. My first thought was a gut reaction, and my second thought, which was milliseconds after, was, "What are people going to think of this?" I had my own feelings about it that were peppered with my feelings about Emilia. You have the growth of the character and the growth of me running along with it. It had gotten to that point where people were like, "They're not talking about you, Emilia, they're talking about the character." I went for a walk and didn't come back for hours because I'm like: "How am I going to do this?"

Clarke reevaluated every previous Daenerys scene and realized that she had helped set up her character's twist without even knowing it—such as Daenerys's chilling reaction to watching her brother die back in season one.

DAN WEISS (*showrunner*): **We didn't know the details until after the third season, but Dany's trajectory was implicit in the first season. You're so rooting for her because she's in this horrible position. But there are a million different ways Emilia could have played watching her brother die, and she played it with a stone-cold-killer-like lack of affect. She has dark currents running through her. Which makes sense when Viserys, the only person she knew growing up, was a sociopath.**

In the first-season finale, Daenerys pledged to the Dothraki, "I am the dragon's daughter, and I swear to you that those who would harm you will die screaming."

In season two, Daenerys warned the leaders of Qarth: "When my dragons are grown, we will take back what was stolen from me and destroy those who have wronged me. We will lay waste to armies and burn cities to the ground."

A couple of seasons later, Daenerys crucified 163 slave masters in retaliation for their doing the same to children. One of the masters later claimed his father was a good man who fought against slavery and didn't deserve his fate. Similarly, after Ser Barristan was killed by the terror group Sons of the Harpy, Daenerys burned a master alive to send a message. She didn't know if the man was guilty or innocent, and she didn't much care.

In season six, Daenerys promised her Dothraki followers, echoing Khal Drogo, that they would "kill [her] enemies in their iron suits and tear down their stone houses."

And in the penultimate season, she ignored Tyrion's pleas and had Drogon torch Samwell Tarly's father, Randyll, and brother, Dickon, after they fought for the Lannister armies and refused to bend the knee. That scene, in particular, was supposed to be a fairly clear hint to viewers that

Daenerys was not okay. But fans had spent so many years on Team Dragon Queen that they had grown accustomed to Daenerys executing her perceived enemies.

BRYAN COGMAN (*co–executive producer*): In our minds, we thought the Randyll Tarly scene was disturbing. Then I watched it with a crowd of people at a friend's house and they were cheering. Weirdly, the audience just didn't care. They loved Dany.

PETER DINKLAGE (*Tyrion Lannister*): Tyrion is like, "Wait a minute, okay, kill the father, but do we need to kill the son? Do we have to kill both? It's senseless to kill the son. . . ."

GWENDOLINE CHRISTIE (*Brienne of Tarth*): The signs have always been there. And they've been there in ways we felt were mistakes or controversial. This show has always been about power, and it was an interesting illustration that [power-hungry] people can come in many different ways and we need to question everything.

KIT HARINGTON (*Jon Snow*): She did some terrible things. She crucified people. She burned people alive. This had been building. So we had to say to the audience, "You're in denial about this woman as well. You're culpable, you cheered her on. You knew there was something wrong."

BRYAN COGMAN: There's a dangerous tendency right now to make art and popular culture feel safe for everybody. I don't believe in that. This is the kind of story that's meant to unsettle you and challenge you and make you think and question. I think that's what George's intent was with *A Song of Ice and Fire,* and David and Dan wanted to do that with the series—make the audience never rest easy.

Over the years, producers sometimes gave Clarke notes about how to play a moment, nudging the character toward her tyrannical destiny.

EMILIA CLARKE: There was a number of times I was like, "Why are you giving me that note?" While I am quite consistently a "How can I help?" kind of person, there were a few moments where I was like, "Don't tell me what to do with my girl. I know what to do!" It's like Daenerys's calling card became cold expressionlessness. I always wanted to infuse that with some humanity because no one's consistently that. I would sometimes fight back a little: "I get that she has to be steely and unforgiving and a powerful force. But in this moment she's also a goddamn human being. So I'm going to give you that and I really pray that you take that in the edit."

Many others on the creative team likewise didn't have any idea that Daenerys was headed for such a dark fate

ALEX GRAVES (*director*): I actually did not know we were telling the story of Daenerys going the way of her ancestors. I thought we were telling the story of her *not* doing that.

Because, of course, there was good in Daenerys too. There were acts of benevolence and restraint. Her hatred of slavery was genuine and unselfish. Daenerys was a character who always *preferred* to do the right thing—so long as doing the right thing didn't entirely thwart her own ambition or undermine her perceived authority to rule. When Daenerys bumped up against such conflicts, it was her advisors who typically pushed her toward the moral choice, and they had to make pragmatic arguments to explain why doing the right thing was also better for Daenerys. Whereas Jon Snow always did the right thing, often foolishly and regardless of consequence.

EMILIA CLARKE: I genuinely did this, and it's fucking embarrassing and I'm going to admit it to you: I called my mom and said, "I read the scripts and I don't want to tell you what happens but can you just talk me off this ledge? I just went walking and I'm having a little cry. It really messed me up." And then I was asking my mom and brother really weird questions, and they were like, "What are you asking us this for? What do you mean,

'Do you think Daenerys is a good person?' Why are you asking us that question? Why do you care what people think of Daenerys? Are you okay?" And I said: "I'm fine! But is there anything she could do that would make you hate her?"

The final season began at Winterfell, where Daenerys clashed with Sansa Stark, despite the queen's best efforts.

EMILIA CLARKE: I think of that as like *Meet the Parents*: "I hope they like me, this dude's wicked, it's a real good thing we got going on, he's the final piece, we're destined for greatness, and world domination is a breath away."

SOPHIE TURNER (*Sansa Stark*): Yeah, not that impressed. Sansa had found her safe place and wouldn't let anyone get near it. She really didn't appreciate someone coming into her home again, her happy place, the one place she really cares about, and basically taking over and taking Jon away from the North. Despite Sansa feeling capable of ruling the North, she knew that she and Jon would do it much better together than on her own. So it's very much a protective thing of Jon and the North, especially considering the Targaryen track record—they're not particularly sane people. And there was a complete frustration that Jon initially wouldn't trust Sansa with the North at all, but he'd trust this stranger whose ancestor happened to be the Mad King.

EMILIA CLARKE: "Can I braid your hair, Sansa? Little Arya, come over here, let's play some cricket!" So there was that, and it very quickly became, "Wait, is it just me, or do they all hate me?" She genuinely started with the best intentions and truly hoped there wasn't going to be something scuttling her greatest plans. The problem is they didn't like her and she saw it and she went, "Okay, one chance." She gave that chance and it didn't work.

Samwell revealed to Jon that the Stark bastard was Aegon Targaryen, the true heir to the Iron Throne. The reveal caused Jon Snow (the character) to do what Emilia Clarke (the actress) did after reading the final-season scripts—reevaluate everything he'd done in the show.

JOHN BRADLEY (*Samwell Tarly*): He knew Jon would rather hear that from Sam than anybody else, because he trusted Sam and he'd deliver it in a compassionate way. But Jon felt Sam was muddying the name of one of the most noble people he's ever known. He felt Sam was basically saying his father figure and the man who'd set the tone of his entire life was built on a lie. Jon could review his entire life backward and see everything completely different and more sinister, even if done for the right reasons. Everything he'd done had been compromised.

KIT HARINGTON: That's the thing I love about Jon, his purity. He didn't fucking want to know. If he could go back in time and say to Sam, "Whatever you're about to say, don't tell me," he would. He'd happily be in ignorance. He didn't want that fucking information. He had no ambition for the throne.

Jon felt compelled to confide in Daenerys what he'd learned and naively hoped she'd be comforted by his lack of ambition.

EMILIA CLARKE: You don't even want it! So support me, it's my turn.

And then, of course, there was the whole incest thing.

EMILIA CLARKE: The related thing to her is so normal. She could have easily married her brother. It's a thing for Jon, but let's just forget about that. The main thing was we were up for the same promotion and I'd been working for it for my entire existence.

KIT HARINGTON: It's the most upsetting thing in the world. The end of the world might be coming soon, but at least he was in love with somebody and knows who he was, and then came a sledgehammer.

In perhaps Clarke's best scene in the series, Daenerys begged Jon to keep the knowledge of his birthright to himself. It didn't matter that Jon didn't want to be king; his legitimacy would undermine and perhaps overthrow her claim. A queen is only legitimate if her subjects believe that she is. Daenerys cycled between showing love, authority, desperation, and fury.

DAVID NUTTER (*director*): I've never worked with a better actress than Emilia. She looks different in different moods and tones she has for the character. She morphs into a different emotional state. In that scene I wanted to have them move around the set so that there would be moments of isolation and also moments of coming together. They kiss each other, and he steps away from her. Then she sits down and faces the other direction. So they're so separate at that point. Then he swoops down and says, "I'll always take a knee for you." It was powerful stuff.

EMILIA CLARKE: This was my whole existence. Since birth! She literally was brought into this world going, "Run!" These fuckers have fucked everything up. There was so much she's taken on as her duty in life to rectify. So much she's seen and witnessed and been through and lost and suffered and hurt. Suddenly these people were turning around and saying, "We don't accept you." She's too far down the line; she's killed so many people already.

KIT HARINGTON: It was a complex scenario between Jon and Dany where she's turning into someone he doesn't like. He was in denial of her power issues and brutality and the fact that when he's kissing her, he can't stop thinking that they're related. [Director Miguel Sapochnik] talked to me and Emilia at length about this, and he had an interesting take on it: Jon is religious, and she's practical. She's the kind of, "Why can't we just lie?" Jon cannot lie to himself. He cannot bury it. He cannot not tell his sister. It frustrates him massively at times. So when he's kissing her he can't forget she's his aunt. Every time they kissed after that, he was the one who stopped it.

What followed was a succession of, as Clarke put it, "strings being cut" for Daenerys. After their victorious battle against the Army of the Dead, Daenerys lost her beloved Ser Jorah. And when Varys heard of Jon's rightful claim, the Spider took steps against his queen, attempting to manipulate a scenario where Jon could sit on the Iron Throne instead. Daenerys, already feeling isolated and paranoid, ordered Varys executed by dragon fire. And that, in turn, further caused Tyrion and Jon to question their loyalty to her.

DAN WEISS (*showrunner*): Tyrion's biggest mistake was finally daring to believe in somebody. His mistake is something we all hope for. To find somebody we trust to lead us.

CONLETH HILL (*Varys*): Varys was absolutely true to his word the whole way through. All he wanted was the right person on the throne and a fair person on the throne. He said it so many times in the scripts. "I don't have the distraction of love or desire or any of those things." And the people he needed to see clearly were both in love. So that made perfect sense. He knew that he had to try anyway to stop her and that it was very possible he would be killed.

EMILIA CLARKE: We love Varys. I love Conleth. But he changed his colors as many times as he wanted. She fucking warned him. That was my only option, essentially.

CONLETH HILL: He was effective, as always. He might not be around to see the results of his effectiveness, but what he did was important. It was a cool death and very dignified, and I swear the dragon thought twice about it.

Jaime Lannister was imprisoned after trying to sneak back to King's Landing to save Cersei from Daenerys's pending attack. Tyrion, feeling he had no choice but to help his brother, betrayed Daenerys by releasing him.

PETER DINKLAGE: Daenerys and her dragons are nitroglycerin. He knew she's going to make the world a better place and understands her passion. He's put his passion in front of himself sometimes and it got the better of him. So he was trying to figure out who he really is. It's okay for him to feel like a traitor to Cersei and Tywin, but then he almost felt like a traitor to his own brother. And with Varys, that's as personal as it gets. Varys was his closest friend outside of Jaime. That's a tough one to get past.

Meanwhile, at sea, Euron managed to shoot down Rhaegal, leaving Daenerys with just one dragon, Drogon. The pirate also captured the queen's dear friend and advisor Missandei and brought her to Cersei. That led to a standoff at the gates of King's Landing, with Missandei's life hanging in the balance and Cersei refusing to surrender.

DAVID NUTTER: That high wall was a real set, but you couldn't get the actors to go that high for an extended period of time. You only saw their faces when we had the actors up there tied in; otherwise we had stunt doubles. As for Missandei, I'm a big believer that when an actor is doing their final scene they get to shine in their last moment. I let them do it until they feel they got it right.

Missandei, knowing her end was inevitable, could see Daenerys in the distance. She defiantly cried one last word in Valyrian for all to hear: "*Dracarys!*"

NATHALIE EMMANUEL (*Missandei*): It comes full circle to my first scene I shot, when Daenerys and I discuss how I might die. Missandei always said she was willing to lay down her life, but we hoped she wouldn't have to. I've said in so many interviews that I don't mind if I die, I'm just happy to be here and be a part of the show. I just wanted it to be really cool and a moment that people remember. I feel like they gave me that moment. She was settled with her fate.

JACOB ANDERSON (*Grey Worm*): I found it heartbreaking. There's like a cruel inevitability in this show where anybody who finds that happiness is going to have that taken away from them. So I thought either Grey Worm or Missandei, that one would be taken from the other. I honestly thought Grey Worm was gone. And I even had that thought, "Take me!" The way they dealt with it in terms of how it affects Dany and Grey Worm makes it even sadder. It's like when she dies, Grey Worm dies too, and he goes back to being a robot death machine.

NATHALIE EMMANUEL: She was so brave and showed her strength and fearlessness even though she doesn't wield a sword. She knew what she was doing and was confident and fierce. I didn't want her to be crying. She believes in her queen and believes in her cause. I wanted to make her strong in that moment, which is really hard when you're feeling emotional. It was a fantastic scene. There's a real sadness to the fact that the character won't go on. She was a catalyst to Dany's crazy fury.

When I watched my character die on the show, I was really sad. I might have shed a tear. I really felt the loss of her.

Emmanuel has also said in interviews that she thought it was unfortunate Missandei didn't have a one-on-one scene with Daenerys in season eight, or perhaps a conversation with Cersei during her captivity. In earlier seasons, *Thrones* typically took advantage of first-time character pairings by giving them at least one conversation together.

DAVID NUTTER: I think that because Missandei was not royalty, how we did it was good, because Cersei treated her as a pawn. That was appropriate. Anything else would have been fun to watch but not honest to the show.

Missandei's death infuriated Daenerys, who readied to attack King's Landing. She turned to Jon Snow once again, seeking love and acceptance.

EMILIA CLARKE: There was just this last thread she was holding on to, this boy. I think he loves me, and that's enough. Is it enough? Is it? There was that hope and will and wishing that finally there was someone who accepted her for everything she was and all of her life choices, that he sees her and "I'll do that with you." And he *fucking doesn't.*

Which led to the final season's fifth episode, "The Bells," and the show's most debated moment. Daenerys destroyed King's Landing's defenses, Euron's fleet, and the mercenary Golden Company army. The city bells rang—a signal of surrender. The Iron Throne was hers. Mounted on Drogon, Daenerys could see the Red Keep in the distance. Cersei stood at a tower window, awaiting her fate. Daenerys could have ordered her armies to take over King's Landing with minimal bloodshed. Instead, Daenerys did something else. She launched a devastating attack, with Drogon firebombing soldiers and citizens alike, punishing all for the sins of their queen.

NATHALIE EMMANUEL: It broke my heart. I knew she lost her mind, but until you see it in all of its glory and the destruction it causes, you can't really comprehend it. I'm not sure Missandei meant that by "*Dracarys.*" Missandei was in heaven somewhere going, "You kind of went over the top there. I meant get Cersei, not, like, *everyone.*"

Committing mass murder to punish a defiant enemy hiding in a castle has a history in the Targaryen family. When Aegon the Conqueror invaded Westeros, King Harren the Black refused to bend the knee and took refuge with his sons, soldiers, and servants inside his massive castle compound of Harrenhal. ("I built in stone," Harren declared. "Stone does not burn.") The Targaryen used his dragon, Balerion the Black Dread, to blast Harren's five towers with so much heat that it turned the castle's impenetrable walls into an oven that roasted everybody inside. "The riverlords outside the castle walls said later that the towers of Harrenhal glowed red against the night, like five great candles," Martin wrote in *Fire*

& *Blood.* "And like candles, they began to twist and melt as runnels of molten stone ran down their sides."

Aegon didn't just end House Harren, but set an example. The lords of Westeros quickly fell into line and swore fealty to Aegon. With Harrenhal destroyed, Aegon built a new city by the sea to serve as the realm's seat of power. The city was named King's Landing.

DAN WEISS: If you think about how long it's taken her to get to this place and what she's given up to get to there—two of her three dragons and her closest friend in the world—and she's looking at the Red Keep with the Lannister logo on it where her family's star of the seven is supposed to be; her family's birthright was taken over by the people who have done this to her.

DAVID BENIOFF (*showrunner*): And in spite of all those injustices, she tried her best to make peace with Cersei in the best interest of the whole country—and got betrayed for it.

DAN WEISS: Also, up north, she sacrificed people she swore to protect. Half of them are dead because she made the decision to be a good actor and then [Jaime] turned on her and defected. It was a perfect storm of bad shit swirling around inside her head.

DAVID BENIOFF: And throughout her career she had people by her side who have been able to temper her worse impulses, whether it was Ser Jorah or Tyrion or Missandei—people who could suggest an alternate path. They're either not there or she doesn't trust them anymore.

DAN WEISS: Dozens and dozens of factors going back to her birth to what she's seeing in her eyes right now a mile away and how that made her feel, all of them stepping on the scale tilting her into a terrible decision. A lot of people we admire and have statues of have made those choices, whether they were coldly rational or made in the heat of battle, that for many thousands of people were horrible life-altering or life-ending decisions.

NATHALIE EMMANUEL: I was really sad she went crazy. I was such a Daenerys fan. She was such a female icon. She had nothing and built herself up and got this army. There was a part of me that was disappointed. But then when you think about it, she's lost everyone around her that meant anything to her. You can understand how it happened. I would have loved it if she only killed her enemies and sat on her throne and was the queen of everything.

PETER DINKLAGE: We love Daenerys. All the fans love Daenerys. And she's doing these things for the greater good. "The greater good" has been in the headlines lately when somebody is lumped in with somebody who's done something far worse, and we think, "For the greater good all these people have to come to the front lines and be held responsible." That's what's happening in our show in terms of the purification of this place. When freeing everyone for the greater good, you're going to hurt innocents along the way, unfortunately. That's what war is. David and Dan talked about decisions made in war like [the United States' dropping the atomic bomb on Hiroshima and Nagasaki in 1945]. Did we make the right choices? How much longer would the war have gone on if we didn't make that horrible decision? You'll never know.

CONLETH HILL: One thing the last season was about was the futility of war and conflict. If you get one thing from the whole show, take that.

BRYAN COGMAN: She's a tragic figure in a very Shakespearian/Greek sense. Emilia threaded that needle beautifully. It was the hardest job anybody had on the show that season.

Daenerys won. She conquered the capital. Cersei and Jaime Lannister were buried in rubble. And the new ruler of Westeros gave an authoritarian speech promising many more wars to come: "We will not lay down our spears until we have liberated all the people of the world!"

Daenerys declared in Valyrian to her armies. "From Winterfell to Dorne, from Lannisport to Qarth, from the Summer Isles to the Jade Sea, women, men, and children have suffered too long beneath the wheel. Will you break the wheel with me?" The speech wasn't entirely different from the ones Daenerys had given in the past. But before her rhetoric had all been hypothetical and, perhaps, exaggeration? Suddenly her promise of fire and blood was all too real.

KIT HARINGTON: Jon was watching the speech. He doesn't speak Valyrian. David and Dan said, "Just pretend you know it." Just the way she's speaking and what she's doing was telling him everything he needs to know.

Tyrion was imprisoned for releasing Jaime, and Jon Snow visited him in his cell. Tyrion was often an ineffective advisor, and he'd made a slew of strategic errors over the years. But in his cell scene with Jon Snow he informally served as Hand to the true king of Westeros, and for once, his advice was effective, correct, and devastating.

"Sometimes, duty is the death of love," Tyrion told Jon, in a callback to Night's Watch maester Aemon Targaryen once telling him that "love is the death of duty." "You are the shield that guards the realms of men, and you've always tried to do the right thing, no matter the cost," Tyrion continued. "You've tried to protect people. Who is the greatest threat to the people now? It's a terrible thing I'm asking. It's also the right thing. Do you think I'm the last man she'll execute?"

Daenerys walked into the ruins of the Red Keep's throne room and saw snow falling on the Iron Throne, just like in her prophetic vision from season two. She laid her hand on the throne and was just about to sit down when Jon Snow entered. He wasn't determined to kill his lover. He first begged his queen to see reason while she insisted her plans were for the greater good. "What about everyone else?" Jon asked. "All the other people who think they know what's good?" And Daenerys replied, "They don't get to choose." That declaration guided Jon's hand.

KIT HARINGTON: This is the second woman he's fallen in love with who dies in his arms, and he cradles her in the same way. That's an awful thing. In some ways he did the same thing to Ygritte by training the boy who kills her. This destroys him.

Harington's word choice was rather fitting. Arguably the best line from Martin's novels that did not make it into the show was a warning that Lord Commander Jeor Mormont gave to Jon Snow: "The things we love destroy us." It's a prophetic quote that proved true for several characters in the series, such as Jon, Daenerys, Ygritte, Drogo, Jaime, and Robb. Though Clarke also offered a humorous take on the twist.

EMILIA CLARKE: He just doesn't like women, does he? He keeps fucking killing them. If I were to put myself in his shoes I'm not sure where he could go with it aside from, I dunno, maybe having a discussion about it? Ask my opinion? Warn me? It's like being in the middle of a phone call with your boyfriend and they just hang up and never call you again. "Oh, this great thing happened to me at work today—hello?"—that was nine years ago. . . .

KIT HARINGTON: We spent a week shooting it. It was hard because you had to keep the emotion at a certain level for a long time and keep returning to it. But it felt fucking epic.

EMILIA CLARKE: We reshot it more than any other scene, trying to get it perfect. It was a big deal, and it was logistically a massive thing. You've got the throne room, it's fallen in, there's some green screen, there's a dragon, there's snow. And I very much wanted her final moment to be childlike in her innocence—because there's nowhere else for her to go. In the penultimate episode, I felt like I slammed against the wall of how manic or crazy she could be. Where else is there for you to go other than right back to the beginning?

I know it sounds completely ridiculous because it's make-believe, but

I've never been killed on camera before. I have an innate understanding of what death looks like because I was pretty damn close to it twice and then I lost my dad. So having Daenerys die, a lot of these things were coming out. It was like grieving my brain hemorrhages all over again, grieving my dad all over again, grieving what Daenerys could have been, and grieving the love that I had for the show, for Kit, for David and Dan, for Jon Snow, and for the dragons. In that one moment, the grief of a thousand deaths came back and it was like, "Oh my God, I'm struggling to find breath right in this moment."

A furious Drogon turned his wrath upon the Iron Throne, destroying the seat of power. The Iron Throne had been forged by Aegon I Targaryen, who had his dragon melt down the swords of his vanquished enemies. Just like the Night King, the Iron Throne was unmade as it was made. Drogon's action was not explained. But given Daenerys's strong connection to her dragon, it's fair to assume the creature understood that his mother had been obsessed with this particular object and that it had somehow led to her doom. Drogon picked up Daenerys's body and flew away. We never learn where they went.

EMILIA CLARKE: People have asked me about that a lot. It's my tendency to be funny with it and say, "Oh, Hawaii." But honestly, if I'm really being very serious about the whole thing: I think he flies around with her body until it decomposes. I literally think he keeps flying until he can't fly anymore. He just keeps grieving.

In Daenerys's vision back in season two, she didn't quite touch the Iron Throne. Instead, she walked out of the room and found herself transported to the Night Lands. There she reunited with Khal Drogo—whom Drogon is named after—who was waiting for her along with their child.

JASON MOMOA (Khal Drogo): The woman just wanted love her whole life. If you see the whole journey she went through and how she was

407

obviously mishandled by her family, and then had a husband she fell in love with, and then has her baby taken away, and then has to kill her husband. And then all the people and dragons and things that she's loved . . . she's just had the shit beat out of her and then she crashed. She goes off on everyone. It's just sad.

BRYAN COGMAN: Jon asked, "Were we wrong?" Tyrion said: "Ask me again in ten years." Which I think is valid.

EMILIA CLARKE: After ten years of working on this, it was logical, because where the fuck else can she go? It's a logical change of events that happens. It's not like she's suddenly going to go, "Okay, I'm gonna put a kettle on and put some cookies in the oven and we'll just sit down and have a lovely time and pop a few kids out." That was never going to happen. She's a Targaryen. And your childhood and upbringing affects your choices in life so greatly. She was brought up with the Iron Throne being the only goal. That need to say, "I did it for my family, for my everything, I went there and we conquered." That no member of her family died in vain for this. That her life hadn't been for nothing. That she hadn't been struggling for nothing. She was *that* close to fulfilling that seal of approval, that thing we all secretly want. That plays a major role as to why she goes there.

But having said all of the things I've just said . . . I stand by Daenerys. I stand by her! I can't not.

CHAPTER THIRTY-ONE

MANY PARTINGS

From survival to annihilation, from finding love to enduring heartbreak, from promotion to exile, the remaining *Game of Thrones* characters experienced an array of final-season storylines. As with Daenerys, each character's fate reflected their journey, either as a reward for their skills and growth or as a consequence of their flaws.

Brienne of Tarth was knighted by Jaime Lannister at Winterfell on the eve of the Army of the Dead battle. The moving scene emerged in an offhand manner, as Jaime made the abrupt decision to reward Brienne with the official legitimacy that was always unimaginable for somebody of her gender and status in Westeros. At first, Brienne thought that Jaime was once again, mocking her. Then the weight of the moment took hold.

BRYAN COGMAN (*co—executive producer*): We wanted to take the audience by surprise. It's not a ceremonial scene on a cliff at sunset with billowing capes. It came out of a throwaway moment. Even some people in the room thought it was a joke, and then they quickly realized it was not. It's a monumental thing. It's a moment of grace and beauty in the middle of a nightmare.

GWENDOLINE CHRISTIE (*Brienne of Tarth*): She was in Renly's Kingsguard but had never been part of the establishment. No matter how much you carve a place for yourself outside of things, there's something about acceptance from people that you love that's irreplaceable. That's what that moment represents. It's also an idea of the possibility of equality in all this fighting and doing the honorable thing. In that moment, she feels it's an acknowledgment of all of that and the body she has doesn't matter; it's about the acts she's performed and how she's behaved.

NIKOLAJ COSTER-WALDAU (*Jaime Lannister*): Jaime understands Brienne and the feeling of being an outsider and people having preconceived opinions about you. With her people think, "She's a woman, she can't fight, she so big"—all the things he used to attack her with when they first met. He now understands her pain and that she just wants to be recognized.

DAVID NUTTER (*director*): Nikolaj said he left his body during that scene. He said afterward, "I don't know what just happened," that he actually became Jaime Lannister for a minute. For an actor, those are the best performances.

After fighting alongside each other in the Winterfell battle, Brienne and Jaime shared a night in bed together.

GWENDOLINE CHRISTIE: Sharing the experience of surviving war together and saving each other's lives continuously, moment to moment, proved a very heady combination. Physicality often releases emotion. Working together unlocked them. If you're facing and survived death, you want to experience everything life has to offer—it wouldn't be as human to not explore that. She's a woman, and that means she has a sex drive, so why shouldn't she?

NIKOLAJ COSTER-WALDAU: I never thought it was going to happen. They survived. There was this party. They buried the dead. There was this enormous relief. We did it. There's drinking and happiness. And there's flirting and she leaves and he goes to see her in her quarters and suddenly it happens.

GWENDOLINE CHRISTIE: It's important to me how these things come about. I felt it was important to see a moment of choice from Brienne where she chooses to do this. As far as we know, Brienne hasn't had a sexual or romantic encounter before. I was pleased about that, as a character who, in the books, sleeps in her armor to protect herself, that if something happened between her and another character, that she wanted it.

NIKOLAJ COSTER-WALDAU: It was really weird [to film]. It was awkward. I was trying to laugh, and Gwendoline was like, "Don't fucking laugh!"

GWENDOLINE CHRISTIE: Yeah, there had to be a few conversations. "Now, you're going to need to be very professional about this. . . ." I care for the character so deeply, it was important that it was taken care of well, and I believe it was. Though . . . personally? I always wanted to see her get together with Dany.

Speaking of Daenerys, Jaime learned the Dragon Queen was readying to attack King's Landing. The Lannister made the fateful choice to leave Brienne and try to rescue his twin sister and lifelong love.

GWENDOLINE CHRISTIE: I was so upset for Brienne. I know it's just a character and I'm an actor who's lucky to do her job. It's just so heartbreaking. That's *Game of Thrones*, isn't it? Just when you think things are going to go well it punches you harder than ever in the guts. I could feel a million hearts breaking.

NIKOLAJ COSTER-WALDAU: You wonder if he's changed and if he's escaped the destructive relationship. He's so bound by this code of honor of family first, and he and Cersei have a strong bond on every level. But he has to go back. She's all alone. He's the last one she has. He has to try to save her. It makes sense even though you don't want it to.

GWENDOLINE CHRISTIE: I believe the reason Jaime left is because he wasn't very good [*laughs*].

NIKOLAJ COSTER-WALDAU: It would have been wonderful if he and Brienne could have had a life together. But he says it himself as he's leaving: "Have you ever walked away from a fight?" I have to do this. The things you do for love . . .

DAVID NUTTER: I wanted her to feel something she didn't expect to feel. So I had Nikolaj say other dialogue that wasn't in the script [when he leaves]. It caught Gwen off guard and she broke down and it was incredible.

The cruel off-script line that Jaime said to Brienne wasn't included in the scene, but it was revealed in the episode's DVD commentary: "I don't love you. No one loves you."

Jaime returned to King's Landing, where he was promptly attacked by Euron Greyjoy. While Jaime won the fight, he was almost certainly mortally injured. One could say the Kingslayer wasn't killed by the Red Keep's eventual collapse, as seen later, but by Euron—which is certainly how Euron, and actor Pilou Asbæk, preferred to see it.

PILOU ASBÆK (*Euron Greyjoy*): The only one who dies with a smile is me. I told Dan and David, "I'm not going to die. You're not going to see me go [*makes a dying wheeze*]." They said: "But you're gonna die." I said, "No, I'm not. I'm not gonna act it." It's a happy ending for Euron Greyjoy.

Jaime located Cersei and attempted to escort her to safety. The two were buried under the collapsing Red Keep, where they were later discovered by Tyrion. Their death mirrored their birth, the twins leaving their lives as they came into them. What Martin has planned for the characters is unclear, but in his books there is a similar hint, with Jaime thinking at one point, "We will die together as we were born together."

NIKOLAJ COSTER-WALDAU: I thought it was a great ending for that couple. She was never going to surrender. Bronn asked Jaime in season four: "How would you want to end?" "In the arms of the woman I love." So it was foreshadowed, and it's what happened. There's at least a moment that they do connect: "Just look at me, just look in my eyes, it's just you and me. . . ."

LENA HEADEY (*Cersei Lannister*): It was a quick season for me. It's more about the other characters and where they go. I genuinely wanted her to have some big piece or fight with somebody. But Nikolaj and I talked about it, and the more we talked the more it seemed like the perfect end. They came into the world together and now they leave together.

CHRISTOPHER NEWMAN (*producer*): Some say they had an ignominious death. But Tywin died on a toilet. There are no heroic endings in life.

LENA HEADEY: The important thing in their last scene is Jaime had a chance at freedom and to liberate himself finally from her, but ultimately they belong together. Cersei realized just how much she loved him and just how much he loved her. It's the most authentic relationship connection she's ever had. It's maybe the first time that Cersei had been at peace.

The last day for me on set was walking up and down the stairs twenty thousand times. During one scene I told Nikolaj, "I've never seen you so sweet and sentimental," and he was all, "What's happening to me?" We kept cuddling and going, "I love you. . . ."

Brienne filled in Jaime Lannister's pages of the White Book of the Kingsguard. In season four, Joffrey had mocked Jaime for his lack of accomplishments in the book. The final entry for the man formerly known as the Kingslayer read: "Died protecting his queen."

NIKOLAJ COSTER-WALDAU: The scene with Gwen where she fills in the last pages [of the White Book] is also Jaime's last scene. It was beautiful. It was a beautiful way of telling his story and her story and how we live on. We make our mark in this world by the impact we have on other people.

After he was crowned king, Bran Stark appointed Brienne commander of the Kingsguard at the capital and gave her a seat on the small council. It was the ultimate fulfillment of her quest to become a knight serving a worthy cause.

GWENDOLINE CHRISTIE: I love that she doesn't crumble from him leaving. She goes back to work. Because she always loved work. That feels refreshing—a woman can be happy without a companion. She chooses to do what she loves, dedicating her life to service. It's what I love about the character. Women don't have to be defined by their partner.

Sandor "the Hound" Clegane faced off against his abusive brother Ser Gregor "the Mountain" Clegane on a stairway in the Red Keep. Their clash had been teased from the first season, when we learned Gregor disfigured Sandor when they were kids. "You know who's coming for you," Sandor warned his brother in season seven. "You've always known."

The Clegane Bowl was one of the last major scenes filmed for *Thrones*, and by the time the actors, Sapochnik, and the crew began to work on the long-anticipated fight sequence, everybody involved felt as half-dead as the Mountain. The fight was even grueling for professional strongman Hafþór Björnsson, who has broken several world records for feats of strength.

HAFÞÓR BJÖRNSSON (*Gregor "the Mountain" Clegane, seasons 4–8*): Modern Icelandic is by far the closest of the Nordic languages to the original Viking language. We have a saying: "Bræður munu berjast," which literally means "brothers will fight." Never has that been more true than in this scene. It was some of the hardest work I've had to do, bar none. I lost over thirty pounds of body weight during the fight. Makeup started at four A.M. and went on for hours and hours. A big part of my body was covered in prosthetics and there were lenses in my eyes. I was in full armor, and it's a proper heavy armor. We were working for up to eighteen hours per day, and a great deal of the time we were shooting the fighting; the whole scene, doing the same actions again and again and again. Rory McCann was great to work with, and I am proud to have been an integral part of one of the most epic fight scenes ever created.

MIGUEL SAPOCHNIK: My least favorite experience on *Thrones*. Hard set, tired crew. Exhausted actors—though Rory saved the day. There were so many details that you would never know about looking at it, but they were the stuff nightmares are made of.

The brothers' fight claimed both their lives.

RORY McCANN (*Sandor "the Hound" Clegane*): I'm very happy with the way the Hound's story ended, thank you very much. My last filming days were the fight. I'm absolutely sure I'm going to be limping for months. It's a glorious death. He's laughing at it. He can see the Mountain can't be killed by sticking a dagger in his eye. He had to be burnt. Of all the things Clegane had to do, it was to go in the fire. That's the sacrifice. But his pain is over.

Yara Greyjoy, having been rescued from captivity by her brother Theon, returned to her home on the Iron Islands, which were reincorporated into the Kingdoms with Yara as its leader.

GEMMA WHELAN (*Yara Greyjoy*): I really wish Yara had killed Euron. But a lot of people wished they could have killed Euron. I'm very happy to have made it to the end, and there's not always space for all the characters to get the full truth of their storyline as they might hope it would be. But Yara got what I feel rightfully should have been hers and did the right thing by winning it graciously.

In the wake of Missandei's execution, Grey Worm regressed to a remorseless order-following killing machine. In the finale, he decided to give up soldiering and fulfill his pledge to his love by traveling to her birthplace of. Naath, an island in the Summer Sea. Never seen in the show, Naath is described as a tropical land of white sands and tall trees.

JACOB ANDERSON (*Grey Worm*): There came a point for Grey Worm where he was like, "Enough is enough." That's why he left. Everybody dear to him was dead, and he had only just learned how to have people dear to him. This was a violent place, and I don't think he wanted that to be his existence anymore. He's keeping his promise to Missandei, and he's sitting on the beach drinking piña coladas and protecting everyone.

Anderson's final day of filming was also the last for Kit Harington and Liam Cunningham (whose Lord Davos Seaworth would end up serving on Bran's small council as the master of ships).

LIAM CUNNINGHAM (*Davos Seaworth*): The last day of shooting was the scene where Jacob was going to kill the King's Landing guards. It was incredibly difficult because, coldheartedly, it was another filming day. Jacob, Kit, and I, during shooting breaks, we were just looking at the fucking ground. Whenever we caught each other's eyes we couldn't prolong the gaze because we knew how momentous the moment was. We knew David and Dan would be there at the end of the day presenting us with shit. It was really weird, trying to be professional while at the same time wanting to bawl your eyes out.

Dan Weiss told Harington after his final shot, "Your watch has ended, and it has been a hell of a watch," in the documentary *Game of Thrones:*

The Last Watch. Harington, in turn, gave a farewell speech—this time, a real one. "I love this show," Harington tearfully told the cast and crew. "It's never been a job for me. It will always be the greatest thing I ever do."

Ser Jorah was laid to rest after the Battle of Winterfell, with Iain Glen among several actors lying on funeral pyres.

IAIN GLEN (*Jorah Mormont*)**:** In that moment, I was aurally saying good-bye, listening to the set operating. What a vast, slick machine it had become, and to hear it orchestrating . . . I got into it. Everything echoes backward over the past decade. Trying to let the whole thing go.

But when Daenerys said farewell to her faithful friend, she bent forward and whispered something in his ear. In the script, her words are described as "something Jorah will never hear, and we will never know." Appropriately enough, Iain Glen will not reveal what Emilia Clarke said.

IAIN GLEN: It was something entirely sincere and true to the moment and something that I will never forget. I'll always cherish it because it's something no one will ever know but the two of us. And that's a memory to hold on to.

Samwell Tarly was perhaps the show's most unlikely survivor, a character who seemed doomed from the moment he struggled to pick up a sword in season one and then somehow made it through so many journeys and battles. Yet Samwell had perhaps the show's happiest ending. He was with Gilly, and they had a child together, Sam; and he joined Bran's council as grand maester, where his scholarly knowledge and gentle wisdom would finally be appreciated and put to good use.

JOHN BRADLEY (*Samwell Tarly*)**:** Sam wanted a domesticated, low-key happiness. So it's a spectacular ending for Sam because the chances of that happening are so outlandish. He's one of the few characters who had been unhappy from the first moments of his life. He's had so much pain and so much darkness that you never think he's going to be happy.

One of the nice things about the final scene at the small council is we left them bickering amongst themselves. We've set up a slightly more comic space. I felt like you wanted to stay with them.

Tyrion Lannister served as Hand of the King to Joffrey, then Hand of the Queen to Daenerys. He struggled in both roles, his compassion and practicality clashing with their self-serving agendas. Tyrion was named Hand of the King yet again to Bran Stark. The position was part honor, part punishment—a chance to correct his past failings.

PETER DINKLAGE (*Tyrion Lannister*): We're so used to the standard formula of bad guys dying and good guys living. David and Dan had a beautiful, gentle touch with some and a hard touch with others. I had all these ideas in my head [for Tyrion's fate], and a version of one of them is how it ended up. He wanted to make amends for what he's done.

DAN WEISS (*showrunner*): Tyrion is the smartest guy and the funniest guy and one of the most pragmatic guys on the show. Wouldn't it be great if he was in charge? By the time you get to the end, like many people who have those qualities, he's made many mistakes. It was a fun way of having Tyrion driving the day-to-day operations of things without having him be on the Iron Throne, which for reasons he himself states wasn't really feasible. He was always going to be doomed or blessed to not be the person in that situation. He was always going to be the person who doesn't show up in the history books but made a lot of decisions that determined things.

Brandon Stark was named Bran the Broken, First of His Name, and Lord of the Six Kingdoms. A central question posed by *Thrones* from the very beginning was: "Who will end up on the Iron Throne?" Many fans wanted their favorite hero to rule the Seven Kingdoms because so many viewed the Iron Throne as a prize to be won. HBO's marketing likewise embraced that idea, teasing different characters ending up in the ultimate seat of power.

But across eight seasons, ruling in *Thrones* was always shown to be a burden, not a reward. The Iron Throne is the Westeros version of the One Ring in *The Lord of the Rings*; it is a quest item many seek for reasons good or ill, but even those with the best intentions are eventually corrupted by its power. The Iron Throne and the One Ring also shared the same fate—each destroyed by the mythical fire that forged it. That's why Daenerys was wrong for the throne—she wanted it too much—and why the Three-Eyed Raven might be right for it, even if the choice feels unsatisfying.

DAVID BENIOFF (*showrunner*): Who's going to rule at the end was an important question. It's got to be somebody who's earned it in terms of the experiences they've gone through, but we also wanted somebody we thought would be a good ruler, which means not somebody who's doing it for the wrong reasons. We try to avoid conversations about theme, but if there's any theme to this show, it's about power—power corrupts people, and a lack of power will also hurt you. Bran doesn't care about power.

ISAAC HEMPSTEAD WRIGHT (*Bran Stark*): I can't imagine his government is a barrel of laughs. It might be quite serious. And I guess for all intents and purposes, Westeros is now a surveillance state, as Bran knows everything everybody's doing. Perhaps there will be something missing in having a real emotive leader, which is a useful quality in a king or queen as well. At the same time you can't really argue with him. He's like, "No, I know everything."

DAVID BENIOFF: It's what Bran says in that scene: "Why do you think I came all this way?" We've been following his storyline for so long. With Arya we see she had an incredibly important role in destroying the Night King. And Sansa becomes Queen in the North. What have Bran's experiences led to? There had to be some purpose for all these things he's gone through. We try to avoid the prophecies for the most part. But there's something about Bran you can't avoid. He has chosen to be the Three-Eyed Raven, and to what end? If that didn't lead to something incredibly consequential, it would feel anticlimactic.

ISAAC HEMPSTEAD WRIGHT: The more I thought about it, the more I thought it made perfect sense. He's an ideal person to be in control of everything. By definition he's levelheaded and totally impartial and armed with an entire knowledge of history—which is quite useful. I think he'll be a really good king.

DAVID BENIOFF: It's a fruition of Varys's hopes all along. Who's going to think about what's best for the realm? In order to be that disinterested in self and family, it almost takes somebody who isn't human. Because we all have those flaws and weaknesses.

Sansa Stark had long sought a sense of security and stability for herself, for her home, and for the North. Appropriately enough, she was named Queen in the North, which would now be an independent kingdom, and she was crowned at Winterfell.

SOPHIE TURNER (*Sansa Stark*): Ever since the end of season one, Sansa has not been about the capital and being queen. She knows her place is in the North, and she can rule the people of the North and rule Winterfell. She has no desire to be ruler of the Seven Kingdoms. She's probably capable with the help of her family and advisors like Tyrion, but on her own but I'm sure she'd feel out of her depth. I thought it was an awesome way to end.

BRYAN COGMAN: In the pilot, Sansa's main function was informing members of her family and the audience that the only thing she wanted was to get out of Winterfell and go live in the big city and become queen—except a very different kind of queen than the one she ended up being. So Sansa's storyline was always meant to have a note of triumph at the end, especially after all that she went through in the middle of the series. It was appropriate that she came full circle at the end. She was the only Stark left in Winterfell and leads the North into this new chapter. She's the best hope for the North's future.

SOPHIE TURNER: I wanted to keep my necklace—the black one with the chain leading down. They wouldn't let me, so I just kept my corset instead, the thing that brought me so much pain. It's the one thing I had that led me through this experience to the end.

On one of my last days on the set, I had a moment where I was just walking in my Sansa costume on the grounds of Winterfell and thinking, "This is one of the last times I will be here, as Sansa, in your home." It was this emotional, powerful moment when I really truly appreciated the character and *Game of Thrones* itself.

Arya Stark, on the eve of the Battle of Winterfell, shared a night with her former traveling companion and friend Gendry, much to his surprise.

MAISIE WILLIAMS (*Arya Stark*): I thought the script was a prank. They're like, "We haven't done that this year." Oh, fuck! When do I shoot this? I need to go to the gym. David and Dan were like, "It's the end of the world, what else would you have her do?" This maybe is a moment where Arya accepts death tomorrow, which she never does. "Not today." So it was that moment where she said, "Tomorrow, we're probably going to die. I want to know what that feels like before that happens." It was interesting to see Arya be a bit more human, speak more about the things people are scared of, and that paved the way for the rest of her story.

JOE DEMPSIE (*Gendry*): It's obviously slightly strange for me because I've known Maisie since she was eleven, twelve years old. At the same time, I didn't want to be patronizing toward Maisie. She was a twenty-year-old woman, so we just had a lot of fun with it.

MAISIE WILLIAMS: David and Dan said, "You can show as much or as little as you want" [in the scene]. So I kept myself pretty private. I don't think it's important for Arya to flash, and this beat isn't really about that. And everybody else has done it on the show, so . . . they did it and I don't need to!

At the beginning [of filming the scene], everyone was really respectful. No one wants to make you feel uncomfortable, which kind of makes you feel more uncomfortable, because no one wants to look at anything that they shouldn't, which, in turn, makes you feel like you look awful because everyone is kind of like [*looks away*]. You want people to act more normal.

Then by the end we were rushing to finish the scene and David Nutter is going, "Okay, you're going to come in and do this and do that and, great, take your top off," and then walked off. I'm like, "Okay, let's do it."

Arya journeyed to King's Landing, intending to kill Cersei and cross a big name off her death list. In several ways, Arya had been on a path similar to Daenerys. They were both heroic young women who were victims of terrible tragedies who then became increasingly skilled at survival, yet also murderous and apathetic. When Arya poisoned a feast at House Frey in revenge for the Red Wedding at the opening of season seven, it was not unlike Daenerys's crucifying the masters—they're evil as a group, yes, but what about as individuals? Did everybody at the banquet deserve the same fate? Arya halted a servant girl from drinking her poisoned wine, but what if she hadn't been right next to her?

BRYAN COGMAN: Both of the Stark girls were taken to the edge, where humanity can get lost. They come right up to that cliff and then come back. The final season for Arya was deconstructing this darker persona she's had to acquire and rediscovering a bit of her lost humanity.

Arya had her final conversation with the Hound. After witnessing so much horror and devastation, she changed her mind about going after

Cersei. She made the opposite choice from Daenerys—to embrace life over death—at almost the exact same moment in the series. It was not a move that gave fans what they wanted, but it arguably gave Arya what she needed.

MAISIE WILLIAMS: I wanted her to kill Cersei, even if it meant she dies. Even up to the point where she's with Jaime, I thought he's going to whip off his face [and be revealed as Arya] and they were both going to die. I thought that's what Arya's drive had been.

LENA HEADEY: I lived that fantasy [of an Arya-Cersei confrontation] as well until I read the script. There were chunky scenes, and it was nothing that I dreamed about. It was a bit of a comedown, and you have to accept that it wasn't to be.

MAISIE WILLIAMS: The Hound said, "You want to be like me? That's what you want, you want to live your life like me?" In my head the answer was, "Yeah." But I guess sleeping with Gendry and seeing Jon, she realized she's not just fighting for herself anymore but her family. All these human emotions that she hasn't felt for a long time. When the Hound asks her that, she has another option. All of a sudden there were so many more things in my life that I can live for, that I can do, that I can see. It was a shock for me. Then I realized there were other things I could play, and bring her back to being a sixteen-year-old again.

Arya said farewell to a lovestruck Gendry, rejecting his offer of a domestic life—"That's not me."

MAISIE WILLIAMS: Arya had always been a lone wolf. She's always felt like a bit of a misfit in her own family. I don't think being with a partner is what would make her feel the most at home or the most fulfilled. They will probably see each other at like a friend's wedding and say, "Oh, hey, it's good to see you. . . ."

Instead, Arya set sail for destinations unknown, to explore "what's west of Westeros," a young woman going into the hostile unknown, but we know she can take care of herself.

MAISIE WILLIAMS: It's not a *Game of Thrones* ending. It's like a happy ending for her. It let me take Arya to a place I'd never thought I'd go with her again. I hope that doesn't sound wanky and actor-y.

Jon Snow could have become the king of Westeros. Many viewers felt that the reveal of his mysterious parentage, teased from the very first episode, should have had greater impact on the final season's storyline.

BRYAN COGMAN: It was a subversion of the expectation. When you have your "main character" discover that he's meant to be king, on any other show he would become king. That's not our show. He was never destined for that. But the truth about his parentage does affect the dominoes of the season and how they fall. Being able to ride a dragon was a factor in the destruction of the Night King—not the ultimate factor, but in the war against the dead everybody had an essential part to play to get Arya to the right spot, and if you took away any one element, the Night King would have been victorious. And his parentage was a factor in the chain of events that led Daenerys to her eventual tragic ending.

Bran Stark agreed that punishing Jon Snow was the only way to keep peace with the Unsullied. So Jon Snow was sentenced to serve out his days in the Night's Watch at the Wall. Like Grey Worm fulfilling Missandei's dashed hope for their future by journeying to Naath, Jon Snow fulfilled Ygritte's dream that he would embrace a life free of the restraints and responsibilities of Westeros. He left his post at Castle Black with his friend Tormund Giantsbane and headed beyond the Wall with the Free Folk, never to kneel again.

KIT HARINGTON (*Jon Snow*): There's no trauma or cheer. He got closure. The closure doesn't necessarily feel joyous. It's just the end of something. There's a satisfaction to that. It's not a happy feeling. "At least this is done and I'll continue to be hurt by this—forever. But it's done and I need to let go of it now." Everyone has told him he belonged in the true north and he's finally going there. I don't think he's coming back.

BRYAN COGMAN: Ultimately this show is about this family, this family that has split apart, and finding a way to bring all that together again. I don't think it's an accident David and Dan ended the series with that montage of Jon and Sansa and Arya going on their separate ways on their new journeys.

ISAAC HEMPSTEAD WRIGHT: One of the cleverest things about the ending is it didn't conclude everything very neatly. The kingdom is in disarray. Arya is going off to start her own journey. Sansa is now Queen in the North. Bran is now king. The Starks are left unfinished. There's no full stop. There's no period. It's almost as if the world of *Game of Thrones* exists, still, somewhere.

CHAPTER THIRTY-TWO

AND NOW THE WATCH
HAS ENDED

F ans were booing. That wasn't good.

Game of Thrones cast members waited anxiously backstage at Comic-Con in San Diego, preparing to step in front of six thousand people and celebrate the show's final season. The show's last episode had aired just two months earlier. HBO had scheduled a final *Thrones* Comic-Con panel for the San Diego Convention Center's massive Hall H and tapped an unsuspecting journalist (me) to serve as the moderator. In the weeks leading up to the event, fans upset with the final season had circulated posts on social media gleefully detailing creative plans to disrupt the panel with protests in the ballroom.

Aware of the threats, a Comic-Con official took the unusual step of going onstage before the panel started to remind the audience that it was in the spirit of the convention to always express support for shows regardless of how fans might feel about them. That's when the boos happened.

"This panel is screwed," I thought, my head filled with visions of taking the stage to fans howling "*Shame! Shame! Shame!*"

The stage lights went down.

A *Thrones* highlight reel played.

Then it was time to face the crowd. . . .

———

Game of Thrones aired its final episode, "The Iron Throne," on May 19, 2019. The seventy-nine-minute series finale was divided into two strikingly different parts. The first depicted the gray postapocalyptic aftermath of Daenerys's King's Landing attack and the rise, and demise, of her fascistic regime (one might say it felt like "the winds of winter"). The latter half picked up months after Daenerys's death and showed Westeros being reborn as the survivors determined the fate of the realm and grappled with their new roles and destinies ("a dream of spring").

With each passing episode in the final season, the volume of fandom debate about the show increased. Every minute detail of the series was passionately discussed. Perhaps the best example of the extraordinary level of scrutiny was when an errant modern-day coffee cup was accidentally left in a shot during a scene at Winterfell, barely visible, and it sparked global headlines.

DAVID BENIOFF (*showrunner*): I couldn't believe it. When we got the email about it the next day, I honestly thought someone was pranking us, because there had been things before where people were like, "Oh, look at that plane in the background!" and somebody had Photoshopped it in. I thought, "There's no way there's a coffee cup in there." Then when I saw it on the TV I was like, "How did I not see that?"

DAN WEISS (*showrunner*): I'd seen that shot one thousand times and we're always looking at their faces or how the shot sat with the shots on either side of it. I felt like we were the participants in a psychology experiment, like where you don't see the gorillas running around in the background because you're counting the basketballs. Every production that's ever existed had things like this. You can see a crew member in *Braveheart*; there's an actor wearing a wristwatch in *Spartacus*. But now people can rewind things and everybody is talking to each other in real time. So one person saw the coffee cup, rewound it, and then everybody did.

The final season was watched by nearly forty million viewers in the United States and tens of millions more around the world. *The Hollywood Reporter*'s Tim Goodman declared that the show, "ended just about as well as one unwieldy, sprawling, complicated epic could end," and *io9*'s Rob Bricken wrote, "The story was the 'best' ending people could have hoped for . . . things worked out shockingly well for everyone but Daenerys and Jon—and that was exactly what *Game of Thrones* needed to get right."

But many critics—as well as the vocal mass of fans—were quite displeased. "Tonally odd, logically strained, and emotionally thin," wrote *The Atlantic*'s Spencer Kornhaber of the finale. And *The New York Times*'s Jeremy Egner opined, "It all could have worked better if the past two seasons had felt less like headlong rushes toward predetermined outcomes. . . . So many of the things that drove fans loudly crazy this season most likely wouldn't have if they'd been given more room to breathe." The season's Rotten Tomatoes and IMDb scores plummeted compared to previous years, and a fan petition was signed by thousands asking HBO to remake season eight.

The decision to end the series at its peak of popularity combined with revealing the oft-tragic and convention-defying fates of dozens of beloved characters over the course of just six episodes was inevitably going to result in some frustration and controversy along with accolades and cheers. Yet the amount of blowback was beyond what was anticipated.

Many of the show's insiders felt that a good percentage of the criticism was a casualty of *Game of Thrones* being a momentous pop culture event that was hyped to a level that no drama series could possibly satisfy. And with *Thrones*, there was the added consequence that its finale marked the end of an era. With more than five hundred scripted shows on television in 2019 and audiences increasingly bingeing or delaying their viewing rather than watching programs live, *Game of Thrones* didn't just conclude a TV show but ended a sense of global community at a time when people were feeling increasingly isolated. "*Game of Thrones* is the last great show to bring us together," mourned *Wired*'s Emily Dreyfuss. "Maybe that's part of why everyone seems so upset about this final season."

Or, as Nikolaj Coster-Waldau put it: "How can any ending be good . . . when you don't want it to end?"

CAROLYN STRAUSS (*former programming president at HBO; executive producer*): No matter what you do in the Twitter age, you're going to get killed. There's always going to be somebody in their comfy chair who has the better ending. It's a very tricky balancing act, and there were a lot of practical and storytelling factors that were never considered by someone doing a theoretical finale. If other people have a better idea, well, they can go do it themselves.

GEORGE R. R. MARTIN (*author, co–executive producer*): I hear both extremes. There are people who say they hate the show and say, "George, write your books and 'fix' things." And there are people who love the show who say, "I don't care about George's version anymore, it's a novelization, it's fan fiction, who cares." When I finish my books people can argue which is right, which is wrong, and which is the "real" story. None are the real story. These are fictional characters. Which one resonates with you more?

DAVID BENIOFF: There definitely are things [over the course of the show] we would do differently. I don't know if there's anything I would want to discuss publicly.

DAVID WEISS: Prince once said something about how any record you listen to that you think is terrible, somebody worked themselves to the bone to make it. So many people work so hard on any aspect of a thing. So when you say something critical it can sound like you're blaming somebody else. And really the only people who are to blame are us—and I sure as hell don't want to blame us.

CHRISTOPHER NEWMAN (*producer*): I have no regrets about the last season. I thought it was the best work we had ever done. Once everybody gets over the anger of the Internet, they will see they wrote some fantastic stuff. The criticism doesn't seem to fairly consider what an extraordinary achievement the whole thing was. When people say, "I wasn't happy with the ending," I think, "If you wrote the ending you wanted, I bet nobody would have been happy with your ending either!"

MICHAEL LOMBARDO (*former HBO programming president*): Most people thought it was an unbelievable season of television. I was at HBO when *The Sopranos* ended and everyone was outraged. Now it's looked at as a perfect ending. When *Seinfeld* ended it was like the world had stopped. It's hard to land those planes. They left an incredible testament. Only time will be the true judge.

In an unprecedented move, HBO put five *Game of Thrones* prequels into script development, all from different writers, in a competitive "bake-off" in hopes of finding a show that might prove a worthy successor. One of them by Jane Goldman (*Kick-Ass*), even shot a pilot in 2019. The project starred Naomi Watts and was set thousands of years before the events in *Thrones,* in the lead-up to the events of the original Long Night. HBO decided not to move forward with the show, perhaps proving once again how difficult it can be to make Martin's world come alive. But HBO hasn't given up. The network gave a full series order to another project, *House of the Dragon,* based on Martin's history of the Targaryen family, *Fire & Blood.* Martin is quite hopeful about the new series, and the network promisingly tapped *Thrones* veteran Miguel Sapochnik as the project's director and co-showrunner (along with *Colony* writer Ryan Condal). The other prequel projects remain in development, while *Dragon* is planned for 2022.

Now let's go back to that Comic-Con panel.

One by one, seven *Thrones* stars (Maisie Williams, Nikolaj Coster-Waldau, Conleth Hill, Isaac Hempstead Wright, Liam Cunningham, Jacob Anderson, and John Bradley) took to the stage.

The massive Hall H audience *roared* at them . . . with love. Fans laughed at their jokes ("What did I steal? The scenes I was in!" quipped Hill). Each panelist had a coffee cup in front of them, a wink to the coffee cup goof. They made heartfelt speeches that brought applause and tears. And when the event concluded, the panel received a standing ovation. No boos, no protests, no shames. It didn't mean everyone in Hall H was thrilled with the final episodes, of course. But it suggested their overall love for *Game of Thrones,* and particularly the work of its cast, had endured.

A couple of hours after the panel, the actors went out to dinner together. A silent question hung over the table. It was the same question that had lingered over all gatherings of *Thrones'* cast and crew ever since the series had wrapped production: *Will all of us ever be together again?*

For the cast, the show ending meant the loss of many things: working with friends, being part of a global sensation, having a steady and rather lucrative job, and, perhaps most important, playing characters they loved in a world that was so immersive that it gained its own reality and permanence.

IWAN RHEON (*Ramsay Bolton*): The thing I'll miss most is when you pick up a script and read it and there's always one scene in every season where I go, "Thank you so much, this is such a beauty."

LENA HEADEY (*Cersei Lannister*): Every time you did your last scene with a character you were like, "That's it, it's over." There was a great sense of grief and we're off to new pastures. There's also a sense of loss, that nothing like this will ever happen again. I'll probably never be on sets as magnificent as these again. There was an enormous amount of gratitude.

JACOB ANDERSON (*Grey Worm*): People think it must have been a very heavy and dark place to work. But I had so much fun. I have a very chaotic mind and can be very restless. I'm quite a panicky person. Sometimes for like five to ten minutes during a scene, I got to be this character who was so in control of themselves and still and calm. That's been a really powerful thing for me, to be able to do that.

KRISTIAN NAIRN (*Hodor*): For me, it hasn't really ended. It's very hard talking about *Game of Thrones* in the past tense. I still feel like I'm still waiting for the next season.

NATALIE DORMER (*Margaery Tyrell*): I got the golden ticket. I watched the first season as a fan. I got on the train in the second season and was part of a beautiful, mad ride, and I had a beautiful arc for five years. Then I got out where I could capitalize on the profile it had given me, which I'm very grateful for. Then I had the beauty of watching the end of the series as a fan again. I'll always have a little yellow rose after my heart.

JOHN BRADLEY (*Samwell Tarly*): It's easier, in a way, for people who had careers before *Game of Thrones*. For people like Charles Dance and Diana Rigg, this is just part of a wider career. But for me and a lot of other cast members, this was the first time I'll be a working actor and not be in *Game of Thrones*. I've never been kicked into the abyss. No matter what job I did in the first half of the year that I might not enjoy as much, at least I had *Game of Thrones* to go back to in the summer and be around that family again and be around all those familiar faces. *Game of Thrones* always felt like coming home.

MAISIE WILLIAMS (*Arya Stark*): There are loads of stories I want to tell. There are loads of stories I want to play. I worry nobody will want me to do it. It will be nice to get back to normality. I also have an app I'm launching that I hope will help people. I've got a production company and there are a couple movies we want to make. I want to direct. There are not many opportunities where you get to do everything with one character and [on *Thrones*] there was a whole spectrum I got to do. So whatever happens after, I made this count.

RORY MCCANN (*Sandor "the Hound" Clegane*): I'm a sailor and spent all my years trying to do up boats. I'm thinking of sailing off into the sunset. That's my dream. I have an old wooden ketch. Two masts, all wood, forty-five years old. Gorgeous thing with a peat fire inside it. I'd like to go away for a couple years.

When asked where McCann plans to sail away to, the actor replied with a Hound-like bark: "That's my fucking business."

KIT HARINGTON (*Jon Snow*): The goal of acting is to gain some recognition and fame. That's not what I'm looking for anymore. This gave me the freedom to try things I want to do. Produce a bit, maybe try directing and try roles that not many people will see but will give me some satisfaction. Maybe do something completely different. I nicked beers from David and Dan's fridge and I left them a note saying, "I owe you two beers and one career." And that's how I feel.

LIAM CUNNINGHAM (*Davos Seaworth*): Because of the timeless nature of it and being a fantasy and because of how good it is, I think *Thrones* will hold up the next fifty years and people will keep discovering it. It's a great honor to be a part of that. Every day it was a pleasure to go to work. I will miss the elegance of it and working with people who are at the absolute top of their game.

GWENDOLINE CHRISTIE (*Brienne of Tarth*): I loved that Brienne, in her last scene, is at work. I love that her last line is, "I think ships take precedence over brothels. . . ." That's what I want to be remembered for, and that's how I want Brienne to be remembered: as a feminist icon and a practical woman.

PETER DINKLAGE (*Tyrion Lannister*): I will miss this so much, but you gotta turn the next chapter of your life. I'm closing in on fifty. I started on this show in my thirties. Like so many people on the show, I've married and had children during the course of this. You got to make room for the new thing. It's heartbreaking. It's the greatest role I've ever had, working with the greatest people who are crazy fucking lovely.

EMILIA CLARKE (*Daenerys Targaryen*): There was a lot of laughter, there were a lot of parties, there was a lot of drinking. Every time we all hung out, I always felt like we'd just come back from working in the mine. Everything about doing the show was so not glamorous, so no one ever stood on ceremony with anyone. It was the most honest working environment I will probably ever experience.

NATHALIE EMMANUEL (*Missandei*): I can never really quite articulate what the show and the people who were involved meant to me. People often give the cast the praise for it all, but it's important to talk about the hundreds, if not thousands, of people who have been responsible for that show's creation who have put in so many hours. Every person who was there made it what it was. I hope they read this book and know I'm eternally grateful.

SOPHIE TURNER (*Sansa Stark*): I'm quite sad about it. This is everything I'd ever known. This has been my home. I spent more time there than I had at home. The saddest part is I don't get to be Sansa, Maisie doesn't get to be Arya. I won't see Maisie in her costume anymore, I won't be able to be in my costume and play this character. We don't get to interact on that level, which is sad, because their relationship is a big part of who Maisie and I are.

CONLETH HILL (*Varys*): This show began ten years into a peace process in Northern Ireland after about thirty years of conflict. What I'm most proud of is the collection of all kinds of different people—young, old, gay, straight, black, white, male, female, Muslim, Jewish, Christian—who all worked together so well and so productively. And to the credit of my homeland, it showed you how beautiful it is there and how we can work together in peace. I couldn't be prouder that it was made in large part in the place where I was from.

IAIN GLEN (*Jorah Mormont*): What we do as actors is ephemeral. We get lost in something and then go get lost in something else. But to live in that for a decade was the best thing ever to be involved in. Until my dying day it will be the most exceptional experience. To be in the biggest hit ever is the best feeling. What you can't do is project ahead and say, "I want more than that," because it ain't going to happen. It's a once-in-a-lifetime thing.

You have your final shot, your final red carpet—all of the "finals" of everything. There's even a final "How do you feel about it ending?" It never hit me that much. It's only looking back now, occasionally, that a shock will go through me: "I won't be doing that again." I can be doing anything, but it's usually around work, when I just get a memory of the *Thrones* world. You had the most amazing support, the most brilliant crew, these great friendships, and a great deal of love for what we were doing, where anything was possible. Nothing will ever compare to it. Nothing will be like that, ever.

DAVID BENIOFF: After the final wrap party, the cast came back to the house that Dan and I had rented. We were there until sunup. There was a really steep hill in the back going down toward the water and all these young actors were drunkenly rolling down the hill. I just remember sitting there, watching them at sunrise, and thinking, "This was a good job."

With no more words left to write, I asked that traditional final question for when something popular and influential concludes: What is its legacy? It's probably not possible to sum up the contribution of *Game of Thrones* to the world. The series had such an enormous and varied impact on so many millions. But striving for the impossible was always the point.

BRYAN COGMAN (*co–executive producer*): The legacy of the show? It's too soon to tell. When you're writing an addendum chapter to this oral history for the tenth-anniversary edition, then you can tell.

DAVID BENIOFF: It would be fun if it were like when you're watching *Fast Times at Ridgemont High*, where people are still watching it twenty years from now and going, "Look, that's a young Alfie Allen," and "That's a young Sophie Turner." It would be really fun on a personal level to know we had a helping hand in launching those careers, and other actors who aren't so young but we gave a boost.

DAN WEISS: I hope people keep watching the show. I hope kids who are the age of our kids now grow up and watch the show and take from it what they take from it. Nobody owns the future of what they make. Once you put something out there, it's not yours anymore. It doesn't belong to the people watching it now either. In twenty years there will be a whole new group of people and they'll either watch it or they won't. If they do, their reaction might be very different from your reaction. So I hope they watch it, and I hope they like it.

GEORGE R. R. MARTIN: We were the most popular show in the world, for a time. We set a record for most Emmys, and that's a legacy. But records are made to be broken, and twelve years ago there was another show that was the most popular in the world and I don't know what it was. I tell you what I hope for in terms of legacy: that we established adult fantasy as a viable genre on television. Now everybody wants "the next *Game of Thrones*." Will anything be the next *Game of Thrones*? Even our prequels? I don't know. If they all flop, then it will be another ten years before somebody tries a fantasy show again. That would be sad. I would like to see fantasy become a permanent genre, like lawyer shows or cop shows. There are good cop shows and shit cop shows, but there are always cop shows coming on. And it doesn't matter if a cop show is good because there's always another coming. That's what I would like to see, every year a new fantasy show or two. That would be the legacy I would like to see for *Game of Thrones*.

NATHALIE EMMANUEL: It was a cultural phenomenon, it affected a whole generation. It was something dreams are made of. If I never work again, I'll be like . . . "You know what? I did fucking *Game of Thrones*."

CREDITS

WRITTEN IN INK AND BLOOD

Like *Game of Thrones* itself, this book reflects more than a decade of passion and often seemed like an insurmountable task that was only possible to pull off with the help of many others.

I wish to thank my former and current *Entertainment Weekly* editors, particularly Henry Goldblatt (who approved the bulk of my set visits), Jess Cagle (who took a leap of faith in hiring me), and my current editor, JD Heyman (for his patient support of this project). At a time when so much entertainment reporting is reduced to quoting celebrity tweets, *EW* has been unmatched in its dedication to conducting on-the-ground reporting on film and TV sets worldwide. I would encourage readers who enjoyed this book to consider getting a subscription to *EW*, and regularly check out EW.com for ongoing coverage of *Thrones* and other popular franchises.

Also thanks to former HBO publicist Mara Mikialian, who accompanied me on each of my eight *Thrones* set visits and tirelessly stood by in the rain and cold while I waited for just one more interview. Thanks also to David Benioff and Dan Weiss, who let me come to their top secret sets and answered hundreds of probing questions. Thanks to George R. R. Martin for his wonderful chats, as well as for his immeasurable contribution to the world of fantasy. Thanks to "third head of the dragon" Bryan Cogman for his terrific insight into the production and creative process (and his own behind-the-scenes book, *Inside HBO's Game of Thrones:*

Seasons 1 & 2). Additional thanks to HBO licensing chief Jeff Peters for approving this book as an HBO project, supplying the photos, and making good on his company's assurance that the manuscript would have creative independence. Also thanks to my agent Rick Richter for proposing the idea. A special thanks to my Dutton editor, Jill Schwartzman, who took a gamble on a first-time author. Also thanks to my former editor Kristen Baldwin (and Hula) for a helpful edit, and to my former *THR* boss Nellie Andreeva for letting me write that fateful *Thrones* pilot story. Gratitude as well to my supportive friends Dan Snierson, Stephanie Mark, Scott Barnett, Hannah Vachule, Caryn Lusinchi, and Keith Goode for putting up with so much of my book stress. Finally, thanks to the cast and crew of *Thrones,* who answered so many of my questions over the years, particularly Emilia Clarke, Nikolaj Coster-Waldau, Liam Cunningham, and Kit Harington, who were among the first of the show's leads to grant interviews expressly for this project, lending it some helpful legitimacy.

Most quotes in this book are from my interviews conducted between June 2019 and April 2020. Others were culled from interviews conducted between 2011 and 2019 and were previously published by *Entertainment Weekly,* except those directly attributed to other outlets in the text. Some of the outside quotes were brought to my attention by Kim Renfro's well-researched book *The Unofficial Guide to Game of Thrones.* Quotes were edited for length, grammar, clarity, occasional pronoun clarification (for example, "Brienne" instead of "she"), and tense consistency, and their order was arranged for narrative coherence so long as it did not alter the speaker's intended meaning.

At one point in this book, Clarke abruptly asked a rather existential question: "What is Daenerys?" One might ask the same of the show. What is *Game of Thrones?* There are many correct answers: an adaptation, a TV series, a fantasy story, a corporate enterprise, a snapshot of the entertainment world during seismic industry and cultural transitions.

I saw the show as a seemingly impossible dream made real. *Game of Thrones* was the filmic equivalent of Roger Bannister breaking the

CREDITS

four-minute mile—proof that with enough determination and sacrifice, a creative human endeavor can portray even the most expansive outer reaches of our storytelling imagination and, in doing so, captivate the world.

—JAMES HIBBERD, AUSTIN, TEXAS, JULY 30, 2020

INDEX

Note: *Game of Thrones* characters can be found alphabetized under their first names.

INDEX

INDEX